Low-Cost E-Mail with UUCP

Integrating Unix, DOS, Windows, and Mac

Low-Cost E-Mail with UUCP

Integrating Unix, DOS, Windows, and Mac

Thomas Wm. Madron

 VAN NOSTRAND REINHOLD
I(T)P A Division of International Thomson Publishing Inc.

New York • Albany • Bonn • Boston • Detroit • London • Madrid • Melbourne
Mexico City • Paris • San Francisco • Singapore • Tokyo • Toronto

Copyright © 1995 by Van Nostrand Reinhold

I(T)P A division of International Thomson Publishing Inc.
       The ITP logo is a trademark under license

Printed in the United States of America
For more information, contact:

Van Nostrand Reinhold
115 Fifth Avenue
New York, NY 10003

International Thomson Publishing GmbH
Königswinterer Strasse 418
53227 Bonn
Germany

International Thomson Publishing Europe
Berkshire House 168-173
High Holborn
London WC1V 7AA
England

International Thomson Publishing Asia
221 Henderson Road   #05-10
Henderson Building
Singapore 0315

Thomas Nelson Australia
102 Dodds Street
South Melbourne, 3205
Victoria, Australia

International Thomson Publishing Japan
Hirakawacho Kyowa Building, 3F
2-2-1 Hirakawacho
Chiyoda-ku, 102 Tokyo
Japan

Nelson Canada
1120 Birchmount Road
Scarborough, Ontario
Canada, M1K 5G4

International Thomson Editores
Campos Eliseos 385, Piso 7
Col. Polanco
11560 Mexico D.F. Mexico

1 2 3 4 5 6 7 8 9 10 RRDHB 01 00 99 98 97 96 95 94

Library of Congress Cataloging-in-Publication Data
Madron, Thomas William, 1937-
   Low-Cost E-Mail with UUCP : Integrating Unix, DOS, Windows, and
Mac / Thomas Wm. Madron.
      p.   cm.
   Includes bibliographical references and index.
   1. Electronic mail systems.   I. Title.
HE6239.E54M33   1994
384.3'4—dc20   94-12594
                                                         CIP

Contents

Readme First

UUCP (Unix-to-Unix CoPy program) has long been a basic tool supporting E-Mail services among UNIX systems over dial-up telephone lines. Versions of UUCP are now available that run on personal computers using MS/PC-DOS and Windows, on Apple's Macintosh computers, as well as a variety of other platforms. The original conception behind UUCP was to provide reliable file transfer facilities among UNIX machines over telephone lines using low-speed, low-cost dial-access modems. Such a concept is uniquely suited for personal computers as well.

In order to set up an E-Mail network using a variety of computers with UUCP it is necessary, at the present time, to become intimately familiar with aspects of UNIX networking and the vagaries of the personal computer UUCP "clones." This requires a major research effort in and of itself. Then, in addition, UUCP has the reputation for being very difficult to set up.

This book was conceived as a "how-to" manual for designing and implementing a UUCP-based E-Mail network using only public domain and shareware products. Such a network may include UNIX, DOS/Windows, and MAC machines, but may also be based only on DOS/Windows systems (or Macs, or UNIX). Because all the software is shareware, the software costs are minimal. An organization, using only existing equipment and the information found in this book, will be able to set up an E-Mail system of almost any dimensions. Moreover, because the primary means of communication is over dial-up telephone lines, the network can operate within the same building, city, state, or nation.

Although this book contains a great deal of information on UUCP that is difficult to obtain elsewhere, it is focused on the use of the system for designing and implementing private E-Mail systems. General literature on UUCP often centers on the use of UUCP as a means for accessing the national and international networks, Usenet and Internet. I have provided a chapter, Chapter 10, addressing this topic, but it is not central to the book. Moreover, this is not a general tutorial on UUCP in a UNIX environment. The UNIX environment is discussed, and where possible the technical discussions apply to all relevant versions of UUCP, including those on UNIX. In other words, the object of this book is at once more universal than some other treatments of UUCP, and more narrowly focused on its use as a low-cost transport mechanism for E-Mail systems. It is, in short, a "how-to" book on structuring a generalized E-Mail system using UUCP.

One other note is also necessary. During the writing of this book during the latter half of 1993 the most recent distribution version of the latest UUCP, commonly called Taylor UUCP, was released as Version 1.04 (version 1.05 was released March 1994). It was released under the GNU Software License. Taylor UUCP provides needed enhancements for UUCP. This newest version of UUCP can, of course, communicate properly with older versions, and its executables will seem familiar to those with UUCP experience. The setup and configuration of Taylor UUCP is substantially different than older versions of the system, using different sets of configuration files. The most obvious to the casual observer is the combination of information required for the operation of UUCP found in the *SYSTEMS* or *L.sys* and *Permissions* files into a more generalized *sys* file. Moreover, Ian Taylor has also provided the capability for the use of multiple *sys* files within the same implementation of UUCP. Over the next two or three years I anticipate that Taylor UUCP will become the common UUCP distribution with most variations of UNIX. Moreover, I would guess (although I have no evidence) that even as you read someone is busy porting Taylor UUCP to other operating environments.

This rapid progress in UUCP software technology is also apparent in products just now coming to market for Windows and other operating systems. When I started writing in mid-1993 there was not a "native" Windows implementation of UUCP that was easily and inexpensively available. Some DOS versions, such as UUPlus, which is extensively discussed in and distributed with this book, can be run under DOS with a screen-oriented MUA, such as **pcelm**, thus making the entire system pleasent to use. Components of UUPlus can also be run in a DOS window under Windows, and integrated with an easily used mail user agent (MUA) such as the Cinetics Mail Manager (CMM) for Windows. Computer Witchcraft, Inc., which operates a commercial Internet access network, has been distributing a Windows software package called WinNET™ Mail, for use with their network services. They have generalized the WinNET™ package, however, to enable access to any other UUCP system. Their product is a good example of a Windows UUCP product specifically tailored for E-Mail. It can be used by a mail user for E-Mail or file transfer to any UUCP host to which the user has access and is very easy to set up. This system cannot, however, be used as a host UUCP system, however, so other products are still necessary to perform that function in a DOS/Windows environment.

All of this illustrates that even for a system now almost 20 years old, UUCP is certainly alive and well. It is especially well-suited to the task of E-Mail transport in situations where dial-access over the telephone system is the norm, or at least important, and where there is an amalgam of diverse computers using different operating environments. Because good implementations (or components) of UUCP are available either free or at very low cost, it can be used as the basis for low-cost E-Mail systems. It is also very useful in situations where corporate MIS functions are performed on a UNIX system. In such a situation, the UNIX system will use UNIX mail facilities, which all interface with UUCP, for a variety of purposes even when other mail systems are available. Through the use of the software technology described in this book you can structure an integrated E-Mail system using UUCP, thus obviating the need for multiple E-Mail products.

I had hoped to distribute some additional utilities and software with this book. Unfortunately, after providing UUPlus™, WinNET™, and Waffle, there was little space left on the two diskettes required for these systems. As a substitute for direct distribution I have tried to provide sources for other software that is discussed and where they may be found for downloading.

A number of people and readers have contributed to this book, although sins of ommission and commission are mine. Members of the Board of Directors of the South Central Chapter of the Data Processing Management Association served as experimental subjects and critics of the distribution diskettes and software, along with some commentary on selected sections of the book itself. Ian Taylor provided some useful feedback in his review of the original manuscript. My wife, Beverly, put up with me as I was working on this project as well as being part of the DPMA experimental group. Thanks must also be extended to the maufacturers of the products distributed with this book. I hope you find this a useful and interesting book.

Deciding What to Install

What you keep is what you finally decide you should use for your installation. In general, you might consider the following:

1. If you are setting up a DOS mail server, then you will need the Waffle installation.
2. If you are setting up a DOS leaf system (a mail user system), then you will need the UUPlus™ installation.
3. If you are setting up a Windows leaf system, then all you will need to do is to install WinNET™.
4. If you are setting up a Macintosh host or leaf system, then you will need either UUPC for Macintosh 3.0, or GNU Mac, along with one of the MUA's for the Macintosh. These are not distributed with this book, although they are discussed.
5. If you want a UNIX-like host, then you will have to buy UNIX, or for a less expensive alternative, Coherent 4.2 with Taylor UUCP v. 1.04. There are also other low-cost UNIX-like systems available, including BSD386 and Linux, among others. The advantage of Coherent over these products is that it is a commercial system with appropriate technical support, whereas the others are more experimental in character.

Regardless of which system you choose, if you will be working on a DOS, OS/2, or Windows system, the extra utilities described in Chapter 5 may also prove to be useful to you from time-to-time. Although not covered in this book, you should also be aware that there are UUCP implementations for systems other than those discussed in this book.

Typographical Conventions

Italics	File names and general emphasis
Bold	Programs and software
SMALL CAPS	References to the UUCP system and its derivatives
/	"slash" or "forward slash"
\	"back slash"

1

An Introduction to UUCP/Mail

The concept and role of "electronic mail" (E-Mail) is widely misunderstood by corporate and other organizational officers. Frequently, therefore, it is not used effectively when available, or it is not provided where needed. Add to the corporate confusion the fact that there are a very large number of mail systems available, and many of them have very high price tags and the situation becomes even worse. On top of everything else, large organizations (and even some smaller ones) frequently have multiple E-Mail systems, many of which cannot communicate with one another.

E-Mail is most broadly defined as a system which sends messages between or among users of an information network and the programs necessary to support such message transfers. When E-Mail systems first became available, the "messages" tended to be simple substitutes for interoffice memos. This is still one of E-Mail's strong points. However, today the use of E-Mail systems goes well beyond an electronic memo system. Virtually all E-Mail systems currently on the market can, for example, send almost any kind of file along with a message so that it becomes a means of collaboration among people. Many application programs, such as accounting systems or operating system utilities, will generate various kinds of automatic mail messages back to designated individuals providing a means of monitoring system activity. Several accounting packages, in fact, have monitoring systems that generate mail messages to controllers when a budget is about to go over its limit, or when other indicators of the financial wellbeing of the organization have reached a critical level. If an organization is having a system developed by an outside software organization, the developers can often update versions of software by sending new programs by E-Mail or by UUCP. It is also a means of maintaining contact with developers on a *very* timely basis.

With our generic definition of E-Mail, then, we must expand our understanding of what is meant both by "messages" and by "users." Messages can be any kind of file, and users can be either human or computer. As Steven Baker has observed, "mail is the lifeblood of many networks."[1] Indeed, it is the lifeblood of many organizations.

If E-Mail is important to many organizations concentrated in one or a few buildings, it can be particularly useful in organizations that are widely distributed. Examples of such organizations are retail businesses with many outlets distributed around a region or the nation. Insurance companies and conventional retail chains are also included in this category. An example of an entity with a similar organizational character is a church which has many local congregations but which must answer to some central authority. Many local, state, and federal government agencies are also organized in this way. Rather than spending a great deal of money on the U. S. Postal Service, Federal Express, or even fax machines, E-Mail can provide a convenient and cost-effective alternative.

Today E-Mail has become an important integration tool. If you wish to have a scheduling system for a workgroup or office, some form of E-Mail is likely to be used as the medium by which the schedules for various people will be posted. E-Mail can be an important tool for enabling a group of people to work as a team. E-Mail might also be the solution to at least partially automating those little pink telephone slips. E-Mail can be of assistance in pushing software development to take place faster. To reduce the cost of intra-office and inter-departmental communications, E-Mail is your answer. If faxing is becoming a major item in a company's budget, it may help reduce the cost. These and a myriad of other possibilities exist for a well-thought-out E-Mail system.

One of the oldest E-Mail systems is that from the UNIX world based on the UNIX-to-UNIX CoPy, UUCP. UUCP has now emigrated from UNIX and is available for a variety of operating environments including MS/PC DOS, OS/2, Microsoft Windows, Apple's Macintosh, and DEC's VMS, among others. What we will do in this book is to demonstrate the way in which UUCP and its affiliated mail service can be used to structure low cost enterprise mail services. It can also serve as an integrating agent for organizations with diverse computing and networking systems. Be aware that "low cost" does not mean "free." It does mean, however, that there is E-Mail software that is well-known and understood, and may already be part of your software inventory. It also means that even if you do not already have access to UUCP, it may be the most cost-effective way for you to implement an extended E-Mail system.

If your organization already uses UNIX, you already have UUCP and **mail** available. From a terminal, you should be able to login and start using **mail** instantly. This is not the approach to use when there are many remote sites in your organization, or you want a "user-friendly" approach to mail, or you want to handle mail in the most cost-effective manner, because it maximizes expense and minimizes functionality. If you do not already have a UNIX machine, the benefits of UUCP may not be readily apparent at all.

This book will show different ways that UUCP can be used in a cost-effective manner as an integration tool, linking together machines with diverse operating systems, with (for the most part) inexpensive personal computers. Some designs may contain *only* DOS machines or Macs. In this case, we will demonstrate the use of UUCP with the DOS-based system distributed with this book, called UUPlus™. Others may require something that at least looks like UNIX, and for this we will illustrate the case with Coherent, a low-cost UNIX clone produced and marketed by the Mark Williams Company. MACs and OS/2 machines can, of course, be used in place of DOS machines, and some of the UUCP software for Macs and OS/2 is briefly described. As noted above, if your organization already uses UNIX, this book can suggest some additional ways in which you can get the most out of UUCP/**mail**. This chapter provides an overview of the major components of a UUCP system, and Chapter 2 deals with the actual design of a network tailored for your environment.

WHO WOULD WANT A UUCP-BASED E-Mail NETWORK?

In answer to this question, the first that comes to mind would be a company or other organization that uses UNIX-based computing for corporate purposes. UUCP/Mail is not for everyone, however. There are, for example, practical, if not theoretical, limits to the size a UUCP/Mail network can grow before it is so unwieldy that it becomes a problem to maintain. What is that upper limit? There is, unfortunately, no fixed answer; it depends upon the individual needs and dictates of each organization. A UUCP/Mail network will be precisely the solution some groups require. Some characteristics of such groups are:

1. Any group that needs a low-cost E-Mail network. "Low-cost" in this case is defined in terms of the initial cost of software and hardware for both the network generally and individual members of the network. Once set up, maintenance of the network can also be distributed among a relatively large number of users of the system so that those costs can be controlled.

2. Any group that needs to communicate primarily across public telephone systems. Examples that come readily to mind are informal groups of friends and colleagues; denominational groups of churches and/or clergy; sales groups within larger organizations; companies with outlying district or regional offices; professional groups that may like or require occasional E-Mail with members or local chapters; civic clubs; amateur sporting groups; hobbyist groups; and other similar organizations. In some areas amateur radio operators already have similar networks running over ham radio.

3. Any group that currently uses fax on a daily schedule to communicate with a relatively well-defined group of people.

4. Consultants and other business people who have customers with UNIX systems.

5. People who like DIY (do-it-yourself) computing projects.

6. Anyone who wants to experiment with electronic mail.

The possibilities are quite large. In the not-too-distant future everyone will need access to E-Mail systems, and this approach is a good first step. Moreover, uucp-based mail systems also can be economically linked into the national and international Usenet which also has gateways into the expanding Internet. Usenet itself, which is probably the world's largest bulletin board, can provide many resources for many different people, as can the Internet. Anyone who has some reasonable experience with personal computing should be able to follow this book. For the more technically inclined, however, it should also serve as a means for clarifying some of the vagaries of uucp and associated E-Mail services. In the course of our discussions, we will, hopefully, even shed some light on E-Mail networks that are based on technologies other than uucp.

FIRST, SOME PRELIMINARIES

Before describing uucp/Mail it may be helpful to review a few networking concepts. If you are already familiar with networking concepts, including the Open System Interconnection (OSI) Model, you can skip this section.

Network Topologies[2]

There are a variety of ways in which networks might be organized, and most networks are in a constant state of change and growth. If the computer network has only a main-site or host computer which does all data processing from one or more remotes, it is a centralized network. If there are remote computers processing jobs for end-users, as well as a main-site computer (which is itself optional), we may have the beginnings of a distributed network. A distributed network can be either centralized or dispersed, but a network that does not involve distributed processing can only be centralized, since all data processing is done on a main-site computer.

A single communications system can provide communications for two or more concurrently operating computer networks. We will review several characteristic (although oversimplified) network configurations: point-to-point, multipoint, star (centralized), ring (distributed), bus structure (distributed), and hierarchical (distributed), with more on local area networks. Figure 1.1 contains diagrammatic representations of the various network configurations or topologies.

Point-to-Point

A point-to-point network is undoubtedly the simplest network. It has only a computer, a communications line (direct or through the telephone system), and one terminal at the other end of the wire. The terminal can be either a remote

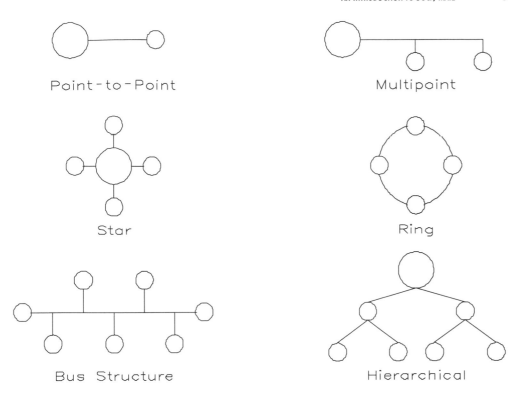

Figure 1.1. Network topologies

batch terminal (RBT), or an interactive terminal. This was the earliest form of network, and many networks still begin in this fashion and gradually develop into more complex entities. In such a system the central computer does not need to be large. A microcomputer can act as a host computer for one or more terminals. Normally, however, such systems have a large computer as the host system.

Multipoint Networks

Multipoint networks originally constituted a straightforward extension of point-to-point systems, with multiple remote stations that dropped off the same communication line rather than having a single remote station. Those remote stations were either RBTs, or interactive, or both. The remote stations may be connected by independent communications lines to the computer, or they may be multiplexed over a single line. In either a point-to-point, or a multipoint system, the characteristics the remote workstations are a function of the work to be accomplished at the remote site. In some of their manifestations, local networks are expansions of the multipoint concept. In its original context, a multipoint system contained only one node with "intelligence"—it had only one computer on the system. A local network will normally have intelligence at all, or most, points on the system without the necessity for any central system.

Centralized (Star) Networks

To reiterate, a centralized network is one in which the primary computing is accomplished at a single site, with all remote stations feeding into that site. Often such a system is thought of as a star network with each remote site entering the central system by a single communications line, although point-to-point and the classical multipoint systems are also centralized networks and are directly incorporated into star networks. Typically, however, a multipoint network does not have distributed processing capabilities, although a star network may have other computers out at the end of its communications lines. The computer which supports a traditional multipoint network might itself have been linked into a star network. Electronic Private Automatic Branch Exchange (EPABX) systems, based on telephone technology, uses a star topology by which the computer that acts as the switch, constitutes the central node, since all information must be passed through it.

Ring (distributed) Networks

A ring network is organized by connecting network nodes in a closed loop with each node linked to those adjacent on the right and the left. The advantage of a ring network is that it can be run at high speeds and the mechanisms for avoiding collisions are simple. As Harry Saal has noted, the " . . . ring topology does not have the flexibility that bus structures [see below] have, yet it forces more regularity into the system. . . ."[3] Ring networks sometimes use *token passing* schemes to determine which node may have access to the communications system.

Bus Structures (distributed)

The bus network depicted in Figure 1.1 is configured, at least logically, with taps (arms, branches, etc.) extending off a central backbone. As a signal traverses the bus network—normally a coaxial, fiber-optic, or twisted pair—the connection listens for the signal that carries an address designation. Bus systems such as Ethernet or most broadband (Cable Television) systems use either a single cable with forward and return paths on the same wire, or a two-cable system, one for forward and one for return signals. With systems based on cable television (CATV), a signal processor exists at the *headend*. It takes a low incoming signal from a device on the bus and upconverts it for retransmission on a higher frequency channel.

Hierarchical (distributed) Networks

A hierarchical network represents a fully distributed network in which computers feed into computers which feed into other computers. The computers used for remote devices may have independent processing capabilities and draw upon the resources at higher or lower levels as information or other resources are required. A hierarchical network is one form of completely distributed network. The classical model of a hierarchical distributed network is that once used by Texas Instruments in which there were several large IBM mainframes at the top, IBM midrange machines in the middle, fed by a combination of minis (such as the TI990), micros, and other machines at the bottom. The TI990s sometimes functioned as a third level, and the micros (or intelligent terminals), at a fourth level.

The Open System Interconnection (OSI) Model

UUCP/Mail is not part of the set of standards associated with the OSI model. However, in order to understand UUCP/Mail, it is helpful to view it in the context of a "layered architecture." In a layered architecture, each open system is viewed as logically composed of an ordered set of subsystems. This is a useful way to understand any system, even one not originally conceived as part of either an open architecture or a layered system. UUCP/Mail, which has its origins in UNIX, comes closest of any system now available to being an "open" operating system (although it is not in any way an official standard). And a related set of networking protocols, called the Transmission Control Protcol/Internet Protocol (TCP/IP), which are often associated with UNIX, is a layered (but non-OSI) architecture. TCP/IP was structured originally by the United States Department of Defense for its AR-PANET network, which later became "The Internet." For a more extensive discussion of this topic, see the references at the end of this chapter.

To understand some of the issues involved in network planning, and to lend credibility to the project itself, it is useful to take a quick look at some of the relevant standards available. There are several standards organizations in North America and Europe, which seek to rationalize electronic systems. Among those organizations are the International Organization for Standardization (ISO) and the Institute of Electrical and Electronics Engineers (IEEE). Standards of any kind for networks are of recent origin, and the lack of standards led to an almost chaotic array of network products.

In 1977, the ISO chartered a committee to study the compatibility of network equipment, a development which eventually led to the publication of the Open System Interconnection (OSI) Reference Model. In this context, "open system" refers to a network model open to equipment from competing manufacturers. As Frank Derfler and William Stallings have noted, the OSI "reference model is useful for anyone involved in purchasing or managing a local network, because it provides a theoretical framework . . ." by which networking problems and opportunities may be understood.[4] The OSI model divides networking issues into functions or layers. These layers are depicted in Table 1.1.

The Reference Model was devised to allow "standardized procedures to be defined enabling the interconnection and subsequent effective exchange of information between users."[5] "Users" in this sense means systems consisting of one or more computers, associated software, peripherals, terminals, human operators, physical processes, information transfer mechanisms, and related elements. These elements together must be capable of "performing information processing and/or information transfer."[6] The importance of the Reference Model is that it will permit various networks of the same or different types to communicate with one another as easily as though they constituted a single network.

TABLE 1.1. OSI Reference Model—Open System Interconnection

Layer	Function
Layer 7 Application	End-user and end-application functions, such as file transfer (FTAM), virtual terminal service (VTP), and electronic mail (X.400)
Layer 6 Presentation	Data translation for use by Layer 7, such as protocol conversion, data unpacking, encryption, and expansion of graphics commands.
Layer 5 Session	Provides for the establishing of a session connection between two presentation entities, to support orderly data exchange.
Layer 4 Transport	Transparent transfer of data between session entities, relieving the session layer of concerns for data reliability and integrity.
Layer 3 Network	Contributes the means to establish, maintain, and terminate network connections among open systems, particularly routing functions across multiple networks.
Layer 2 Data Link	Defines the across strategy for sharing the physical medium, including data link and media access issues.
Layer 1 Physical	Definition of the electrical and mechanical characteristics of the network.

At the outset it is important to keep in mind that conformance with the Reference Model does not imply any particular implementation or technology. In other words it does not specify a medium (such as fiber optic cable, twisted pair, or coax), nor does it specify a set of recommendations such as the IEEE 802.3, 802.4, or 802.5 networks in the United States. The Reference Model is designed to support standardized information exchange procedures, but it does not provide details, definitions, or interconnection protocols.[7] The Model, therefore, is a frame of reference for open systems, with implementation details being left to other standards. Because the Model is a frame of reference, it provides the framework for the definition of services and protocols, which fit within the boundaries established.

AN OVERVIEW OF UUCP/MAIL

Ian Lance Taylor, the author of the newest version of UUCP, recently wrote that the "UUCP suite of programs is widely used in the UNIX world to transfer mail and news between computers. UUCP implementations are also available for many types of personal computers."[8] Along with the simple mail transfer protocol (SMTP), UUCP is, in the UNIX world, synonymous with mail. SMTP started as an official network mail protocol to handle message transfer for TCP/IP. UUCP, in contrast, was built in 1976 as a research project at AT&T Bell Laboratories by Mike Lesk. UNIX originated at Bell Laboratories. Version 2 UUCP was distributed by AT&T with its UNIX System 7 (Release date: 1977). UNIX System V Release 3 (Release date: 1983) UUCP is referred to as Basic Networking Utilities (BNU), or, more popularly, as "HoneyDanBer" UUCP, after its authors, Peter Honeyman, David A. Nowitz, and Brian E. Redman. BNU was an attempt by AT&T to rationalize many of the inconsistencies that had crept into uucp by 1983. The latest UNIX version of uucp is a complete rewrite of the program suite from scratch, in order to distribute it in source code-form under the GNU Public License. Ian Taylor's implementation is called Taylor UUCP.

Distinctions are sometimes made between "real-time" networks and "store-and-forward" networks. The former is just what it implies: a network to which a user may be connected at all times and through which a user has access to resources at will. LANs are examples of such real-time networks. Even on LANs, however, some software may be structured to perform in a store-and-forward manner. Networks based on dial-access over the telephone system are often structured as store-and-forward systems in order to reduce overall operating costs. uucp is an example of store-and-forward software technology. Requests for file transfers (such as mail) or remote execution of commands on another system are not executed immediately. Rather, they are spooled for execution when communication is established. Depending upon how a system is configured, attempts at communication may be made whenever something is in the spool, or communication may be established only at designated times (for example, when telephone rates are lower or to make more effective use of inbound and outbound modems).

In the late 1980s uucps started being produced for MS/PC DOS, the Apple Macintosh, and more recently, for DEC's VMS. The PC version that will be focused on here is UUPlus™. UUPlus™ is a relatively full implementation of uucp, and it is currently (V. 1.50) available as shareware. A Microsoft Windows version, WinNET™ Mail and News, is also discussed extensively and will be found on the distributed diskettes. Both UUPlus™ and WinNET™ are designed for the use of end users. We have, therefore, also included Waffle, a shareware bulletin board system, that can also be used as a uucp host system under DOS.

uucp provided network mail and file transfer among UNIX machines earlier than these features were available on other operating systems. At least some of the dramatic growth of UNIX is likely due, at least in part, to the existence of uucp. Because uucp allowed software to be easily shared, it helped create demand for the operating system, according to Baker. An entire national network, Usenet, based on uucp, grew up that became the primary means for transferring "news" among those with access. In fact, it became the largest bulletin board with current postings of about 40MB a day.

As was noted above, uucp stands for UNIX-to-UNIX CoPy. It was originally conceived primarily as a utility to copy files between UNIX machines, extending the UNIX copy command, **cp**. uucp, in any of its incarnations, is not a single program; rather it is a suite of programs that implement several protocols which allow for file transfers and remote execution of programs. The original design was focused on doing these things via modem over telephone lines. In 1977 that meant slow 300 b/s modems. uucp in a point-to-point system, which means that it is used between two computers at a time. The system has two layers, a session layer and a transport layer. When the usual mail agent is added, along with the programs necessary to queue the mail for transport, it expands to at least four layers. Mail is treated by uucp simply as another file to be transferred. The two computers use the session layer to identify each other and to agree on which files should be transferred. The session layer relies on the transport layer to provide error-free data transfer across the communication link.

THE UUCP PROGRAM SUITE

No truly definitive list of programs which constitute UUCP exists. One way to think about this issue is to look at the set of UUCP programs distributed with formal versions of UNIX from AT&T (or, since AT&T sold UNIX to Novell in 1993, subsequent Novell releases). The difficulty with this is that AT&T also licensed UNIX to a number of other corporations which require more tailored versions, and those companies, in turn, often enhanced UUCP. Various other people have added to the list of UUCP utilities, and some of these additions are very widely distributed. As already noted, UUCP has also been widely rewritten both to run on operating systems other than UNIX and because AT&T's ownership of the code precluded certain kinds of new development. The fundamental list of UUCP and related programs (since **mail** is not technically a part of UUCP) necessary to set up a UUCP-based mail network is the following.

> **uucp**
> **uucico**
> **uux**
> **uuxqt**
> **mail**
> **rmail**

These, and a few other programs common in UUCP are listed and briefly described in Table 1.2.

Not all PC-based UUCP systems designed primarily to support E-Mail contain a program called "**uucp**." Versions of UUPlus™ prior to 1.50 (when it was still called

TABLE 1.2. Common UUCP and related commands

Command	Function
mail	Mail user agent (MUA) that allows the exchange of electronic mail either on the local system or on the other systems via **uucp**.
rmail	Mail delivery agent (MDA); writes to local mailboxes and/or queues for remote sytems.
uucico	Transmit data to or from a remote site.
uucp	Ready files for transmission to other systems.
uulog	Examine UUCP operations.
uuname	List UUCP names of known systems.
uux	Requests the execution of a command on a remote system.
uuxqt	Execute commands requested by a remote system.
Notes	All these commands (except **uucico**, of course) funnel messages/directives/requests, etc., through **uucico** for delivery on remote systems.

FSUUCP) were distributed without **uucp**, for example. The reason for this is that **uucp** (the program, not the system) is designed to set up a file for transmittal. When UUCP (the system, not the program) is used as the foundation for E-Mail, the mail user agents perform that task. Programs such as **mail** (in UUPlus™), **pcelm**, **cmm**, and the Windows and Mac versions discussed in this book have all been optimized for E-Mail and do not, therefore, require a program called "**uucp**." At appropriate points we will illustrate how to transfer files with E-Mail. The program that you will find with all systems is **uucico**; it is the communications program that performs the transmission of a mail message (or other file) from one point to another. Users will still be able to receive files set up by **uucp** on a UNIX or other system. If a user finds that he or she needs a DOS-based version of **uucp**, he or she will need to install the appropriate packages. Both UUPlus™ and Waffle, distributed with this book, contain a **uucp** program, so you should not have any problems.

UNDERSTANDING THE PIECES

The suite of UUCP programs cover the range of functions outlined in Layers 4 through 7 of the OSI Model. It is sometimes suggested that UUCP consists only, or primarily, of session layer (Layer 5) and transport layer (Layer 4) protocols. As you can see from Table 1.3, that is not an adequate portrayal of the situation. In fact, one of the programs in the suite, **uucico**, contains virtually all of the session and transport layer protocols alluded to.

It is true, however, that the session and transport layer protocols, and **uucico**, can probably be described as the "guts" of the UUCP system. The negotiations between two machines take place in the session layer and the actual file transfer protocols are a function of the transport layer. The "negotiations" that take place

TABLE 1.3. Comparison of OSI, TCP/IP, and UUCP

Layer	OSI Standards	TCP/IP	UUCP
Layer 7 Application	X.400	SMTP	**mail, r-mail**
Layer 6 Presentation	ISO 8823		**uuencode, uudecode**
Layer 5 Session	ISO 8327	TCP	**uucp, uux, uuxqt**
Layer 4 Transport	ISO 8073		**uucico**
Layer 3 Network	ISO 8473	IP	IP, X.25, Telephone System
Layer 2 Data Link	LLC/MAC HDLC	X.25/HDLC 802.x/LLC/MAC	Async. Serial, 802.x/LLC/MAC
Layer 1 Physical	Modem Stds., IEEE 802.x, etc.	Modem Stds., IEEE 802.x, etc.	Modem Stds., IEEE 802.x, etc.

Notes X.400 is the ISO message handling service (mail); SMTP is the Simple Mail Transfer Protocol for TCP/IP. The ISO *nnnn* standards are simply some appropriate standards for the various layers noted. LLC is the 802.2 Logical Link Control and MAC is the 802.x Medium Access Control protocols. X.25 actually overlaps the Network and Data Link Layers. Nothing listed for Layers 1 or 2 are part of either TCP/IP or UUCP specifications. UUCP "equivalents" have been listed by program/command rather than by specification standard.

include the login dialog, as well as other options, such as the type of transport protocol to be used for file transfer. Today, in addition to the original *g* protocol, there are several other methods **uucico** can use to transfer files from one machine to another. They are all designed to provide ways of getting information from "here to there" in an error-free manner.[9]

From Figure 1.2 it can be seen that **uucp**, **uux**, and **mail** do not actually transfer files, execute remote commands, or deliver mail to a remote system. When **uucp**, **mail,** or **uux** are invoked two basic things happen:[10]

1. A temporary file containing appropriate information is created in the UNIX directory */usr/spool/uucp* or the DOS directory *\fsuucp\ spool\uucp*. This file contains selected information to get both it and any associated files to be transferred from here to there.
   a. The *source* and *destination* files which, in the case of the *destination*, include the destination machine.
   b. The type of request, which may be: *send*, *receive*, or *execute*.
   c. Any data files, including mail messages, that are to be copied for transfer.
2. The transfer is then made using **uucico**.

Configuration Files

Only a small proportion of the information **uucico** needs for a successful transfer is contained in the temporary files just described. In effect, they tell **uucico** what to do, but not how to do it. The information on how to do it is contained in a set of configuration files, the more important of which is called *SYSTEMS* or *L.sys* (or *sys* in Taylor UUCP). We shall consistently refer to this file as *SYSTEMS/L.sys*. Just remember that some UUCP implementations use *SYSTEMS* (BNU, UUPlus™, UUPC), while others use *L.sys* (Version 2, Coherent prior to v. 4.2, DOSGATE), or *sys* (Taylor UUCP). The *SYSTEMS/L.sys* file contains a list of systems known to your local systems and instructions on how to reach them. Because the configuration files used by Taylor UUCP are quite different than previous versions, we have occasionally referenced Taylor's system independently of other discussions.

In addition to *SYSTEMS/L.sys* UUCP uses several other configuration files in order to know how to do its work. All these files will be discussed in detail in other chapters. Suffice it to say at this point that some or all of the following files may be necessary for a particular implementation of UUCP to operate.

1. *L-devices* or *devices* which link a device name, such as COM1, or tty008, to the actual hardware used to communicate.
2. A system configuration file defining the local system.
3. A user configuration file defining each local user.
4. A modem definition file called *acucap* or *modemcap* in Version 2-based UUCPs; *Dialers* in BNU; and individual modem definition files (*.mdm) for UUPlus™ (and UUPC/Extended).
5. A *Permissions* (BNU), *permissn* (UUPC), or *USERFILE* and *L.cmds* (Version 2) file that controls which parts of your local system are

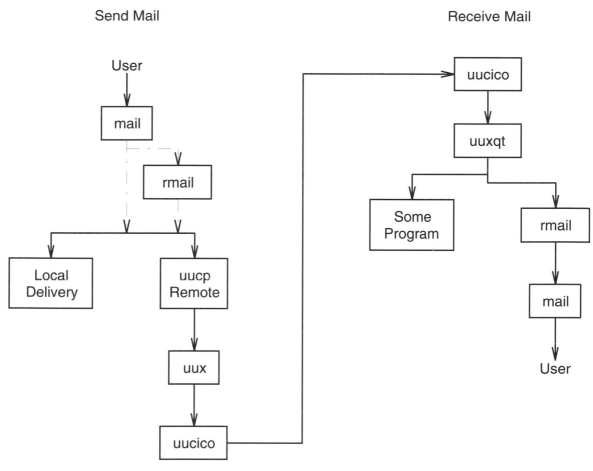

Figure 1.2. Flow diagrams of UUCP/Mail

accessible to remote systems. In Taylor UUCP the information in *Permissions* is combined into *sys* and in UUPlus into *uuplus.cfg*.

6. A *passwd* file that controls whether remote machines can log into a system and identify legitimate local users of the system.
7. Optional files may provide some routing information or system aliases.
8. *SYSTEMS* / *L.sys*.

The most difficult part of setting up UUCP is constructing these configuration files. One reason for choosing UUPlus for distribution with this book is that UUPlus comes with an installer program that helps considerably with specific configura-

tions. WinNET™ constructs the necessary files through typical Windows dia-
logues, thus making it very easy to set up.

Other Items of Note

In addition to the configuration and program files on both UNIX and DOS, it is
necessary to set up some environment variables. In DOS this is done usually in
the *autoexec.bat* file, and in UNIX, in either the system configuration file, or the
user's own configuration file. These variables, which are discussed in detail
elsewhere, tell the computer such things as where the programs are to be found,
where to find the configuration files, and the time zone in which you live.

UUCP also requires that some directories be defined for its use. On UNIX it is
likely that you will find */usr/spool/uucp*, which is used for all those files created
when a transfer is requested. On some UNIX systems this "spool" directory may
be found in */etc/spool/uucp*. The equivalent UUPlus directory on DOS systems is
\uuplus\spool\uucp. For security purposes remote systems are usually restricted
to reading and writing files to a "Public" directory often named */usr/spool/uucp-
public*. Because of the differences in name lengths between DOS and UNIX, the
equivalent DOS directory is *\uuplus\spool\uupc\public*. There are some other
directories we will use as well, and these will be described in appropriate sections.

Some Notes about Mail

UUCP is used most frequently when people use electronic mail under UNIX. The
principal program we see when this happens is a not-very-friendly "mail user
agent" (MUA) called, appropriately enough, **mail**. **mail** is essentially a reading
and composing program for UNIX E-Mail and may be interfaced with SMTP as
well as with UUCP. This is why we suggested earlier that *mail* is not actually part
of UUCP. Part of our quest in this book is for a more friendly MUA that people will
be happier about using.

One attempt for friendliness is **elm** (ELectronic Mail), a program written for the
UNIX environment. **elm** provides the utility of *mail* through a menu-driven user
interface. A DOS program inspired by **elm** (although otherwise unrelated) is
pcelm. While an improvement over *mail*, **elm** (**pcelm**) is still far from intuitive
in its use and is certainly not what people who use Microsoft Windows are coming
to understand as "easily used" software. Fortunately, there are packages, usually
distributed as Shareware, that are Windows applications that can (and do) provide
"front ends" to UUPlus and other DOS-based UUCP systems. One such product, the
Cinetic Mail Manager (**cmm**). Both **pcelm** and **cmm** are fully configurable so that
if you find yet another UUCP system for DOS, you can probably still use these
mailers (MUAs). And, of course, WinNet is a full implementation of UUCP with an
integrated MVA under Windows.

cmm comes ready to use with UUPlus (actually its predecessor, FSUUCP), and
with a little creativity in the use of the UNIX Network File System (NFS), **ccm**
can be made to function more or less directly with UNIX. In subsequent chapters
we will suggest ways to do this. In the diagram found in Figure 1.2, **cmm** is simply

substituted for **mail**. On a LAN **cmm**, along with **rmail**, and a minimum of other files from UUPlus, a UUCP-based mail system can be set up that is very inexpensive and that functions easily and well. Adding the necessary components to allow dial-access to that same mail system then becomes a relatively simple matter. This enables people traveling, or those in remote offices, to have the same use of E-Mail as the people in the central office. This latter component, access from outside, provides the reason why, even on a Microsoft Windows for Workgroups LAN which comes with Microsoft Mail, you might wish to use a UUCP-based system rather than the native mail application. If you happen to be using some variety of Novell LAN, it is necessary to acquire a mail system outside the basic LAN network operating system (NOS), so UUCP might well be a viable alternative.

REFERENCES

1. Steven Baker, "From UUCP to Eternity," *UNIX Review*, April 1993, vol. 11, no. 4, p. 15 (8 pages).

2. This section is based on similar discussions in related books by the author: *Microcomputers in Large Organizations* (Englewood Cliffs, NJ: Prentice-Hall, 1983), pp. 22–28; *Local Area Networks in Large Organizations* (Hasbrouck Heights, NJ: Hayden Book Company, 1984); *Micro-Mainframe Connection* (Indianapolis, IN: Howard W. Sams & Company, 1987); *Local Area Networks: The Next Generation* (New York: John Wiley & Sons, 1988, 1990); *Enterprise-Wide Computing* (New York: John Wiley & Sons, 1991); and *Peer-to-Peer LANs: Networking Two to Ten PCs* (New York: John Wiley & Sons, 1993).

3. Harry Saal, "Local Area Networks: An Update on Microcomputers in the Office," *Bytes*, May, 1983, p. 62.

4. Frank Derfler, Jr. and William Stallings, *A Manager's Guide of Local Networks* (Englewood Cliffs, NJ: Prentice-Hall, 1983), p. 79.

5. The actual text of standards are sometimes difficult to obtain. An easily accessible compilation of many of the more important standards can be found in Harold C. Folts, ed., *McGraw-Hill's Compilation of Data Communications Standards*, Edition III (New York: McGraw-Hill, 1986), 3 volumes. The ISO 7498 standard (OSI) was adopted from the CCITT Recommendation X.200. X.200 has been used as the basics for discussion in this chapter and references are made to that document, designated as *Fascicle VIII.5 - Rec. X.200*. In references following the identification of the actual standard, volume and page references to the standard as found in *McGraw-Hill's Compilation of Data Communications Standards*. Fascicle VIII.5 -Rec. X.200, p. 3 (Vol. 2, p. 2235).

6. Ibid.

7. Ibid., p. 3 (Vol. 2, p. 2235).

8. Ian Lance Taylor, "The UUCP g protocol," *C Users Journal*, Jan., 1993, vol. 11, no. 1, p. 63ff (9 pages).

9. For more detail concerning OSI, TCP/IP and other issues related to this discussion, see Madron, *Enterprise-Wide Computing*, Chapter 7. Note also the explanation of file transfer protocols in Chapter 9. While the UUPC file transfer protocols are not discussed, several others are, and Chapter 9 provides details on discussion in the section on the *SYSTEM/L.sys* file in this book.

10. The discussion on how the process works is based on an excellent book by Tim O'Reilly and Grace Todino, *Managing UUCP and Usenet* (Sebastopol, CA: O'Reilly & Associates, Inc., 1990), Chapter 1.

2

Designing a UUCP Network

Much of what has been written on UUCP has focused on how to use the system for the purpose of connecting to national and international networks. Indeed, a later chapter of this book also discusses this issue. The primary focus of this book, however, is how to use this software technology as the basis for integrated networking *within* an organization rather than *between* unrelated organizations or individuals. The design suggestions given in this chapter are just that—*suggestions*. The UUCP system is very flexible, and it is capable of being configured in a wide variety of ways. I have tried to develop some approaches which may be useful to systems managers when deciding how to approach your specific needs. I have also tried to suggest some of the easier ways of setting up a network. Depending on an organization's own local conditions, managers may find it is appropriate to organize their network differently than suggested here. How to do that can be discovered by paying close attention not only to this book, but also to the documentation of the system(s) being used.

For the moment, let us assume that we are not talking about corporations, or other bureaucracies. Assume that you and a group of your friends want to communicate by electronic mail, and that you want to do it inexpensively. Moreover, we will also assume that you each already have some sort of a computer with an operating system. Under these circumstances we might have the following.

Name	Computer	OS
John	IBM (compatible)	MS/DOS
Mary	IBM (compatible)	DOS/Windows

Name	Computer	OS
Tom	IBM (compatible)	Coherent
Beverly	Macintosh	System 7
Dick	Sun Workstation	UNIX
Jane	IBM (compatible)	OS/2

Under these circumstances, one simple approach would be for everyone to buy a membership in CompuServe, BIX, or some other national computer utility, and use whatever mail system was provided. However, for some reason you may determine that you really want to have a completely private mail system. The solution is UUCP, as some version of it runs on each of these machines. Other than UUCP, another possiblity would be to simply use one of the small multi-user systems on a dial-up basis to obtain mail through a simple bulletin board mechanism. Indeed, some situations might be that simple to solve.

However, what a UUCP-based mail system provides is the more generalized ability to transfer a variety of files and to schedule all transfers, (whether mail or other files), in an orderly fashion. Another advantage of this system is that its components are easily and inexpensively available. Moreover, if you have a need, or a desire, for more expansive mail and file transfer capabilities to the world at large, they can also be provided.

In "real life" you probably would not run into quite this variety of operating systems. MS/DOS is, of course, Microsoft's familiar single-user PC operating system, and it is the most limited of those listed. When we add Windows, we obtain multi-tasking and a graphical user interface (GUI). Windows/NT, which is a version of Windows that does not require DOS, can now be obtained. Coherent is a UNIX-like operating system from the Mark Williams Company. The versions of UNIX that normally run on a Sun Workstation are actually called Sun/OS (old version) or Solaris (new version). OS/2 is the IBM/Microsoft multi-tasking operating system and Apple's Macintosh uses System 7. Integrating this variety of machines and operating systems can become a nightmare. However, through the use of UUCP, the process can become an interesting and enlightening experiment in low-cost networking.

The details on how to set up the various files and programs mentioned in this chapter will be left to subsequent discussions. Suffice it to say at this point that you will each need to acquire some version of UUCP, at least some of which are listed in Appendix C. Both Coherent and UNIX come with UUCP as part of their software distribution so that aquisition is already taken care of for Tom and Dick in our example. UUPlus and Waffle are available for DOS, WinNET™ Mail and News for Windows, UUPC/Extended for OS/2, and either GNU UUCP for Mac or UUPC for Mac 3.0. There are several others available that are noted in the Appendix. We have now taken care of John, Mary, and Jane. Beverly will use one of the Mac versions. This book contains distributable versions of UUPlus, WinNET™, and Waffle. Sources for each of the other systems listed may be found in Appendix and they are discussed in Chapter 4.

PRELIMINARIES

In order to design an electronic mail system that works smoothly, automatically, and at a low cost, there are a few points that need to be understood. First, it is desirable to be able to have each machine communicate with the others, without having to place a voice telephone call telling the recipient to turn on the machine and bring up the software. This implies that if Tom is sending Beverly a message, then Beverly's machine should be waiting to receive a call. In order for this to happen, with UUCP, a program named **uucico** must be running on Beverly's machine waiting to receive calls.

Since Beverly's machine is multi-tasking this is not too much of a problem because she can still use her computer for other purposes even while it is waiting for communications. However, for John, who only has DOS, this could be disruptive since only one program can be run at a time. John's solution is to get Windows or some other multi-tasking software such as *DesqView*. This problem can also be overcome by scheduling software (on UNIX systems usually called **cron**). In this way everyone could be set up so that communications would take place at a known time. Shareware "cron" software is available for DOS and Windows. Many popular PC software packages, such as PCTools, Norton Utilities, and even WordPerfect 6.x now come with scheduling programs that allow the execution of other programs at specific times. This also has the advantage of being able to schedule calls when phone rates are lowest and so that your modem is not monopolized by UUCP. An alternative, still not precluding scheduling, is to designate a particular machine as a server for UUCP and mail.

Other software that is not a formal part of UUCP is a MUA that allows you to prepare and read mail, programs for encoding and decoding binary files so that files can be sent through "seven-bit" systems without corruption, and programs to translate text files into formats required by DOS, UNIX, and MACs. A program called **mail** is actually distributed with virtually all implementations of UUCP or its capabilities are built into other programs. PC implementations of **mail** are normally patterned after the standard UNIX **mail**, which is *very* primitive. Fortunately, programs that enhance the user interface are available, either as shareware or in the public domain. Examples are the Cinétics Mail Manager (**cmm**) for Windows, and the PC (DOS) version of ELectronic Mail (**pcelm**) that provide better user interfaces. With all these programs, it is usually possible to designate the editor you wish to use to compose and read mail. In DOS, for example, you might use the full screen editor in DOS 5 and 6, called **edit**. Under Windows you would probably use **notebook**, while with UNIX you might opt for **vi,** or some version of **emacs**. In the case of WinNET™ Mail both the MUA and the editor are integrated into the total package.

The encoding and decoding programs that are distributed with UNIX are usually called **uuencode** and **uudecode**. They translate binary files to standard ASCII characters so that they can pass over the most primitive of networks. "Primitive," in this case, means networks that cannot pass 8-bit data, or that become confused when confronted by embedded control characters. Programs for the other operating environments, using the same method for encoding and decoding data, are available. DOS and Windows versions are found with this book. Finally, it may be necessary for you to translate text files from one OS standard to another in order to read or use them comfortably (although the mail systems usually take care of this for you). The reason for this is that each of these operating systems uses a different ASCII character to delineate the end of a line. DOS uses a carriage return and a line feed (CR/LF). The MAC uses a carriage return (CR), and UNIX uses a line feed (LF). Utilities for this are also included in this book. If your operating system supports "pipes," it may be possible for a sending station to automatically do a translation based on knowledge of the receiving station. Conversely, a receiving station may be capable of being set up to handle this automatically. If you want a completely generalized network, however, (as in the case of national or international mail) it is probably more desirable to have all the messages go out in UNIX format, which is closer to a standard than either the DOS or MAC conventions.

The most common means for communicating via UUCP is over the telephone system. You may also be able to do this over a local area network (LAN), or via an X.25 network. We will discuss the telephone and LAN options in this book. The X.25 approach is simply an extension of the telephone system (at least for our purposes). If you will be operating over the telephone, then you will also need a modem to be attached to a serial port on your computer. The vagaries of serial communications are discussed in Appendix K.

NETWORK DESIGN

In some respects, the easiest way to put our UUCP network together would be simply to have everyone, all six members of our group, connect to everyone else as needed. This kind of "any-to-any" configuration may be seen in Figure 2.1. It would be easiest because it would take the least overall coordination, but it would be almost impossible to set up to run automatically. It would also mean that everyone would have to have **uucico** running all the time in order to answer the phone on demand, or there would have to be individual pair-by-pair negotiations to determine a set of schedules. Even for so small a group, the number of schedules would be 2^{6-1}, or a total of 32 across the entire group. In other words, the any-to-any approach would likely create the maximum amount of aggravation with the minimum amount of convenience. While the amount of network-wide coordination might be minimal, it would create the maximum amount of person-to-person oversight.[1]

A better approach would be for one of the group members with a multi-user, multi-tasking operating environment (in this case either Tom or Dick), to volunteer to be the coordinator for a "mail server." In this case, we would set up a star topology similar to the one in Figure 2.2. Just from the number of lines on the two drawings it can be seen that the complexity of the network has just been reduced from 32 individual negotiations to either 6 or 10, depending on your interpretation. If Tom or Dick is willing to dedicate a modem and a telephone line, it drops to five; in this case, only the other five must make decisions on how and when to connect. Alternatively, the

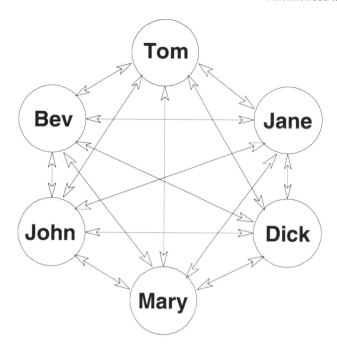

Figure 2.1. Any-to-any topology

number could remain at five if there was an agreed upon time of day when the server would be open to calls from the others. This would free up the telephone line and modem at other times. The positive side of this is that most group members would have a relatively simple configuration. The down side is that the owner of the server—Tom or Dick—would have a more complicated setup. Overall, however, the topological design of Figure 2.2 is probably the superior one.

This is not to say that we cannot make the star topology more complicated, or at least as complex as our situation demands. For example, if Beverly were actually part of a LAN, and all the others on the LAN wish to communicate with John, Mary, Tom, Beverly, Dick, Jane and with one another, the system could be set up to accommodate that eventuality. What we would actually be structuring in such a case are two networks—the main one as depicted, and another one on the LAN subsidiary to the main network. If that were the case, intra-LAN messages would not have to leave the LAN at all and the software setup for each LAN connection would be *very* simple, although each LAN member that needed to be known individually and uniquely across the entire network would have to be known to the central mail server.

Addressing Messages

On the host end, under ordinary circumstances, forwarding of mail to systems known to the server, but not to the end user, can be automatic. In fact, while **uucp** file transfers often have automatic forwarding inhibited, it is normal for mail files

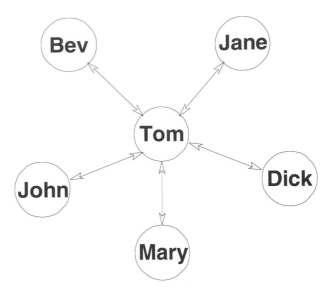

Figure 2.2. Star network

to be forwarded automatically. This means that the descriptions of how to forward mail explicitly do not need to concern the end user. If your server has been set up appropriately (which usually means taking the default conditions), then Beverly can simply address a mail message to Jane by the simple expedient of sending the message to `jane@mach2` or `mach2!jane` and the message will arrive safely, assuming that the server knows about mach2. *Unless you are told differently by the manager of your mail server, you should assume that this default method of addressing may be used.* There may be times, however, when you will have to use more explicit addressing techniques.

Assuming that Tom must take care of the server, we will look at the configuration issues for both the server and each of the other UUCP nodes. For purposes of this discussion (and for the configuration and addressing of mail and other files), it is necessary not only to have user names, such as Tom and Beverly, but each machine must also be assigned an unique name. In Figure 2.3 simple machine names, "Mach1" through "Mach6" have been added to the user names already there. The basic structure of a UUCP address is:

`machinename!username`

Beverly would address a message to Tom with the address mach1!tom. The machine name and user name are separated with an exclamation point. Some software can translate an Internet-style address of the form `username@machinename` or even a fully qualified Internet-style address. For purposes of this discussion, however, we will confine ourselves to using the standard UUCP addressing scheme. For Beverly to send a message to Jane, assuming that Tom allows

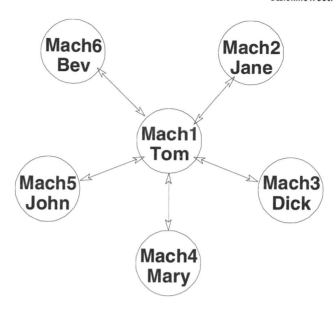

Figure 2.3. Star topology with machine and user names

message forwarding on the server, it can be accomplished through the use of an extended address:

```
machinename1!machinename2!username
```

for the general case and

```
mach1!mach2!jane
```

for the specific case. In this case, the message is first sent to mach1; then, if mach1 knows about mach2, to mach2. There are other methods for transferring files across extended networks, but this simple approach is sufficient for our purposes at this time.

The actual setup on each computer can actually be made friendlier since UUCP systems, or at least mail user agents, have the capability of using "alias" files. An *alias* file is something like a telephone directory that typically gives a common name to be used when addressing someone on the network, such as "Tom," and it associates that common name with a specific address, such as "mach1!tom." Thus, when the MUA requests that the "TO:" (or address) field be filled, all that is necessary is to type in "Tom." If an *alias* file exists, then the full address is pulled and substituted for the common name.

Larger groups and organizations may require more complicated routing addresses in order get from "here-to-there." While more detail on network maps will be given elsewhere, there is a UUCP Mapping Project maintained at Rutgers

University (mail addresses: *uucpmap@rutgers.edu* or *uunet!rutgers!UUCPmap*). The "maps" are actually the data for a database of locations of UUCP sites, and updated data are posted monthly on Usenet in the *comp.mail.maps*. Usenet is a network of systems designed to exchange "news," allowing users to read and post messages. It is, in essence, a very large, distributed bulletin board system. Many of the maps produced by the Mapping Project are also available elsewhere, such as on the UNIXFORUM on CompuServe. To participate in Usenet, you must have a registered site (see the Appendix for details). The most commonly used program to access the map database is **pathalias**, which calculates the least expensive routing of a UUCP transfer and provides the extended address required by **uucp**. The point of this comment is that specific groups and organizations can maintain their own map database and access it with **pathalias**, thus allowing relatively easy use of complex routes.

Defining the Domain

The term "domain" is used technically to refer to a particular kind of addressing scheme that is centrally maintained. We will, in fact, discuss it in detail later in this book. Here we use the word "domain" more generically to discuss how we want to think about our own UUCP-based mail system. In this more general sense, "domain" refers to all the people and machines that will participate in our UUCP/mail network. This domain needs to take into consideration all those people of immediate concern as well as support staff, mobile units (such as laptops carried when out of the office), activities from home, and any personnel that may be in offices that are not at the central site. The reason this issue is important is that it has implications for how we configure the UUCP network and even how we assign user names. It also has implications for how complicated or easy it will be to maintain the system in the future.

If, for example, John, Mary, Tom, Beverly, Dick, and Jane all work in the same office, and are connected by a LAN, the problem is very easy. There is no need for an independent server, other than one on which files can be accessed by everyone, and the installation on each workstation is very simplified. If we add to this simple setup the need to service people in the field, people from home, and remote offices, however, then the problem becomes greater, and the administration of the system can become more arduous. However, a little advance planning can reduce the problems and make the system both easy to use and relatively user friendly as well as inexpensive.

Thus, the first step in planning your mail network is, therefore, to define both the membership of that network and the needs for flexibility and future growth. Will some people be coming in over a LAN? Will others have to access the system by telephone? Is more than one group going to share a common mail network? If the latter, we may need more than one mail server to prevent all mail from having to be sent through the most expensive routing. Are the routes simple, as in the case of our illustration, or should they be more complicated in order to reduce the communication costs? How often during a twenty-four hour period should mail be updated? Do you need something every half-hour, every hour, once a day, or once a week?

MAIL SERVER ISSUES

Once we know the magnitude of the system we need to design, we can turn our attention to how to actually structure it. An important part of this is an understanding of a *mail server*. Generally, a server is a computer in a network that is shared by multiple users such as a file server, print server, or communications server, or it can be a computer in a network that is designated to provide a specific service as distinct from a general-purpose, centralized, multi-user computer system, although it does not need to be dedicated only as a server. The most recent model of cooperative computing is called *client-server*. This is a model of interaction in a distributed system in which a program at one site sends a request to a program at another site and waits for a response. The requesting program is called a *client*; the program satisfying the request is called the *server*. When UUCP was originally designed, the client-server concept had not been articulated, but the concept was present in the product: it was called a *master/slave* relationship. The slave makes requests of the master. Regardless of the nomenclature, the relationship is dynamic because in an interaction between two systems during the same session, the roles may change.

When designing a UUCP-based network we have a number of possible options regarding servers. We can use an existing central UNIX machine, we can use a small, stand-alone system running UNIX, or some UNIX clone. We can do without a server at all, or we can use a DOS-based machine as a server. There are other options we might imagine, but these will serve to illustrate the issue and allow you to decide how to design your system. Actually, UUCP systems can function as servers, although there are some that are designed primarily as leaf systems. Both WinMail™ and UUPlus™ are examples of the latter. Since UUCP was originally conceived as a point-to-point file transfer system, no server is needed. A user simply needs all the relevant telephone numbers or network addresses. This situation is illustrated in Figure 2.1.

As we have already seen a pure point-to-point network becomes very cumbersome when there are even just a few users. When there are many users, it becomes impossible. Hence the desirability of a server. A server allows us to streamline the way in which the network is ordered. The term "server" in this case is used differently than it is when we talk about the "client/server" model. With the former we are focusing as much on physical conditions as on anything else. "Server" in the client/server (or master/slave) model is more of a functional than a physical issue. Even in the point-to-point system in Figure 2.1, during the passage of files back and forth between any two systems there will be times when one side is the client (slave) and the other the server (master), and the situation may be reversed if files must also flow the other direction.

In Figure 2.3 everyone's life has been simplified because there is only one phone number that needs to be known. The server, Mach1 (Tom), can also be made to *never* call another machine. Initially, then, Mach1 is a physical server as well as a server in the client/server or master/slave context. If Mach1 knows about the others, it will simply hold (or *queue*) mail and other files until the next time a recipient calls in. In essence, Mach1 has become the central post office. As with any postal service, a postmaster is necessary. This is usually set up as a dummy userid so that undeliverable mail can go somewhere. In our case, however, Tom would have to also function as a postmaster because he would need to manage the configuration of the system, dispose of undeliverable mail, add and delete users as group membership changes, and provide the computing and storage resources for the network. It needs to be clearly understood, that every electronic mail system must have someone to serve these functions, not just one based on UUCP.

The problem in having a physical mail server somewhere is largely one of cost. If a machine must be dedicated to the mail server function, the cost of the mail system just went up by whatever expense is necessary to acquire that system. Fortunately, a dedicated machine is rarely needed for the server in a UUCP network. For example, if your organization already has a UNIX system that is used for central computing, or for workgroup computing for that matter, you already have a computer on which UUCP is available. In that case it might be best simply to use that machine as the mail server. This would make sense especially for a small group, as such systems usually will have multiple communication ports already hooked to modems and phone lines, and/or connected to a LAN. Such a machine will hardly notice it is supporting the mail service.

Another common situation today are workstations using Microsoft Windows. Since Windows is a multi-tasking system, several processes can be running at the same time. The mail server function can run in the background, and the owner of the machine will still be able to do useful work. However, that the process is not completely transparent and there will be times when work is interrupted by actions of the mail server function. Up to two ports can be enabled for mail activity, assuming that the workstation does not have a serial mouse attached. With the normal COM1-COM4 configuration only COM1 and COM2 (or COM3 and COM4) can be used for intensive serial applications at the same time. This is a function of the design of the IBM-type PC which uses the same interrupt for COM1 and COM3 on the one hand and COM2 and COM4 on the other.

Since a standard DOS machine is a single-user system, unless some multi-tasking software is being used, such as DesqView (or Windows), a DOS machine must be used as a dedicated mail server rather than one that shares the mail service with other functions. This brings us to the issue of why you might actually wish to have a dedicated mail server. If the mail and file transfer function becomes important to your operation, and with the price of 386, 486, or later machines dropping dramatically, it may be useful to think in terms of a dedicated server.

The primary advantages of a dedicated server are its ability to tune the software to optimize the communications process and the stability when a system is used for only one function. If properly managed, a large multi-user system is also very stable, but such a system may not be available for your use.

Any approach to building a dedicated server will require the use of a 386 or 486 microcomputer. Such machines, with substantial memory and disk storage, are now available for prices ranging from $800 to $1400 in the United States. The use of DOS, with a multi-tasking add-on such as DesqView or Windows, will allow support of more than one port, since multiple copies of **uucico** can be running at the same time. DOS plus Windows or DesqView will cost an additional $100 to $150. If a single phone line will suffice for your situation (as it would for our six member illustrative group), then DOS is all that is necessary. An alternative would be to use either a true UNIX system (which costs $700–$1500), or a UNIX clone such as Coherent (which runs about $99). The advantage of UNIX, or Coherent is that they are true mult-tasking/multi-user operating systems, and they come equipped with UUCP. No add-ons are necessary to run multiple instances of **uucico** in order to answer multiple phone lines. Once properly configured, the stand-alone mail server can sit in a corner, and you can more or less forget about it.

EXPANDING THE DESIGN

Thus far we have considered some relatively straightforward design issues. To summarize the status of our design, we might consider the following points:

1. **Physical layer:** The public telephone system.
2. **Transport mechanism:** UUCP or some variation thereof.
3. **User interface:** Some appropriate MUA (mail user agent).
4. **Distribution mechanism: rmail** implied, see below.

Up to this point we have not discussed how mail gets distributed in a UUCP-based system. Just as there is a need for a MUA so that mail can be constructed by a human being, so there is need for a Mail Delivery Agent (MDA). The MDA normally associated with UNIX-oriented E-Mail systems is called **rmail**. On non-UNIX UUCP-based mail systems an MDA is also required, and it is usually a clone of the UNIX **rmail. rmail** or its equivalent is invoked on a remote system by **uuxqt**, or on a local system by an MUA, such as **mail** for local delivery. The primary function of **rmail** is to interpret the address on incoming E-Mail and either deliver it locally or pass it on to the next machine named in the **uucp** path. The address that most **rmail** programs interpret must usually be one that is valid according to the rules of RFC-822 (see Appendix G). The UUPlus™ applications depend only peripherally on an external **rmail** program, since they use an internally linked version of that program. A command-line independent **rmail** program is distributed with UU-Plus™, however, so that other programs can link to the mail facility. An example of such use is the Cinetics Mail Manager that uses **rmail** to deliver mail locally or to queue for transmittal by UUCP. The program **uuxqt** executes commands locally as requested by a remote system. When UUCP is not required as a transport mechanism, **rmail** may be called directly by the MUA for direct local delivery. This is the typical situation found when this E-Mail system is used over a local area network (LAN).

Integrating LANs with E-Mail

All of this brings us to the point of this section. One way in which the design may be expanded is to include people and workstations connected via a LAN into the E-Mail network. This concept is illustrated in Figure 2.4. In the illustration there are two LANs: ALAN and BLAN. Tom (Mach1) is the postmaster for the E-Mail star network and is also a node on the ALAN. The other machines on the ALAN are named ALAN1 . . . ALAN*n*. Similarly, the machines on the BLAN (apart from

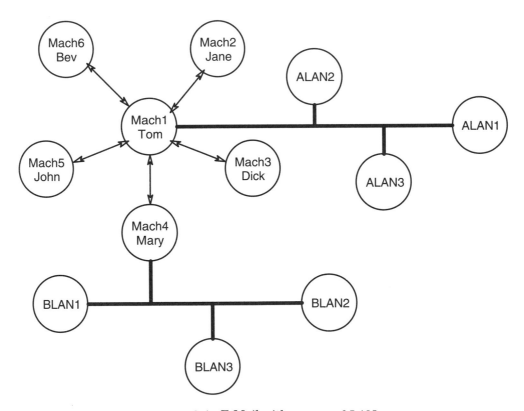

Figure 2.4. E-Mail with connected LANs

Mary's, which is named Mach4), are named BLAN1 .. BLAN*n*. Please note at the outset that the communication issue for ALAN is different from BLAN's.

The first design issue we will address, when considering E-Mail on LANs, is whether it is appropriate to use a UUCP-oriented mail system on a LAN at all. There are many powerful commercial E-Mail systems available for use on LANs, some of which may have features that we will not be able to implement through UUCP/E-Mail. The advantages of such packages include: a richness of features; good integration with the LAN technology, and support of a commercial enterprise. Even price is often not at issue since some LAN network operating systems (NOS), such as Artisoft's LANtastic and Microsoft's Windows for Workgroups (WFW), come with E-Mail packages. There are also low-cost (but often with fewer features) shareware E-Mail packages for the most popular LAN NOSs. For a large Novell network, several high-end E-Mail systems are available, although they tend to be a bit costly. So why would we want to use a UUCP/E-Mail system?[2]

The first reason is that many of the commercial LAN E-Mail packages cannot be easily, or inexpensively, integrated into an E-Mail network which require interaction with UNIX, IBM, DEC, or other large-scale operating environments. With add-on options, it will be possible to make such connections with MS-Mail as it comes with WFW (and other versions of Windows). These options come at additional cost and with complexity. Appropriate mail gateways are also available for several of the commercial mail programs, but, again, at additional cost and complexity. Another option, is to run two or more E-Mail networks: one for the LAN and another for those external to the LAN or on some "foreign" computer system. However, the latter solution, creates operational problems for both end-users and system administrators.

A second reason for using a UUPC/E-Mail system is that while the configuration of a UUPC/E-Mail system can sometimes be arduous (although with this book we hope to reduce that problem), adding users on a LAN is very simple and easy. The reason for this is that with any of the commonly used LAN NOSs, the only necessary requirement is to properly configure the file system on which E-Mail is based. Since a LAN workstation can simply use disk storage on a server as if it was another local disk drive, no special transport mechanism, including UUCP, is necessary. Basically all that is necessary is an MUA, an MDA, a subset of the standard configuration files, and an appropriately configured set of common directories. **mail** (or some other MUA) will also have to be available (although this may reside on the server), and **rmail** (which may also reside on the server). The setup on the server is more complex because **uucico** must be periodically executed to send queued files on their way. However, **rmail**, is sufficient to deliver mail local to the LAN. Appropriate files on the server must also be configured so that the LAN users will be known to the local E-Mail system. All users are accessed by external systems via the machine name of the server. In the case of our illustration, that would be Tom's machine, Mach1.

Since ALAN is connected directly to Tom's machine, very little additional configuration would have to take place. It would work very much as described above. This is because the LAN would be linked into the common file system on Tom's machine. The internal setup for BLAN would not be much different either. Each LAN node would be set up as described above. In the case of BLAN, however, Mary's machine must store and forward messages from all users on the LAN to other users in the E-Mail network. This means that Mary's configuration would share some of the characteristics of Tom's machine, but the added management cost is small and incremental. However, there will be a little overhead involved.

If a UNIX machine is attached to one of the LANs, an additional level of complexity is introduced. If it was desirable for UUCP/E-Mail to be handled by the UNIX machine, for systems using other operating environments to be integrated, it would be necessary to run some version of the UNIX Network File System (NFS) that encompassed all machines. This is so that the *same* file system could be used to organize the E-Mail system. Once this is accomplished, it is no more complicated on a node-by-node basis than the descriptions given above. If a UNIX system is the basis for the LAN, it is possible that the LAN will not use a common NOS, such as Novell's NetWare, Banyan's VINES, or WFW. Instead, it is possible that TCP/IP will be used as the transport mechanism without a server other than the UNIX machine. If this is the case, then it would be necessary for each of the PC workstations to be able to communicate with TCP/IP protocols and NFS would be a requirement. Conversely, if the UNIX machine was running NetWare on UNIX, then that would also take care of the integration for the use of a common file system. If you plan on using WinNET™ Mail, Computer Witchcraft has promised a LAN version for some time in 1994.

Other Expansion Opportunities

Although the use of the telephone system and LANs will be the most common physical media for a UUCP-based E-Mail network, it is possible that you may run into other variations that must be taken into account. Examples might be the requirement for the use of an X.25 network, leased lines, or even radio links. Each of these variations may require modifications in the configuration, but most are solvable. Some of the details on how to handle such variations will be discussed in subsequent chapters. For the moment, remember that the UUCP technology was developed for serial communications over dial-up telephone lines. This requires the use of **uucico** to handle the serial communications and transport of the mail files. As we have implied in the case of LANs, neither **uucico** nor **uucp** is necessary, and the mail service would be "UUCP-based" in only a very peripheral manner until a message was sent or received over an attached serial line. The serial lines do not have to be dial-access telephone lines. They can be lines that travel across X.25 networks or directly attached devices. In either case both **uucico** and **uucp** would be used. Most physical network variations that you will encounter can be handled as analogues to either the dial-access serial mechanism or LAN-based configurations. Some UUCP implementations allow use over TCP/IP networks, standard in almost any UNIX environment.

A New E-Mail Group?

The distance Tom might be from any of the other members of our illustrative E-Mail group is, for the most part, irrelevant, except for the fact that long distance calls cost more than local calls. Suppose, for example, Dick gets transferred to some other part of the country, or even to an assignment outside the country. In that case, Dick might have associates or employees that need E-Mail access to the network we are building, yet most of the E-Mail traffic for this new group may well be among themselves. One approach, of course, is to simply have all the new E-Mail users dial directly into Tom. If the distances are very great, this will probably not be very efficient. The alternative may be seen in Figure 2.5. A new E-Mail group has been set up around Dick with a link between Tom and Dick. Through this type of design, we have expanded the E-Mail network in the simplest possible way.

If you have been careful in your reading, however, you might start wondering what kind of a statement you might need in order to properly address some of the others on this expanding network. The short answer is: "a long one." This is actually the situation faced in the national UUCP-based network called Usenet. One disadvantage of UUCP is that since it was originally defined as a point-to-point transport mechanism, there is no such thing as a central directory service. For extended networks, however, a substitute for a directory service has been invented using a database of "maps" of the network that contain the linkages necessary to get "from here to there." A single organization can also use such maps and the associated software to make life easier for members of a more extended, but private, E-Mail group. Maintaining the maps can sometimes be a problem, but it is feasible to do so.

Fax Integration

A somewhat more esoteric possibility might be the incorporation of fax into the E-Mail network so that messages can be sent to people who only have a fax machine. If Tom's machine were equipped with a fax board, it might be possible for anyone on the E-Mail network to send a message to someone only accessible by fax. This could be done by forwarding a message through Tom's machine to the fax board. Ordinarily, when a message is received, **rmail** is invoked in order to distribute the mail. It may be possible to invoke a program which would send the message out the fax board rather than being configured locally or being queued for forwarding through **uucico** and **uucp** to another node on the E-Mail network. If such a feature is desirable, this should be noted in the conceptual and topological design that is being built. Please note, however, that with the falling cost of fax boards, and with good, relatively low-cost LAN-oriented fax software increasingly available, this may not be as useful an option as it was only a few months ago.

File Transfer, Report Distribution, and Event Notification

In an organizational context, other features may be more helpful. One such feature might be the passing of "printed" reports from an accounting system, not to a

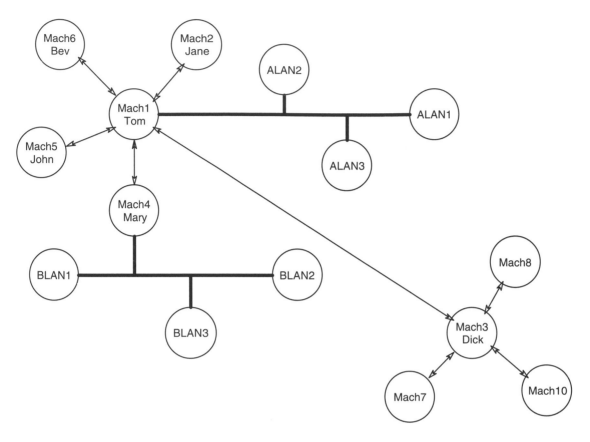

Figure 2.5. Further expansion

printer, but to the E-Mail system so that the report will be automatically transferred to the appropriate recipient for local printing or for incorporation into
another application. Many corporate and system applications today are enabled to
automatically generate mail messages to designated users in the case of errors,
problems, or specific event occurrences. One accounting package for example, had
an option to send an automatic mail message to the corporate controller in the
event of a departmental purchase requisition exceeding the budget of the department. This would allow the controller to either approve or disapprove the requisition in a very timely fashion. Similarly, if an unattended backup of a computer
system failed, for example, it would be helpful for the system administrator to be
automatically informed via E-Mail. This was the reason why we noted above that
rmail was designed to be called from other programs rather than being directly
used by an end-user. An error-trapping routine in a commonly used program could,
for example, be designed not only to print an error message but also to format a
mail message including the error message, and call **rmail** to send it along its way.
When using an E-Mail system that is based on commonly accepted procedures (if

not necessarily on formal national and international standards), this is possible. However, a proprietary E-Mail system may not have the "hooks" available to make such services possible.

Security

Before leaving the matter of E-Mail network design the issue of security should be noted. E-Mail messages in the system being described are usually readable ASCII files. This means that anyone who happens to list out a mail message file will be able to read it in its entirety. Most E-Mail systems confront this problem in one fashion or another. If the content of your E-Mail messages is sensitive, however, it would behoove you to consider the methods for security. The only acceptable method for doing this is to encrypt the text of the E-Mail message. Encryption of the entire E-Mail document cannot be done because the header information, which contains the address of the recipient, must be readable for the various UUCP programs in the network. The body of the message can, however, be encrypted and placed in the mail "envelope." With the mail system we are building this procedure will not be entirely automatic, but it can be workable. Some commercial E-Mail packages have built-in systems for mail encryption, and if most of the messages crossing the E-Mail network are sensitive, then such a commercial package may be desirable. An important design issue, therefore, is what is the estimate of the security threat involved if some unauthorized person were to read the mail on the network?[3]

COMPLETING THE DESIGN

The first and most major step in designing an E-Mail network is to decide what you want that network to do. Who is to be attached? How are they to be attached? What kind of information is to be transmitted (simple notes, graphics, documents, reports, documents with embedded sound or video, and so forth)? Once these questions are answered, a "topological" design similar to the figures in this chapter can be drawn. Once a topological design is completed, then the system can be configured. Without such a topological and conceptual design, however, E-Mail is not likely to work as needed or intended. These design questions, and any others that might arise, are common to the successful implementation of *any* E-Mail network, not just one that is based on UUCP. Since a UUCP-based E-Mail network will probably be more of a DIY (Do-It-Yourself) project, it is especially important that these questions be answered. It is also important to remember that "design" is not static. In a growing, changing group, flexibility is the key word, and the design may have to be updated frequently.

A "technical" point you might wish to keep in mind is that much of the activity of a network consists of the transfer of files from one place to another. This is particularly true of E-Mail systems. When using UUCP as the transport mechanism this point becomes abundantly clear since UUCP was designed to copy files from one point to another. It just happens that it can be used to copy specialized files, such as E-Mail messages, as well as other kinds of files. This also means, as in the case of report distribution, that files of any sort can be distributed through the network once it is established.

As used in this chapter, "design" is essentially conceptual and topological. Once we know what we want to do, we can figure out how to do it. In this book, our intent is to "figure out how to do it" through the use of UUCP-based mail systems. There will be other solutions, and perhaps you should look into them, but they are not the subject of this book. Our focus here is relatively narrow: how to design and configure an easily used, low-cost, enterprise-wide mail service using reliable, low-cost, easily available components. The distinct advantage of a UUCP-related mail system is that the components are available for a very wide variety of platforms, the software cost is low, and we can capitalize on low-cost hardware.

REFERENCES

1. For a complete discussion of enterprise-wide networking, see Madron, *Enterprise-Wide Computing* (New York: John Wiley & Sons, 1991).

2. For more detail on many of the issues discussed in this section on LANs, see Madron, *Local Area Networks: The Next Generation* (New York: John Wiley & Sons, 1990) and *Peer-to-Peer LANs: Networking Two to Ten PCs* (New York: John Wiley & Sons, 1993).

3. For a more complete discussion, see Madron, *Network Security* (New York: John Wiley & Sons, 1992).

3

UUCP on UNIX

Since UUCP was born to UNIX, it sometimes does not make much sense, unless you know something about the UNIX environment. UNIX is a general purpose, multi-tasking, multi-user operating system which runs on a very wide variety of computer hardware from PCs to mainframes. Both the strengths and weaknesses of UNIX relate to the portability of UNIX. It has been portable because it was written in a language, C, that is very similar from one system to another. This means that the source code for UNIX has been relatively easy to take from one platform to another by the simple means of recompilation. The two or three preceding sentences vastly oversimplify the problems in porting an operating system from one hardware technology to another. It is, however, a fairly accurate description of the end result of what has happened with UNIX.

The UNIX operating environment consists of a kernel, a shell, a file system, and assorted utility programs. The kernel is the fundamental operating system that controls the functions of the computer. The shell is the user interface, and there are several in common use including the bourne shell, the korn shell and the c shell. The bourne and korn shells are the ones most often seen other than in software development organizations. The "assorted utility programs" are usually called "commands" and are files that are executable. Executable files may be compiled programs or shell scripts (similar to MS/DOS batch files). One characteristic of UNIX is that it is often possible to write a program with a new function by combining existing executable files together in a shell script. Large systems are often constructed using either existing subprograms in a new (usually C) program, or by combining existing programs in shell scripts.

UUCP takes advantage of this characteristic of UNIX environments as well as contributing to it.

In general, a *file system* is a method for cataloging files in a computer system. A *file* is any collection of data that is treated as a single unit residing on a peripheral device such as a disk drive. UNIX, MS/DOS, OS/2, and the Macintosh System 7 are all examples of operating systems that use *hierarchical file systems*. Such a file system stores information in a top-to-bottom organizational structure. All access to the data starts at the top and proceeds throughout the levels of the hierarchy. The topmost (starting) directory in UNIX, DOS, and OS/2 is called the *root directory*. Files can be stored in the root directory, or directories can be created off the root and hold files and subdirectories. With the Macintosh, the *disk window* is the starting point. Files can be stored in the disk window, or folders can be created that can hold files and additional folders. Although it is easiest to think of a directory as some kind of a container, it is, in reality, a specialized kind of file.

There are some differences between the file systems of UNIX and DOS (and the others). In DOS, all directories have a name. The name of the DOS root directory on a hard disk system is usually "C:\". In contrast, the root directory of a UNIX system is symbolized only by a forward slash ("/"). DOS uses backslashes ("\") to distinguish between directories in a path, while UNIX uses a forward slash. Under DOS, a filename can have only two levels, a file name and a file extension. The file name may not be any longer than eight characters, and the file extension may not be any longer than three characters. These restrictions also apply to the naming of directories. UNIX allows names longer than eight characters and allows multiple levels to a name, separated by periods. In either system a *path* consists of all directory names from the root directory to a specific file of interest. A file in UNIX is often referred to by its full path name, such as */bin/pwd*. The program pwd reports the current working directory path name and is a file that resides in */bin*.

In Chapter 1 we briefly discussed some of the fundamental components of UUCP. As a system for supporting networking, it was designed to take advantage of the way in which UNIX is organized. Thus, rather than being a single monolithic program, UUCP has several programs that can be used in conjunction with one another in varying combinations. In addition, although they are not a "formal" part of UUCP, other programs have been written to work with that system, and they are now almost universally available under the auspices of UNIX. Examples of such programs are **uuencode** and **uudecode**. In addition to the executable files (programs), there are the standard configuration files which are used by several of the UUCP programs to determine the operating characteristics of a particular site. Finally, there is the subset of the UNIX file system that is specified for the use of UUCP.

HOW IT WORKS

In this book we are concerned not only with how UUCP works, but also with how UUCP is used to transport E-Mail. To understand that process generally, it is useful to understand the process under UNIX, for it has been the model for other implementations of UUCP and **mail**. As we have already seen (see Chapter

1), the entire UUCP communications process operates through a number of programs using various configuration files. The detail of the contents of those configuration files will be described in later chapters, as will the operational details of the various commands. At this point it is necessary only to remember that the **uucp** command was originally designed to allow files to be transferred from one UNIX machine to another. It was not designed as an E-Mail transport system. It is, therefore, still possible to invoke **uucp** to do file transfers. As a side note, in the illustrations that follow, when a dollar sign appears ("$"), it is used to connote a common UNIX prompt symbol, much like the DOS "C:\>" prompt.

UUCP File Transfers from System-to-System

The general syntax for the **uucp** command is almost identical to that of the UNIX CoPy (**cp**) command:

```
uucp [options] source destination
```

For the moment we will not worry about the "options." The "source" is the local filename that is to be sent while the destination is the network and file system path that will receive the file. The destination might be something like the following:

```
ewc!/usr/spool/uucppublic
```

In this case, "ewc" is the destination machine name; the exclamation point ("!") is a required delimiter; and "/usr/spool/uucppublic" is a directory path known to be write-enabled on the destination machine for **uucp** file transfers. If you wish to have the transferred file go to some other destination directory, your system must have appropriate permissions on the target machine. If the source file was named "tom.txt," then it might look like this:

```
tom.txt, or
/usr/tmadron/tom.txt.
```

In the latter case I have specified the full path to my "home" directory. We will discuss "home" directories in the following pages, but suffice it to say at this point that a user's home directory is the one assigned at the time the account was established on the source UNIX system. Thus, the fully qualified **uucp** command would look something like this:

```
$ uucp /usr/tmadron/tom.txt ewc!/usr/spool/uucppublic
```

This would allow my file, *tom.txt*, to be transferred to the target system which has a machine name of "ewc." In Figure 3.1 you can follow a flow chart that describes more completely the steps require for getting *tom.txt* "from here to there."

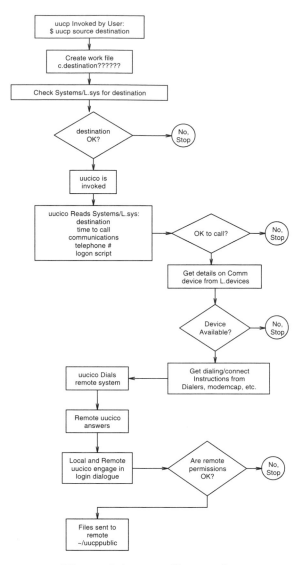

Figure 3.1. uucp file transfer

When I invoked the **uucp** command to send *tom.txt* **uucp** first checked a file called *Systems* or *L.sys* or *sys* (depending on the versions of UUCP and subsequently referred to as *Systems/L.sys*), which contains a list of all the remote UUCPs my system knows about. If the destination exists (as far as I am concerned), a temporary work file, beginning with "C." is created. The temporary file name has the general form of *C.destination??????*, where the question marks represent an assigned number for the file. Thus, in the illustrative case, the work file might be named *C.ewc123456*. **uucp** then invokes **uucico**, the program that actually handles communications. **uucico** also reads *Systems/L.sys* and obtains from that file not only the remote system name, "ewc," but also information concerning what time of day the call may be placed, through what communications medium (telephone, a TCP/IP network, a LAN, etc.), the telephone number, and a login script consisting of *send/expect* tokens. The *send/expect* tokens will be discussed later in conjunction with the detailed discussion of *Systems/L.sys*.

If everything to this point is OK, then our local **uucico** dials the remote system, "ewc." Ewc's **uucico** will be invoked during the login dialogue, when the remote system recognizes that this is a UUCP call. On UNIX systems, **uucico** is provided to UUCP as the shell for a calling UUCP system. It is invoked as a byproduct of the login process. Remember, we noted that UNIX consists of a kernel, a shell, and some utilities. The shells, noted above, were interactive user interfaces for human beings. **uucico** acts as a shell specific for the needs of UUCP. The remote **uucico**, the one on "ewc," checks the *Permissions* to be sure that my machine can call "ewc," and if that is OK allows the transfer of the file (*tom.txt*) to ~/uucppublic. Actually, it used to check the *Permissions* file. Since shifting to Taylor UUCP it now checks the *sys* file. The tilde, by the way, stands for the preceding full path name which should be specified via a system environmental variable. With a PC operating system (DOS, Windows, OS/2, System 7, etc.), **uucico** will handle the login process, as well as communications, since remote logins are not intrinsic to those environments.

Getting a File to a Particular User

Under many UNIX systems there are at least three ways, using UUCP, that we can send a file to a particular person. We can properly code a **uucp** command, we can send the file via **mail**, or we can send the file by **uuto**. The first is the direct use of **uucp**, while the latter two use **mail** and **uuto**, respectively, as "front-ends" to **uucp**.

Transferring Files with *uucp*

If you look closely at that fully qualified **uucp** command, you may have jumped to the correct conclusion that *tom.txt* may get to "ewc" all right, but that no particular person is designated as the receiver. If "ewc" is a single-user system, there is no problem, except for the fact that the owner of "ewc" may not know that the file has arrived. Even on a single-user system, therefore, you might want some method of notifying the user or owner that a file has arrived, and that it should be retrieved. There are at least three ways of handling this issue, all of which make use of the E-Mail system.

1. Using one of the options of **uucp** we ignored earlier.
2. Using a shell script called **uuto** instead of directly using **uucp**.
3. Using **mail** to transfer the file as an "attached" file.

Remember that the general case of the **uucp** command was:

```
$ uucp [options] source destination
```

and the specific case:

```
$ uucp /usr/tmadron/tom.txt ewc!/usr/spool/uucppublic
```

One option we might add is –n<userid>. If I wanted to send *tom.txt* to beverly at "ewc," I could add that information to the **uucp** command:

```
$ uucp -n beverly /usr/tmadron/tom.txt ewc!/usr/spool/uucppublic
```

When *tom.txt* has safely been copied to ewc!/usr/spool/uucppublic, the –n option would inform the remote system that a mail message should be sent to beverly indicating that the file had arrived. The disadvantage of this approach is that Beverly will still have to move the file from ~/*uucppublic* to her home directory.

Using *mail* to Transfer Files

An alternative to using **uucp** directly is to transfer the file to Beverly by **mail**. The syntax of the line that would be typed to send an ordinary mail message would be:

```
$ mail [options] [-f file] [user] [<file]
```

The details of this command are described elsewhere in this book and will not be repeated here, save for one or two comments. The optional "–f file" parameter specifies that mail will be read from a particular file rather than from the default, which is usually /*usr*/*spool*/*mail*/*userid*. It is rarely used. In order to send a simple E-Mail message, it is normally necessary only to type something like the following:

```
$ mail ewc!beverly
```

Here we simply tell **mail** that we want to send a message to *system!userid*. *System* must be listed in the *Systems* file and *system* ("ewc" in the example) must also be given suitable permissions in the *Permissions* file. Other information required by **mail** will be requested interactively (or it could also be typed following *system*/*userid*). If we wish to mail a file, which is the point of this section, then we use the simple expedient of the shell's redirection operator "<":

```
$ mail ewc!beverly <tom.txt
```

mail in particular, and all of the other MUAs noted in this book, allow the use of Internet-style addressing in the **mail** command:

```
$ mail beverly@ewc[.domain]
```

In addition, it is possible to define two other files which will be used in the mail process, that help simplify the use of **mail**: *.aliases* and *.signature* (*.sig.mail* under

Coherent), both of which will be in the user's home directory. The *.aliases* file allows the use of a short name to "stand in" for a long, convoluted address and *.signature* provides a means for automatically transmitting a "signature" file containing standard information on the sender, such as real name, address, telephone number, E-Mail address, and so forth. **mail**, by the way, is used to send and read E-Mail. **mail** "front ends" **uucp** to send E-Mail or a file. This process can be followed in Figure 3.2, which is an expanded version of Figure 1.2 from Chapter 1. Keep in mind that as far as **uucp** is concerned E-Mail is simply another file that is no different than a document or a program file. The E-Mail system simply provides a better user interface so that the human user does not have to deal with all the vagaries of sending and receiving messages.

From Figure 3.2 it may be seen that two additional programs (commands) have been introduced: **uux** on the source system and **uuxqt** on the destination system. The **uux** command queues other commands for execution on remote systems. It is used by other facilities, such as news functions and the **uucp** command, to handle processing more complex problems than simple file transfers. On the receiving end, **uuxqt** takes the information transmitted from **uux** (on the sending system) and actually executes the commands that are queued. In the case of an E-Mail transfer, the command that is queued is **rmail**, which is then executed on the receiving machine for E-Mail distribution. Even with E-Mail, however, it might be useful to execute something other than **rmail** at the receiving end.

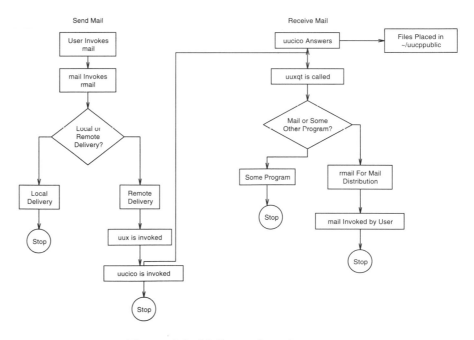

Figure 3.2. Mail transfer using **uucp**

Using *uuto* to Transfer Files

Some systems provide a command, which is usually implemented as a shell script, called **uuto**. The purpose of **uuto** is to provide the user with mail-like simplicity in the specific task of sending a file. Although **uuto** is widely (but not universally) available on UNIX systems, it is less frequently available on non-UNIX implementations of uucp. Where it is available, however, it is helpful. Its syntax is:

```
$ uuto [options] file system!user
```

Thus, in order for me to send Beverly my file, *tom.txt*, I would code:

```
$ uuto tom.txt ewc!beverly
```

When the file arrives at "ewc" it will be found at the bottom of a somewhat convoluted directory path.

```
/usr/spool/uucppublic/receive/userid/system/filename
```

for the general case, or:

```
/usr/spool/uucppublic/receive/beverly/madron/tom.txt
```

for our continuing example. The "userid" subdirectory designates the recipient, while the "system" subdirectory represents the sending system. "Receive" is a subdirectory of the public directory that is specifically used by **uuto**. This is not all one has to do, however, Beverly will still need to use an associated command, **uupick**, to retrieve *tom.txt* and place it in her home directory for further use.

What Should I Use?

One of the premises of this book is that E-Mail is rapidly becoming more than just a message-passing system. Even using the standard UNIX **mail**, it is apparent that it may be much easier from an end-user's perspective to use **mail** rather than **uucp** directly in order to send a file, such as a report, to someone else. Likewise, **uuto** can also be helpful where it is available, but it is still more difficult to use than is **mail**. Moreover, under UNIX at least, if we use an MUA such as **elm**, that is menu-driven, the entire E-Mail process, if not intuitive, is at least relatively simple. To ensure that a message or a file has actually arrived properly at the designated address, by the way, **uucp** provides the "-m" option which is carried over to both **mail** and **uuto**, that a notification via E-Mail that the **uucp** copy was actually successful.

So why not use E-Mail exclusively for transferring files with **uucp**? One reason on UNIX systems is that when the file arrives, the user will have to manually (usually with an editor) remove the E-Mail header from the file, then remove the signature, which is essentially a footer, if the sender uses a signature file. If the file is very large, or if it is a binary file, or has some other characteristics that tend to defeat systems designed for short text files, problems can occur. There are at least two solutions to this problem: 1) use **uucp** or **uuto**; or 2) use an MUA that will recognize that E-Mail has been used to transfer a file rather than a message and will automatically remove headers and footers from the transferred files. In subsequent chapters and pages we will discuss these possibilities.

THE UUCP FILE SYSTEM

Except with reference to specific systems, there is probably little chance of being able to accurately describe the UUCP file system. One reason is that local systems managers may alter the basic structure. Another reason is that different versions of UNIX handle the files somewhat differently. In addition, UUCP itself may use various commands which are common to the entire UNIX system. An example of the latter is the MUA. The illustrations above are given in terms of **mail**, but there are other public and commercial MUAs that might be used on a particular system.[1]

The UUCP Directories

In general, UUCP has three primary directories and uses other standard UNIX directories:

1. */usr/lib/uucp* contains the UUCP database files *L-devices/Devices)*, *Systems/L.sys, Permissions*; administrative shell scripts or other programs such as **uuclean**, and **uutouch**; and "daemons," which are background utilities often run at periodic intervals by **cron** (the standard UNIX scheduling program). In (AT&T) SVR4 and in SunOS Release 4.0+, the administrative programs and database files have been moved to */etc/uucp*.
2. */usr/spool/uucp* is used to store workfiles, data files, and execute files for spooled transfers. Sometimes simply called *the spool directory*, in SunOS 4.0 it is located in */etc/spool/uucp*. Depending on the particular version of UUCP you are using, both the */spool* and the */spool/uucp* (sub)directories may contain numerous other subdirectories.
3. */usr/spool/uucppublic* provides at least one place on a UNIX system that is open to public access. That is, it is one place on every UNIX system to and from which **uucp** can copy files. Because of the power of UUCP and its ability not only to copy files but also to initiate the execution of programs, system security demands that UUCP access to the entire UNIX file system should be limited. This particular directory is sometimes referred to as the *public directory*, or for historical reasons, simply *pubdir*.
4. Executable files that are accessible by end-users are stored in the */usr/bin* directory. UUCP commands which end-users can execute are

also stored here. These commands include (but probably are not limited to) **uucp**, **uuname**, and the related **uudecode** and **uuencode** programs.

The "wonder" of this file structure can best be appreciated by looking at the diagram found in Figure 3.3. This figure contains only the file structure directly related to UUCP. It does not contain the related directories and files associated with **mail** or **cron**.

The directory structure as depicted in Figure 3.3 looks more imposing than it is in reality. Most of the structure is set up automatically at the time of installation. Some of the subdirectories, such as the */sitename* directories, are added dynamically, since sites are added and subtracted from the *Systems/L.sys* file, found in */usr/lib/uucp*. It should also be noted that while this is a fairly typical structure, it is probably not precisely the one you will find on any UNIX system to which you have access. In fact, you may find that much or all of what is listed in */usr/spool/uucp* may even have been moved to */usr/etc/uucp*. This relatively elaborate directory structure does, however, simplify the actual operation of UUCP, because it allows every component to know the precise location of the files for which a particular program is responsible. When **uuxqt** must execute a program specified by a remote site, for example, it executes remotely spooled commands in */usr/spool/uucp/.Xqtdir*, to gain better control over security.

The UUCP Files

Without question the files that are most central to the operation of UUCP are *Systems/L.sys*, *Permissions*, and *L-devices* or *sys, dial,* and *port* in Taylor UUCP. These three files are usually located in */usr/lib/uucp* and they provide the major configuration for the UUCP system. They are also the files that create the most headaches because they must usually be created by hand with an editor, or at least be "tweaked" with an editor. Most UNIX/UUCP systems do not have a configuration program. As we have already noted in Chapter 1, and as we will describe in detail in subsequent chapters, the *Permissions* file provides information on what a remote system can do, and where it can do it, on the local system. *Systems/L.sys* identifies the remote systems the local UUCP knows about, the logon details, and the general method for communications (modems, LAN, TCP/IP, etc.). *L-devices* contains statements about the hardware ports that are being used.

With the exception of a few programs, most of the UUCP executables will be found in */usr/bin*. The other executables are probably in */usr/lib/uucp*. In the figure executable files are denoted with an asterisk/star ("*") while a forward slash ("/") following a file name designates a (sub)directory. Each of the four primary UUCP programs, **uucico**, **uux**, **uucp**, and **uuxqt** all generate log files specific to a particular remote site so that the system manager can see what has been going on. These are particularly useful in debugging any problems. These log files are kept in */usr/spool/uucp/.Log/programname*. In the */usr/spool/uucp/.Sequence* directory is kept information concerning the sequence numbers of pending UUCP tasks.

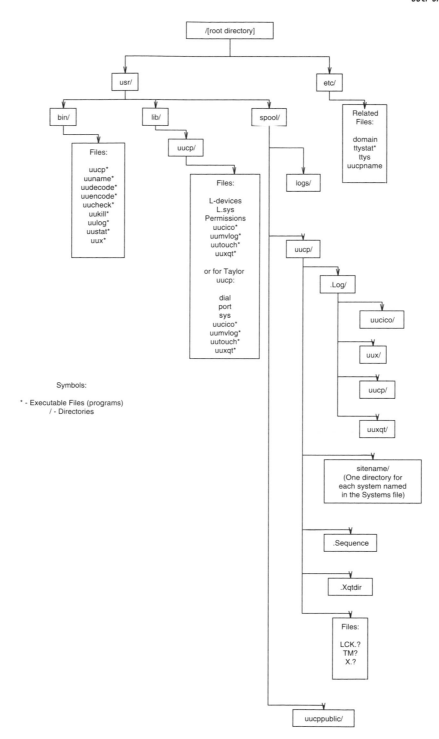

Figure 3.3. The UNIX UUCP file system

When a new remote site is added to the *Systems/L.sys* file, a new sitename subdirectory is also created to contain files specific to that remote site. The files in */usr/spool/uucp* and */usr/spool/uucp/sitename*, noted as LCK.?, TM?, X.?, C.?, and D.?, in some books and articles on UUCP are represented as LCK.*, TM*, and so forth. Since I have used the asterisk for other purposes, I have here used the question mark ("?") as the wildcard symbol. When in use, all these file prefixes will be automatically assigned extensions.

/usr/spool/uucp/LCK.?

The *LCK.?* files are used by UUCP to coordinate its resources. In order to prevent UUCP from accidently trying to access the same remote site more than once at the same time, a lock file is written. When the program that writes the lock file terminates successfully, it erases the file. This ensures that remote sites are polled in an orderly manner. Sometimes, of course, UUCP fails or crashes. It will then neglect to clean up its lock files and they may have to be done manually. Under Coherent, **uurmlock** is provided to ensure that old lock files are removed. This program should not, of course, be run while there are any active instances of a UUCP command, since **uurmlock** will remove all lock files. Normally, however, UUCP can detect a stale lock through other means.[2]

/usr/spool/uucp/TM?

When **uucico** is functioning, it generates temporary files of the form, *TM?*. These are written when the local **uucico** is receiving files from a remote site. Like the *LCK.?* files, these should also be erased at the end of the receiving session.

Control Files (/usr/spool/uucp/sitename/C.?)

Control files are used to instruct the local system to either send or receive files. For each site they contain as many lines as there are requests issued in a single **uucp** command. A **uux** command generates a control file for each system used in the command string. The file has eight fields for receiving files and nine for sending, separated by white space.

1. Each line starts with either an "S" or an "R" to indicate sending or receiving (Taylor UUCP also uses an "E" line with somewhat different fields.)
2. Source file.
3. Destination.
4. Local user.
5. Options field. Options indicating whether to create directories as needed, and if the file is being transferred from a copy, or the true source.
6. The name of the data file (see below) that contains a copy of the destination file. *This field is not present* when the request is for files

being received from a remote system. In the case where the true source file is used, the data file field is a dummy place holder.

7. The mode of the source file (as established by **chmod**).
8. The name of the user to be notified in case of problems (may be specified with the –n option).
9. The file in which to report the transfer status, as supplied with the –s option. This field may be null.

Data Files (/usr/spool/uucp/sitename/D.?)

The data files, noted in the previous subsection (#6), are work files for outgoing and incoming files. Since these files are usually a temporary copy of whatever it is that is being transferred, there is no defined format. They can be anything. They may be created by users of **uucp** with the –C option, or by **uux** to place an execute file on the remote system.

Execute Files (/usr/spool/uucp/sitename/X.?)

When a remote site dictates that a command will be run on the local system, the remote **uux** command generates the files which are then transferred. When **uuxqt** runs on the local system, these files, because they contain the specifications for executable files on the system, are executed (providing that the remote system has the properly established rights in the *Permissions* file). The format is somewhat flexible. Each line begins with a one-character field specifying the meaning of the remainder of the line. The **uux** command also generates comment lines that are inserted into each *X.?* file. The line types are:

1. # = comment.
2. F = a file necessary for execution and without which execution cannot take place.
3. I = standard input.
4. O= standard output.
5. C = the command to execute.
6. U = username to notify for command execution status.
7. B = an instruction to **uux** to return the standard input to the user if the command fails.
8. M = the *filename* in which to write the execution status report.
9. R = the return address for mail.
10. Z = notification if the command fails.
11. N = do not send notification even on failure.
12. n = send notification if the command succeeds.

While it is unlikely that most users would need to look at any of these files, the system manager may find it necessary when debugging a failed execution requested by a remote site.

The UUCP Files in Perspective

This section is not a catalogue of all the files that are generated during a UUCP file transfer. They are among the more important ones, however. Other temporary files assist UUCP to keep track of what it is doing. For the most part, the end-user certainly does not need to be concerned with such issues. The system manager may, on occasion, need to clean up some of these files manually and may need to read them in order to debug a problem with UUCP. What I have tried to provide is some sense of the file structure that UUCP uses.

A CONCLUDING NOTE

In order to have orderly and successful file transfers, and for the entire UUCP system to succeed in its various tasks, a file system has been devised which will allow any given directory to contain limited information and any given command to accomplish basically a single task (or small group of tasks). It is difficult (and in fact, probably not very useful) to be encyclopedic in a book like this. Most readers probably will never see the temporary files described in this chapter. The commands, many of which will never be seen by an end-user, are documented in a separate chapter. Similarly, the major files, *Systems/L.sys*, *Permissions*, and *L-devices*, are all discussed extensively elsewhere in this book. When used primarily for E-Mail, at least two additional commands are of importance: **mail** and **cron**. In addition, a command called **ttystat** is helpful in order to check the status of asynchronous ports. All of these will be discussed in their proper order.

REFERENCES

1. This disucssion is based on UUCP as it existed on Coherent v. 4.0 and 4.2. That version was based more or less on Version 2 UUCP. With Coherent v. 4.2, the Mark Williams Company started distributing Taylor UUCP with its operating system. However, they retained a file structure very similar to earlier versions.
2. A process creating a lock writes its process ID into the lock file. When another process finds a lock file, it checks whether the named process still exists. Thus UUCP can usually detect a stale lock.

4

UUCP on DOS/Windows, OS/2, and Macintosh

This chapter will look at a number of UUCP packages for personal computers that are easily available. Not all of those discussed are distributed with this book. An additional list of products, updated just before publication, may be found in Appendix C. The products on the distribution diskettes include UUPlus™ for DOS, WinNET™ Mail for Windows, and Waffle for DOS. When trying to decide which UUCP package to use, several criteria might be helpful to consider.

1. How easy or difficult is the installation process? This can be a major consideration. The two that are clearly "front runners" for IBM (compatible) PCs are UUPlus™ (DOS) and WinNET™ Mail and News (Windows).
2. Will the component products operate successfully in a DOS Window under Windows, if the target machine runs with MS/DOS?
3. Does the mail subsystem adhere as closely as possible to the several Internet recommendations contained in various "requests for comment" (RFC) documents that form the body of "standards" for E-Mail?
4. Is there a Windows mail user agent (MUA) that will work easily and successfully with the UUCP package chosen for implementation?
5. What are the classes of software that are useful for a fully developed, operating UUCP system?
6. Related to Number 5, what parts of a UUCP system do you really need?

There are actually a number of PC-based UUCP packages available, including several commercial packages and some shareware products. This book concentrates on the shareware products because they are very inexpensive, and they work. At this point, you should be aware of the range of products available. These include at least the following:

Shareware UUCP products for DOS/Windows included with this book

- UUPlus™ Utilities by UUPlus Development[1]
- WinMail for Windows by Computer Witchcraft, Inc.[2]
- Waffle by Darkside International (Thomas E Dell)[3]

Other DOS UUCP Systems

- DOSGATE by Ammon R. Campbell[7]
- UUPC/extended for DOS by Kendra Electronic Wonderworks[8]

UUCP for the Macintosh

- Gnu UUCP for Mac ported by Jim O'Dell[4]
- Macintosh UUPC 3.0 coordinated by Dave Platt[5]

OS/2 UUCP Systems

- UUPC/extended for OS/2 by Kendra Electronic Wonderworks[6]

Commercial Products

- The MKS Toolkit from Mortice Kern Systems[9]
- UFGATE from Late Nite Software[10]
- UULINK from Vortex Technology[11]
- "UMail" UUCP for the Macintosh by ICE Engineering[12]
- UUCP/Connect (for the Macintosh) by Intercon[13]
- Coherent 4.2 with Taylor UUCP from the Mark Williams Company[14]

Mail User Agents (MUAs)

- Cinetics Mail Manager (CMM) for Windows by Cinetic Systems[15]
- PCElm (for DOS) by Wolfgang Siebeck and Martin Freiss[16]
- Fernmail or Eudora for the MAC[17]

Scheduling Software (CRON)

- WCRON for Windows from Cinetic Systems[18]
- CRON for DOS[19]

Related Products

- PC-NFS from Sunselect (Sun Micro Systems Inc, a commercial product)[19]
- PC/TCP by FTP Software Inc. (Commercial product)[20]
- Pathway by The Wollongong Group Inc. (Commercial product)[21]

There may be others available; the endnotes to this chapter provide the sources for each of the products. All of the shareware/freeware may be downloaded from CompuServe and other information utilities, as well as from bulletin board services.

The products listed above vary in quality and price. Some packages, such as UUPlus™ are relatively complete, seemingly stable, and work without many problems under a variety of conditions. However, there is a distinction not previously made that is important: the difference between a *host* node implementation and a *leaf* node version. The former can operate as a full-blown UUCP host, the latter only as a client. A host system can receive calls from other UUCP systems; it can also place calls. A typical leaf system can only place calls to host systems. For the purposes of this book, that situation is quite acceptable because a private UUCP-based mail network will most likely operate with a central mail server (the host) that receives calls from other members of the network. Consequently, the most efficient methods of operation might well be to establish a more or less dedicated mail server running either a DOS or UNIX (compatible) UUCP system, while the users in the field may wish to have a friendly leaf system running under Windows or on a Macintosh. It is certainly feasible to set up such a system quite inexpensively.

SHAREWARE UUCP PRODUCTS

This class of products are UUCP implementations for personal computers. Their authors have, for the most part, sought to duplicate the facilities of standard UNIX UUCP implementations on DOS, OS/2, Windows, and the Macintosh. All the products are either free or low-cost shareware. Some of these products are redistributed with this book. Two additional products, GNUUCP and Taylor UUCP, both distributed under the GNU software license, also fall in this category. "GNU" is produced under the auspices of the Free Software Foundation.[22] GNU products are free and everyone is permitted to copy and distribute copies of such software. There is a license agreement that is designed to keep such software publicly available by imposing distribution restrictions. Many GNU products have been ported to DOS (from UNIX). I have not, however, been able to find an available port of the Taylor UUCP package to DOS or Windows, but such a version may become available and information may be acquired from the Free Software Foundation. As you may have noted from the list of Shareware/Freeware UUCP products, there is one that claims to be a port of the GNU product. It is not a port the Taylor UUCP. However, the GNU products are designed to be easily ported to a variety of platforms.

UUPlus™ UTILITIES BY UUPLUS DEVELOPMENT

UUPlus™ 1.50 (previously, FSUUCP) is a shareware implementation of UUCP by Christopher Ambler from UUPlus Development. If you decide to use the software regularly you should register it. The product may be copied and distributed as long as no files are altered in any way whatsoever (with the exception of configuration files, of course), the documentation is included intact, no charge is made for *any* reason, and those that receive it may also redistribute it under the above conditions. UUPlus Development reserves the right to modify distribution conditions at any time without prior notice.

The documentation for UUPlus™ was written with the assumption that those trying to install it have some basic knowledge of Usenet news and electronic mail facilities. This software system was designed to be a DOS implementation of UUCP that reflects the UNIX version. According to one note in the accompanying material, it " . . . can be considered a subset of the UNIX™ utilities of the same name, but with certain enhancements and/or compromises in the name of functionality." The latest version at the time of writing was 1.50. It has no password protection, as it is intended for standalone use. UUPlus™ is, essentially, a local utility for the exchange of UUCP/Internet electronic mail and Usenet news. It is also a transport engine for third-party readers/posters, such as **pcelm** or **cmm**. Version 1.50 is a leaf (end-user) implementation of UUCP and does not have the capability to act as a host system. Upon registration a printed version of the documentation is made available.

A major advantage of UUPlus™ over its DOS competitors is that it is relatively easy to install. It incorporates an installer program that makes installing and configuring this package relatively easy, if not fully automatic. To install, simply type "a:install" or "b:install" (depending on which drive contains your installation diskette), or copy the installation diskette to a temporary hard disk directory and from that directory, type "install". Then do the following.

1. Type "install" and follow the prompted instructions.
   The installer creates the proper directories and moves the files into them. It also creates certain configuration files, some of which will need to be hand-edited.
2. Edit the configuration files, as provided in the installer, or with an external editor. For specific information about each file, see either the comments in that file, or the appropriate manual section.
3. Create the proper environment variables. While there are several environment variables (UUPLUS, TZ, USERNAME, and FULL-NAME) that may be used, only one, UUPLUS, is mandatory; for it gives the directory path to the *uuplus.cfg* configuration file. As in all else, the distributed documentation should be carefully read before installation.

UUPlus™ supports both the standard "g" and the Taylor UUCP "i" protocols. Multiple mail users can receive mail on the same DOS system since they can each of separate mail configuration and mail files. Parts of the UUPlus™ file system can be spread on a local machine and on a LAN file server, thus making "multiuser" systems configuration possible.

Unfortunately, there is not a list of system requirements that comes with UUPlus™, nor is there any mention made of operation in a multi-tasking environment. It would appear, however, that an Intel-based PC, running a later version of MS/DOS, with at least 512 MB of memory is necessary. The modules do not appear to operate well in a multi-tasking environment, such as Windows or DesqView, although I have not tested that possibility.

The version of **uucico** distributed with UUPlus™ Utilities 1.50 will not operate reliably under Microsoft Windows. All the other programs do seem to work properly in DOS windows under Windows. If you habitually use a Windows environment, you will probably wish to implement one of the Windows versions of UUCP rather than UUPlus™. On the other hand, if you normally work in a DOS environment, then this is a good product and should be carefully considered.

WinNET™ MAIL AND NEWS FOR WINDOWS BY COMPUTER WITCHCRAFT, INC.

The WinNET™ Mail and News system was originally devised to provide friendly access to Computer Witchcraft's Internet access service, WinNET™. There are a rapidly growing number of Internet service providers (see Appendix B) of which WinNET™ is one. As far as I know, Computer Witchcraft is the only company that has taken the trouble to produce a good, user-oriented access system so that dealing with the Internet is pleasant rather than arduous. The result of this is that WinNET™ for Windows is a leaf system tailored specifically for use with the WinNET™ host. Their approach has been to give the software away, through shareware channels, in order to entice people to subscribe to their network services (which are quite moderately priced). They have, indeed, made it easy to exchange Internet mail and Usenet News with anyone around the world connected or gatewayed to the Internet or Usenet networks.

A byproduct of this activity has been an interest in a more generalized version of the WinNET™ software which is capable of connecting with any UUCP host. That product is actually only a modification of their network services version and is still easy to install and use. And it works with other systems without difficulty. I have tested it with Taylor UUCP running on a Coherent 4.2 host and with a UUCP/Extended host. It works as advertised in both cases. There are some slight problems in that the setup program must currently be rerun if you want to change hosts. This is not a major problem (we are not talking about reinstallation), but it would be nice to have a menu of hosts that could be contacted. As a component of a private E-Mail network, this would not be a problem at all. At this writing, this product was in the last phases of beta testing and a final price had not been established, although it will initially be distributed as shareware. The likely price on registration is $99.

When the primary program, **wnmail.exe**, is executed by clicking on an appropriate icon, the screen illustrated in Figure 4.1 appears. If there were any messages waiting, they would be displayed. Part of the package is a cron-like daemon that will, at periodic intervals, execute **uucico** and call the host you have configured. The icon for the daemon is visible but unobtrusive. After a call has been placed, and mail or news has been received, another mail icon shows up that indicates you have mail waiting. In Figure 4.1 there is a button on the button bar, labeled "call", that may be clicked to send a message immediately. Any messages queued from you to anyone else will be sent at standard times as specified in the setup for the mail daemon. In either case, as with any UUCP system, a version of **uucico** is

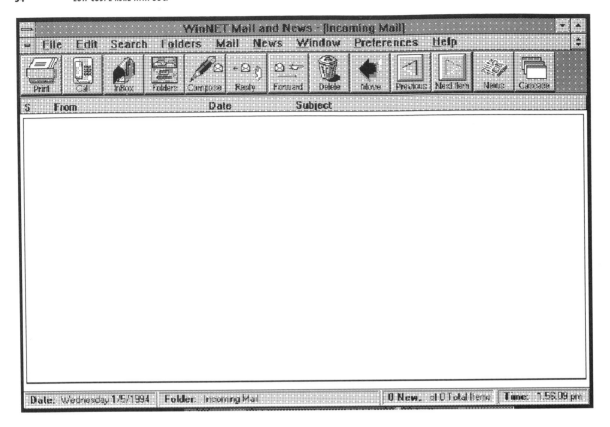

Figure 4.1. WinNET Incoming mail screen

executed that handles the actual communications. This normally works as a minimized icon, but by double clicking on the **uucico** icon, you get the screen in Figure 4.2. From that screen you can watch file transfers take place as well as accessing the **uucico** logs and error logs.

There are some enhancements that are planned for 1994 that will increase the utility of WinNET™. Specifically, the product is being expanded to work in a LAN environment. The LAN version will be very similar in appearance to standard WinNET. What will be different is that there will be a user id/password screen. The user id may be picked up from the environment, but the password will still be requested. After that, WinNET™ will come up. If you look closely at the WinNET™ structure, you can see that it is largely already set up for multiple users. There is a \usr directory with the user's name as a directory name. A system administrator will be able run an Add User screen in setup to add new users to the WinNET™ system. Mail intended for postmaster will go to the person designated as System Administrator. Local mail will be addressed by omitting the @ portion of an address.

News is designed to work on a group basis. The cleanup program can be used by the sysadmin to cleanup news. Otherwise, there is a per-user file to track news

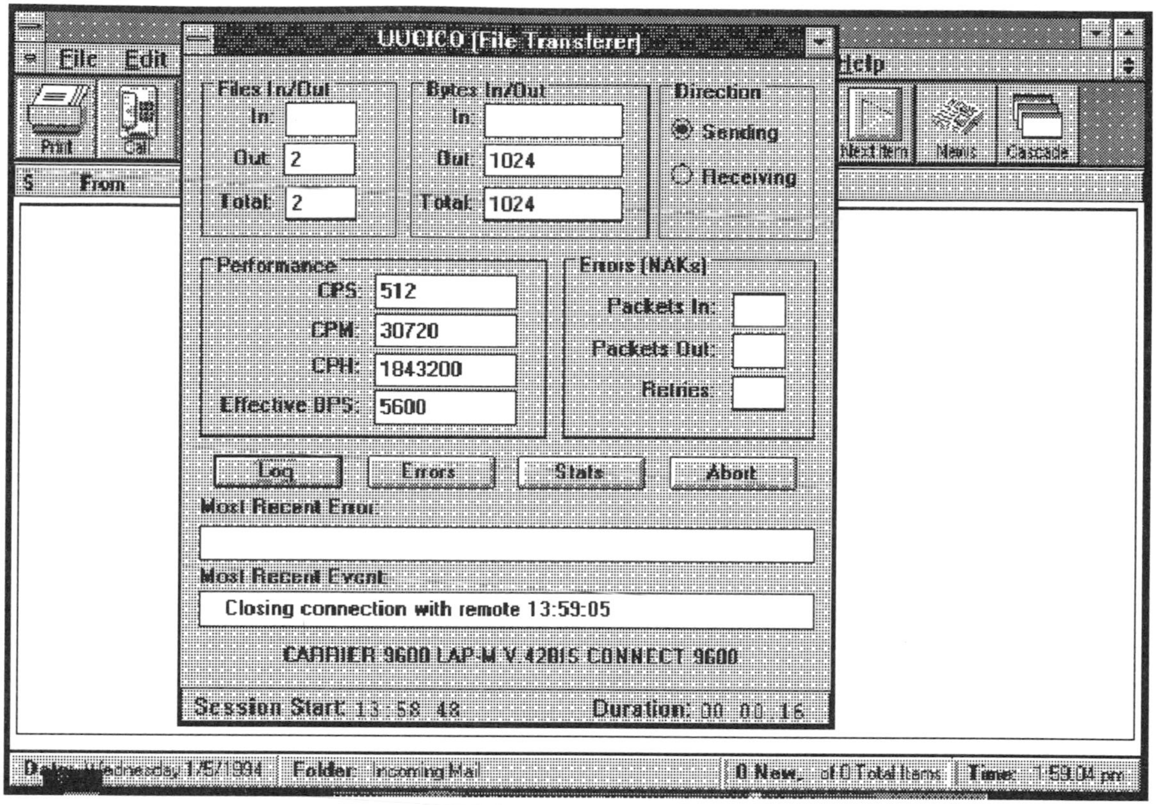

Figure 4.2. The WinNET *uucico* file transfer screen

subscriptions on a per-user basis. WinNET™ was designed, according to Michael Tague, President of Computer Witchcraft, "with Multiuser in mind, most of the functions are there, just a few administrative screens need to be added and some checkout." Once these enhancements are completed, it appears that WinNET™ would be able to function as a local LAN-based mail system as well as accessing other UUCP hosts.

Waffle by Darkside International

The two products reviewed above, UUPlus™ and WinNET™, are "leaf" systems, in the parlance of networking. That is, they are designed for use by end-users rather than for providing support to a generalized UUCP-based mail server. There are several ways in which a mail server might be established. Probably the most common is to simply have UUCP running on an UNIX or UNIX-like system such as Coherent (see below). A single-line DOS server can also be set up using products like UUCP/Extended or DOSGATE. A multi-line DOS server might be successfully established by running multiple instances of the more general DOS products under a multi-tasking operating add-on, such as DesqView. OS/2, since it is a multi-tasking operating system, might also be set up with multiple instances of an OS/2 UUCP server. Perhaps the most interesting possibility, and the one that we will highlight in this book, is a product called Waffle from Darkside International.

Waffle is basically a bulletin board system available for both DOS and UNIX. Like most bulletin board systems, Waffle supports E-Mail. The difference between Waffle and others, however, is that UUCP is used as the transport mechanism to support E-Mail. The system also supports links to Usenet mail and news feeds, allowing newsgroups to function under the bulletin board. The DOS version is shareware while the UNIX product is commercial software. The cost of registering the DOS version is $30 and the cost of purchasing the UNIX version is $120. Among the machine-readable documents distributed with the DOS version is a short "readme" file that summarizes the capabilities of Waffle as follows:

- Allows a PC to communicate with Unix systems using the UUCP "g" protocol, giving them capability to exchange UUCP mail and Usenet news. Contains DOS equivalents for UUCICO, UUXQT, UUX, UUQ, UUCP, RMAIL, RNEWS, and a news and mail reader.
- Can be run as an single-user, individual UUCP node.
- Can be run as a BBS program, including electronic mail, messages, editor, transfer section, access controls, external programs, cookies and numerous other amenities.
- A scheduler can execute DOS commands (such as polling neighboring sites) at specific times, or on a regular basis.
- Mail facilities include mail aliases, address routing, folders, and gatewaying of E-Mail into Usenet newsgroups.
- Usenet News facilities include support for batched and compressed news, the ability to give other sites newsfeeds, access control on a per-newsgroup basis.
- Hooks are provided for gating mail and news into external networks (or specific programs).

The attribute of Waffle that is interesting in the PC environment is that the product does double duty by providing UUCP mail and file transfer services as well as the features of bulletin boards. Particularly in a corporate or other organizational environment, the dual features of Waffle are very compelling. Even for an individual or a small group or business, having a private bulletin board system can by very useful. On the other hand, if a microcomputer is to be dedicated to the task of being a mail server, a fundamental issue that must be resolved is whether to go with a flexible system like Waffle under DOS, or a flexible and much more generalized solution by using UNIX or one of its variants. There is not a single solution answer to this problem (or opportunity?), rather, it is a function of need, support capabilities, and related issues.

The use of Waffle has spawned a number of "third party" shareware products. We do not have the space to describe all the products nor the disk space to distribute them. They are available via Internet from the Simtel 20 MSDOS archive. If you do not have Internet access, then you may buy this archive on CD-ROM.[23] The Waffle archive, as it existed in mid-1993 consisted of the following:

```
Directory MSDOS/WAFFLE/
Filename Type Length Date Description
ALLFIL62.ZIP  B  41590   930406   Allfiles 6.2: Waffle BBS file listing compiler
APSIG105.ZIP  B  13953   920510   Signature control/selection utility for Waffle
ARBITRON.ZIP  B  17074   910814   Waffle BBS arbitron program (perl)
ASER28.ZIP    B  64201   920131   Mail-based archive file server for Waffle BBS
ATMOVE.ZIP    B  7892    920312   Move Waffle BBS files and @files description
BAT164A.ZIP   B  13985   920312   Tom Dell's batcher for Waffle - can feedbymail
CHKFLS12.ZIP  B  31495   920813   Waffle BBS file area consistency checker v1.2
CLINF012.ZIP  B  25173   920131   Top Ten caller display utility for Waffle BBS
CWEXP104.ZIP  B  24147   911104   Free expire program for Waffle; includes C src
DISKHOG.ZIP   B  14418   920312   List the top 10 Waffle BBS users by disk usage
EXPIRE10.ZIP  B  16235   910325   Expire program for Waffle BBS Usenet files
EXPLODE.ZIP   B  13135   920911   Convert Waffle 1.65 BBS mailbox to 1.64 mails
FAQFIL10.ZIP  B  33072   930406   FAQ file searcher and archiver for Waffle BBS
FILDR201.ZIP  B  42545   910605   External file section door for Waffle's BBS
FSEDWAFL.ZIP  B  2560    920312   Examples of how to use fsed with your Waffle
FXL142.ZIP    B  41854   920131   Text filter/newline conversion for Waffle BBS
FXUC03B.ZIP   B  42086   930831   Enhanced UUCICO for Waffle 1.65 BBS
GENPASS.ZIP   B  6568    920312   Generate passwords for Waffle BBS
GRAFFITI.ZIP  B  46075   920312   Allows Waffle BBS users to generate graffiti
HK_SET.ZIP    B  24441   920312   Hunt & Kill message file delete for Waffle BBS
HPV101B.ZIP   B  276504  930709   HDPF threaded offline news/mail reader for DOS
LINES.ZIP     B  10575   920312   Add Lines: headers to Waffle BBS postings
MAILSUM.ZIP   B  14480   910814   Waffle BBS mail log reporter v1.00
MKDOOR11.ZIP  B  11264   910705   Creates DORINFO1.DEF door file for Waffle BBS
NETSUM25.ZIP  B  32014   911104   Waffle BBS net log file reporter v2.3
NEWUSER.ZIP   B  12757   920312   Push files into Waffle BBS user directories
NEXP20.ZIP    B  8745    921116   Perl expire program for Waffle BBS, V2.0
POLL100.ZIP   B  22279   910814   Multiple tries for UUCP connects in Waffle BBS
PRIVLIST.ZIP  B  10520   920312   List Waffle BBS users with certain priv level
PURGEDIR.ZIP  B  9214    920312   Delete old user directories on Waffle BBS
PWPL165.ZIP   B  6016    920722   Perl scripts for Waffle BBS SysOp utilities
QUOTA01.ZIP   B  19409   920312   Jonathan Herr's Disk quota program for Waffle
REQ.ZIP       B  10067   920312   Display requests file entry for a Waffle user
REQ101.ZIP    B  10926   920817   Shows user info from the Waffle REQUESTS file
RETRY10.ZIP   B  17194   920312   Poll pgm for Waffle, more flexible than PPOLL
RFILES23.ZIP  B  37440   920131   Rfiles v2.3: File list compiler for Waffle BBS
RNF074B.ZIP   B  54116   930205   Rnf: Local newsreader/mailer for Waffle 1.65
RUSN_101.ZIP  B  102589  930325   Threaded newsreader for Waffle BBS, w/source
SEX100.ZIP    B  19326   921201   Waffle BBS utility for news & dir expiration
SOLAR93B.ZIP  B  177745  930709   HDPF offline reader door for DOS Waffle
SUBN120B.ZIP  B  44544   930823   SUBNET for Waffle, works on spooled mail & news
TMA114.ZIP    B  30641   920910   Newsgroup moderator's tool for Waffle BBS
VAC162.ZIP    B  16086   930103   VACation: Automatic reply to email, for Waffle
VOTE.ZIP      B  17419   920312   A voting booth for Waffle BBS
W165PEG7.ZIP  B  75190   930417   Pmail UDG kit for Waffle 1.65. Pmailuucp
WAF165.ZIP    B  545609  920810   Waffle BBS v1.65, with UUCP mail & Usenet News
WAFCOL12.ZIP  B  10885   930308   Merge unread Waffle news into 1 file for dwnld
WAFDAY.ZIP    B  21074   920312   Display Waffle BBS daily usage statistics
WAFDB.ZIP     B  9410    920312   Convert the waffle 1.64 password file to ASCII
```

```
WAFDL111.ZIP   B   21344    920312   External file section door for Waffle's BBS
WAFM10.ZIP     B   66733    920312   WafMail 1.0: Offline mail door for Waffle BBS
WAFPROT.ZIP    B   1421     920312   Waffle BBS external protocols - sample setups
WAFSRTR2.ZIP   B   17014    911023   FILESORT: Waffle BBS @FILES editor program
WAFTRIM.ZIP    B   6980     920312   Trim Waffle BBS logfiles to N lines
WFS302.ZIP     B   198400   930724   Mail-based archive/mail list server for Waffle
WINFO100.ZIP   B   34344    921201   Infocom game interpreter for Waffle BBS (DOS)
WUP100.ZIP     B   18314    910313   Waffle BBS utility programs, version 1.00
WUTL10.ZIP     B   19485    920312   A collection of Waffle BBS (mail) utilities
WWCP120.ZIP    B   111007   920510   Waffle  WWIVnet gateway software for Waffle
XFAX006B.ZIP   B   29696    930702   XFax v0.06b: FAX receiving S/W for Waffle 1.65
ZNEWS97C.ZIP   B   52119    930731   ZipNews News DOOR; Waffle, PCBoard, Wilcat! BBSs
ZNR092I.ZIP    B   98052    930731   ZipNews QWK-like newsreadr but Internet format
```

If you inspect the foregoing list, you will find that there is at least one replacement for the Waffle **uucico** command: *FXUC03B.ZIP*. As of this writing the current version is actually *FXUC04B.ZIP* (the "B" meaning Beta version). This zipped archive contains the **uucico** replacements and the instructions for installation. The FX version of **uucico** provides major enhancements and is included on the diskettes with this book. To use this version of **uucico**, you will have to read the instructions contained in the archive. If you become a serious user of Waffle you will probably want to make use of several of these add-ons.

The UUPC Products

"UUPC" is, of course, a word play on "UUCP." The UUPC products consist of closely related versions for DOS and OS/2, and a more distantly-related version for the Mac. The current version, supported by Kendra Electronic Wonderworks, is called UUCP/Extended. This package is as extensive a PC implementation as any, and more extensive than most. With selected exceptions, the DOS and OS/2 versions adhere closely to UUCP as it is found on UNIX systems. The software has few restrictions placed on it and it "may be used and copied freely so long as the applicable copyright notices are retained, but no money shall be charged for its distribution beyond reasonable handling costs, nor shall proprietary changes be made to this software so that it cannot be distributed freely. Whenever possible, the source must be distributed with the executable files."[24]

Installation for UUPC/Extended can be somewhat arduous. The basic distribution of the software does not include any installation tools, other than a manual. Installing the system may be easier if you have had some experience in setting up complex systems. This, and other books, along with the distributed documentation, should be sufficient for a successful implementation. As the documentation suggests, trying to install the software " . . . with no experience and no resources can cause pain and suffering for a very important person—you."[25] Although the software is "free," it may be registered for a small fee, thus insuring you of notification of future updates which occur with some frequency.

To install UUPC/Extended only a relatively minimal system is required. The minimum configuration is an IBM/compatible PC running MS/DOS or OS/2, with at least 512 KB of RAM (memory) and 2 MB of hard disk space. In addition, you will need a modem and its manual (documentation), preferably a "Hayes compatible" modem. To configure or "tweak" the various configuration files you will need a text editor, such as **edit**, which comes with DOS 5 and 6. An editor such as Windows **notepad** will also work, although it is the better part of valor to get the system running first under DOS before you attempt to run it under Windows. More will be said of this below. Another requirement, is, of course, access to another UUCP or UUCP/Extended system so that you can communicate with someone. This may be a second system that you own, or someone else's. A copy of **pkunzip.exe** is required to decompress the "zipped" distribution files.

UUCP/Extended comes with a program called **uupoll.exe**. It is designed to run **uucico** and **uuxqt** automatically at specified times. As noted, when **uucico** is live, and awaiting a call, it is the only program that can run under DOS. However, you can run these and other programs under MS-Windows 3.x in 386 enhanced mode, or under OS/2. DESQView should also work. Even on a DOS machine, however, UUCP/Extended can support multiple users on the same machine. During the installation process you will configure a file called *personal.rc*, where the *"personal"* part of the filespec is changed to a specific username. Thus, you can have multiple *personal.rc* files, each with unique usernames, thereby allowing each user to receive E-Mail on a DOS machine. The active user must be changed in order to read the appropriate mail, but this is accomplished with a small batch program, properly configured, named **su.bat**. In all likelihood if you are using Windows, you will want to use the Cinetics Mail Manager (**cmm**) as your MUA. **cmm** takes care of this problem for you in a somewhat more elegant manner. In addition to the DOS and OS/2 versions of UUCP/Extended, a Windows version is now being distributed as well. UUPC/Extended can be used as a host system. Versions for Windows and Windows/NT became available as this was being written.

DOSGATE by Ammon R. Campbell

DOSGATE Release 0.07 and the accompanying documentation and materials are Copyright 1988, 1991–1993 by Ammon R. Campbell. DOSGATE is a software package designed to emulate a subset of the functions of a typical UNIX UUCP mail system installation. The software allows a suitably equipped IBM PC or compatible computer to exchange electronic mail with other UUCP-capable computers–potentially all over the world. The current release of DOSGATE also includes a limited facility for receiving a Usenet news feed. Users who are familiar with UUCP mail systems may find DOSGATE somewhat familiar in that it emulates some of the arcane but "standard" setup of UNIX-like UUCP mail systems. The system can be configured as a multi-user or single-user mail system.

In recognition of the fact that UUCP has a reputation for being difficult to configure, the documentation contains the following warning: "Users who are not familiar with UUCP mail systems may find DOSGATE to be an extremely obtuse and unfriendly software package." Moreover, the documents state, "be warned that DOSGATE is NOT user-friendly, it is NOT a commercial software product, and there is NOT a technical support hotline for it." This same statement can probably be made concerning other DOS-based UUCP systems described in this book, although part of the reason for writing this book is to make such installations somewhat less arduous.

DOSGATE will run on any IBM-PC or PC/AT compatible computer, if it has a hard disk, at least 384K of free memory (540K for a news feed), a modem or serial connection to another UUCP-capable computer, and MS-DOS or IBM Personal Computer DOS version 3.0 or newer. The modem or serial device must be configured as COM1 or COM2. DOSGATE does not support devices as COM3 or COM4. While DOSGATE will run on an IBM-PC/XT compatible computer, a 286 or better CPU is strongly recommended. A high-speed modem is also strongly recommended for installations that receive Usenet news or transport high volumes of electronic mail. The software uses approximately one megabyte of disk space, plus whatever additional space is needed to accommodate any electronic mail that will be sent or received and/or news articles that will be stored. For a single-user setup with a moderate volume of electronic mail and no news articles, two or three megabytes is often sufficient. For a multi-user setup, or a large news feed, many megabytes may be needed depending upon the level of activity.

Installation must be done manually, although it isn't particularly difficult. The examples in the documentation assume the software has been installed in a directory named "c:\dosgate," but another directory may be used if desired. Once the software has been placed in a suitable directory, several files must be modified before the software can be used. Specifically, the *dosgate.cfg*, *L.sys*, and *passwd* files must be modified appropriately. The *active* file should also be modified if you plan to receive Usenet news. Once the configuration files have been modified, several empty directories must be created. Specifically, the directories that were selected as the *tmpdir*, *pubdir*, *spooldir*, *maildir*, and *newsdir* directories in the *dosgate.cfg* file must be created. The directory for the log files selected in the *dosgate.cfg* file must also be created if the logfiles will not be stored in one of the directories just named. This procedure is rather common to all three DOS products, and a comparison of their directory structures will be found later in this chapter.

Since UUCP implementations must be able to handle filenames from systems that are usually not MS-DOS compatible, some of the DOSGATE commands will convert filenames from remote systems into filenames that are acceptable to MS-DOS. This is a feature of DOSGATE that is not clearly available with the other systems, or at least it is not well documented. DOSGATE attempts to preserve these filenames as closely as possible. Generally, DOSGATE will handle non-standard filenames from remote systems by stripping all periods out of the filename and inserting a period after eight characters. If a filename contains more than eleven non-period characters, however, the first eight non-period characters will be retained and the remaining characters will be hashed into a three-digit hexadecimal number that can be used by the software to uniquely identify the file.

DOSGATE does not seem to work well in a multi-tasking environment. In order to get it functioning it was necessary to run it under DOS, rather than from Windows under a DOS window. It also had a problem with the network drivers for Windows for Workgroups. With the drivers loaded the system hung, regardless of the amount of conventional memory available. This is a potentially serious problem for many people.

Gnu UUCP for Mac Ported by Jim O'Dell

This package is being presented in a somewhat uncritical fashion because I have not personally tested it. Like the comments for the Mac implementation of UUPC, this commentary is taken from the documents distributed with the software. The system consists of two programs. The first is a HyperCard Mail management stack from which you will be able to read and reply to mail. The second program is called Mac/GNUUCP, and it performs the actual mail delivery to local machines and remote computers.

This implementation of Mac/GNUUCP assumes a full 8-bit connection to the remote UUCP site. Furthermore the line that is used cannot have any type of flow control, such as ^S, ^Q control on the line. If you call your computer through a terminal concentrator, check with the system administrator about the connection requirements.

A typical interaction would be to start up Mac/GNUUCP to call your mail forwarder or any other site that may have mail for users at your site. Mac/GNUUCP will collect this mail and place it in a file in the Mail directory. The HyperCard stack can then be started up and told to retrieve new mail. Each message will be placed in a separate card in the stack.

Mac/GNUUCP grew out of a desire to be able to send and receive electronic mail directly from a Macintosh computer to others on Usenet and the Internet. As the project evolved a HyperCard interface was added in order to ease the growing volume of mail. The actual interface to the GNUUCP portion of the code remains very UNIX-like to keep the project limited in scope. The program has connected to SUNs, VAXs and to other instances of itself running on remote Macintoshes. Perhaps the most interesting part of this package is the HyperCard Mail Reading and Replying Stack. Without that program and the ability to easily use Mac/GNUUCP to deliver the mail, Mac/GNUUCP might be difficult to use.

According to O'Dell, the project would have never have been completed without the GNUUCP code supplied by the Free Software Foundation. Although O'Dell suggests that the original author of GNUUCP is unknown, it was mostly assembled by John Gilmore. Whether any improvement would come by upgrading to the Taylor UUCP code is unknown, but the code used is certainly prior to Taylor UUCP. Because of the reliance of the product on GNU code, this product is essentially "freeware," although a small registration fee of $20 is requested for membership in the Mac/GNUUCP electronic mailing list and for being kept up to date on the future development of this program.

O'Dell suggests that while Mac/GNUUCP can probably be run on a machine without a hard disk, he has never tried it. The program requires 256K of system memory. The Mac/GNUUCP files require about 600K of disk space. In order to call other computers you will need a modem. The program uses the Hayes modem command set to deal with the modem, so a Hayes, or "Hayes compatible," modem is required. Any modem with a Hayes compatible command set should function correctly. The sources for Mac/GNUUCP require about 1 Megabyte of space. The biggest space requirement will be for disk space to hold the mail that will be coming to your machine should you decide to acquire an Internet or Usenet connection.

The installation, based on a reading of the documentation, seems to be straightforward. The documentation comes as a Word for Mac 4.0 doc file and is attractive and apparently complete.

UUCP 3.0 for the Mac Coordinated by Dave Platt

The Mac version of UUPC is a program which allows a Macintosh to communicate using the UUPC protocols, and to exchange files and electronic mail with other UUCP sites. UUPC 3.0 is MultiFinder-friendly, running under System 6.0.x and under System 7. It supports fast modems, is domain-aware, allows for both outbound calls and for inbound (slave-mode) calls, has an automatic call-scheduler. It supports the "g" protocol (7-packet window, packets up to 256 bytes) and the "f" protocol (for use with error-correcting modems or with X.25 links). As noted above, the Macintosh UUPC 3.0 software release was coordinated by Dave Platt. Like its DOS and OS/2 counterparts, code in this release was written by a number of individuals, including Dave Platt, Gary Morris, Drew Derbyshire, Sak Wathanasin, and others.

UUPC 3.0 is distributed as "freeware." You may use it, give it away, pass it around, or upload it to your friendly neighborhood BBS. It may not be used as the basis for a commercial product, and portions of it are copyrighted by their respective authors. Like UUPC/Extended, UUPC 3.0 is provided without any warranty whatsoever. According to Platt, "if you feed it after midnight, and it gets nasty and shreds your living room furniture, that's your problem, not mine." Full source code to UUPC 3.0 is available, so if you don't like the way some aspect of UUPC 3.0 works, you can customize it to suit your own preferences. This package is distributed without further comment or instruction on the diskette with this book. It contains its own documentation and installation instructions.

COMMERCIAL PRODUCTS

The commercial UUCP packages for PCs are few and far between. During a product search, I was able to identify only three for the IBM family (one of which never responded to inquiries), and possibly two for the Mac. In the following sections these products are briefly described with the information taken from product announcements or brief review articles. I present this information for the sake of completeness, since I have concentrated on *low-cost* shareware or freeware products for this book and have not personally tested these commercial products. All the commercial packages seem a bit pricey and somewhat out of line with the pricing for other personal computer products. However, if a commercial package seems appropriate, then perhaps these products are for you.

The MKS Toolkit from Mortice Kern Systems

The MKS Toolkit (V.4.1) is a set of DOS and OS/2 utilities that provide some UNIX functionality for those operating systems. Toolkit is comprised of programming and utility commands such as MKS Korn Shell, MKS Vi editor, MKS AWK, UUCP, Make and 180 other commands. It includes an on-line reference manual with a man command that will find and display command information and a readable interface for viewing command options and descriptions. Raw device support is provided including **dd**, **tar**, **cpio**, and **pax**, as well as multi-volume support and automatic disk density detection and adjustment. A related product is also available: MKS Toolkit for Windows NT (V.4.1). The two products each sell for $299, require a minimum of 256 KB of RAM, 10 MB of hard disk storage and support EMS. UUCP is clearly a byproduct of providing these UNIX functions in a DOS, OS/2, and Windows NT environment.[26]

UULINK from Vortex Technology

UULINK is a software package for DOS which allows PCs to communicate with standard UNIX-based systems and between DOS PCs for electronic mail and automated file transfers. This product is a relatively full implementation of UUCP for DOS. It will operate with as little as 256KB of memory, and while a hard disk is recommended, it is not required. It can also operate on any version of DOS from 2.0 on. All of this means that UULINK can operate on everything from the original PC on. Its cost, especially compared to the shareware products, is expensive with a single-user price of $335. According to Vortex Technology, UULINK is compatible with all standard versions of UNIX UUCP, including support of full-duplex, multiple packet transmission/reception windows for optimum communications throughput. This product provides the full range of services of "standard" UUCP as well as selected extensions. It supports both mail and news feeds. Software is provided that allows scheduling of access to remote systems while other utilities are provided to enhance the integration of the various programs, to simplify complex polling setups, and to deal with special communications or compatibility situations. It is not clear whether the various modules will run under a DOS window in Windows. The product is apparently well supported and this may be sufficient reason for its adoption over less expensive alternatives.

"UMail" UUCP for the Macintosh by ICE Engineering

In 1990, ICE Engineering announced its intent to open a Mac window on the wide world of UNIX communications with uAccess, a telecommunications product shipped in October of that year for an introductory price of $275. The program offered a full Mac interface. **uAccess** users were able to generate, forward or reply to UUCP mail, and post or follow up on news articles. **uAccess** works in the background under MultiFinder. Users can define scripts to handle even complex dialing or login procedures and to specify a list of tasks to be performed at specific times and dates. **uAccess** was described as a Mac version of the UUCP, letting Mac users create, send, receive, and forward messages and files over wide-area links. The standard price for **uAccess** was $375 per Mac.[27] As can be seen, the product was fairly expensive, and ICE Engineering is relatively small. As of this writing, it is unclear whether the product continues to exist in this guise, since, the technology was sold by ICE to Intercon Systems in 1993.

UUCP/Connect (for the Macintosh) by Intercon

In January 1993, Intercon Systems reached an agreement with ICE Engineering to license ICE's Macintosh-based UUCP product. This product is called UUCP/Connect and is sold and supported by Intercon. UUCP/Connect provides a UUCP G level protocol access to Macintosh computers. This is especially useful to Macintosh users who are not on a network with UNIX users, but who would still like to take advantage of Internet services. Because UUCP/Connect is UUCP-specific, it is not necessary to acquire a complete UNIX-like communications package which would have NFS, TCP/IP and other features that a Mac user may not need. Intercon has not, apparently, enhanced the product much over the offering by ICE, although Intercon believes the product rounds out its line of communications offerings. Like its predecessor, UUCP/Connect offers the user file copying by using the UUCP G protocol. It also offers E-Mail delivery and notification to the user through the Apple menu. There is a mail reader and an electronic news reader. Finally, the package offers modem control features for any Hayes-compatible modem and VT102, VT320, and TTY terminal emulations.

There are two levels of the package available. Single users are offered the UUCP/Connect Client version which retails for $295. For a network of Macintoshes, Intercon is selling the UUCP/Connect Host version for $395. Bundles for 10, 25, 50, and 100 users are also available.[28] The product converts a Macintosh into a UUCP host or client computer that can connect with other UUCP hosts using a dial-up connection or a direct link, such as Ethernet or AppleTalk. UUCP/Connect provides network communication using any Communications ToolBox connection tool, a serial port, a modem, a MacTCP link, or a MacISDN connection.[29]

Coherent 4.2 with Taylor UUCP from the Mark Williams Company

Coherent is a professional operating system designed for use on machines that can run MS/DOS. It has the features and functionality (the "look and feel") of the UNIX operating system, but it is the creation of Mark Williams Company. Coherent provides a 386 or 486 computer with true multi-tasking, multi-user capabilities without the cost required by current versions of UNIX. There are currently two editions of Coherent: Coherent 286 and Coherent 386. The latest version is 4.2, which was shipped in late 1993 and includes X-Windows, the graphical user interface for UNIX systems. Describing Coherent in detail would simply be describing UNIX, and this book is not the place for that. Coherent retails for an impressively low price of $99.

Version 4.2 comes with Taylor UUCP v. 1.04, the latest version of UUCP. If your environment requires a powerful UUCP host, especially one that supports multiple lines, Coherent can be the basis for a relatively low-cost system that works like UNIX. There are other UNIX "clones" available, but they are not, for the most part, distributed as commercial products and do not have the technical support available from Mark Williams. The current price of Coherent is to be compared to 386/486 versions of UNIX that range up to $1,500 for full-blown development systems. With the acquisition of UNIX by Novell in 1993 (actually, the acquisition was of USL, to which AT&T transferred ownership of UNIX), we may see lower priced, more easily installed versions of UNIX in the near future, but for the moment Coherent is probably the best suited for applications of the sort described in this book.

More will be said of Coherent in subsequent chapters and the assumption is made that what is said of Coherent can also be said of UNIX and *vice versa*. The assumption is also made that since we are discussing the design and implementation of "low cost" E-Mail systems based on UUCP, if you need a more powerful host than can be provided on DOS machines, you should seriously consider Coherent. The most severe limitation of Coherent is that it does not currently have the drivers for supporting Ethernet LANs (it can handle ARCNet), does not have developed TCP/IP software, and does not have NFS (Network File System) software. Ethernet and TCP/IP have been promised for mid-1994.

MAIL USER AGENTS (MUAs)

Before mail can be moved from one place to another by UUCP, there must be a method for composing it and reading it when it arrives. Each of the DOS packages reviewed above have a command called **mail**, which is similar to, if not identical with, the UNIX counterpart, also called **mail**. The **mail** command performs several functions, the most important of which is to provide a user interface to the entire UUCP-based E-Mail system. There are at least three MUAs that are in widespread use in the UNIX world: **mail**, **mailx**, and **elm**. **mail** comes with every UNIX system and provides the basic means for formatting and addressing E-Mail. Mail forwarding (see below) may also be supported. Some versions of **mail** only understand the simple UUCP address, *sitename!username*. Others have the capacity to parse Internet domain addresses. Alternatively, the MUA may only pass an address to **rmail** or an associated MDA, **smail**.

smail (for Smart Mailer) was originally designed to handle addresses and addressing with some intelligence. **smail** will do such things as parse an Internet address of the form *username@sitename* into the UUCP format, *sitename!username*. It may also access a "map" database by which an extended addressing path is generated to get a message to a system to which you are not directly connected. The program **pathalias** generates the database from the basic map data supplied by the user, or taken from the Usenet mapping project. **smail** can make use of these data to generate an extended address for your mail message. As already noted the functions of **rmail** and **smail** may be folded into other commands, such a **mail**, or, as under Coherent, merely alternative names linked to a common program.

The **mail** programs that come with UUPlus™, DOSGATE, UUPC/Extended all have varying capabilities, but generally they combine attributes of **mail** and **smail**. This is one reason why they are not precisely compatible with the UNIX **mail** command. Likewise, it is often desirable for an MUA to read a "signature" file that contains standard information (such as name and address of the sender of mail) that is appended to every E-Mail message, and an "alias" file that allows the end-user to use short names, like "Bob," rather than the more extended *sitename!username* format. Indeed, if you use forwarding, you might well end up with something like *site1!site2!site3!username* or something even more obtuse. Forwarding, which is something we will deal with in detail later in the book, can also be used, by the way, to assist in making E-Mail messages available to you even when you are traveling and forwarding the messages to your laptop, on which another UUCP system is defined.

All this goes to say, if a third party MUA is to be used it must at least do most of the things just noted. It must also provide a friendlier user interface than the line-oriented **mail** program. Three such MUAs are described in the following paragraphs: **cmm**, the Cinetics Mail Manager; **pcelm**, a DOS, menu driven MUA; and **fernmail** for the Mac, that can "front-end" either Mac UUPC or GNUUCP for the Mac.

Cinetics Mail Manager (CMM) for Windows by Cinetic Systems

Cinetic Mail Manager (**cmm**) is a mail reader/composer that lets you manage UUCP mail under Windows. The main purpose of CMM is to let the user read, reply, forward, and create messages. There are also other functions to simplify the reader's task. CMM is not a mail transport package or a UUCP system; it acts as a front end to such packages. To send a mail message, **cmm** calls a third party MDA that does the distribution part of the mailing process. In the case of the DOS packages we have discussed, that mailer program is the routing agent, **rmail**. **cmm** currently supports directly the following systems:

- FSUUCP by Fubar Systems (and its successor, UUPlus™)
- UUCP/extended by Kendra Electronic Wonderworks.
- PC-NFS from Sun Micro Systems Inc.
- PC/TCP by FTP Software Inc.
- Pathway by The Wollongong Group Inc.

Cinetic Mail Manger is fully configurable to support other systems.

Since CMM is fully configurable, you may use your PC as a multi-user mail system by creating as many users as you wish. Cinetic Mail Manager is a shareware product. If you decide to use it, after a reasonable trial period (30 days), you are obligated to purchase a license for its use at the cost of $30 US ($35 Canada). The shareware version of CMM is distributed with this book. Suffice it to say at this point that CMM is both easy to use and very flexible if you are a Windows user. The CMM window is shown in Figure 4.3.

PCElm (for DOS) by Wolfgang Siebeck and Martin Freiss

PCElm is an MUA with a user interface closely modeled after the Usenet ELectronic Mail (ELM) program for UNIX. To avoid confusion, the authors stress

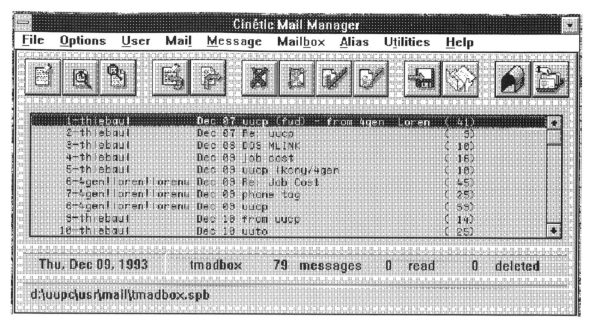

Figure 4.3. Cinetics Mail Manager window

that **PCElm** and Usenet **ELM** are not related. **PCElm** is intended to be used as a drop-in replacement for **mail** when using DOS version of UUCP. It can also be used for other mail systems, since all relevant things for compatibility with MTAs (Message Transfer Agents) are configurable. As seen in Figure 4.4, PCElm provides a full screen, menu-driven DOS interface.

Considering the limitations of DOS character-based screens, **PCElm** has a helpful user interface with easy-to-learn and easy-to-use commands. UNIX users will already be familiar with the more important commands. It can be made to work with most mail systems available for PCs, as **PCElm** makes no assumptions at all about the underlying network software. Finally, **PCElm** is multilingual; you can make all messages appear in your favorite language. As might be expected, given the fact that the authors are German, message files are provided in both English and German.

PCElm was written in part as the user interface for amateur radio packet networks that use TCP/IP and a variety of UNIX derived software. Thus, it has a ham radio mode that creates text- and workfiles directly usable by two widely used ham radio systems (NET or NOS) for distribution with SMTP (simple mail transfer protocol, a part of the TCP/IP protocol suite). In UUCP mode, **PCElm** executes a mailer (usually **rmail**) to feed E-Mail to your UUCP system. Since there are several UUCP systems for PCs, it is up to you to find the correct way to execute the mailer.

The executable **pcelm.exe** may be freely copied and distributed, provided that all files in this package are distributed with it, and provided that the copyright notices are retained. No money may be charged for copying **PCElm**. A license is

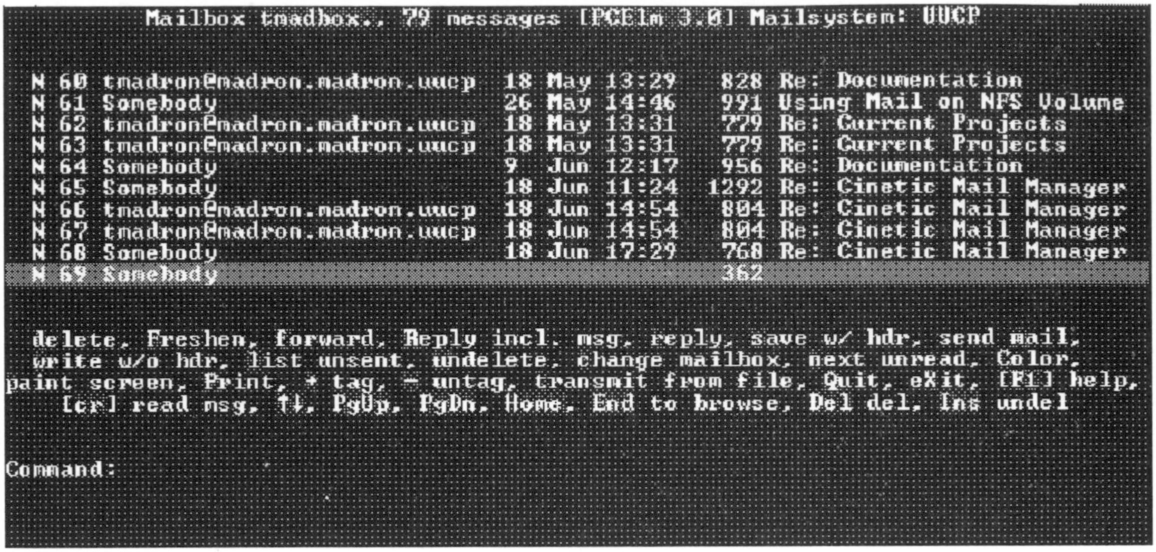

```
        Mailbox tmadbox., 79 messages [PCElm 3.0] Mailsystem: UUCP

 N  60 tmadron@madron.madron.uucp   18 May 13:29    828 Re: Documentation
 N  61 Somebody                     26 May 14:46    991 Using Mail on NFS Volume
 N  62 tmadron@madron.madron.uucp   18 May 13:31    779 Re: Current Projects
 N  63 tmadron@madron.madron.uucp   18 May 13:31    779 Re: Current Projects
 N  64 Somebody                      9 Jun 12:17    956 Re: Documentation
 N  65 Somebody                     18 Jun 11:24   1292 Re: Cinetic Mail Manager
 N  66 tmadron@madron.madron.uucp   18 Jun 14:54    804 Re: Cinetic Mail Manager
 N  67 tmadron@madron.madron.uucp   18 Jun 14:54    804 Re: Cinetic Mail Manager
 N  68 Somebody                     18 Jun 17:29    768 Re: Cinetic Mail Manager
 N  69 Somebody                                     362

 delete, Freshen, forward, Reply incl. msg, reply, save w/ hdr, send mail,
 write w/o hdr, list unsent, undelete, change mailbox, next unread, Color,
paint screen, Print, + tag, - untag, transmit from file, Quit, eXit, [F1] help,
    [cr] read msg, ↑↓, PgUp, PgDn, Home, End to browse, Del del, Ins undel

Command:
```

Figure 4.4. PCElm DOS screen

given to use **PCElm** for an unlimited time in non-commercial environments. Like
all programs of this genre, no warranty, expressed or implied, is given " . . . that
PCElm does what you think it does."

A version of PCElm for Windows (WinElm) was released as this book went to
production.

Fernmail or Eudora for the MAC

Although I did not have much information on these two products at the time of
writing, there are at least two Macintosh MUAs in the shareware/freeware
category of software that are easily available. These are **fernmail** and **eudora**.
They are noted here for informational purposes rather than for the depth of
information available.

Fernmail is a mail reader program for owners of Mac/GNUUCP or Mac UUPC.
You must have one of these two UUCP transport programs in order to use
Fernmail. Fernmail is an application for sending and reading mail via UUCP.
You will need a UUCP connection with another computer (using one of the two
Macintosh versions of UUCP mentioned above) in order to make any real use of
Fernmail.

Eudora is an Internet-compatible mailer for Macintoshes. It can be used with
MacTCP, the Communications Toolbox, or any of the UUCP implementations for
the Mac. The Eudora software, source code, and manual are Copyright © 1989–
1992 by the University of Illinois Board of Trustees. Parts are Copyright ©
1992–1993 by Qualcomm, Inc. Permission is granted to copy the software and the

manual is provided at no charge beyond reasonable reimbursement for duplication and handling costs. Eudora is free and will be found in *fsuucp**macintos* after you install the diskettes.

SCHEDULING SOFTWARE (CRON)

On several occasions we have alluded to scheduling software being useful in the operation of a UUCP network. There are several reasons why one might wish to schedule the operation of UUCP.

1. The mail hub, or postoffice, is only available at specified hours.
2. It is necessary to make long distance calls, and the user wishes to call at the most economical times.
3. The user wishes to collect and send E-Mail frequently during the day, but does not wish to send/receive every time he, or she, writes a note.
4. There is a desire to operate in an orderly manner.

The UNIX command used for this purpose is **cron**. **cron** is a standard scheduling program that reads a file that specifies the operations to be accomplished, the time of day they are to be run, and the day of the week they are to be run. In a multi-tasking, UNIX environment, the operation of **cron** is relatively easy and straightforward. It simply runs as a task in the background, executing tasks as instructed. Many organizations have used scheduling systems, both simple and complex, for many years in order to do repetitive tasks that can be automated, particularly at night when no one else is around. Backups of hard disks, standard report generation, and automated communications tasks are examples of processes that might be scheduled.

When LANs became popular, most of them operated in a DOS environment which meant that each node, apart from the file server, was a single-tasking, single-user machine. To automate processes across the LAN, when the scheduling software was run on one of those machines, typically required the dedication of the machine, at least during the hours the scheduler was active. There were semi-solutions to this problem.[30]

1. The scheduling program could be written as "terminate and stay resident" (TSR) software that would load into memory and just sit there "in the background" until it was required to run a task. This was a multitasking-like solution, but it took up memory and machine cycles, thus reducing the usefulness of the program. Considerably less memory might be available for doing "real" work, particularly when network drivers were also loaded. Even with the advent of expanded and extended memory and memory managers that can load such programs into "high" memory (between 640KB and 1 MB), there is a

limit to what can be loaded high. This approach was a "last resort," although some schedulers still are designed using this approach.

2. A foreground program could be made that loads the tasks as child processes. The problem with this approach, since a second copy of the DOS command interpreter (**command.com**) must be run, is that the scheduling software still remains in memory. In addition, memory is required for the second copy of **command.com**, so very little memory is left for the task that must be run. This can be remedied by so-called "memory swapping" software, but that complicates the operational problem.

3. A transient program could be made that is only in memory when it is needed. With this solution, all memory is available for the task. The scheduler is running most of the time, but when the time comes for a task to be run, a batch file is run that terminates the scheduler, runs the task, then runs the scheduler again. This is actually just a lower key version of alternative #2 above, except that it does not require a second copy of **command.com**, nor does it require memory swapping software to provide sufficient memory for the scheduled task.

The serious problem with alternatives #2 and #3 is that in a DOS environment—at least at some hours—a machine must be dedicated to the task of scheduling. In a high-powered production environment this may well be the correct approach, but in a lower-key or personal environment either of these alternatives is probably unacceptable, unless scheduling is to take place only in the dead of night. The real solution to this kind of problem is that which UNIX has always had available: use at least a multi-tasking (if not a multi-user) operating environment. If you are dealing with 80386 (or later) Intel-based machines or with the Macintosh, multi-tasking is either built-in or easily available. If you must run in a DOS environment, a multi-tasking system such as DesqView from Quarterdeck allows the concurrent operation of several DOS tasks, as do several of the multi-tasking DOS clones (rather than using MS/DOS), one of which could be a scheduling system that runs all the time. If you have moved to Windows or you have a Macintosh, your problems are more or less solved since you are already using a multi-tasking operating environment. OS/2 is another option which is more powerful than DOS.

However, we would like to be able to suggest ways in which virtually any computer, including the older DOS-based machines using the 8088/8086 processor, or the 80286 processor, might be included in an orderly UUCP network. Consequently, if you must incorporate a single-tasking DOS machine into your UUCP network, scheduling must be partly automated and partly human. This occurs because the DOS machine will be monopolized by UUCP while its components are running.

One other point should be noted. Although we will describe some scheduling software below, several popular software packages for the IBM-oriented computers come with scheduling software. Tape backup software for DOS, for example, usually comes with a TSR scheduling program, so that the backup can be done at night. These programs may or may not be sufficiently generalized to accomplish other tasks, but often they are structured to run batch files. Those batch file can contain other commands in addition to, or instead of, the backup software. General purpose utility systems, such as Norton Utilities and PCTools, typically have some sort of scheduling assistance, and their Windows versions certainly do. Even WordPerfect 6.x for Windows (I have not checked the DOS version) now comes with a scheduler. The point is, this sort of software is becoming very widespread. In some of the software you own, you may already have a scheduler that you can use and with which you may be familiar. In the case of WinNET™ it comes with a scheduler called the "Mail Server Daemon."

When designing a UUCP network, part of the process will include decisions concerning the availability of the mail server. If it is available 24 hours a day, seven days a week, scheduling is then a problem for the remote sites. However, if the mail server can be made available only periodically, scheduling becomes an issue for the host and remote sites, and they must be properly merged. In general, however, if you wish to use scheduling software at a remote site, you will need to integrate it into your own environment. In my office, for example, I have a telephone line dedicated to data communications. Under normal circumstances I have a mini-BBS system waiting to answer the phone. Twice a day **wcron** terminates the BBS and runs the UUCP system so I can send and receive one of my clients' E-Mail. After the E-Mail transfer, the BBS is executed and is back on-line. This is an entirely automated procedure of which I am mostly unaware. For high-volume mail transfers, you might wish to have more than two mail deliveries a day, or in a more relaxed situation, you may wish the mail deliveries to take place late at night while everyone is sleeping.

WCRON for Windows from Cinetic Systems

WCRON for Windows from Cinetic Systems is very nice, easy to use, scheduling shareware program that works well and is easy to set up. According to the developers of WCRON, it was inspired by the UNIX **cron** utility. WCRON lets you specify the time of execution of specific tasks. It can be used for one-shot executions and for periodic executions. People use it to make regular backups, remind them of something, and start background tasks such as file transfer or automated BBS systems. WCRON is not free. If you decide to use it after a reasonable trial period, you are obligated to purchase a license for its use. A license for the use of WCRON can be obtained by filling out the Registration form found in the Help file and by sending a check or money order in the amount of $25 US ($30 CN) to Cinetic Systems. There are, by the way, a number of Windows-based, easily-used, low-cost shareware scheduling programs available, and virtually any of them will perform the scheduling of E-Mail. *The main criterion is that they be able to execute DOS as well as Windows commands within the Windows environment.* The reason is, at this point, the UUCP commands are all DOS commands, and they must be run in a DOS window.

CRON for DOS

There are several shareware programs for DOS that use the "CRON" name. One such program is CRONJR. It is included on the diskette with this book. CRONJR may not fit your operating mode precisely, but it is an example of the programs available.

According to the author of CRONJR, " . . . the reason for designing CronJr was for lack of anything better in the MS-DOS world. Simple but powerful programs like CRON (part of AT&T's UNIX) or Sleeper (public domain for HP's MPE) are nonexistent for PCs." Even if this was entirely correct when it was written, it is no longer true. The author is correct to say that "With more and more companies moving from mini-computers to PC based LANs, one of the many things that has been lost was the ability to schedule the nightly reporting and maintenance programs needed to keep a business working during the day."

The program requires an MS-DOS-based machine running MS-DOS 3.30 or higher. MS-DOS versions below 3.30 may be used, but they are not recommended since they require CRONJR to use more memory. The following points describe the way CRONJR works:

1. The schedule file *CronJr.SCH* is created by you. It contains the timing parameters for the tasks to be executed.
2. The master batch file, **CronJr.BAT**, is loaded from the command line. That is your last intervention.
3. The work file, **CronWk.BAT**, is deleted by **CronJr.BAT**.
4. The scheduler program, **Cron.EXE**, is loaded and the schedule file *CronJr.SCH* is read.
5. When the time comes to execute a process **Cron.EXE** dumps its scheduling information to *CronJr.JOB*, writes the **CronWk.BAT** file and unloads from memory to return control to **CronJr.BAT**.
6. If **CronJr.BAT** can find **CronWk.BAT** then the **CronWk.BAT** work file is called/executed.
7. Upon completion of **CronWk.BAT**, control is returned to **CronJr.BAT** which then executes **CronJr.BAT** (thus ending the original **CronJr.BAT** execution) with the parameter RELOAD. This is passed to **Cron.EXE** from Step 4, which causes the file *CronJr.JOB* to be loaded, rather than the file *CronJr.SCH*.

The following line summarizes the process:

```
CronJr.BAT -> Cron.EXE -> CronWk.BAT (YOUR TASK) ->CronJr.BAT
```

If this program conforms to your operating environment and you use DOS primarily or exclusively or you are dedicating an old DOS machine to the task of collecting mail, then perhaps this program is for you.

RELATED PRODUCTS

There are several other kinds of products that allow the functionality we have discussed thus far. This is provided that the PCs exist on a LAN, with an attached UNIX host machine. Developed by Sun Micro Systems, Inc., a manufacturer of high performance work stations using UNIX, the Network File System (NFS) provides a means for a host system to mount a remote file system, or part of it, as its own. When this happens, depending on the configuration, either or both machines can transparently use the other's disk resources. This means that if a PC could look at a UNIX file system as part of its own, it could then use UUCP and the related E-Mail system on the UNIX system, as if it resided on its own hard disk. Thus, the PC would need only an MUA and an MDA (mail delivery agent), and UNIX would take care of the rest. It would not be necessary to have a full-fledged UUCP system on DOS, OS/2, or Mac in order to use the facilities of UUCP. This is the basic thrust of the products described in this section.

While there are some very good reasons for using such a system, the cost of the software usually precludes its use when budget is a primary issue. Moreover, it addresses a relatively narrow problem because a LAN environment is probably the only practical one in which such systems can be used successfully. There are several of these products available. The ones mentioned are among the most widely used for IBM PCs, and at least one, *Pathway* from The Wollongong Group, is available not only for DOS and Windows, but also for OS/2 and the Mac.[31]

PC-NFS from Sunselect (Sun Micro Systems Inc., a Commercial Product)

Sunselect's $415-per-license PC-NFS 5.0 network software offers connectivity between IBM and IBM-compatible microcomputers and UNIX-based computers running the Network File System (NFS). The software is also available for $345 per license without documentation. PC-NFS is chiefly intended for UNIX networks but may also serve as an adequate network operating system for MS-DOS-based enterprises. The software can also work with Novell's NetWare and Microsoft's LAN Manager. Installation on UNIX and PC-NFS environments is straightforward, but in NetWare local area networks (LAN) it is slightly more difficult. Many of PC-NFS's commands will be familiar to experienced UNIX users, but DOS users will need some time to familiarize themselves with them. PC-NFS's documentation is thorough for the most part, but the guide listing customizable DOS applications is somewhat outdated. NFS allows resource-sharing and interhost printing to enhance network efficiency.[32]

PC-NFS connects IBM PCs compatible with one another, with UNIX-based computers that use the Network File System (NFS). Although it can be used in networks composed solely of MS-DOS-based machines, PC-NFS's UNIX ancestry, culture, and compatibility are apparent throughout its installation and use—whether or not UNIX or VMS NFS also live on the network. PC-NFS can also work concurrently with Microsoft's LAN Manager and Novell's NetWare.

In general, NFS lets a client mount an NFS host's filing system (or a part of it) as an extension of its own resources. NFS's resource-sharing mechanisms encompass interhost printing. The transactions among NFS systems traditionally ride across TCP/IP and Ethernet, but NFS will work with any network that supports 802.3 frames. PC-NFS comes with a character-based program to build a network and can be managed through DOS batch files or through Windows programs.

SunSelect includes instructions for adding PC-NFS to an existing LAN Manager or Windows for Workgroups network—using Network Driver Interface Specification (NDIS) drivers. Novell's Open Datalink Interface (ODI) drivers work only if the network card's driver interface supports 802.3 frame types.

PC/TCP by FTP Software Inc
(Commercial Product)

FTP Software Inc.'s $400 PC/TCP 2.2 network software offers a comprehensive set of TCP/IP internetworking functions. Both DOS' and Microsoft Windows' commands are bundled with PC/TCP, along with programs such as terminal emulation, file transfer agent, network utilities, and remote print/file access for both environments. PC/TCP includes an NFS (Network File System) utility called Interdrive that allows sharing, transfer, reading, and editing of remote files between a microcomputer and a UNIX host. The Windows File Manager will display long UNIX filenames or DOS filenames under PC/TCP, but users may be required to change configurations and restart Windows to achieve the desired result. PC/TCP's installation procedure is extremely difficult and assumes knowledge of advanced networking terminology.[33]

FTP Software's PC/TCP for DOS/Windows, Version 2.2, is bundled with a complete set of both DOS and Windows commands. With specific TCP/IP utilities, both a Windows and DOS command are available. For example, PC/TCP offers both commands for PING, Telnet, and FTP. The Windows programs include a terminal program, message transfer agent, PING, file transfer, network utilities, and access to remote file systems and printers. There are equivalent DOS programs, plus other DOS utilities for print management, mail, remote login, and remote program execution. Any of the DOS programs will run under Windows.

Interdrive allows you to transfer files to and from the host, read and edit files on the host; run local DOS applications on the host; and share remote files. For $400 the product is pricey, but FTP offers substantial functionality for the money. According to one review, it is one of the easiest products to use for connecting network drives and remote printers. According to Evan Birkhead, "You have to be a network guru to understand its installation program, but fortunately, their technical support is quick on the trigger and very knowledgeable."[34]

Pathway by The Wollongong Group Inc. (Commercial product)

Release 2.0 of Pathway Client NFS for DOS/Windows (PCNFSD) provides support for DOS 6.0, linked file systems, Pathway Server NFS for DOS/Windows 2.0, and the **rpcinfo** utility, a common application on UNIX-based NFS clients that gives the user a list of TCP- and UDP-based NFS services that are available on NFS Servers. In addition, printing services have been expanded to offer higher speed and more capabilities. Through PCNFSD 2.0, the Browse function in Windows can be used to locate and mount a remote printer. Current jobs in the print queue can be viewed by any user and deleted by the owner.[35]

PathWay Access 2.1 provides network printing services, a Workplace Shell user interface for OS/2 that features Telnet, FTP, and terminal emulation capabilities, including IBM 3179G and Tektronix 4150 and 4010. PathWay Runtime provides TCP/IP transport applications to PathWay applications such as Access, as well as third-party software. PathWay API 1.2 provides a 32-bit Windows DLL implementation developed by Berkeley Sockets.[36]

Pathway NFS for Macintosh 2.0, priced at $295 per copy, lets users on an Ethernet network (or LocalTalk network connected via a TCP/IP-aware router) directly access remote NFS servers. The new version is 50 percent faster, according to the company. The upgrade also lets users access NFS servers via the Chooser or browse an extended dialog box of all available NFS servers. The previous version only offered access via a control panel. Users can now mount multiple volumes at start-up. The product also gives users the option to make remote volumes more Mac-like by hiding certain UNIX files, such as those pertaining to directory structure. Pathway now supports MacTCP 2.0.2, lets users log onto multiple servers by letting them change group IDs or names. Users are also notified after files have been transferred successfully.[37]

CONCLUDING NOTES

This chapter reviews the range of UUCP products available for non-UNIX platforms. The availability of such products makes the use of UUCP viable as an integration tool. A large number of these products have been written specifically to provide access to Usenet and more globally to the Internet in general. Although a chapter is included concerning more extended networking and how to do it, the focus of this book is on the use of UUCP and its derivatives for private networks. Both in terms of quality and support, it is not clear that the commercial products are superior to some of the shareware/freeware systems. However, as a general rule it is probably true that the commercial products will be somewhat more integrated, providing features that you may have to acquire from other sources to ensure the same level of functionality. On the other hand, if cost is an issue, the average price for commercial UUCP-like products is around $300 for a single user whereas the cost for the non-commercial products range from free to less than $50. Moreover, there is no clear indication that the non-commercial products are, for the most part, inferior to their commercial counterparts. The burden of the successfull use and installation of the shareware/freeware products is entirely yours.

The choice of UUCP products is varied providing a wide range of possibilities for configuring both servers and leaf systems. The range of products is growing constantly. It is likely, that by the time this book is published, good Windows-based server software will be available or on its way, thus providing even more variety. The three packages distributed with this book will certainly get you started and include the following:

- UUPlus™ Version 1.50.
- WinNET™ Mail and News.
- Waffle, archived as *waf165.zip*.

Each of the packages has its own documentation and installation instructions, although some installation instructions on selected packages will be found in Chapter 7.

REFERENCES

1. UUPlus™ Utilities is manufactured by UUPlus Development, P. O. Box 6991, Los Osos, CA 93412; Telephone: 805-534-1425; Fax: 805-534-5902; E-Mail: info@uuplus.com.
2. Computer Witchcraft, Inc., may be reached at Post Office Box 4189, Louisville, KY 40204; Telephone: (502) 589-6800; Fax: (502) 589-7300; Internet Mail: winnet@win.net; CompuServe Mail: 76130,1463.
3. Waffle is a product of Darkside International, Thomas E Dell, P.O. Box 4436, Mountain View, CA 94040-0436. The preferred method of contact is via electronic mail; you can contact the author at: dell@vox.darkside.com (...vox!dell). If you don't have E-Mail access, you can contact the author by sending FEEDBACK at : The Dark Side of the Moon; 300/1200/2400 bps 24 hours 8N1; +1 408/245-7726. There also exists the comp.bbs.waffle and alt.bbs.waffle Usenet newsgroups.
4. Information may be requested from Jim O'Dell, Fort Pond Research, 15 Fort Pond Road, Acton, MA 01720; E-Mail: fpr!jimuu.psi.com, or you might try, from CompuServe, >INTERNET:jimuu@psi.com.
5. Macintosh UUPC 3.0 is coordinated by Dave Platt who may be reached by E-Mail at dplatt@snulbug.mtview.ca.us, or, presumably, through CompuServe at >INTERNET:dplatt@snulbug.mtview.ca.us. The product can be downloaded from the Macintosh Communications forum on CompuServe.
6. UUPC/Extended for DOS and OS/2 is currently supported by Drew Derbyshire, Kendra Electronic Wonderworks, P.O. Box 132, Arlington, MA 02174-0002.
7. The author, Ammon R. Campbell, may be contacted via CompuServe mail at: 71441,2447 or UUCP mail at: or uunet!compuserve!71441.2447 or uunet!sequent!jli!ionz!ammon or Internet mail at: >INTERNET:71441.2447@compuserve.com.

8. UUPC/Extended for DOS and OS/2 is currently supported by Drew Derbyshire, Kendra Electronic Wonderworks, P.O. Box 132, Arlington, MA 02174-0002.

9. From Mortice Kern Systems, Inc., 35 King St., N. Waterloo, ON, CD N2J 2W9; 800-265-2797; 519-884-2251; Fax: 519-884-8861; Tech support: 519-884-2270.

10. This product is listed in the materials from UUNET, an international networking organization providing domestic and international communications and information services to its customers including services as an UUCP mail and news feeder. Late Night Software, 671 28th Street, San Francisco, CA 94131, Telephone: 415-695-7727. During the writing of this book I placed several calls to Late Night Software requesting information on their product. None were returned nor was any information forthcoming by U. S. Mail.

11. Vortex Technology may be reached at P. O. Box 1323, Topanga, CA 90290; Telephone: 310-455-9300.

12. ICE Engineering may be reached at 8840 Main St., Whitmore Lake, MI 4818; Voice: (313) 449 8288; E-Mail: time@oxtrap.aa.ox.com or uunet!oxtrap!time.

13. Intercon may be contacted through Clint Heiden at 703-709-5503 or via CompuServe Mail's Internet connection at address >INTERNET:clint@intercon.com.

14. Coherent is a UNIX look-alike selling at the very reasonable price of $99. It is available from the Mark Williams Company, 60 Revere Drive, Northbrook, IL 60062; Telephone: 708-291- 6700; Fax: 708-291-6750.

15. Cinetic Systems may be reached at 4933 Verreau, Montreal, Quebec, Canada, H1M 2C7; or by E-Mail at Internet: Cinetic@Speedy.CAM.ORG or CompuServe: 71640,666.

16. PCELM is a shareware product. Support may be acquired from the authors at the following addresses:

    Wolfgang Siebeck -or- Martin Freiss
    Rosstr. 38-40   Muehlenfloessstr. 60
    D-W 5100 Aachen   D-W 4792 Bad Lippspringe
    Germany   Germany
    E-Mail: E-Mail:
    siebeck@infoac.rmi.de freiss.pad@sni.de

17. Both of these are available from the Macintosh/Communications Forum on CompuServe.

18. See the endnote for Cinetics Mail Manager for an appropriate address.

19. For more information call SunSelect, 2 Elizabeth Dr., Chelmsford, MA 01824, (508) 442-2300.

20. FTP Software, North Andover, MA, can be reached at (800) 282-4387.

21. For more information, contact The Wollongong Group, 1129 San Antonio Rd., Palo Alto, Calif. 94303; (415) 962-7100.

22. Free Software Foundation, Inc., 675 Mass. Ave., Cambridge, MA 02139, USA.

23. Available from Walnut Creek CDROM, Suite 260, 1547 Palos Verdes Mall, Walnut Creek, CA 94596; Telephone: 510-674-0783; Fax: 510-674-0821; or via Internet E-Mail: info@cdrom.com. This CDROM is updated periodically.

24. Except as otherwise noted, quotations for this and other shareware/freeware products come from distributed, machine-readable documents.

25. Two books that are referenced elsewhere, and that are specifically referenced in the documentation for UUCP/Extended, and for all the other systems described in this chapter, are the following: Tim O'Reilly and Grace Todino, *Managing UUCP and Usenet* (Sebastopol, CA: O'Reilly & Associates, Inc.,

1990); and Grace Todino and Dale Dougherty, *Using UUCP and Usenet* (Sebastopol, CA: O'Reilly & Associates, Inc., 1991). Both of these are useful adjuncts to this book.

26. A recent book featuring the MKS UUCP system is Jame Gardner, *A DOS User's Guide to the Internet: E-mail, Netnews, and File Transfer with UUCP* (Englewood Cliffs, NJ: Prentice-Hall, 1994). A diskette is included with this book containing the MKS UUCP.

27. Margie Wylie, "UUCP application offers access to Unix mail, nets" *MacWEEK*, April 16, 1991, vol. 5, no. 15 p. 26(1). Carolyn Said, "ICE breaks barriers between Mac, Unix UUCP", *MacWEEK*, Sept 25. 1990, vol. 4, no. 32, p. 13(1).

28. Naor Wallach, "New for Mac–Intercon UUCP product: Intercon Systems licenses ICE Engineering's Macintosh-based communications product", *Newsbytes*, Jan 22, 1993, p. NEW01220012.

29. Anon., "InterCon licenses Mac software," *Digital News & Review*, Feb. 1, 1993 vol. 10, no. 3, p. 12(1).

30. This section, and the three point analysis, is based on comments made by the documenter of one of the cron programs for DOS: *CronJr ver 2.36*, Software Shorts, Suite 101, 14101 Yorba Street, Tustin, CA 92680, U.S.A., author unknown.

31. Note the following articles for discussion of this approach to the integration of DOS/Windows/Mac and UNIX: Nicholas Petreley, Nancy Durlester, and Laura Wonnacott, "Discovering a world beyond NetWare; InfoWorld tests eight TCP/IP NFS products for remote network services," *InfoWorld*, May 24, 1993, vol. 15, no. 21, p. 108(10); and Tom Henderson and Casey Gaynor, "Four paths from PC to TCP/IP. (TCP/IP software connection services from Beame and Whiteside, FTP Software, Novell and NetManage)," *LAN Magazine*, Nov. 1993, vol. 8, no. 12, p. 184(7).

32. This section is based on Tom Henderson, "DOS and Unix: mounting the net," *LAN Magazine*, August 1993, vol. 8, no. 8, p. 177(4)

33. Nicholas Petreley, Nancy Durlester, and Laura Wonnacott, "PC/TCP version 2.2", *InfoWorld*, May 24, 1993, vol. 15, no. 21, p. 115(3).

34. See also, Evan Birkhead, "FTP further refines PC/TCP," *LAN Computing*, Feb. 1993, vol. 4, no. 2, p. 8(1).

35. Anon., "Wollongong upgrades Pathway Client NFS (new release 2.0 of The Wollongong Group's Pathway Client NFS for DOS/Windows)," *Digital News & Review*, June 21, 1993, vol. 10, no. 12, p. 14(1).

36. Anon., "PathWay Access for OS/2," *LAN Computing*, August 1993, vol. 4, no. 8, p. 52(1).

37. Nathalie Welch, "Wollongong Group carves out a new Pathway to NFS volumes. (Network File System) (Pathway NFS for Macintosh 2.0)," *MacWEEK*, Sept. 6, 1993, vol. 7, no. 35, p. 24(1).

5

The UUCP and Mail Programs

This chapter is a quick reference guide to the major commands in UUCP and other support programs. Each UUCP command is presented with both the Taylor UUCP and the UUPlus™ options so that some sense of the similarities and differences may be observed. The Taylor versions of the commands are used for comparative purposes because it is new and is likely have a major impact on UUCP over the next few years. BNC (HoneyDanBer or HDB) is probably the more commonly used UUCP at the present time. The commands are divided into two groups: end-user commands and system commands. For the sake of completeness I have included some commands that appear in only one system or the other to demonstrate the variations that can take place.

You will find from a reading of this book, as well as from other literature on UUCP, that the concepts of what are the essential and basic commands vary from system to system. The contemporary versions of UUCP all have enhancements not particularly envisaged by the early authors. Moreover, as UUCP has been ported to operating environments other than UNIX, it has also been necessary to provide support programs that those working with UNIX—even fifteen years ago—took for granted.

Note that in this chapter several non-UUCP commands, most notably the mail-related commands, **uuencode** and **uudecode**, and GNU versions of **gzip**, a file compression utility, are included. **uuencode**, **uudecode**, and **gzip** appear in neither the Taylor nor the UUPlus™ versions of UUCP because they are not part of the UUCP system. They are, however, often required for the transmission of binary files across networks of unknown character. The mail user agent (MUA) for

Windows, the Cinetics Mail Manager, and the WinNET™ Windows implementation of UUCP (on the distribution diskettes), include **uuencode** and **uudecode**.

This chapter does not summarize all the programs that are mentioned in this book, nor does it summarize all those that are on the distribution diskettes. Rather it focuses on what is necessary for a working UUCP system that supports E-Mail. You will need to read other parts of this book and read the documentation provided by the authors of the distributed software for additional information.

MAIL COMMANDS

In addition to having UUCP, in order to have a mail system, it is necessary to have a mail user agent (MUA) and a mail delivery agent (MDA), although these may be combined in a single program. The discussion in this chapter of the commands and programs available is restricted to the software distributed with this book. The two basic commands which come with UUPlus are **mail** and **rmail**. After you get UUPlus™ running properly as a DOS-based UUCP system, and after you have experimented with **mail**, you can substitute either **pcelm** (under DOS) or the Cinetics Mail Manager (**cmm**) (under Windows) for **mail**. The latter two programs are described in some detail in Chapter 7 and 8 along with figures illustrating their screens. Much the same advice is also appropriate on UNIX or UNIX-like systems, such as Coherent. First get UUCP running properly, then be sure it can send and receive mail using the basic UNIX E-Mail command **/bin/mail**. At that point, you can move on to the use of **elm** or other MUAs, perhaps even one under X-Windows, one of the graphical user interfaces (GUI) for UNIX. If you are setting up a client workstation that will not act as an UUCP host, and if you normally use Windows, you should probably skip all this chapter and install WinNET™.

mail/pcelm/cmm/WinNET™

Since this is in the nature of a "handy reference" chapter, the more elaborate mail user agents will not be described here. They are discussed extensively in other chapters and all have more documentation files that come with the packages. However, a few considerations should be kept in mind when deciding what MUA to use. If you are setting up a client machine, and the user uses Windows, then use WinNET™. The primary executable file is named **wnmail.exe**, and it is a Windows program. It is an excellent system, easily installed and used.

Simply take the zipped file, copy it into a temporary directory, then unzip it with **unzip** (see below). Then read the readme file followed by running the installation program from Windows. It will default to setting up a directory called *d:\wnmail*. You will find a small configuration file called *chat.rc* that may need a little editing. The program is quite intuitive in its use and the help system is very good.

Doing a full installation of UUPlus™, is necessary when setting up a client in a DOS environment. This means primarily editing the configuration files. Get it running first using **mail** as the MUA. Then, when you have an operating system that can communicate with your mail server, you can install **pcelm**. **pcelm** is much easier to use than **mail**. It, too, has its own configuration file, called *pcelm.rc*, which must be correctly edited. Once you have done a couple of client workstations in a DOS mode it will become routine, but the first one might be troublesome.

Finally, if the mail server host is set up using WAFFLE, then you will need to install that product. For a PC-based mail server, choices are currently limited since, at least at the writing of this book, early 1994, no low-cost Windows host systems are available. Waffle provides a flexible, well-documented, moderately easy-to-install server system with the added advantage of a "standard" bulletin board. Because of its BBS design, Waffle does not use, nor does it require, a traditional **mail** command. The other alternative, of course, is to acquire a low-cost UNIX-compatible operating system, such as Coherent, and use it. In either case, even though you may use **elm** or **pcelm** with those systems, you will probably be wise to have **mail** fully functional as well. In other words, unless you are using Windows, a Macintosh, or Waffle exclusively for a client ("leaf") installation, do not try to circumvent the use of **mail**.

The on-line manual distributed with UUPlus™, which can be accessed from the Install program or a DOS reader or text editor, explains the **mail** command in some detail. The name of that document is *uuplus150.doc*. You can read that documentation on-line, once you have installed UUPlus, with an ascii text editor or file lister. The **mail** program is used both for sending and receiving mail. The options available depend on whether you wish to send or receive mail. They also differ slightly from implementation to implementation.

Sending Mail

For sending mail interactively in UNIX or Coherent, the basic syntax is:

```
mail -s "subject" addressees
```

If the *-s "subject"* is omitted, the user is prompted for a subject. *Addressees* must be specified. For sending mail from UUPlus:

```
mail [-i] [-r filename] [-s subject] name [name ...]
```

UUPlus **mail** has one additional option that allows you to see the setup parameters for the command: **mail -a**.

Receiving Mail

For receiving mail, the syntax for UUPlus™ is:

```
mail [-f filename]
```

In the examples just given *filename* is the mailbox to be read using the syntax described below for filenames. The default is to read the user's own system mailbox.

Consequently, under normal conditions, the end-user need only enter the command, **mail**.

Sending Files

mail can be used to send files as well as standard E-Mail. To send mail which already exists in a text file, or to send some other kind of file, the procedure is as above, but under UNIX the standard syntax for file redirection is added to the end of the command line:

```
mail tmadron@madron.uucp < tom.txt
```

UUPlus, however, provides the "-r" option for file transfer:

```
mail -r tom.txt tmadron@madron.uucp
```

In either case, the file *tom.txt* would be sent to tmadron at madron.uucp in a mail "envelope."

Binary files, which include many word processing files, must be sent very carefully using the **mail** command. Generally the **uucp** command is normally used for transferring binary files to directly connected systems, rather than to **mail**. You will find, however, that in many cases, even with binary files, **mail** may be your best choice. In either case, you can use a program such as **uuencode** to convert a binary file to printable characters before transmission, and it is a requirement when mailing binary files to distant systems. Some variants of these programs will automatically encode binary files or have menu options for so doing. This is the case with both the Cinetics Mail Manager and for WinNET.™ Both, of course, have the capability of restoring the files once they are transferred.

Typical **mail** command line options can be summarized as follows:

```
Sending mail:
Coherent: mail -s "subject" recipients
UUPlus™: mail [-i] [-r filename] [-s subject] recipient [recipient ...]
Receiving mail:
mail [options]
```

Coherent (Unix)	UUPlus™	Description
	-a	Print the setup parameters for the UUPlus mail command.
-f file	-r file	Read mail from file instead of from the default, /usr/spool/mail/user.
	-i	Enter sending options interactively.
-m		Send a message to the terminal of user if he is logged into the system when mail is sent. *(continues)*

Coherent	UUplus™	Description
-p		Print all mail without interaction.
-q		Quit without changing the mailbox if an interrupt character is typed. Normally an interrupt character stops printing the current message.
-r		Reverse the order of printing messages. Normally mail prints messages in the order in which they were received.
	-r file	Import *file* as the mail message.
-s subject	-s subject	Subject of the mail message.
-v		Verbose mode. Show the version number of the mail program, and display expanded aliases.

Once **mail** has been executed, and you are busy reading your mail, there are several commands that can be used to save, delete, or send each message to another user interactively. These commands provide **mail** with considerable flexibility:

Summary of Interactive **mail** Commands		
Coherent	UUPlus™	Description
d		Delete the current message and print the next message.
	d	Delete the current message.
	dp	Delete the current message, and print the next message.
	h	Display headers for each message.
	i	Display information about current message.
m [user]	m [user]	Mail the current message to each user given (default: yourself).
	n	List next message (same as <Return>).
q	q	Quit and update mailbox file to reflect changes.
r		Reverse the direction in which the mailbox is being scanned.
	r	Reply to sender.
	R	Reply to sender, recipient(s), and Cc(s)
s filename	s filename	Save mail, with header. If filename exists, message is appended. *(continues)*

Coherent	UUPlus™	Description
t user		Send a message read from the standard input, terminated by an end-of-file character or by a line containing only "." or "?", to each user (default: yourself).
	u	Undelete message.
	v	Show mail version.
w filename	w filename	Save the curren message, without headers. If filename exists, message is appended.
x	x	Exit without updating the mailbox file.
\<Enter\>	\<Enter\>	Print the next message.
-		Print the previous message.
EOF		Quit updating mailbox; same as q.
?	?	Print a summary of available commands.
!command		Pass command to shell for execution.

rmail

It is more difficult to generalize about **rmail** than to generalize about the UUCP commands. First, there is no Taylor equivalent of **rmail** since it is a mail delivery agent (MDA). In UUPlus™, other programs such as **mail** and **uuxqt** pass **rmail** mail for delivery on standard input (see also the "react file" parameters for E-Mail), and **rmail** then handles the actual writing to local mailboxes and/or queuing for remote systems. **rmail** is designed to be invoked only from other programs, and as such, end-users should never have to invoke **rmail**. On UNIX systems **/bin/mail** can usually act as its own MDA without invoking **rmail**, although **rmail** or **smail** may still have to be used by other MUAs. The general syntax of RMAIL is as follows:

RMAIL: UUPlus™	
RMAIL recipient mailfile sender	
Arguments	Description of Options.
recipient	argv[1] is the recipient of the mail. A valid RFC-822 address is required here (or the name of a local mailbox).
mailfile	argv[2] is the file to read from. This should contain the text of the message in addition to all necessary header fields.

(continues)

Arguments	Description of Options.
sender	argv[3] is the person sending the mail, if local; if there is no argv[3], it's assumed that the mail is from offsite and no "From" header will be constructed.

The function of **rmail** for UUPlus™ is to provide third-party support to the UUPlus mail mechanism. Several of the UUplus™ applications themselves use an internally-linked version of rmail. The **rmail.exe** application, however, provides a command-line link to the rmail facility. If you install **pcelm** or **cmm**, for example, you will find that it is necessary to use **rmail** as the means those programs have of delivering mail appropriately.

THE UUCP COMMAND SET

In late 1978, D. A. Nowitz, one of the people who worked on Version 2 of UUCP, defined the system as "a series of programs designed to permit communication between UNIX systems using either dial-up or hardwired communication lines."[1] The UUCP system consisted of four primary and two secondary programs. Nowitz listed the four primary programs as **uucp**, **uucico**, **uux**, and **uuxqt**. These remain the center of UUCP to this day. The secondary programs at that time were **uulog** and **uuclean**. **uulog** updates the log file with new entries and reports on the status of UUCP requests, and **uuclean** removes old files from the spool directory. Both of these programs or their equivalent continue to be part of most contemporary UUCP systems. However, there are others that have also become important and essential to the operation of the system.

I have attempted to divide the UUCP commands, as they are available under Taylor UUCP and UUPlus™, into two categories: "end user commands" and "system commands." In the presentation of these commands, where applicable, I have listed the Taylor UUCP options for a particular command along with the UUPlus™ options. This has been done to provide you with a frame of reference for understanding the differences among UUCP systems. You will find, as you read along, that both Taylor UUCP and UUPlus™ contain enhancements beyond those basic commands listed by Nowitz. They also contain commands that are unique to each system. Not all the commands for Taylor UUCP are documented here, since we did not include it on the distribution diskettes.

End-user Commands

This section summarizes the commands that end-users will need when dealing with E-Mail or when sending files with UUCP. The next section details those commands that are largely called by other programs or are used primarily by the "system administrator," that person who is using this book to actually set up the systems. The last section in the chapter provides some documentation for a few utilities that you all will likely need as your mail network develops. Remember that the MUAs are not part of uucp. They are, however, essential in a mail system.

The uucp Command

uucp queues files for transfer between two systems. The basic **uucp** command syntax is:

```
uucp [options] file1 system!file2   or
uucp [options] system!file3 file4
```

The first example copies a local file (file1) to a remote host (system) as file2, the second example copies a file (file3) on a remote host (system) to the local file 4. Filenames may be specified as an absolute path name, relative to a user's home directory (~user/file), or relative path to the uucp public directory (~/name).

Different versions of **uucp** vary somewhat in the range of options, although common options have retained their definitions since the beginning.[2]

Taylor UUCP version 1.04, copyright (C) 1991, 1992 Ian Lance Taylor Usage: uucp [options] file1 [file2 ...] dest UUPlus™ Usage: uucp [-c] [-system] [-filename]		
Taylor Options	UUPlus™ Options	Description of Options
-c	-c	Do not copy local files to spool directory.
-C,-p		Copy local files to spool directory (default).
-d		Create necessary directories (default).
-f		Do not create directories (fail if they do not exist).
	-f	Filename of the file to be sent or received.
-g grade		
-m		Report status of copy by mail.
-n user		
-R		Copy directories recursively.
-r		Do not start uucico daemon.
-s file		
	-s system	Remote system name.
-j		Report job id.

(continues)

Taylor Options	UUPlus™ Options	Description of Options
-W		Do not add current directory to remote filenames.
-t		Emulate uuto.
-u name		Set user name.
-x debug		
-I file		Set configuration file to use.

uuname

uuname reports names of the remote systems defined to you via the *SYSTEMS/L.sys* or *sys* file. Using the "-l" option, it also reports the name of your local system. In the case of UUPlus™ this is the local system name (nodename) defined in UUPlus.cfg. On UNIX, it resides in the */etc/uucpname* file. The **uuname** command distributed with this book for UUPlus™ is not a standard or "official" part of the UUPlus system.

Taylor UUCP version 1.04, copyright (C) 1991, 1992 Ian Lance Taylor UUPlus™ version 1.5 unofficial utility by Thomas Wm. Madron, 1994 Usage: uuname [options]		
Taylor UUCP Options	**Madron UUNAME Options**	**Description of Options**
-a	-a	Display aliases.
-l	-l	Display local system name.
-I *file*		Set configuration filename; alternate configuratons not supported by UUPlus.
The default is to report all the defined remote systems to which the local system may connect.		

uustat (uuq, uusnap)

Under Taylor UUCP, the **uustat** program does many things. By default **uustat** displays all jobs queued up for the invoking user, as if given the -u option with the appropriate argument. **uustat** can be used to remove any of your jobs from the queue. It can also be used to show the status of the UUCP system in various ways, such as showing the connection status of all the remote stations your system knows about. It can output detailed or summary information for one or all systems directly connected to the local host. The same information can be obtained for UUPlus™ by using **uusnap.exe** and **uuq.exe**. **uusnap** provides essentially the same information on the job queue as does **uustat** without any options. More formally, **uusnap** displays a "snapshot" list of all UUCP jobs queued and ready for transfer, as well as jobs in the queue waiting to be processed. In a manner more analogous to **uustat**, **uuq** displays detailed information about the list of all UUCP jobs queued and ready for transfer. A summary of **uustat**'s operands (along with **uuq** and **uusnap**) follows.

Taylor's version of **uustat** extends the capability of the command over traditional versions. The following uses work similarly in most systems that have the **uustat** command:

uustat	displays all jobs queued for the current user
uustat -a	displays all jobs queued by all users
uustat -q	displays statistics for jobs queued for all remote systems
uustat -m	displays the status of all remote systems and their last connection time

Taylor UUCP version 1.04, copyright (C) 1991, 1992 Ian Lance Taylor			
Usage: uustat [options] or uuq [options]			
Taylor Options	UUPlus™ Options		Description of Options
	uuq	uusnap	
-a			List all UUCP jobs.
-B num			Number of lines to return in -M or -N mail message.
-c command			List requests for named command.
-C command			List requests for other than named command.
-e			List queued executions rather than job requests.
-i			Prompt for whether to kill each listed job.
-k job	-d job		Kills job "jobid."
-K			Kill each listed job.
	-l		Display the information in "long" format, providing more detailed information regarding queued jobs.
-m			Report status for all remote machines.
-M			Mail report on each listed job to UUCP administrator.
-N			Mail report on each listed job to requestor.

(continues)

| Taylor Options | UUPlus™ Options | | Description of Options |
	uuq	uusnap	
-o hours			List all jobs older than given number of hours.
-p			Show status of all processes holding UUCP locks.
-q			List number of jobs for each system.
-Q			Don't list jobs, just take actions (-i, -K, -M, -N).
-r job			Rejuvenate specified UUCP job.
-s system	-s system		List all jobs for specified system.
-S system			List all jobs for other than specified system.
-u user			List all jobs for specified user.
-U user			List all jobs for other than specified user.
	-v		Verbosely reports scan progress.
-W comment			Comment to include in mail messages.
-y hours			List all jobs younger than given number of hours.
-x debug			Set debugging level (0 for none, 9 is max).
-I file			Set configuration file to use.

System Commands

The "system commands" are those UUCP commands that are designed to be called by other programs or used by systems administrators.

uucico

uucico is the program which actually calls the remote system and transfers files and requests. Under UNIX, **uucico** is normally started automatically by **uucp** and **uux**. Most UNIX systems will start it periodically to make sure that all work requests are handled. **uucico** checks the queue to see what work needs to be done, and then calls the appropriate systems. If the call fails, perhaps because the phone line is busy, **uucico** leaves the requests in the queue and goes on to the next system to call. It is also possible to force **uucico** to call a remote system even if there is no work to be done for it, so that it can pick up any work that may be queued up remotely.

To make **uucico** call all connected systems to deliver and pick up remote mail and files, simply type:

```
uucico -s all
```

Here **uucico** is directed to poll all the systems listed in the *systems/L.sys* or *sys* files. The full list of options supported by **uucico** follows:

```
Taylor UUCP version 1.04, copyright (C) 1991, 1992 Ian Lance Taylor
Usage: uucico -[options]
UUPlus™, 1994
Usage: uucico [-s system] [-x debug] [-h] [-g grade] [-ln]
             [-v] [-f filename]
```

Taylor Options	UUPlus™ Options	Description of Options
-s system -S system	-s sysname	System: Call system (-S implies -f in Taylor UUCP).
-f		Force call despite system status.
	-f	Allows debug information to be diverted to a file.
	-g grade	Will run uucico at the specified grade and above. The highest grade is "A" and the lowest is "Z."
	-h	This option tells uucico to ignore the host name sent by the remote machine. It has the same effect as the ignorehost on option in the UUPLUS.CFG file. If -h is used, the ignorehost command in the UUPLUS.CFG file will be ignored.
-r state		1 for master, 0 for slave (default).
-p port		Specify port (implies -e).
-l		Prompt for login name and password.
	-ln	Allows the maximum length (number of characters) of the sitename to be specified when calling a remote system. This switch is intended to provide compatibility with systems that do not follow the UUCP standard of a maximum of 8 characters in a sitename. The value specified here will override any value set in the UUPLUS.CFG file.
-e		Endless loop of login prompts and daemon execution.

(continues)

Taylor Options	UUPlus(tm) Options	Description of Options
	-v	Prints the current version number of UUPlus Utilities.
-w		After calling out, wait for incoming calls.
-q		Don't start uuxqt when done.
-x,-X debug	-x debug	Set debugging level.
-I file		Set configuration file to use.

uuclean (UUPlus™)

UUClean will remove old UUCP queue files from the spool. Time is based on the number of days old the files are, rounded down to the nearest day. The syntax of the **uuclean** command is:

uuclean

Optional parameters:

-o days	Number of days to expire all spool files.
-C days	Number of days to expire C. files.
-D days	Number of days to expire D. files.
-X days	Number of days to expire X. files.
-T days	Number of days to expire temp files.
-s system	Restrict uuclean to single system, else, uuclean runs on all systems.

uux

uux is used to request a program to be executed on a remote system. As with **uucp**, programs and files on remote systems may be named by using *system!* In his documentation file, Ian Taylor gives the following example: "to run the **rnews** program on ‹airs› passing it standard input, you would say ‹uux - airs!rnews›. The ‹-› means to read standard input and set things up such that when ‹rnews› runs on ‹airs› it will receive the same standard input."

Remember that neither **uucp** nor **uux** do any work immediately. They only queue requests for later processing. The requests are processed automatically (by **cron** calling uucico, for example) and the appropriate systems are called. Normally the system will also start the daemon periodically to check if there is any work to be done. The advantage of this approach is that it all happens automatically. You don't have to sit around waiting for the files to be transferred. The disadvantage is that if anything goes wrong, it might be a while before anybody notices. **uux** does not exist in UUPlus™ although its functionality is embedded in the programs.

For the sake of completeness, and because **uux** is of considerable importance, the Taylor version is presented below. If you opt to use Coherent 4.2 on your host system, this is the version you will use.

Taylor UUCP version 1.04, copyright (C) 1991, 1992 Ian Lance Taylor Usage: uux [options] [-] command	
Options	Description of Options
-,-p	Read standard input for standard input of command.
-c	Do not copy local files to spool directory (default).
-C	Copy local files to spool directory.
-l	Link local files to spool directory.
-g grade	Set job grade (must be alphabetic).
-n	Do not report completion status.
-z	Report completion status only on error.
-r	Do not start uucico daemon.
-a address	Address to mail status report.
-b	Return standard input with status report.
-s file	Report completion status to file.
-j	Report job id.
-x debug	Set debugging level.
-I file	Set configuration file to use.

uuxqt

The function of **uuxqt** is to read and process executable files (i.e., under UNIX or Coherent, those marked with the prefix **X.**) normally found in */usr/spool/uucp/ sitename*. These systems will only allow it to process execute requests for which the remote system has permission. **uuxqt** may be called by either **uucp** or **uucico**. It is not normally considered a user-callable program. For UUPlus™ **uuxqt** places incoming data files from a **uucp** transfer in the appropriate directory structure (i.e. mail is delivered to the proper mailbox and news is placed in the proper directory). This is the equivalent of executing **rmail** or other mail delivery agent. **uuxqt** should normally be invoked after a call with **uucico**. UUPlus™ recommends that you do this via a batch file, for example:

uucico -s%1 -x3
uuxqt -s%1

where the system name will be substituted for the %1 variable, when given on the command line. If no system name is given, **uuxqt** will ask if you wish to process all systems.

Taylor UUCP version 1.04, copyright (C) 1991, 1992 Ian Lance Taylor Usage: uuxqt [-c cmd] [-I file] [-s system] [-x debug]		
UUXQT: UUPlus™, 1994 Usage: uuxqt [-a] [-f filename] [-s system] [-xdebug]		
Taylor Options	UUPlus™ Options	Description of Options
	-a	Run UUXQT in automatic mode, not prompting the user at any time.
-c cmd		Set type of command to execute.
	-f filename	Send all debug output to filename.
-s system	-s system	Execute commands only for named system.
-x debug	-x debug	Set debugging level (0 for none, 9 is max).
-I file		Set configuration file to use.

USENET NEWS

The news transfer functions are well developed in all three of the systems distributed with this book: UUPlus™, Waffle, and WinNET™. One of the reasons is that all three were developed, at least in part, to assist people in the use of Usenet. There is nothing equivalent in Taylor UUCP, of course, since the news functions are not a part of UUCP. There are a number of news processing utilities on UNIX systems, however, and many of those also run on Coherent. The news-related commands will not be documented here since that is outside the scope of this book. The documentation that may found with each of the three distributed systems should suffice for you to use those programs if that is your desire.

Alternative Approaches

To summarize comments made throughout this chapter, we need to have a good understanding of what we are trying to accomplish. UUPlus™ provides a good DOS alternative to the UNIX UUCP system. If you usually use Windows, then WinNET™

Mail and News is the product for you. If you must establish a DOS-based mail server, however, then your choice will probably be Waffle. When deciding on the appropriate mix of software for your E-Mail network, however, you must make some decisions about what software is the most appropriate. There are a large number of alternatives and they are growing day-by-day. In terms of the software distributed with this book you might wish to use WinNET™ rather than UUPlus™ on a client workstation, for example. And on the host you might wish to use a low-cost UNIX look-alike (not distributed), such as Coherent 4.2. There are hybrid alternatives, as well, such as replacing the use of **mail.exe** with **pcelm.exe** under DOS or with Cinetics Mail Manger under Windows with **rmail** and **uucico** running in a DOS window. **uucico** itself should be run directly under DOS, or at least full-screen if run under Windows.

GENERAL (BUT NECESSARY) UTILITIES

There are a few essential utilities that you will need in order to deal with the files that come with this book, or with files that you are apt to confront along the line in your use of E-Mail. You will probably find that you need others than those supplied, but these will get you started. There are a number of UNIX utilities that have been "ported" over to DOS. Virtually all of them may be found somewhere on the Internet (see Chapter 10). In the meantime, if you have accounts with CompuServe or BIX or Delphi, you can get them without too much difficulty. On CompuServe go to the Unixforum forum and take a look at the files in the section labeled "DOS under UNIX" if you find you need something that I have not provided.

uuencode/uudecode

A problem occurs when trying to send 8-bit binary files over some networks that are limited to 7-bit ASCII characters. The standard within the UNIX community for handling this situation is the process known as "uuencoding" the file. **uuencode** prepares a file for transmission to a remote destination via uucp. It takes binary input and produces an encoded version, consisting of printable ASCII characters, on standard output, which may be redirected or piped to uucp. On the receiving end the file is passed through the companion program "**uudecode**", which converts the ASCII version back into the original binary file.

   uuencode is chiefly used for mail. You cannot mail a binary file, even when you may be able to **uucp** it. But you can mail a **uuencode**d binary. The standard way to mail a binary is to compress it (see the section on **gzip**), **uuencode** it, split it into pieces less than or equal to about 50 kilobytes each, then mail each piece. The reason for this restriction is that many systems do not allow mail items greater than about 64 KB, and some overhead is consumed by headers and signature files. There is a standard format to these files which is described in Chapter 10.

Joan Riff's UUENCODE/UUDECODE for the PC, version 3.0 (Mar 11 1992)
Copyright (c) 1992 Computerwise Consulting Services. All rights reserved.
This software may be used by individuals from whom CCS receives a licensing
fee of $10. Any other use is a violation of our rights under copyright
law. Computerwise Consulting Services, Phone: (703) 450-7175, P.O. Box 813,
McLean, VA 22101, Internet: bob@grebyn.com.

Usage: **uuencode** [-cdem] *[filename]>outfile*

Options	Description of Options
-c	Use DOS-standard \r\n (CRLF) as line terminator, instead of UNIX-standard \n (LF) by itself.
-d	Decode filename to whatever output file is encoded into the file. This is the same as running the uudecode program on the file.
-e	Encode filename to stdout. This is the default action and need not be explicitly specified.
-m	Encode the true DOS file mode in the output file. This is not very useful, since the DOS file mode is very different from the UNIX file mode. Any UNIX decoder of the resultant file will attempt to set some nonsensical mode on the resultant file. This flag may be useful if the eventual decoder will be a DOS system. In the absence of this flag a constant mode of octal 666 will be used.

'filename' is the name of a file to be encoded. If no file is specified,
then stdin will be used.

'>outfile' redirects the encoded output of this program to whatever output
file you specify.

This is a relatively simple program to use consistent with the typical UNIX version of **uuencode** that usually has a syntax similar to the following:

```
uuencode [ source ] file_label [  source ]  output
```

The decode program is equally simple. Moreover, when decoding, if the file is part of a mail message the **uudecode** program will ignore the headers and signature file information, dealing only with that portion of the message that is **uuencode**d.

Joan Riff's UUENCODE/UUDECODE for the PC, version 3.0 (Mar 11 1992)
Copyright (c) 1992 Computerwise Consulting Services. All rights reserved.
This software may be used by individuals from whom CCS receives a licensing

(continues)

fee of $10. Any other use is a violation of our rights under copyright law. Computerwise Consulting Services, Phone: (703) 450-7175, P.O. Box 813, McLean, VA 22101, Internet: bob@grebyn.com.	
Usage: **uudecode** [-dem] *filename*	
Options	Description of Options
-d	Decode filename to whatever output file name is encoded in the file. This is the default action and need not be explicitly specified.
-e	Encode filename to stdout. This is the same as running the uuencode program on the file.
-m	Obey the file mode as encoded in the file. This flag causes a chmod() to be performed for whatever mode value was encoded into the file. This makes little sense on DOS, because the UNIX mode as encoded into the file means something very different on DOS. Nevertheless, this flag may be useful if the original encoder of the file was a DOS system.
'filename' is the name of a uuencoded file to be processed.	

In a manner similar to **uuencode**, the UNIX version of **uudecode** is very simple:

```
uudecode [ file ]
```

uudecode takes a file encoded by uuencode and translates it back to binary. Any leading and trailing lines added by uucp are discarded. If the file is not specified, standard input is read. Consider the following example using a file called *tmp*:

```
begin 644 sys
M5&AE('%U:6-K(&)R;W=N(&9O>"!J=6UP<R!O=F5R('1H92!L87IY(&1O9RX*
end
```

Note that the third line is a space followed by a new line. To decode it, type:

```
uudecode tmp
```

The output contained in file *sys* will be:

```
The quick brown fox jumps over the lazy dog.
```

Tar

If you start using Usenet or the Internet much (see Chapter 10), you will undoubtedly obtain files that have an extension, ".*taz*", or ".*tar*". The first is an archive file generated with the UNIX **tar** command, then compressed with the UNIX **gzip** command (see below). The second is just an archive. In order to sort all this out, you will need a DOS rendition of **tar**. The approach to the issues of archiving and compression have been somewhat different on UNIX and DOS. Two common DOS programs, **pkzip** and **pkunzip**, do both the tasks of **tar** and **gzip**: they archive *and* compress. Because some materials you may receive will have originated on UNIX systems, however, you need to be prepared to deal with UNIX usage.

```
tar: you must specify exactly one of the c, t, or x options
tar: valid options:
```

-b N	blocking factor N (block size = Nx512 bytes)
-B	reblock as we read (for reading 4.2BSD pipes)
-c	create an archive
-D	dump record number within archive with each message
-f F	read/write archive from file or device F
-h	don't dump symbolic links; dump the files they point to
-i	ignore blocks of zeros in the archive, which normally mean EOF
-k	keep existing files, don't overwrite them from the archive
-m	don't extract file modified time
-o	write an old V7 format archive, rather than ANSI [draft 6] format
-p	do extract all protection information
-S X	device for -V option is X Kbyte drive
-s	list of names to extract is sorted to match the archive
-t	list a table of contents of an archive
-T F	get names to extract or create from file F
-u X	add X to list of file extensions to be opened in BINARY mode (use '.' to denote 'files with no extension')
-V X	use drive X (X=A..D) in multivolume mode; ignore -f if present
-v	verbosely list what files we process
-x	extract files from an archive

File Compression: gzip

gzip (GNU zip) is a compression utility designed to be a replacement for "compress." Its main advantages over compress are much better compression and freedom from patented algorithms. The GNU Project uses it as the standard compression program for its system. It is distributed here, in addition to the more common DOS compression utilities, **pkzip.exe** and **pkunzip.exe**, to preserve consistency with UNIX systems on which it is widely used and with which you may be communicating. The current version, as of this writing, was 1.2.4 on both UNIX and DOS. For this reason there are only minor differences that result from the differences between operating systems. This material was abstracted from those documents.

Read also *gzip.doc*, and in particular the description of the -N option which is very useful for MSDOS to restore to UNIX the original file names that have been truncated. You can set it by default by adding:

```
set GZIP=-N
```

in your *autoexec.bat* file.

If you get the error message "DMPI: Not enough memory", you are using a memory manager which allocates physical memory immediately instead of allocating on demand when pages are used for the first time. This problem occurs only when using DMPI. (Try under plain DOS without loading any memory manager in *config.sys*.) This problem will be fixed in future versions. As a side note, I have not observed this problem using *qemm386*, v. 7.0 or later. I have not used it with earlier versions of QEMM. Forewarned is forearmed, however. **gzip** is the generic program. By the simple operation of copying **gzip.exe** to **gunzip.exe**, you automatically acquire the decompression program. Alternatively, you can simply use **gzip** with the "-d" option to decompress. Similarly, **gzip** can be renamed to **zcat**. This was done to preserve consistency on UNIX systems with earlier decompression programs and is pointless under DOS.

NAME: gzip, gunzip, zcat - compress or expand files, Version 1.2.4

SYNOPSIS: gzip [-acdfhlLnNrtvV19] [-S suffix] [name ...]
gunzip [-acfhlLnNrtvV] [-S suffix] [name ...]
zcat [-fhLV] [name ...]

```
gzip 1.2.4 (18 Aug 93)
usage: gzip [-acdfhlLnNtvV19] [-S suffix] [file ...]
```

DOS and UNIX Options	Description of Options
-a —ascii	ascii text; convert end-of-lines using local conventions
-c —stdout	write on standard output, keep original files unchanged
-d —decompress	decompress
-f —force	force overwrite of output file and compress links
-h —help	give this help *(continues)*

DOS and UNIX Options	Description of Options
-l —list	list compressed file contents
-L —license	display software license
-n —no-name	do not save or restore the original name and time stamp
-N —name	save or restore the original name and time stamp
-q —quiet	suppress all warnings
-S .suf —suffix .suf	use suffix .suf on compressed files
-t —test	test compressed file integrity
v —verbose	verbose mode
-V —version	display version number
-1 —fast	compress faster
-9 —best	compress better
file...	files to (de)compress. If none given, use standard input.

File Compression: unzip

One compression system that is widely used for the distribution of shareware and other software is based on the compression algorithm in the programs **pkzip.exe** and **pkunzip.exe** from PKWARE, Inc. Some of the software distributed with this book has been placed in zipped archives by the authors. You will need, therefore, a program to decompress and extract the files. A program widely distributed across the Internet, and one that is freely available is **unzip.exe** from Info-Zip. According to the multiple authors of **unzip.exe**, "As far as we are aware ... the UnZip code is now 'clean' in the sense that an UnZip executable may be distributed with a commercial product SO LONG AS IT IS CLEAR THAT UNZIP IS NOT BEING SOLD ..." Because of the licensing restrictions related to the PKWARE products, **unzip.exe** is provided for you to use in unzipping any distributed zipped files. A complete set of instructions for its use may be found in the file *unzip.doc*. Because "third party" unzipping programs may not always follow a commercial product, an investment in the PKWare products is probably appropriate, although shareware versions are available from many bulletin boards and from CompuServe. If you wish to acquire the PKWare products, they may be reached at PKWARE, Inc.; 9025 N. Deerwood Drive; Brown Deer, WI 53223. The current version is Version 2.04g. **unzip.exe** as well as other zip-related files can be found in the Simtel archive: *msdos/zip*.

To use UnZip to extract all members of the archive *waffle.zip*, creating directories as necessary, just type:

```
unzip waf165[.zip]
```

To extract all members of waffle.zip to the current directory:

```
unzip -j waf165
```

It would behoove you to read *unzip.doc* for further information.

To restore the full Waffle file system, copy *waf165.zip* from the distribution disk to your C:\ root directory, copy **unzip.exe** to a directory in your path or to your C:\ root directory, then type:

```
unzip waf165
```

This will create a *c:\waffle* directory and a number of subdirectories to *waffle* which will contain the files and programs for the Waffle system. Then follow the instructions in Chapter 6 for configuring Waffle.

UNIX2DOS AND DOS2UNIX

One of the annoyances of dealing with both DOS and UNIX is that text files have different delimiters at the end of lines in the two operating environments. DOS uses a carriage return and line feed combinations (CRLF), while UNIX uses only a line feed (LF). This means that if you receive a text file from a UNIX system, you may have to add a CR to the existing LF to make sense of the file. You will find two programs that will do this task for you: **dos2unix** and **unix2dos**. These two programs are invoked as follows:

```
dos2unix filename and
unix2dos filename
```

The actual filename is left "as is" by both these programs. If your text file is processed by one or the other or both, however, the "end-of-line" delimiter is changed to correspond with which direction the adjustment is being made. It is not necessary to use these programs on mail files, however. That is done automatically for you.

cat

cat reads each file in the file list and prints it to standard output. If no files are given, or a ‹-› is encountered in the file list, input is taken from standard input. **cat** is similar to the DOS command **type**, but can be used for some other purposes as well. In particular, if you must break down a large **uuencode**d file into several smaller segments (with **split**, see below), there must be some method for reassembly *before* **uudecod**ing it. This operation can also be accomplished with **cat**. If, for example, you have used **split** to subdivide a file called *sample*, the resulting set of files might be called *sampleaa*, *sampleab*, *sampleac*, and *samplead*. **split** adds the "aa" through "ad" tags to the original filename. In order to reassemble this file, simply type:

```
cat samplea* > sample.uue
```

The asterisk, "*", at the end of the input file name simply indicates that it is to take all four files that were generated by **split**. The greater-than symbol, ">", specifies that output is to be redirected from "stdout" (your screen) to a file named *sample.uue*. The output filename is arbitrary and may be anything you choose so long as it is a standard DOS file specification. You could then apply **uudecode** (see above) to *sample.uue* in order to retrieve the original file. The use and syntax of the command is the following:

cat [-nsv] files ...	
-n	With the -n option, cat displays the line numbers of each file before each line. A -b option given with the -n option will cause cat to omit line numbers from blank lines.
-s	With the -s option, cat will suppress the printing of multiple adjacent lines.
-v	With the -v option, cat displays non-printing characters so that they are visible. Control characters are printed preceded by a '^'. The delete character is printed as '^?'. Characters with the high-bit set are printed as 'M-' followed by the character of the lower seven bits. Specifying the -e option with the -v option causes cat to display a '$' at the end of each line. A -t option with the -v option will cause tab characters to be printed as '^I'.

split

This program splits text input into multiple output files, each n lines in length. The default n is 1000 lines. Split creates unique output filenames by concatenating 2 trailing characters to the base output filename (default output filename is "x"). The trailing characters begin at "aa" and are incremented for each output file (i.e. "aa", "ab", "ac", ...). Each character cycles through all lower-case letters, so that the maximum number of output files is $26 * 26 = 676$.

Arguments to split provide user-specified line counts (-n) as well as input and output file names. Note that all arguments are optional. If no input filename is given, or "-" is used for the input filename, standard input is assumed.

split [-n] [infile [outfile]]	
-n	User-defined length for output files in number of lines.

REFERENCES

1. D. A. Nowitz, "UUCP Implementation Description," October 31, 1978. This document, in machine-readable form, still floats around the Usenet/UNIX/Internet community.
2. See Todino and Dougherty, pp. 23-29, and pp. 181–182.

6

The UUCP System Files

The functions of three files are required for any UUCP installation on any platform. Those files are: *SYSTEMS/L.sys, passwd*, and *Permissions (permissn)*. The latest version of UUCP, Taylor UUCP, uses a file named *sys*, which is a combination of *SYSTEMS* and *Permissions*. Over the next two or three years the Taylor UUCP will, most likely, become common on UNIX systems, and it is also likely that the Taylor UUCP will be ported to non-UNIX platforms before long. Taylor UUCP is very flexible in the ways it can be configured, is more efficient in some of its internal workings than older versions, and the UUCP critical literature seems to have been taken into account in its design. This book is not the place for a complete tutorial on Taylor UUCP, although an overview of the *sys* file will be given at the end of this chapter. The *passwd* file is a standard UNIX file used by systems other than UUCP, and it does not change in Taylor UUCP. DOS, and other implementations of UUCP, will likely continue dependence upon the older structures of UUCP for sometime into the future. *At this point in time (1994), in order to structure a UUCP network using multiple platforms with multiple operating systems, it is essential to understand all the commonly-used UUCP System files.*

THE SYSTEMS/L.sys FILE

The function of the *SYSTEMS/L.sys* file is to provide information to the suite of *uucp* programs concerning how and with whom the local system may communicate. When **uucico** is called, it first scans the *SYSTEMS/L.sys* file for the name of the system being called, notes whether the current time is a valid time to call, and checks what device is to be used to make the call. On UNIX systems the *SYSTEMS*/*L.sys* file always resides in a directory called /*usr*/*lib*/*uucp*/. On DOS machines the location is often defined by an environment variable pointing to the location of the configuration files or to a primary configuration file that itself points to *SYSTEMS*/*L.sys*. In UUPlus™, for example, the UUPlus™ environment variable points to *uuplus.cfg* which, in turn, points to *libdir*.

Depending upon the parentage of the UUCP system you are using, this file will be called either *SYSTEMS* or *L.sys*. *L.sys* derives from Version 2 UUCP, which was distributed by AT&T with its UNIX System 7 (Release date: 1977). Version 2 UUCP was, in turn, an upgrade of the original system built in 1976 as a research project at AT&T Bell Laboratories by Mike Lesk. *SYSTEMS* replaced *L.sys* with UNIX System V Release 3 (Release date: 1983). Under the later releases of System V UUCP is referred to as Basic Networking Utilities (BNU), or, as noted above, more popularly as "HoneyDanBer" UUCP after its authors Peter Honeyman, David A. Nowitz, and Brian E. Redman.

UUPlus™ follows the BNU naming convention, as does Waffle, while some UNIX clones, such as Mark Williams Company Coherent 4.0 and earlier retain the *L.sys* nomenclature. With Coherent 4.2, Taylor UUCP became the standard UUCP. Taylor UUCP defines a file called /*usr*/*lib*/*uucp*/*sys*. /*usr*/*lib*/*uucp*/*sys*. It is an enhanced combination of *SYSTEMS*/*L.sys* and *Permissions*. There are other revisions and emendations of the original UUCP, as well, such as those distributed with Berkeley Software Distribution (BSD 4.*x*), DEC's Ultrix, and Sun's SunOS, all of which are tailored versions of UNIX. Apart from the differences in names, *SYSTEMS*/*L.sys* uses a similar (though not always identical) format to define a foreign UUCP to your local UUCP. We will consistently use the term *SYSTEMS*/*L.sys* to refer to this file and indicate where differences may intervene.

Setting Up *SYSTEMS/L.sys*

Setting up *SYSTEMS*/*L.sys* is actually the first step in setting up UUCP. You have already laid out an appropriate file system and defined a *sitename*, *domainname*, and *username*. Some systems, UUPlus™, Coherent 4.0 and Xenix for example, come (or came) with menu-driven programs to assist in setting up *SYSTEMS*/*L.sys* and other required files. The coherent program is called **uuinstall**, while under UUPlus™ it is called **install.exe**. In order to properly set up a UUCP node, it is important that the content and structure of *SYSTEMS*/*L.sys* be properly understood, and that is the objective of this section.

On many UNIX systems, communications parameters are defined in the *L-devices* file. In Taylor UUCP the *deal* and *post* files handle the function. For UUPlus™ and UUPC/Extended running on MS/DOS, the equivalent is a modem definition file with the file name and extension *mdmname*.MDM.

In order to communicate with another UUCP site, it is necessary to define that site by the operations required to contact it. Some basic information is required in order to accomplish this task and to successfully configure *SYSTEMS/L.sys*. The "standard" *SYSTEMS/L.sys* file consists of a single line for each remote system with which you will communicate. If you communicate with only a single foreign system, it requires only a single line. That line is usually subdivided into six fields:

1. The node (system, machine) name of the foreign (remote) system. This may also be the system you define as your Smart Host, a system that can deal with the transmission of mail to sites with which you are not directly connected.
2. A schedule (days of the week, hours of the day) for communicating with the remote system.
3. The device name through which you can connect with the remote system.
4. The line or modem speed at which you will communicate.
5. If the connection is through a dial-access modem, the phone number through which you can dial the remote system.
6. A "script" that specifies the procedure to be used when the remote system answers the call in order for your system to log into the remote system.

The *SYSTEMS/L.sys* File Format

As noted above, each remote system with which your local system may communicate is defined by a single line or *record* consisting of several items or *fields* (or *tokens*). Each field and the usual order of the fields are more completely defined in Table 6.1. In addition to the fields explicitly listed, some systems may have optional fields available. Where optional fields are possible, they are described below. Each line in *SYSTEMS/L.sys* is either a comment or a site-descriptor. When a line begins with a pound sign (#), it is a comment. Any other line is treated as a site descriptor. Fields are separated by one or more white-space characters (or sometimes tabs). Some of the UUCP-related files, most notably *Permissions* (UNIX) or *permits* (Waffle), allow long records to be split by using a back slash as a continuation character at the end of a record segment. That is not true of *SYSTEMS/L.sys*. You should not use the back slash to break up long records. Keep all the fields for the record on a single line.

The Site Name

Each system in a UUCP network must have a name. A more extended treatment of system or site names may be found in the discussion on setting up your local UUCP node. In the context of the *SYSTEMS/L.sys*, the site name refers to some remote system with which you wish to communicate. Among the various versions of UNIX and UUCP some inconsistencies concerning the length of the name have occurred. A common length in many UUCP implementations is seven characters. If a given

TABLE 6.1. Field Definitions in *SYSTEM/L.sys*

Field	Function
site name (system)	The site (or node/system/machine) name of the remote system—the UUCP your local system may contact. A given site name may occur only once in *SYSTEM?L.sys*, although there may be many sites defined. This is a fixed-length postional field, seven characters or less in length, beginning in column one (1) of the record. The site name is obtained from the remote UUCP administrator of the system you intend to call.
schedule	The times when the remote site may be called. This is a function both of local policy and remote policy. If the word *Any* is entered the remote system may be called any time of the day or night, any day of the week. The remote system may be contacted as soon as a UUCP request is generated.
device type	The type of device to be used for the call, such as a modem, a TCP/IP conncection, a local area network (LAN) connection, or a direct serial connection.
speed	For a serial connection either direct with a modem, the speed in bits per second for the device. Some systems allow the specification of a range of speeds (e.g., 2400–9600). although with the variety of "smart modems" now on the market this is less useful than it may have been at one time and, in fact, may be detrimental.
phone	The dialing sequence that will be used by the modem to call the remote system. This modem is dependent, although most dial-access modems today use the Hayes AT dialing conventions. Some systems, such as UUPlus, require the "AT" preceded the telephone number, others simply supply it by default.
protocol	The error-correcting file transfer protocol to be used between systems. The original UUCP specification used what is called the "g" (lowercase g) protocol although others are now in use and most contemporary UUCP implementations automatically detect the protocol. In most recent versions of UUCP running on UNIX machines, the protocol field is not required and is usually omitted.
chat script	A string that describes the conversation between the local and remote machines in order to complete a login procedure.

UUCP node has a seven character limitation, it will truncate longer names to seven characters.

BNU allows a 14 character name; BSD 4.3 allows a 64 character name (in keeping with Internet specifications) which is truncated to 14 characters for UUCP. A few UNIXs allow only six character UUCP site names. Coherent truncates to seven. In order to be universal across all UUCP systems, the first six characters must be unique to a particular node. That way all UUCPs can communicate with one another. The names should also normally be specified as lower case. The site name for one of my systems is, for example,

```
ewcuucp
```

It is pure happenstance, by the way, that this name is exactly seven characters long. The "ewc" portion of the name stands for my company, Enterprise-Wide Computing, Inc.

Schedule

A local UUCP system administrator has considerable latitude for specifying when a remote system may be called. The purpose of this flexibility in scheduling is to design a network node that can be operated in both a cost-effective and a computer resource-effective manner. You can control the time your system will dial out through the *schedule* field. The *schedule* field consists of three subfields with no separating punctuation or spaces:

1. The *day* of the week. This is specified by using one or more of the keywords **Wk, Su, Mo, Tu, We, Th, Fr,** and **Sa**. These keywords must be entered in upper and lower case letters as illustrated. The **Wk** keyword can only be used by itself. If **Wk** is coded, then queued jobs will be sent during any weekday. Two additional global keywords are also valid: **Any** and **Never**. **Any** means the local system can call out on any day. **Never** is used when the local system should only wait for incoming calls and never call out.

2. The *time* of day to contact other systems is controlled by entering a range of times with two 24-hour clock times separated by a hyphen (-). If you wanted to take maximum advantage of night telephone rates, for example, you might want to use times like 0000-0059 (12 midnight to 1:00 a.m.) or 2200-2359 (10:00 p.m. to 11:59 p.m.). The range can also span 0000 (midnight). If your system was normally shut down from 1:00 to 8:00 a.m. you could enter 0800-0059, for example. In effect, you would be saying that anytime except 1:00 to 8:00 a.m. is all right.

   uucico, the program that actually does the communications, operates only within a single 24-hour day. It would interpret 0800-0059 as 0800-2359 *and* 0000-0059. This rather fine distinction does have an impact when using one or more of the day keywords. For example:

```
Tu0800-0059
```

would truncate the 0000-0059 time period because it would be on Wednesday, rather than Tuesday. Similarly:

```
Wk0800-0059
```

means 0800-2359 *and* 0000-0059 Monday through Friday, but not 0000-0059 Saturday morning. If **Any** is combined with a time, then the time reference will apply to every day of the week.

The *time* subfield can be omitted. This means that the local system can call the remote system any time during the day (or **Wk**) specified. *The time, however, cannot be specified without a day*. A direct link, or one over a LAN, might well be configured to operate any time and any day. A dial-access link, however, might be best configured to obtain the best telephone rates. Specifying days and times does not limit when a user can actually queue a UUCP job. It only specifies when the job(s) in the queue will actually be communicated.

Systems patterned after BNU and BSD 4.3 allow some latitude in differentiating days of the week. This is accomplished by separating day/time pairs with a comma. Most implementations of Version 2 do not support multiple day/time pairs. When they do, they do so by substituting a vertical bar (|) for the comma. If we wanted calls to be made on weekdays from 5:00 p.m. to 7:00 p.m. and all day on Saturday and Sunday we might code:

```
Wk1700-1900,SaSu
```

Some later versions of BNU and BSD 4.3 allow the day or time subfield to be followed by a maximum *grade* specification demarcated by a slash. The grade is a single character in the range [0-9][A-Z][a-z]. Grade 0 has the highest priority, grade z the lowest. Grades are not supported on all systems, or they are only partially supported. If this feature has been implemented for your system, something like the following statement will allow, for example, grade C or better messages to be sent during business hours:

```
Any0900-1700/C
```

3. The minimum waiting period (in minutes) following an unsuccessful call to the remote system may optionally be governed by the *retry* field. The local system must wait until the retry period has expired before retrying the call. The default for Version 2 is 55 or 60 minutes. UUCPs based on BNU or BSD 4.3 use an exponential retry. These systems start with a five minute retry period which becomes longer as the number of unsuccessful attempts increases.

The retry period is coded by adding a comma and a time period in minutes following the time/date fields:

```
Any0900-1700,20
```

In this example, if the local system failed to login on the first try, it would have to wait *at least* 20 minutes before trying again. The maximum number of retries defaults to 26. Shorter retry times may be desirable in many cases, although shortening the time may cause you to reach the maximum number of retries before the remote system comes back online. Retries may be scheduled for a variety of reasons, but the most likely symptom is either a busy signal or endless ringing. If **uucico** is already running, merely changing the retry time will not make the currently running **uucico** retry any sooner.

Device (or Dialer) Type

Depending upon what UUCP you are using, the entries for this field may be one of the following:

```
ACU
DIR
comxy (where x=com port number, y=l [el] or r, for Coherent)
/dev/tty00x (where x=UNIX com port number)
TCP
modem-name (used by UUPlus™ for DOS)
```

The mechanisms for handling devices differs somewhat depending on the flavor of UUCP being used. In general, for UNIX systems the connection is handled through the *L-devices* or *Devices* file. This is particularly true for BNU-based systems. Suffice it to say at this point that if your local system follows the conventions of Version 2, **uucico** reads the device type from the *SYSTEMS/L.sys* file then branches to the *L-devices* file to see what to do about the device type. If the device to be accessed is a modem, then there will be an entry in *L-devices* that defines an Automatic Call Unit (ACU).

ACU is probably the most commonly used since it allows access through the public telephone lines via a modem. If your UUCP is based on Version 2 or the BSD 4.x extensions of Version 2, all that needs to be coded is **ACU**. The entries in *L-devices* are, in turn, linked to the way in which your particular system allows you to define communications ports. Because of the differences between DOS and UNIX, DOS-based systems approach this issue differently.

UUPlus™ (and others systems, such as UUPC/Extended) provides for the definition of *.mdm files, each of which defines the characteristics of a particular modem including initialization strings, speed, and other attributes. Thus, the entry HAYES refers to a file named *HAYES.MDM*.

DIRECT, or **DIR,** for direct connection, is used if there is a dedicated line between the local and remote systems. This is available only for the BSD 4.x extensions and for various DOS systems. In BSD 4.x **DIRECT** is an additional entry in *L-devices*. For UUPlus™ the reference is to a "modem" file called *DIRECT.MDM*. *DIRECT.MDM* defines the appropriate communications port on the DOS. Other Version 2-based UUCPs require the specification of the device name. The usual UNIX reference to a communications port is by reference to a special file in the */dev* directory that defines a communications port and takes the form *tty008* (or whatever the number of the port may be). The equivalent reference in Coherent is to *com3l* (or some other port number). The developers of Coherent simply used the DOS conventions to name the ports rather than the *tty* references more common with UNIX. The *l* makes note that the com port is defined for local (non-modem) activity.

Under BSD 4.3, the keyword **TCP** provides for Ethernet connections using TCP/IP protocols. If you have access to this keyword then a services name (usually "uucp") is entered in the *speed* field, and the remote system name is repeated in the phone number field. BSD 4.3 supports several other keywords that are not of great importance to this discussion, including **Micom** (a Micom terminal switch),

PAD (an X.25 PAD connection), **PCP** (PC Pursuit), and **Sytek** (Sytek dedicated high-speed modem port). One or more of these is obsolete. In BNU the device type field is used more consistently; it always acts as a pointer to an entry in *Devices*. Any keyword can be used, but it must have a corresponding definition in *Devices*.

Speed

A byte, or character of information, is eight bits in length. The standard ASCII character set uses only seven of those bits. In a data communications environment the eighth bit may be use for parity checking (a *very* basic kind of error checking), or it may be used to provide an additional 128 characters beyond the 127 defined by ASCII. Data transmission speed is measured in the number of *bits-per-second (b/s)* passed across the line. Sometimes you will hear the word *baud* used as a synonym for *b/s*, although it is technically inaccurate to do so. Baud is the same as "bits per second" only if each signal event represents exactly one bit, and this does not happen at higher speeds.

Speed is actually encoded as a *b/s* number only when a serial connection, using either a modem or direct connection, is being used. Under other circumstances there will be other coding for this field, as has been already noted. Assuming a dial-access telephone connection, however, you would normally encode this field with a number like 2400 (for 2400 *b/s*) or 9600 (for 9600 *b/s*):

```
2400
```

File Transfer Protocol Selection

UUCP was designed to provide error-free file transmissions from one system to another. There is sometimes a confusion between the "UUCP protocol" and the file transfer protocols used by UUCP. According to Ian Taylor, the UUCP protocol is a conversation between two UUCP packages. A UUCP conversation consists of three parts: an initial handshake, a series of file transfer requests, and a final handshake."[1] Between the initial handshake and the final handshake, if a file is to be transferred, a file transfer protocol is used. A file transfer protocol is a communications methodology for transmiting files without loss of data. The early versions of UUCP were provided with the *g* protocol which uses small, 64-byte packets that are checksummed and immediately retransmitted when errors are detected. This approach was optimized for noisy telephone lines. When a link is reliable and quiet, as with LANs and X.25 packet networks, or when you are using newer error correcting modems, the 64-byte packet imposes substantial overhead and reduces throughput. As a result, several newer protocols have been added. A contemporary implementation of UUCP will always include the *g* protocol, the original 8-bit packet protocol by Greg ("g") Chesson, and, in addition, may include some or all of the following: *f, t, e, G, i, x, d, h,* and *v.* These protocols may be defined as follows:

> *f*   An entire file (*f*) is transferred, encoded using only seven-bit char-acters with a single file checksum. It was originally intended for X.25 links (added with BSD).

t   Intended for network transfer using TCP/IP (*t*) or other reliable connections using port 540 (added with BSD versions).

e   This protocol assumes error-free (*e*) channels that are message-oriented (added with HoneyDanBer).

G   The *g* protocol, except that it guarantees support for all possible window and packet sizes (added with SVR4 UUCP).

i   The "i" protocol was written by Ian Taylor and was introduced in Taylor UUCP version 1.04. It is a sliding window packet protocol, like the "g" protocol, but it supports bidirectional transfers (i.e., file transfers in both directions simultaneously). It requires an eight-bit clear connection.[2]

x   Intended for use on X.25 (*x*) or TCP/IP that guarantees delivery (SVR2).

d   Used for DataKit (*d*) muxhost (not RS-232) connections. Operates in a somewhat obscure and proprietary manner.

h   Used with HST modems, does no error-checking, and is similar to the "t" protocol.

v   According to Taylor, the "*v*" protocol is used by UUPC/Extended. It is simply a version of the "g" protocol which supports packets of any size, and it also supports sending packets of different sizes during the same conversation. There are many "g" protocol implementations which support both, but there are also many which do not. Using "v" ensures that everything is supported."[3]

Information on these other protocols is sketchy at best and can often be deduced only from the source code that implements them.[4]

As we have already noted, the *g* protocol can produce significant performance degradation under some circumstances. This problem relates to the original 64-byte packet size. The result has been ongoing criticism of the performance of UUCP. When complaints are lodged about the performance of UUCP using the standard *g* protocol, the problem really lies with the software coding rather than the protocol design. Many UUCP implementations limit the datasegment size to 64 bytes and a sliding window of three packets (so as not to overrun statically allocated buffers). This limit may have been adequate for slower modems, but the current high-speed modems waiting for acknowledgements can benefit from much larger

---

Some UUCPs support all these protocols, others only support *g* and possibly *G*. Every UUCP supports *g*. If all this sounds complicated, do not fear. During the period when a local UUCP is attempting to establish communications with a remote UUCP, the two will compare notes and arrive at a protocol both can use. Because of this feature, most modern UUCP variants do not require that the protocol field be coded. When users are required to code the field, they should use whatever the remote UUCP administrator recommends, whatever their documentation suggests, or they should simply use *g* (or possibly *G*).

packet sizes and a larger sliding window. As Taylor noted, "protocol efficiency using seven sliding windows and large (1K to 4K) data segments should work well even over packet-switching phone lines."

At this point we have coded a line in our *SYSTEMS / L.sys* file that might look something like this for a UNIX system:

```
ewcuucp Any ACU 2400 ...
```

or for a DOS system using UUPlus, it might look like this:

```
ewcuucp Any HAYES 2400 ...
```

Multiple protocols can be specified for some systems, such as "*eg*", which means that the remote system should try the "*e*" protocol first, and if that doesn't work, try the "*g*" protocol. In BNU the protocol is specified as a subfield of the *device* field, separated from *device* by a comma.

Telephone Number

A telephone number is a telephone number, right? Wrong! Today we learn to do telephone dialing almost instinctively without much analysis of our "dialing behavior." Computers, on the other hand, must be told explicitly, step-by-step, what their dialing behavior should be. When UUCP was originally devised, there were no standards, either actual or *de facto*, for regulating a computer's dialing behavior. In fact, every manufacturer of modems dictated different dialing behavior. The popularity of the Hayes modems, and the command structure they devised, has become so ubiquitous that virtually all manufacturers are now "Hayes compatible." What "Hayes compatibility" means is the use of the Hayes "AT" command set.

Part of that command set (and other aspects of the command set which are discussed in Appendix K), are commands that deal with answering and dialing another computer. At this point we are concerned only with dialing out, not answering the phone. You may have to encode a very long phone number which requires pauses or waits for new dialtones. If your data phone line passes through an EPBX, you may have to first dial a "9", for example. An EPBX is an Electronic Private Branch eXchange (also called a PBX or PABX). An EPBX is a switching network for voice or data. The "9" gives you access to the outside world, but there will need to be a pause or a wait for a second dial tone. If the call is a long-distance number, the long-distance access code (a "1" in the United States) must be dialed. If the call is international, a two- or three-digit series must be called to access the international telephone system ("011" for Great Britain, for example). If you happen to be traveling and your UUCP is installed on your laptop, and you want to use a credit card from a hotel room, you may need to dial a long-distance carrier's access number, wait for yet another dial tone, then enter your credit card number, wait for another dial tone, then dial the telephone number with an area code as well as the basic seven digit (in the United States) telephone number. It may also be necessary to send codes such as "*70" to turn off features of the phone system such as "call waiting."

The *pause* and *wait* commands are the most important in encoding the telephone number. In general, although there are some implementation dependent inconsistencies, UUCP uses the "=" (equal) sign for *wait* (for a secondary dial tone), while "-" (hyphen) generates a one-second *pause*. Early in the development of this technology, these two characters were simply mapped to whatever the local modem supported. Because the hyphen ("-") is also used to make phone numbers more readable, they should not be encoded in the phone number itself except to produce a pause. The equivalent Hayes commands are the "," (comma) for *pause* and a "W" for *wait*. Today the most common method of encoding the telephone number is to use the Hayes commands directly, since **uucico** will simply pass these on to the modem. Avoid using the hyphen ("-"). Thus, the coding for a telephone number might be as simple as,

```
5551212
```

or it might be more complicated:

```
9W1,8005551212
```

In the more complicated example just given, a comma (",") might be substituted for the "W" if your EPBX responds rapidly. Similarly, the comma following the "1" might be omitted entirely or might be changed to an at sign ("@"), which means "wait for silence." All of this depends on the characteristics of your local phone system and how complicated your dialing procedure must be. These examples are also specific to the United States and may differ in other countries. Dialing from a hotel room can frequently present serious challenges. Some hotel EPBXs use "8" to access long distance under any circumstance, others use the more common "9" for an outside line if you are calling an "800" number. A possible number might be the following, however:

```
┌Hotel long distance access code
│┌Wait
││┌long distance access code       ┌Wait for dialtone
│││┌long distance carrier          │┌long distance access code
││││           ┌Wait               ││┌pause 1 second
││││           │┌Credit Card #      │││┌long distance number
││││           ││                   ││││
8W18009999999W12345678901111W1,08005551212
```

This is to be taken only as an illustration that has not been tested. In principle, however, it should work, and it is illustrative of the issues involved in encoding a phone number.

Conventions vary from one UUCP to another on how the telephone number field is handled for a direct connection. In Version 2 the device name is repeated; in

BNU just a hyphen ("-") is placed in the field; for Coherent two double quotes ("")
replace the number; and in UUPlus at least a return should be sent using \r. Up
to this point, then, a cumulative record in *SYSTEMS/L.sys* might look like this:

```
ewcuucp Any ACU 2400 ATDT19085551212 ...(for UUPlus).
```

For UUPlus it is necessary to code the Hayes commands, "ATDT", in upper case
letters, along with the telephone number.

Chat Script

The primary, though not the only, use of *chat scripts* is in *SYSTEMS/L.sys*.
The remainder of a *SYSTEMS/L.sys* record consists of such a script. The *chat
script* defines the login conversation which occurs between local and remote
systems. It does this by telling UUCP what prompts to expect from the site called,
and how to respond to each prompt. Each prompt-response pair is called an
expect-send string. The two components of *expect-send* pairs are separated by
spaces, with optional *subexpect-subsend* pairs separated by hyphens. Structuring
appropriate *chat scripts* can be one of the more difficult tasks in setting up a
UUCP system.

When a remote system answers the telephone call from your local system the
first prompt cannot always be expected to appear instantly. Your local system
needs to wait for a few seconds. The first *expect-send* string should, therefore,
expect nothing, then wait a few seconds and send out one or more carriage returns
(DOS) or line feeds (UNIX) to ensure that the remote system returns a **login**
prompt. In order to generate this behavior the following *expect-send* string should
be the first one in the series:

```
"" \r\d\r
```

The pair of quotation marks ("") tell UUCP to expect nothing. The **\r** sends a carriage
return character, and **\d** provides a one second delay. The letters preceded by
backslashes are called *chat script escape sequences*. The full set of *escape sequences*
may be seen in Table 6.2. Under ordinary circumstances it will not be necessary
to use many more *escape sequences* than those illustrated above; but for more
complicated situations, they are available. The *SYSTEMS/L.sys* record we are
working on should now look something like this:

```
ewcuucp Any ACU 2400 19085551212 "" \r\d\r ... (for UUCP), or
ewcuucp Any HAYES24 2400 ATDT19085551212 "" <CR> ... (for UUPlus).
```

Note that in the example from UUPlus the token "<CR>" is used as a more intuitive
and less obscure form of "/r" to symbolize the carriage return character. It also
automatically sends a return once each second, for a total of ten tries, or until a
response is acquired from the remote system.

TABLE 6.2. Chat Script Escape Sequences.

Escape Sequence	Description
""	Expect a null string.
EOT	Send an end-of-transmission character.
BREAK	Cause a BREAK. This may be simulated using line speed changes and null characters and may not work on all systems.
\b	Send a backspace character. On BSD 4.2, send a break.
\c	Suppress new line at the end of the *send* string.
\d	Delay for one (1) second.
\D	Taylor, telephone #.
\K	Insert a BREAK (BNU, Taylor).
\m	Taylor, requires carrier.
\M	Taylor, no carrier.
\n	Send a newline or linefeed character.
\N	Send a null character (BNU). Use \000 (slash zeros) to send a null in other implementations.
\p	Pause for a fraction of a second (BNU).
\r	Send a carriage return.
\s	Send a space character.
\t	Send a tab character.
	Send a backslash (\) character.
\\	Send the octal code (*ddd*) for a single ASCII
ddd	character.
Note:	Specific implementations may extend this set of escape sequences extensively. Consult local documentation. Taylor UUCP, for example, has several additional escape sequences.

At this time, the remote system should be sending a **login** message. It might include a banner but at the very least it will have the word "login:". An example with a banner might be something like the following:

```
ewcuucp
Enterprise-Wide Computing, Inc.
login:
```

It might be something as simple as:

```
Coherent 386 login:
```

Or, it might be more complex, as in the following illustration from Waffle:

```
50 Last caller: tmadron (tmadron)
UUCP (ewcuucp)
Test UUCP & Mail site,
Enterprise-Wide Computing, Inc.
Waffle version 1.65, out of the box.
<New> or login:
```

The Waffle illustration, by the way, is not quite "out of the box" since—the distributed login line reads "login or ‹New›:" rather than "‹New› or login:". That line may be changed any way the system operator (sysop) wishes; I changed it to better conform to the UNIX norm. Whatever comes back, however, there is obviously some verbiage that needs to be ignored. In fact, some UNIX sites may have changed the word "login:" to "Login:" so we should not test or expect the entire word: only the last few characters and the colon.

The send part of the pair might be something like **nuucp** (the login name). A simple *expect-send* pair could be:

```
ogin: nuucp
```

Unfortunately, this gives **uucico** only one chance to login before it fails. If we add two hyphens and another statement of "ogin:", then at least it has at least a second chance:

```
ogin:--ogin: nuucp
```

What this script communicates is the expectation of "ogin:". If that doesn't come through, then nothing except a carriage return is sent since that is the effect of a null *subexpect-subsend* string ("--"). It then looks again for "ogin:". Similarly, we must now wait for "Password:", then send one:

```
word:--word: public
```

where the word "public" is the password. A normal *expect-send* string only sends if the expect string *is* received. The *subexpect-subsend* string sends only if the preceding subexpect string *is not* received. The entire minimal chat script now looks like this:

```
"" /r/d/r ogin:--ogin: nuucp word:--word: public (for uucp), or
"" <CR> ogin:--ogin: nuucp word:--word: public (for uuplus).
```

A given installation may require other information, but this is an example of a standard UUCP login sequence. In order to login into this system, the only thing the remote UUCP administrator needs to do is add your installation to his or her own *SYSTEMS/L.sys* file, and give you an entry in the remote's *Permissions* file. The remote system might be set up to require additional information, thus requiring you to expand the chat script. You may also have to use one or more of the *escape sequences* which have already been described in the event that there are any peculiarities specific to the remote system you are attempting to contact.

Note one important item: The site record, such as the one we have just constructed, may not continue beyond a single line. The entire site record consists of everything from the remote system/site name to the last password. In some systems there may also be a limitation on the length of the record (for Coherent it is 511 bytes/characters), and a limitation on the number of *expect-send* pairs (again, for Coherent, it is 27). If you have followed these instructions carefully, you will be able to build successful chat scripts. Your *SYSTEMS/L.sys* file must contain one line/record for each remote system that you will allow to login. In addition, you have the option of defining "anonymous logins," something that will be discussed elsewhere.

You also need to be aware that other UUCP systems may vary considerably from the "standard" procedure illustrated above. Waffle, for example, links the site record in its *Systems* file to a *scripts* file that has named records corresponding to a specific field in the *Systems* site record. The named field in *scripts* contains the expect/send dialogue rather than encoding it directly in *Systems*. In the following example the token "toewc" is the name of the record in the *scripts* file that contains the expect/send script.

```
ewcuucp Any g HAYES toewc 18005551212 nuucp public
```

The *scripts* file record that contains the "toewc" script is:

```
toewc   ogin:--ogin: \L word:--word: \P
```

where "\L" and "\P" stand in for login name and password, respectively, taken from the login name ("nuucp") and password ("public") tokens in the *Systems* file.

With Taylor UUCP the expect/send dialogue is encoded in the *sys* file using the **chat** command. The other information needed for a successful login is contained in other statements in the *sys* file. An illustrative chat script is the following:

```
chat "" \r in:-\n-in: nuucp word: public
```

This example also illustrates the use of another escape sequence, \n, which sends a linefeed character, that UNIX systems may prefer to the carriage control character (\r).

For WinNET™, there is not a *SYSTEMS/L.sys* file at all. The information that would normally be encoded in *SYSTEMS/L.sys* is saved as a byproduct of setting up the system. It does have a small file that can handle the chat script, however, called *chat.rc*. A typical *chat.rc* file is the following:

```
INITIATE
\,\n

ogin:
nuucp\n

word:
uucpudwm\n
```

The first two lines are simply the "wake up" process similar in character to the beginning "expect nothing, send a return" in earlier examples. The other line pairs have the same meaning as the expect/send pairs discussed earlier. Only the format is different in that each pair is on a separate line rather than on a single line. The "\n" sends a line feed character. Any expect/send script required can be set up with *chat.rc*.

THE *PASSWD* FILE

A file central to the security of UNIX systems is */etc/passwd*. As the name implies, it contains password information for every user which can log on to a particular system. It contains the login passwords. It also contains other information which the system needs to know about each user. UUCP makes use of */etc/passwd* as do other components of the UNIX operating system. When UUCP is implemented on operating environments other than UNIX, a *passwd* file may also be implemented to maintain the security of the system and to provide UUCP with the information it needs about each user. Remember, too, that a "user" can be either a human being or computer process which possesses the right to log into a particular computer system.

/etc/passwd can be read by anyone. If access to it were refused to a user, he or she could not log on. Thus, the passwords encrypted within it can be read and copied by anyone, and so may be vulnerable to brute-force decryption. For this reason, close attention should be paid to passwords: they should not be common words or names; preferably they should mix cases or use unique spellings, and be at least six characters long. When *passwd* is implemented on non-UNIX systems there is even greater vulnerability since the passwords may not be encrypted at all. The DOS/Windows versions of UUCP often handle the password issue differently, depending on their designs. DOSGATE and UUPC/Extended, for example, both use a "standard" *passwd* file. Neither UUPlus™ nor WinNET™ maintain a password file at all since they are designed as leaf systems that always poll other systems rather than being polled themselves (there is no login to either system). Waffle maintains a password system that has more in common with other Bullten Boards than with UUCP. These variations are , of course, a result of differing design considerations regarding security.

When you give a remote system the ability to copy files and execute commands on your system some security mechanism is required. This is the fundamental purpose of *passwd*. An incoming call to your system (usually called a "Slave," while the calling system is termed a "Master," although during the process these roles may be reversed) from a remote **uucico** must login to your system just like any other user. By assigning a password to such a system you can keep unauthorized users from logging on. Alternatively, the system can be set up to allow even "anonymous" UUCP logins. Through the process of using a local copy of **uucico** as a shell (see the subsection shell, below), the only work that can be done on your system is that which you have allowed.

Setting Up *passwd*

On UNIX systems the *passwd* file is set up independently of UUCP since the file is used for general UNIX security functions. The usual method for editing the file is with a text editor, such as **vi**. If you are using a private UNIX workstation (or Coherent) then you are probably the "system manager." For a corporate UNIX system you will not have permission to alter */etc/passwd* even though you can read it. In that instance you will have to work through your corporate system manager.

The *passwd* File Format

Each line or "record" in the *passwd* file consists of seven fields, delimited by colons (":"), and has the general format:

```
id:password:UID:GID:user info:home:shell
```

The meaning of some of these fields may vary for different operating environments and UUCP implementations on platforms other than UNIX, but all UNIX variants share this particular format. The function of each field may be found in Table 6.3.
  One example of a *passwd* file, taken from my own Coherent system, is very similar to a typical UNIX *passwd* file. Because that system is a very private development system I have omitted some passwords in this example which in any reasonable production environment would be tantamount to committing a major sin. The /etc/passwd file was simply listed with the utility **cat**. The "$" sign is one relatively standard UNIX prompt. The information in **bold-faced** characters is to

TABLE 6.3. Field Definitions for the *passwd* File.

Field	Function
id	The user's login name—the name given to the "login" prompt. For a normal terminal session this is the login name assigned to a human user. For a call from **uucico**, with a **uucp** file transfer, it also may be any assigned name but is conventionally some variation on "uucp," such as "nuucp." In other words, for a UUCP session, the incoming "user" is another UUCP system.
password	*password* is the user's encrypted password. The password is optional and may be omitted. If, for example, the system allows "anonymous" UUCP activity, *password* will not be used. If the field is an asterisk (*), this *id* cannot be used to log in. This feature is required because the *passwd* file is used for purposes other than providing password information. Consequently, if a "user" is defined for some other reason than password verification, we do not want security compromised by the possibility of someone logging into the system using such an *id*.
UID	For UNIX systems, user_id is a unique number that is also used to identify the user.
GID	Group_id identifies the group to which the user belongs, if any, for UNIX.
user info	*user info* holds miscellaneous data, such as names, telephone numbers, or office numbers for UNIX.
home	*home* gives the user's home directory, such as /usr/tmadron on UNIX systems.
shell	Finally, *shell* gives the program that is first executed when the user logs on. For human users this is, in most instances, an interactive shell (default, **/bin/sh**). For UUCP the shell is normally **uucico**. For particular UUCP variations, this may be able to be used for other purposes, as well.

be typed in by the user. If you have access to a UNIX system you can issue the same command:

```
$ cat /etc/passwd
root::0:0:Superuser:/:
remacc::::Remote access::
daemon:No login:1:1:Spooler:/usr/spool:
sys:No login:2:2:System information::
bin::3:3:System administrator:/usr/src:
xmail::4:4:Secret Mail:/usr/spool/pubkey:
uucp::6:6:Coherent-Coherent
copy:/usr/spool/uucp:/usr/lib/uucp/uucico
msgs:No login:7:7:System messages:/usr/msgs:
tmadron:nkQknkkvWwtee:8:5:Thomas Wm. Madron:/usr/tmadron:/bin/sh
bmadron:kxzzKiQWEj6an:9:5:Beverly B. Madron:/usr/bmadron:/bin/sh
sbbs::1000:1000:SBBS user:/u/sbbs:/u/sbbs/programs/initial
$
```

When anyone or anything first makes contact with a UNIX system, a "login" sequence is initiated by the operating system. At the very least, the login sequence consists of the following items, and may, on a particular system, include others:

1. Asks for the login name (*id*).
2. Asks for a password (*password*).
3. May print the "Message of the Day" to the user's screen.
4. Notifies the user if new mail is waiting to be read.
5. Sets the working directory to the user's home directory (*home*).
6. Sets the user id (*UID*) and the group id (*GID*).
7. If a program (*shell*) is specified, **login** first reads */etc/profile* and inserts any system-wide environmental variables, then executes the *shell* program. By default, **login** will execute some shell program dictated by the particular UNIX installation, such as the Bourne shell, **sh**, the Korn shell, **ksh**, or the C-shell, **csh**. If this happens, **login** then executes the content of the *$HOME/.profile* if it exists, which sets user-specific environmental variables, such as the terminal type you may be using. For UUCP the "shell" should be **uucico**.

From this login sequence, it is easy to see how heavily dependent the procedure is on the *passwd* file.

The Login Name (id)

The login (or user) name is a meaningful "natural language" designator for a given user. This parameter may be a user's initials, a nickname, or a construct dictated by the local installation. It must be unique to a system, however. Consequently, for real systems of any size, there are usually some standards about choosing a login name. There are also some standard login names for processes or users that require them. root, for example, is the login name that the systems manager must use to make some changes in the UNIX environment. uucp or nuucp are often used as general login names for other UUCP systems that may require them.

A new user is always added by someone designated with that responsibility. This is true for UNIX, and it is true for non-UNIX UUCP systems. For UNIX there may be a specific command, such as **/etc/newusr** (this is actually the Coherent command), that lets the system administrator assign a new entry in *passwd*. The system manager may also assign the new user a password using the **passwd** command. A user may change his or her password at any time by also using the **passwd** command. The **/etc/newusr** command in Coherent is very helpful because it automatically adds an entry to the file */etc/passwd*, creates a home directory for the user, installs the user in the mail system, and performs other tasks necessary to add new users. If your system does not have a **newusr** command, or something equivalent, this process must take place by hand.[5]

The login name for UUCP purposes will often include *uucp* or *uucpadm* for administrative logins; any login name for working logins, although *nuucp* is probably the most common; or a specific system name such as *ewcuucp*. At this point the entry in *passwd* for a new UUCP users should probably be one of the following:

nuucp:

or

youruucp:

Please note the *required* colon, which separates the login name from the next (password) field.

If you are setting up a system that will be available to a large number of remote UUCP systems, a **mail** server, for example, it might be better to use the generic nuucp name rather than assigning each incoming UUCP a login name. If, however, the system requires more security, a unique login name along with a unique password for each remote system should be given to each user. The issue of security presents no easy answers. Maximum security requires a separate login name and password. Moreover, the use of separate login names makes it easier to trace problems, and it makes it possible to eliminate an incoming site without affecting other users. On the other hand, such an approach is much more difficult to administer than one that requires a generic user name and password. Within a single organization it is often possible to make use of a more generic approach.

The password Field

The *password* field is initially left blank, at least on UNIX systems, since it must be set by running the command **passwd**. It may be left blank, in which case an incoming UUCP call does not need to know a password. This, of course, has the potential for setting up a security problem. When the **passwd** command is used, an encrypted password will be placed in this field. From the standpoint of an external threat this is not a major problem, since an ordinary terminal user cannot use the UUCP login names for normal interactive access. Moreover, through the *Permissions* file the *passwd* file should not be available for downloading and examination.

In general, it is not appropriate to eliminate passwords even if a single user name is used for all remote UUCP sites. Even though a potentially large number of people would have to be given the password, it is still minimally more secure than allowing anyone to get in. Consequently in building a record in the *passwd* file, once you have constructed the base record without the password, and then run **passwd**, your record is now complete to this point:

nuucp:*password*:

or

youruucp:*password*:

where *password* is either an encrypted UNIX password or a readable password in some DOS systems.

UID and GID

The user id number (*UID*) and the group id number (*GID*) are additional means that UNIX has for keeping track of users and their security. It is actually the *UID*, not the login name, that UNIX uses to distinguish among users. It is important, therefore, to assign unique *UID*s to each user. When users all have unique *UID*s and *GID*s they cannot, in general, have access to one another's files. Hence security is at its highest. In some instances, however, within a work group, it may be desirable to have some mutually accessible files. This is the reason for the group id. If two or more users are assigned the same *GID*, they will have mutual access to their files. The worst-case scenario is one in which multiple users are assigned the same *UID*, since then there is little or no security on what happens to their mutual files. Occasionally, however, it is appropriate for some users (*uucp* and *uucpadm*) to share a *UID* so that ownership of files will stay with a particular *UID*. The user listed first in *passwd* is the one that most software understands as the owner of a file, so if you wish to have the "owner" of a file be "uucp," for example, user "uucp" should come before "uucpadm" in *passwd*.

By convention the *UID*s from 0 to 99 are reserved for system ids (root, bin, uucp, etc.). If no groups are developed, the group id should be the same as the user id. If the user ids are all different in a multiuser group, but all members have the same *GID*, the members will be able to access one another's files, but ownership will be unique. If multiple login names are required on the same system, it is appropriate to assign each of the login names the same *UID* and *GID*. This allows authorized users access to any shared files, regardless of what login name is used. Our growing *passwd* record should now look like this:

```
nuucp:password:6:6:
```

or

```
youruucp:password:6:6:
```

User Info[rmation]

The *user info* field is just what the name implies: miscellaneous information about the user in question. On UNIX systems, it is used for information about the user, such as name, phone number, office numbers, or other information that a system manager might need about users from time to time.

This field is mostly informational in character. For specialized "users," with some sort of specialized *shell* (see below), the field might be put to use for other purposes. Since any program can read the *permissn* file, such a program can also parse the file's records and extract information from the various fields. It would even be possible to subdivide this field into subfields containing additional information. For this example, however, we will put in a name only:

```
nuucp:password:6:6:EWC, Inc.:
```

or

```
youruucp:password:6:6:Tom Madron:
```

Home Directory

The user's *home* directory is placed in this field. On UNIX this directory is assigned when an individual is allowed to use the system and is given a login name. The home directory is typically a directory subsidiary to */usr*, such as */usr/tmadron*, where "tmadron" is my login name. It is important to remember that we are dealing with two different kinds of "users" in the *passwd* file. The first is individual humans. If UUCP is to be used as an internal mail system over a LAN, as well as one operating over a wide area network (WAN) based on the telephone system or on X.25 networks, then a *passwd* entry is required for each machine, or for each LAN. In this case the password helps UUCP to find the places to deliver mail. The second class of "users" is other UUCP systems that may need to login in order to deliver or pick up mail. For foreign UUCPs, the appropriate directory entry for UNIX is */usr/spool/uucppublic* for working logins or */usr/lib/uucp* for administrative logins. Thus, the resulting *passwd* record might, at this point, look like the following:

```
nuucp:password:6:6:EWC, Inc.:/usr/lib/uucp:
```

or

```
youruucp:password:6:6:Tom Madron:/usr/lib/uucp:
```

Shell

Under UNIX *shell* gives the program that is first executed when a user logs on. In most instances this is an interactive shell such as **sh** (Bourne Shell), **ksh** (Korn Shell), or **csh** (C-shell). On DOS machines a similar purpose is served by **command.com**, which is the DOS interactive shell. Similarly, when a foreign UUCP system logs on, it, too, needs a shell. In this case, however, it is not an interactive shell, but something that will give access to UUCP. That shell us usually **uucico** for working logins while an administrative login will require */bin/sh* (or other interactive shell). Assuming that the shell we will use is **uucico**, our sample *passwd* entries end up looking like this:

```
nuucp:password:6:6:EWC,   [continued ...]
     Inc.:/usr/lib/uucp:/usr/lib/uucp/uucico
```

or

```
youruucp:password:6:6:Tom   [continued ...]
     Madron:/usr/lib/uucp:/usr/lib/uucp/uucico
```

UNIX is equipped with other access and security considerations which should be observed. This is not the book for general UNIX security, however. The book by Wood and Kochan has already been cited. Chapter 5 of O'Reilly and Todino is also very useful.[6] Because DOS, Windows, OS/2, and MAC/OS were conceived as single-user operating environments (although several are multi-tasking), security arrangements are minimal or non-existent in this context.

THE *PERMISSIONS (PERMITS, PERMISSN) FILE*

The use of the Permissions file (called *permits* in Waffle) is a security feature of UUCP. It is used to control interactions with remote machines regarding file access, remotely requested command execution, and login permissions. It is not universally implemented in DOS versions of UUCP although the functions (or at least some of them) implied by *Permissions* are present. Having a *Permissions* file allows greater flexibility in dealing with multiple remote hosts. This file is used to modify defaults system-by-system or for a group of remote systems. The *Permissions* file has entries associated with either or both of two main entries:

- LOGNAME entries allow you to define specific permissions for login ids used when *remote systems call you*.
- MACHINE entries allow you to specify permissions for particular systems, or groups of systems, on your machine, *when you call them*.

The function of the *Permissions* file is to protect *your* machine and system. These two classes of entries can be somewhat confusing when structuring a *Permissions* file. This has led to the comment that "It is unclear why this somewhat confusing approach was taken, instead of one in which it is simply possible to state the permissions for a remote machine name, regardless of who initiates the call."[7] With the advent of the *sys* file (see below) in the Taylor UUCP, this problem has been remedied somewhat along these lines and has, in addition, combined elements of the *Systems* and *Permissions* files.

If you wish to have complete control over access to your machine by remote systems, you must write a separate MACHINE/LOGNAME entry for each remote system that can access your system. When your system is to be used as a mail server, it may be appropriate, depending on your security needs, to define what amounts to a group entry, but this could create serious security holes in your system. On UNIX machines it is generally possible to list multiple entries for the MACHINE= and LOGNAME= parameters. In the comments that follow we will describe a more-or-less "standard" UNIX UUCP *Permissions* file. If you digest this information, setting up the *permits* file for Waffle will make sense, even when the *permits* file differs from the more common UNIX implementation. This is also the case when dealing with the Taylor UUCP *sys* file.

Setting up the *Permissions* File

A record in a *Permissions* file consists of one or more fields, each with the syntax <Option>=<Value>. The option is normally typed in upper case letters. A list of the available options may seen in Table 6.4. As noted above, the *Permissions* file has two main entries, LOGNAME and MACHINE, and a series of additional entries associated with one or the other or both of the two main entries. The entries or fields are separated by a space and a backslash ("\") may be used as a continuation character so that the record may be entered on more than one line. An example of a *Permissions* file with a single entry is the following:

```
#    Sample Permissions File
#

LOGNAME=dpma MACHINE=ewc REQUEST=no \
    SENDFILES=yes \
    READ=/usr/spool/uucppublic:/tmp \
    WRITE=/usr/spool/uucppublic:/tmp \
    NOREAD= \
    NOWRITE= \
    CALLBACK=no \
    COMMANDS=rmail:rnews:uucp \
    VALIDATE=ewc \
    MYNAME=
```

Blank lines are ignored, and lines starting with a pound sign ("#") are comments. Any ASCII text editor can be used to set up the file. Beware of the fact that the Waffle *permits* file, while similar, is far from identical to this UNIX (actually,

TABLE 6.4. Summary of *Permissions Fields*.

Field	Function
LOGNAME	Specifies the login ids that can be used by remote sites to log into the local (your) system. The *LOGNAME* may be specific to a particular remote site, the same for all remote sites, or a small set of common *LOGNAME*s that specify different classes of permissions to which remote sites are assigned. The *SENDGILES, CALLBACK*, and *VALIDATE* fields refine the permission granted to *LOGNAME*. Some other fields are shared with *MACHINE* permissions.
SENDFILES	Accepts a "yes" or "no" value to determine whether files queued for a remote system will be sent if that system calls. The default is SENDFILES=no. This ensures that files are sent *only* when your system calls out, not when some other system calls you. This field has no meaning if *LOGNAME* is not defined.
CALLBACK	Accepts a "yes" or "no" (the default) value. If the value is "yes," a system that calls you will be terminated and your system will call back to the remote system to establish a legitimate link.
VALIDATE	Ties machine name to a login name. It is used to verify the calling system's identity. The value is a remote system name to which you have assigned a specific name.
MACHINE	Machines that the local system can call with specified conditions in effect. The value of this field *must* match a corresponding entry in the *passwd* file. This field relates to what you, or your users, can do when calling another system. The *COMMANDS* and *MYNAME* fields modify *only* the *MACHINE* field entry.
COMMANDS	Specifies a list of commands that the remote machine may execute on your system. The typical default commands are **rmail** and **rnews**. The keyword "ALL" allows a remote site to execute any and all commands available on your system. This keyword should be used very cautiously.
MYNAME	Used to link another system (machine) name to the local system. This may be useful for debugging purposes or to sort out duplicate machine names. This is normally not used.
REQUESTS	This and the remaining fields, may modify either *LOGNAME* or *MACHINE* name entries. *REQUESTS* takes a value of either "yes" or "no" (the default). The value of this field determines whether a remote site can request file transfers from the local system on its own.
READ	List the directories that **uucico** can use for requesting files. The default is */uucppublic* on UNIX systems.
WRITE	List the directories that **uucico** can use for depositing files from a remote system on your system. The default is */uucppublic* for UNIX.
NOREAD	Exceptions to *READ* options or defaults.
NOWRITE	Exceptions to *WRITE* options or defaults.
PUBDIR	Used to redefine the public directory, which on UNIX systems is usually */usr/spool/uucppublic*. corresponding entry in the *passwd* file

Coherent 4.0) example. The options with no values may omitted. Users of Waffle, should read its documentation carefully.

Even though there may be defaults with some of the entries in the *Permissions* file, it is good form to go ahead and define each field for each record, thus creating a self-documenting file. On a UNIX system the file is "owned" by UUCP and cannot, therefore, be changed by the average user, although it must be capable of being read by a user-generated process.

The *Permissions* File Format

A UUCP can be very secure or very open, depending upon how the *Permissions* file is configured. It is important, therefore, to pay some attention to how this file is set up. *For every LOGNAME entry there must be a corresponding entry in your passwd file.*

When writing the *Permissions* file, keep in mind the following general rules:

1. White space is not allowed either before or after the equal ("=") sign.
2. Each line corresponds to one entry, although an entry may continue to the next line by ending the current line with a backslash character.
3. If a field has more than one value, a colon (":") is used to separate the fields.
4. White spaces are used only to separate fields.

LOGNAME

LOGNAME specifies the login ids that can be used by remote systems calling you to log into your system. This can be set up to be very general or very explicit. Whatever is defined as a LOGNAME for a particular system must also have an entry in the *passwd* file. For a private E-Mail system, it may be appropriate to provide a LOGNAME common to all the members of the mail group. If this were the case, it would also be necessary to provide a common password that everyone used. This approach has potential security risks, but it has the advantage of simplicity in setting up the mail system. If you are to be a mail user, but not the mail server, and the only system you can call is the mail server, then the only entry you would need would be one that defines the mail server. If your machine will be the mail server, you may need an entry for each mail user, or a single entry that covers all potential mail users. If the VALIDATE and MACHINE fields are used, then you will need an entry for each system remote to the mail server. Three additional fields, SEND-FILES, CALLBACK, and VALIDATE, are specific to further refining the operation and functionality of LOGNAME. In the context of an E-Mail system, this has most relevance for the mail server rather than the mail user.

SENDFILES

Part of the security issue revolves around whether you call a remote system, or whether it calls you. The SENDFILES entry can take on the values "yes," "no," or "call," with either "call" or "no" being the defaults (depending on the implementation of UUCP). The values of "no" and "call" have the same meaning: files can be sent to a remote system *only* when your system does the calling. If you code SEND-FILES=yes, when a remote system calls you, and it logs in properly, it can queue a request for file transfers on your system that will be honored by your system when other work has been accomplished. Remember the master/slave roles in UUCP? The system that does the calling always starts off as the master. The passive machine (the one receiving calls), starts out as slave. When the master has completed its work on a remote machine it then offers to terminate the call. If the slave accepts the offer, the line is dropped. If, however, SENDFILES=yes, then the slave *will not* accept the offer to terminate, and the master/slave roles for the machines reverse. At that juncture, if the receiving machine has work queued for the calling machine, it now takes care of those requests. Thus, SENDFILES normally defaults to either "call" or "no" and you must change that if you want the behavior to differ from the default.

CALLBACK

CALLBACK provides a security enhancement, and the entry takes a value of either "yes" or "no" with "no" as the default. One security threat to any system that is accessible through dial access is "masquerading." Masquerading is the attempt to gain access to a system by posing as an authorized client or host. Although callback techniques are not foolproof, they do provide an additional level of security that allows greater assurance of communication with an authorized system. If a system codes CALLBACK=yes, then any system that dials into that system must be called back by the host system before any transactions can take place. This option also allows the choice of which machine gets the phone bill for the call and may have an application in some organizational situations. Note that if you require CALL-BACK, then the permissions that will take effect are those associated with MACHINE, not those associated with LOGNAME. Moreover, if two systems that both require CALLBACK try to communicate with one another, they will never communicate. Similarly, if one system requires CALLBACK and the other has SENDFILES=call, the second system will never be able to send out work of its own.

VALIDATE

VALIDATE ties a machine name to a login name. When a remote system calls yours, if VALIDATE=yes, then the remote machine is asked for its uucpname. On UNIX systems this is contained in a file called *uucpname*. For example:

```
LOGNAME=madron VALIDATE=ewc
```

In this example, if your system requires that my system login is "madron," and my system name is "ewc," then my system must verify that system (machine) name. A very secure system can be set up by requiring the use of both CALLBACK and VALIDATE. For many situations, however, this may be too restrictive, or too costly to maintain.

MACHINE

MACHINE entries define permissions for specific systems *when you call them*. Consequently, these entries have the most relevance for mail users rather than for the mail server, assuming that the server will be passive and be called by the users. If you are a mail user, and your E-Mail system is configured with a single server through which all users must communicate, then this entry, along with associated fields, can be very explicit. The value of MACHINE is either a remote system name, or the special value "OTHER." If "other" is specified, then permissions will be granted to any machine not explicitly mentioned by name. A default UUCP entry might, therefore, be written that would almost cover the universe:

```
LOGNAME=uucp MACHINE=other PUBDIR=/usr/spool/uucppublic
```

This says that anyone can log into your system with the LOGNAME "uucp;" that when you call another machine you do not care about its name (although you will still have to have an appropriate entry in the *systems/L.sys* file); and that the only accessible directory on your system is */usr/spool/uucppublic* (on UNIX systems).

LOGNAME and MACHINE entries (and their associated fields) can either be separate records or combined records. The examples given thus far have all been combined. If, however, there are some systems that only call into you (and you never call them), then only a LOGNAME record is required for that system. Conversely, if there are systems, such a mail server, that you call, but that never call you, only a MACHINE record is necessary. On UNIX systems multiple LOGNAMEs can be specified for the LOGNAME field, separating the login names with colons. With UUCP/Extended only a single login name can be specified per LOGNAME field. The latter format works for all UUCP systems that use a *Permissions* file.

COMMANDS

The COMMANDS= field defines the set of commands that a remote system may execute on your machine. It is used in conjunction with the MACHINE field, and it typically defaults to **rmail**. Under normal circumstances you would also want to enable **rmail** and **uucp**. Keep in mind, however, that the larger the number of commands a remote system can execute on your system, the lower is your level of security. There is a special value, "ALL," that will give a remote user access to any command on your path, which would create a huge security hole. A typical entry might be something like the following:

```
MACHINE=xyz COMMANDS=rmail:rnews:uucp.
```

MYNAME

MYNAME links another system (machine) name to your local system for use when you call out to a remote system. This may be used for debugging purposes or, if the remote system you are calling has already defined entries for a system with the same name as yours, the remote system can request that you use an alternative system name. Another use for this parameter might occur if you changed your system's name, but you did not want everyone you communicate with to have to change their configuration files to accommodate you. You might, therefore, retain your old system name for some contacts using the MYNAME= field. The use of this field might open you to masquerading, although if you were to use the VALIDATE option, it would be set to a remote's "real" machine name, while other uses of MACHINE names would refer to the alias name defined in the MYNAME parameter. Under testing conditions, the use of MYNAME= can allow your machine to call itself.

REQUEST

This, along with the remaining fields, may modify either LOGNAME or MACHINE entries. The REQUEST keyword allows or disallows file transfer requests by a remote site. The default is "no," which means that file transfer requests *must* originate with you rather than with the remote system. If SENDFILES=call and REQUEST=no, remote systems are very restricted in what they can take from your system. By setting REQUEST=yes for all remote systems or for a particular remote system, you are giving permission to a remote system to make file transfer requests independently of you.

READ/NOREAD, *WRITE/NOWRITE*

READ and WRITE list the directories that **uucico** can use for requesting or storing files. The UNIX default is */usr/spool/uucppublic*. NOREAD and NOWRITE are the opposite of READ and WRITE because they provide the option for listing directory exceptions to READ/WRITE options or defaults. For example, if you had the following entries,

```
READ=/ NOREAD=/usr/mydir
```

you would be granting permission to read your entire directory structure (the root directory ("/") and by implication, everything under it, except for your own directory, */usr/mydir*. Some permissions should probably be avoided. For example,

```
LOGNAME=uucp MACHINE=OTHER \
READ=/ WRITE=/ REQUEST=yes SENDFILES=yes
```

would be very dangerous. It grants read and write permissions to your entire directory structure; the remote system can request any files on its own and send any file to you, anywhere on your system. The only saving grace of this is that the login name "uucp" may require a password (but it may not), and only the default COMMANDS can be executed (since COMMANDS is not listed). The only thing that would make this statement worse is to add COMMANDS=ALL.

There are a few conditions under which you might want to allow other systems this level of access. For example, if you own two or more systems that pass files and mail from one to the other over dedicated lines, this level of access might be desirable, although you would probably still need to use a LOGNAME other than "uucp" and have it password-protected. The example above would allow a remote system to read and replace files like *Systems* and *Permissions*. This is because both these files, on UNIX systems, are owned by uucp, and the remote **uucico** runs set-user id **uucp**. This means that the normal UNIX file permissions will not be operative.[8]

Conversely, however, READ and WRITE can also be used, in what should be fairly obvious ways, to further restrict what a remote system can do on yours.

PUBDIR

The public directory is the one which, by default, remote systems may read files from and to which they may write files. No matter what the security requirements are for your system, for communication to take place, there must be somewhere on your system where reading and writing files is possible. For UNIX systems the default directory is usually */usr/spool/uucppublic.* For one reason or another there may be a need to rearrange this or extend the number of directories to which remote systems have common access. This is done with the PUBDIR option. Under normal operating conditions, there is no real need to alter this parameter.

THE TAYLOR UUCP CONFIGURATION FILES[9]

Introduction to Taylor UUCP

This section is not designed to be a complete introduction to, or an explanation of, Taylor uucp. It is, however, designed to introduce some of the differences between Taylor uucp and previous or other versions, as they are discussed in this book. Taylor uucp is a complete uucp package. It is covered by the GNU Public License, which means that the source code is always available. It is composed of several programs; most of the names of these programs are based on earlier uucp packages. Please note that the term "command" is used in two ways by Taylor: 1) to refer to the programs (such as **uucp**) that can be invoked when the system is used; and 2) the options used within the configuration files. The programs are as follows:

> **uucp** The **uucp** program, as usual, is used to copy files between systems.
>
> **uux** The "uux" program is used to request a program to be executed on a remote system. This is how mail and news are transferred over uucp. Remember that neither **uucp** nor **uux** actually do any work immediately. Instead, they queue up requests for later processing. They then start a daemon process that processes the requests and calls up the appropriate systems.
>
> **uustat** The **uustat** program does many things. By default it will simply list all the jobs you have queued with "uucp" or "uux" that have not yet

been processed. **uustat** can also be used to remove any of your jobs from the queue.

uuname   The **uuname** program, by default, lists all the remote systems your system knows about. You can also use it to get the name of your local system.

uulog   The **uulog** program is used to display entries in the UUCP log file. It can select the entries for a particular system or a particular user. You can use it to see what happened to your queued jobs.

uuto and **uupick uuto** is simply shell script interface to **uucp**. It will transfer a file, or the contents of a directory, to a remote system, and notify a particular user on the remote system when it arrives. The remote user can then retrieve the file(s) with **uupick**.

cu   The **cu** program can call another system and communicate with it, as though it is directly connected. It can also do simple file transfers, though it does not provide any error checking.

These eight programs just described, **uucp, uux, uuto, uupick, uustat, uuname, uulog,** and **cu** are the user programs provided by Taylor UUCP. **uucp, uux**, and **uuto** add requests to the work queue, **uupick** extracts files from the UUCP public directory, **uustat** examines the work queue, **uuname** examines the configuration files, **uulog** examines the log files, and **cu** just uses the UUCP configuration files. Most of these commands are replacements for commands of the same name in previous systems. The difference is the that not all these programs were part of the original UUCP and Taylor has provided a consistent set of commands.

As with other versions of UUCP, the real work is actually done by two daemon processes, which are normally run automatically rather than by a user.

uucico   The **uucico** daemon is the program which actually calls the remote system and transfers files and requests. **uucico** is normally started automatically by **uucp** and **uux**. Most systems will also start it periodically to make sure that all work requests are handled.

uuxqt   The **uuxqt** daemon processes execution requests made by the **uux** program on remote systems. It also processes requests made on the local system which require files from a remote system. It is normally started by **uucico**.

So far, Taylor UUCP commands follow the previous versions of UUCP and their emendations. Taylor UUCP is equipped with a few other programs that are useful when installing and configuring the system and are, therefore, specific to this implementation.

uuchk   The **uuchk** program reads the UUCP configuration files and displays a rather lengthy description of what it finds. This is useful when configuring UUCP to make certain that the UUCP package will do what you expect it to do.

uuconv   The **uuconv** program can be used to convert UUCP configuration files from one support format to another. This can be useful for administrators converting from an older UUCP. Taylor UUCP is able to read and use old configuration file formats, but some new features can not be selected using the old formats.

uusched   The **uusched** script is provided for compatibility with older UUCP releases. It starts **uucico** to call, one at a time, all the systems for which work has been queued.

tstuu   The **tstuu** program is a "test harness" for the UUCP package, which will help ensure that it has been configured and compiled correctly. It does not test everything, however. It only runs on UNIX systems that support Berkeley style pseudo-terminals or STREAMS style pseudo-terminals. It can, however, be useful when initially installing Taylor UUCP.

Taylor UUCP Overall Installation
Configuring Taylor UUCP

You will have to decide what types of configuration files you want to use. This package supports a new sort of configuration file. It also supports V2 configuration files (*L.sys, L-devices*, etc.) and HoneyDanBer (HDB) configuration files (*Systems, Devices*, etc.). All types of configuration files can be used at once, if you are so inclined. Currently using just V2 configuration files is not really possible, because there is no way to specify a dialer (there are no built-in dialers, and the program does not know how to read *acucap* or *modemcap*); however, V2 configuration files can be used with a new style *dialer* file or with a HDB *Dialers* file.

Use of HDB configuration files has two known bugs. A blank line in the middle of an entry in the *Permissions* file will not be ignored as it should be. Dialer programs, as found in some versions of HDB, are not recognized directly. If you must use a dialer program, rather than an entry in *Devices*, you must use the "chat-program" command in a new style dialer file. You will have to invoke the dialer program via a shell script, since an exit code of 0 is required to recognize success.

The **uuconv** program can be used to convert from V2 or HDB configuration files to the new style (it can also do the reverse translation, if you are so inclined). It will not do all of the work, and the results should be carefully checked, but it can be quite useful.

If you are installing a new system, you will, of course, have to write the configuration files. You must also decide what sort of spool directory you want to use. If you will only be using these programs, Taylor recommends *SPOOLDIR_TAYLOR*; otherwise select the spool directory corresponding to your existing UUCP package.

When mail is to be sent from your machine to another machine via UUCP, the mail delivery agent will invoke "uux." It will generally run a command such as "uux - SYSTEM!rmail", where SYSTEM is the remote system to which the mail is being sent. It may pass other options to "uux," such as "-r" or "-g." News also invokes "uux" in order to transfer articles to another system. The only difference is that news will use "uux" to invoke "rnews" on the remote system, rather than "rmail."

You should arrange for your mail and news systems to invoke the Taylor UUCP version of "uux" when sending mail via UUCP. If you simply replace any existing version of "uux" with the Taylor UUCP version, this will probably happen automatically. However, if both versions exist on your system, you will probably have to modify the mail and news configuration files in some way.

Actually, if both the system UUCP and Taylor UUCP are using the same spool directory format, the system "uux" will probably work fine with the Taylor "uucico" (the reverse is not the case: the Taylor "uux" requires the Taylor "uucico"). However, data transfer will be somewhat more efficient if the Taylor "uux" is used.

Receiving mail or news via UUCP

Mail is sent by requesting a remote execution of "rmail." To receive mail, then, all that is necessary is for UUCP to invoke "rmail" itself.

Any mail delivery agent will provide an appropriate version of "rmail;" you must simply make sure that it is in the command path used by UUCP (it almost certainly already is). The default command path is set in "policy.h," and it may be overridden for a particular system by the "command-path" command.

Similarly, for news UUCP must be able to invoke "rnews." Any news system will provide a version of "rnews," and you must ensure that is in a directory on the path that UUCP will search.

Taylor UUCP Configuration Files

The configuration files are normally found in the directory NEWCONFIGDIR, which is defined by the *Makefile* variable "newconfigdir;" by default NEWCON-FIGDIR is "/usr/local/conf/uucp." However, the main configuration file, "config," is the only one which must be in that directory, since it may specify a different location for any or all of the other files. You may run any of the UUCP programs with a different main configuration file by using the "-I" option; this can be useful when testing a new configuration. When you use the "-I" option, the programs will revoke any setuid privileges.

In many cases, perhaps most, you will not need to create a "config" file at all. The most common reason to create one is to give your machine a special UUCP name. Other reasons might be to change the UUCP spool directory or to permit any remote system to call in.

If you have an internal network of machines, it is likely that the internal name of your UUCP machine is not the name you want to use when calling other systems. Taylor gives one example of the situation at the company for which he works. At "airs.com" their mail/news gateway machine is named "elmer.airs.com" (it is one of several machines all named "LOCALNAME.airs.com"). If they did not provide a *config* file, then their UUCP name would be "elmer"; however, they actually want it to be "airs." Therefore, they use the following line in *config*:

```
nodename airs
```

This example deals with situations where the MYFILE parameter might be used in the *Permissions* file of other implementations of UUCP.

Configuration File Names

In order to get some understanding of Taylor UUCP it may be useful to define the range of configuration files the system uses. First, there are standard default names for the configuration files, but they can be changed or modified through the use of the *config* file. The references that follow assume that you are defining the configuration file names in *config*, but if you use the default names this is not necessary. The first parameter is a "command," while the second ("STRINGS") is one or more fully qualified file name.

`"sysfile STRINGS"`

Specify the system file(s). The default is the file *sys* in the directory NEWCON-FIGDIR. These files hold information about other systems with which this system communicates. Multiple system files may be given on the line, and the "sysfile" command may be repeated; each system file has its own set of defaults.

`"portfile STRINGS"`

Specify the port file(s). The default is the file *port* in the directory NEWCON-FIGDIR. These files describe ports which are used to call other systems and accept calls from other systems. No port files need be named at all. Multiple port files may be given on the line, and the "portfile" command may be repeated.

`"dialfile STRINGS"`

Specify the dial file(s). The default is the file *dial* in the directory NEWCONFIG-DIR. These files describe dialing devices (modems). No dial files need be named at all. Multiple dial files may be given on the line, and the "dialfile" command may be repeated.

`"dialcodefile STRINGS"`

Specify the dialcode file(s). The default is the file *dialcode* in the directory NEWCONFIGDIR. These files specify dialcodes that may be used when sending phone numbers to a modem. This permits using the same set of phone numbers in different area-codes or with different phone systems, by using dialcodes to specify the calling sequence. When a phone number goes through dialcode translation, the leading alphabetic characters are stripped off. The dialcode files are read line by line, just like any other configuration file, and when a line is found whose first word is the same as the leading characters from the phone number, the second word on the line (which would normally consist of numbers) replaces the dialcode in the phone number. No dialcode file need be used. Multiple dialcode files may be specified on the line, and the "dialcodefile" command may be repeated; all the dialcode files will be read in turn until a dialcode is located.

`"callfile STRINGS"`

Specify the call out login name and password file(s). The default is the file *call* in the directory NEWCONFIGDIR. If the call out login name or password for a system are given as "*", these files are read to get the real login name or password. Each line in the file(s) has three words: the system name, the login name, and the password. This file is only used when placing calls to remote systems; the password file described under "passwdfile" below is used for incoming calls. The intention of the call out file is to permit the system file to be publicly readable; the call out files must obviously be kept secure. These files need not be used. Multiple call out files may be specified on the line, and the "callfile" command may be repeated; all the files will be read in turn until the system is found.

`"passwdfile STRINGS"`

Specify the password file(s) to use for login names when "uucico" is doing its own login prompting, which it does when given the "-e", "-l" or "-w" switches. The default is the file "passwd" in the directory NEWCONFIGDIR. Each line in the file(s) has two words: the login name and the password (e.g. "Ufoo foopas"). The login name is accepted before the system name is known, so these are independent of which system is calling in; a particular login may be required for a system by using the "called-login" command in the system file. These password files are optional, although one must exist if "uucico" is to present its own (secondary) login prompts. Multiple password files may be specified on the line, and the "passwdfile" command may be repeated; all the files will be read in turn until the login name is found.

THE SYSTEM CONFIGURATION FILE

By default there is a single system configuration, named *sys* in the directory NEWCONFIGDIR. This may be overridden by the "sysfile" command in the main configuration file. The first set of commands in the file, up to the first "system" command, specify defaults to be used for all systems in that file. Each system file uses a different set of defaults. As has been noted elsewhere, the *sys* file is primarily a combination of the *Systems* and *Permissions* files of older systems.

Subsequently, each set of commands from "system" up to the next "system" command describe a particular system. Default values may be overridden for specific systems.

Each system may then have a series of alternate choices to use when calling out or calling in. The first set of commands for a particular system, up to the first "alternate" command, provide the first choice. Subsequently, each set of commands from "alternate" up to the next "alternate" command describe an alternate choice for calling out or calling in.

When a system is called, the commands before the first "alternate" are used to select a phone number, port, and so forth; in theory, if the call fails for some reason, the commands between the first "alternate" and the second are used. Well, not quite. Actually, each succeeding alternate will only be used if it is different in some relevant way (different phone number, different chat script, etc.). If you want to force the same alternate to be used again (to retry a phone call more than once, for example), enter the phone number (or any other relevant field) again to make it appear different.

The alternates can also be used to give different permissions to an incoming call based on the login name. This will only be done if the first set of commands, before the first "alternate" command, uses the "called-login" command. The list of alternates will be searched, and the first alternate with a matching "called-login" command will be used. If no alternates match, the call will be rejected.

The "alternate" command may also be used in the file-wide defaults (the set of commands before the first "system" command). This might be used to specify a list of ports which are available for all systems or to specify permissions based on the login name used by the remote system when it calls in. The first alternate for each system will default to the first alternate for the file-wide defaults (as modified by the commands used before the first "alternate" command for this system), the second alternate for each system to the second alternate for the file-wide defaults (as modified the same way), and so forth. If a system specifies more alternates than the file-wide defaults, the trailing ones will default to the last file-wide default alternate. If a system specifies fewer alternates than the file-wide defaults, the trailing file-wide default alternates will be used unmodified. The "default-alternates" command may be used to modify this behavior.

This can all get rather confusing, although it is easier to use than to describe concisely. The "uuchk" program may be used to ensure that you are getting what you want.

CONCLUDING NOTE

In this chapter we have attempted to provide a detailed set of instructions on the use of the *SYSTEMS* / *L.sys*, *passwd*, and *Permissions (permissn)* files that provide the configuration information for UUCP. An introduction to Taylor UUCP has also been given because it is a version of UUCP that will be come increasingly important in the near future. Even today, if you decide to use Coherent 4.2 (the current version as this was being written) on one of your systems, perhaps for the mail server, you would receive Taylor UUCP as the "standard" UUCP package. For the versions of UUCP distributed with this book, an understanding of the older configuration file structure is necessary.

REFERENCES

1. Ian Lance Taylor, "UUCP FAQ." From: ian@airs.com (Ian Lance Taylor); Date: 24 Jan 94; Originally Posted On: comp.mail.uucp; Archive-name; uucp-internals; Version: $; Revision: 1.23; Last-modified: $Date: 1994/01/23 04:36:38 $.
2. This and other protocols are described in greater detail in Ian Lance Taylor, "UUCP FAQ," referenced previously.
3. *Ibid.*
4. In addition to the general references on UUCP cited elsewhere, two recent and easily-available articles provide additional detail on the protocol issues: Steven Baker, "From UUCP to eternity," *UNIX Review*, April, 1993, vol. 11, no. 4, pp. 15ff (8 pages); and Ian Lance Taylor, "The UUCP g protocol," *C Users Journal,* Jan., 1993, vol. 11, no. 1 p. 63ff (9 pages). Much of this discussion of the UUCP protocols is based explicitly or implicitly on these articles as well as on Taylor's "UUCP FAQ" cited earlier.
5. For a detailed description of how to perform this process by hand, see Patrick H. Wood and Stephen G. Kochan, UNIX System Security (Carmel, IN: Hayden Books, 1990), pp. 138–141.
6. Tim O'Reilly and Grace Todino, *Managing UUCP and Usenet* (Sebastopol, CA: O'Reilly & Associates, Inc., 1990), pp. 95–120.
7. O'Reilly and Todino, p. 110.
8. These and other technical issues regarding UUCP in a UNIX environment, and UNIX-dependent issues such as file ownership, are discussed further in books and articles cited elsewhere.
9. The material in this section is taken from Ian Taylor's documentation files that are distributed with or generated by Taylor UUCP 1.04. The material is only lightly edited or is taken verbatim from Taylor's files under the copyright permissions granted by Taylor, as noted below. Under these terms, this section of this chapter may be copied along with the appropriate Taylor copyright and the copyright notices from the book.

7

Installing UUCP on Your System

Now that you have found out what UUCP and E-Mail is all about, and having designed your E-Mail system, it is time to take a look at installing the appropriate software on your computer. The software distributed with this book is all shareware or public domain. Shareware is *not* "freeware" and it is not in the public domain. It is, rather, commercial software that is distributed in a way that allows you to try it out first. If you use the software regularly, you are obligated to register it and to pay the registration fee. If this software is to be used in a company or other organization with multiple employees or members, then either a site license should be purchased or multiple licenses should be acquired.

In order to install any of the versions of UUCP distributed with this book you will need about one or more megabytes of hard disk storage available on an Intel-based machine. Each of the packages on the distribution diskettes have their own documentation files. Throughout this book I have attempted to be complete, however, the specific documentation for a particular software system will be much more complete than I can be. Consequently, once you have read this chapter, then retrieved the system you want to use, you should then read the documentation from the authors of the software. Even after you have done all these things and installed one of the UUCP systems, however, it is still possible to run into some difficulties. The most common set of problems revolves around your modem and whether it is properly initialized. In Appendix K, I have provided a few tips on dealing with modems and related matters. If you have any problems communicating with your mail server, you should immediately read Appendix K.

THE DISTRIBUTED FILES

Before proceeding further, it will be useful to take a more detailed look at the distributed files and what they contain. The diskettes distributed with this note contain a UUPlus™ Utilities for MS/DOS, WinNET™ Mail and News for Microsoft Windows, Waffle for DOS, and several support programs. This section is a brief description of the UUCP and other software contained on the associated diskettes. The software, which includes UUCP implementations for DOS and Windows, is spread across two diskettes in "zipped" archive files. In order to install the software, it will first be necessary to "unzip" the archives into an appropriate subdirectory on your hard disk. The systems present on the diskettes are the following:

```
                Disk 1                                      Disk 2
Volume in drive A is DISK1                  Volume in drive A is DISK2
Volume Serial Number is 203E-13F1           Volume Serial Number is 164A-17DB
Directory of A:\                            Directory of A:\

UTILS    ZIP      145,706 06-27-94   4:12p  INSTALL  EXE      366,346 06-23-94   1:12p
WAF165   ZIP      509,807 01-01-80  12:00a  ORDER    FRM        1,748 06-20-94   6:58p
WNMAIL   ZIP      788,854 06-27-94  12:10p  UU150    ZIP    1,027,245 06-23-94   2:31p
        3 file(s)   1,444,367 bytes         UNZIP    EXE       30,581 01-17-93   9:47p
                   12,800 bytes free               4 file(s)   1,425,956 bytes
                                                              30,720 bytes free
```

First, select a directory in your DOS path and copy *utils.zip* to it. Copy **unzip.exe** to the same directory. Execute **unzip.exe** on *utils.zip* by typing `unzip utils`. This will unarchive several utility files. Next, decide which UUCP system you wish to use. If you need to install a leaf (end-user) system, then use either WinNET™ or UUPlus™, depending on whether you work in a Windows or DOS environment. If you need to set up a UUCP host, then use Waffle.

If you want to use **wnmail**, *then, at a DOS prompt, do the following:*

1. Copy *wnmail.zip* to a *temporary* directory on your hard disk.
2. From the temporary directory type `unzip wnmail`.
3. Go to Windows, Program Manager, File, Run; then type: `c:\temp\setup`, where "c:\temp" is the disk drive and temporary directory name to which you copied *wnmail.zip*.
4. Follow the setup instructions as you would with any Windows program.

If you want to use Waffle, then, at a DOS prompt, do the following:

1. Copy *waf165.zip* to a root directory on a hard disk, such as "C:\".
2. Type `unzip waf165`. This will create the Waffle file system in a subdirectory called *c:\waffle*.
3. Read and follow the remaining installation instructions for Waffle later in this chapter and in the document *c:\waffle\docs\dos.doc*.

If you want to use UUPlus, then, at a DOS prompt, do the following:

> **1.** Place Disk 2 in your floppy disk drive, then type a:install or b:install (depending on the diskette drive), and follow the installation instructions.

The remainder of this chapter is given over to the actual installations in which you may be interested. First, the installation procedure for UUPlus™ is specified. Even if you plan to implement either WinNET™, Waffle, or a version of UUCP on OS/2 or a Mac, it is still instructive to read through the UUPlus™ installation since most of the problems with UUCP installations are reviewed. The second installation description is for WinNET™ Mail and News for UUCP under Windows. Waffle installation instructions are given on the premise that it is the appropriate choice for setting up a mail server. Finally, you will find some brief comments concerning the OS/2 and Mac implementations of UUCP, although the detailed instructions given for DOS and Windows are not repeated for these products.

INSTALLING UUPlus™

Beginning with release 1.40 UUPlus incorporated an installer program that helps make installing and configuring this package easier than it would be otherwise. The installation of release 1.50 is even more automatic.

The Installation Program

To start the installation, simply type install. Your hard drive is checked for a previous installation to determine how to proceed. The installer can also be used to edit the various configuration files, so you are given a choice for managing your system or doing a new installation. You are, presumably, doing a first-time installation so the result of this command is the screen in Figure 7.1. The installer creates directories, allows you to assign machine/system names, user names, set up your modem, and to specify other information. It also creates selected configuration files, some of which may need to be hand edited (see below). Samples of the UUPlus™ configuration files may be seen in Appendix D, entitled, "Sample UUPlus Configuration Files."

There is a sequence of screens which elicit various items of information. All are self-explanatory and most will not be reproduced here. Several of them are worth noting, however. First, in Figure 7.2, you will see the beginning of a series of screens dealing with the file system. Unless you have some compelling reason not to use the defaults, the defaults should be used.

The second series deals with the "domain name" you will use and your own machine name. Assuming that you are participating in establishing a private E-Mail network, use "UUCP." Otherwise, if you are connecting with a service provider then the service provider will probably assist you in obtaining a registered domain name. In any event, the screens provided for entering your domain name, and your machine/system name, may be found in Figure 7.3, Figure 7.4, and Figure 7.6.

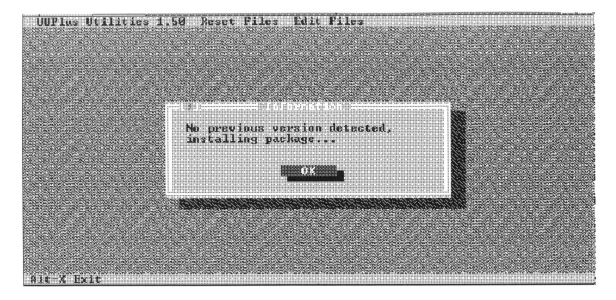

Figure 7.1. Initial UUPlus installation for screen for a new installation.

The UUPlus File System

The result of answering this sequence of questions is the screen found in Figure 7.4, Figure 7.5. As you can see, the installer will create appropriate directories. Once created, it will move the files from the installation directory or diskette into the directories in *c:\uuplus*. If you wish to change any of the directory assignments, you

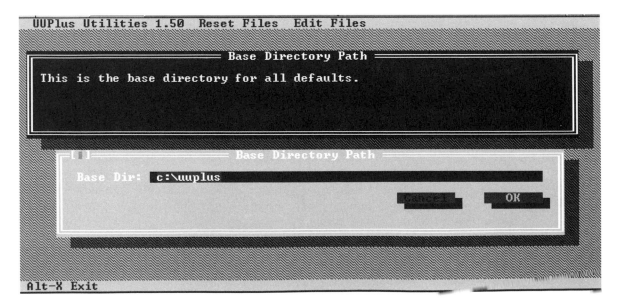

Figure 7.2 Choose your base directory.

```
UUPlus Utilities 1.50   Reset Files   Edit Files
```

```
============ Full Domain (FQDN) Name ============
This is the Fully Qualified Domain Name, or FQDN, of your system.
In the configuration file, this will be refered to as the sysname.
If you do not yet have an FQDN, use the psuedo-domain .UUCP for now,
but remember to apply for a domain!
```

```
[ ]========== Full Domain (FQDN) Name ==========
Full Domain Name:
                                        Cancel       OK
```

```
Alt-X Exit
```

Figure 7.3. Specify domain name

may do so at this time since this is the general editing screen you will get if you run **install** again. The "Exes" files are the actual programs for the system consisting of both batch files and ".exe" programs. I happen to place these files in *c:\uuplus\bin* rather than leaving them in the UUPlus™ root directory because I find it easier to manage and maintain them if they are in a separate subdirectory by themselves.

```
UUPlus Utilities 1.50   Reset Files   Edit Files
```

```
============ Site Name (UUCP Name) ============
This is the single-word UUCP site name of your system.
In the configuration file, this will be refered to as the logname
```

```
[ ]========== Site Name (UUCP Name) ==========
Site Name: uucp
                                        Cancel       OK
```

```
Alt-X Exit
```

Figure 7.4. Select site/machine/system name.

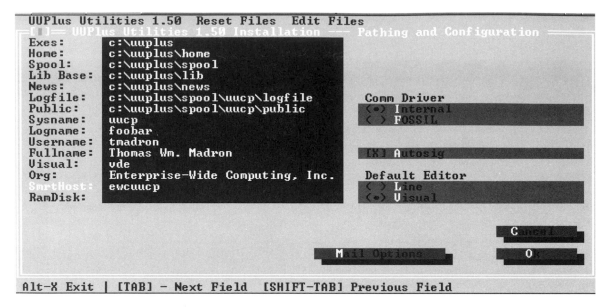

Figure 7.5. Installation summary editing screen.

Specifying Names

From the illustrations already presented, it may be seen that some additional information is important for the installation. Two variables are *essential* for UUPlus™ operation, "logname" and "sysname." "logname" is the single UUCP name of your machine (eg. foobar, ewc, etc.) and "sysname" is the domain-style name of your machine (eg. ewc.love.com). Domain names are discussed elsewhere, and in detail in Appendix H. If you do not have a domain name, enter your machine name followed by the pseudo-domain ".UUCP" (eg. ewc.UUCP), and look into getting a domain name. As is made clear in *install.man*, the use of "UUCP" as a domain is usually inappropriate, particularly if you intend to obtain Internet/Usenet access. For the purposes of this book, however, since we are dealing primarily with private networks, "UUCP" will suffice for a domain name at this point. The "logname" is also called the "machine name" in other contexts in this book. This name *must* be unique in the network.

The "username" is your user id on the system you are building. It must be unique for your local installation. Multiple users can receive E-Mail on your machine, but each such user must have a username unique to your system. A good compromise for unique usernames is often the user's first initial plus last name. Thus, my username on system ewc is "tmadron". The "Fullname" parameter is just what it implies, your full name. These two parameters may be left blank and filled through the use of environment variables (see below). If you will be the only person to receive mail on your machine, then code them at this time (or enter them later into the *UUPlus.cfg* file). If, however, there will be other mail users on your machine, then leave them blank at this time and use appropriate environmental variables.

Other names that can be entered at this point include the name of a full-screen ("visual") editor, the name of your company or organization, if appropriate, and the name of your "smarthost". If you put a name in for a full-screen editor, such as **edit**, which comes with DOS 5 and 6, highlight the "Visual:" line, then type "edit". In Figure 7.5 you will note that I have entered "vde," which is the name of the editor I use. All of these parameters are requested if you select "Mail Options." If you use a "visual editor" you may also change the "default editor" from "Line" to "Visual" by pressing "v" or by highlighting "Visual" under "Default Editor" and pressing <Enter>.

You name your organizational affiliation with the "Org:" parameter. If you do not wish to name an organization, you can at least erase the product name that comes as the default. Finally, specify your E-Mail server (host) with the "SmrtHost:" parameter. My "smart host" is owned by my company and is named "ewcuucp". If you use a ram disk, you can also indicate the drive letter assigned to it.

A final sequence of screens deals with the setup of your modem. The first of these screens may be found in Figure 7.6. In this particular screen you need to indicate which communications port you are using for your modem (mine is on COM2), take the default on the trigger level, and indicate what speed your modem uses. If you are using a new, high speed modem, (one that has a nominal speed of 14,400 b/s) you can choose either 9600 (or possibly 19200) or you can enter the maximum speed with which the modem can communicate with your computer. The new modems can be set for a local speed (57600 b/s in the illustration), but they will "autobaud" to whatever is needed to connect to the remote modem. Thus, most 14,400 b/s modems will connect locally at up to 57600 b/s. Check your modem manual for suggestions regarding the speed issue. You should read Appendix K for more information on modem setup.

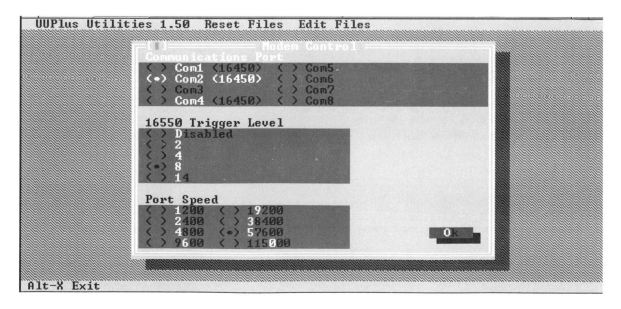

Figure 7.6. Modem setup.

During the installation procedure additional information may be requested, including the name of a "signature" file. This file typically includes your real name, company name, telephone number, E-Mail address, and similar information. You do not need a signature file, but it is useful for people receiving messages from you. You will, however, have to create a signature file named "sig": *c:\UU-Plus\home\username\sig*. My signature file may be seen in Figure 7.7. It should contain no more than four lines of text.

Configuration and Control Files

The installer will, during this process, generate several configuration and control files. For the most part, they can be re-edited through **install**, or you can edit them with an ASCII text editor, such as the DOS **edit** command. For specific information about each file, see either the comments in that file, or the appropriate manual section.

Some configuration files are optional, and will work as supplied, while others *need* to be edited, and are marked with a bullet. The global and mail files that must be edited, or at least reviewed, are the following:

- \UUPlus\UUPlus.cfg
  \UUPlus\home\[user]\mailrc
  \UUPlus\home\[user]\aliases
  \UUPlus\home\[user]\sig
- \UUPlus\lib\uucp\systems
- \UUPlus\lib\modem*.mdm (whichever one you're using as reflected
      in the systems file entry)
  \UUPlus\lib\mailrc
  \UUPlus\lib\aliases

If you will also be using news, then the following files will be needed, and the bulleted files will need to be edited:

- \UUPlus\lib\news\active
- \UUPlus\lib\news\batcher.cfg
- \UUPlus\lib\news\dist
- \UUPlus\lib\news\explist
  \UUPlus\lib\news\headers
  \UUPlus\lib\news\modrecdg
  \UUPlus\lib\news\recordin
- \UUPlus\lib\news\sys

```
Tom Madron                    Telephone: 1-908-274-3616; FAX: 1-908-274-3615
EMail: tmadron@ewc.win.net              Address:    417 Georges Road
tmadron@ewcuucp.uucp (private system)              Dayton, NJ 08810
```

Figure 7.7. Signature file for Tom Madron

DOS Environment Variables

In order for UUPlus™ to work properly, or at all, one or more DOS environment variables must be set. Environment variables are specified with the DOS **set** command and are usually set in the *autoexec.bat* file. They can also be set from the DOS command line or from other batch files. The full list of all possible environment variables includes the following:

```
UUPlus=
TZ=
USERNAME=
FULLNAME=
```

The UUPlus™ environment variable is mandatory. UUPlus provides the directory path to the *UUPlus.cfg* configuration file. If that file is found in the *UUPlus* root directory, then you should issue the following command:

```
set UUPlus=c:\UUPlus
```

If you placed *UUPlus.cfg* in the *UUPlus* directory, then you would point to that subdirectory with the **set** command:

```
set UUPlus=c:\UUPlus
```

Although the TZ variable is optional, it should probably be set. TZ specifies your time zone using standard abbreviations (EST/EDT, CST/CDT, MST/MDT, PST/PDT, etc.), and allows the calculation of mail movement ultimately relative to Greenwich Mean Time (GMT). The UUPlus default is Eastern Standard Time (EST). The TZ variable is set like the following:

```
set TZ=EDT
```

The USERNAME and FULLNAME variables specify the person using the current UUPlus™ session. This variable determines which mailbox to use and also which return paths are used by mail and news. The analogous settings in the *UUPlus.cfg* file are overridden by these environment variables. Examples of setting these variables are the following:

```
set USERNAME=tmadron
set FULLNAME=Thomas Wm. Madron
```

In addition to the environment variables, it is also helpful to add the *c:\UUPlus\bin* subdirectory to your path statement (also found in your *autoexec.bat* file). An easy way to handle the environment variables is to write a small batch file that you execute prior to any UUPlus™ session, or that you call from *autoexec.bat*. An example of such a batch file is the following, which I call *setfs.bat*:

```
rem SETFS.BAT
rem usage:  SETFS username fullname
c:\utility\pathman +c:\UUPlus\bin;c:\UUPlus
set UUPlus=c:\UUPlus
set USERNAME=%1
set FULLNAME=%2
set TZ=EST
```

The **pathman** command allows one to add to the existing path. Such utilities are widely available. Alternatively, you can simply repeat the path statement already in your *autoexec.bat* file to **setfs.bat,** adding the two subdirectories indicated. When I use **setfs** I type the following:

```
setfs tmadron Thomas_Wm._Madron
```

The underscores (or some other characters) are needed when this batch file is used or the DOS batch file processor would understand the first, middle, and last names to be separate parameters, rather than the same parameter. The "%1" and "%2" are standard batch file command line variables.

Testing the Installation

To test the installation thoroughly you will need a UUCP host with which to communicate. For the moment, however, simply send yourself a piece of E-Mail so that you can verify that **mail** and **rmail** can manage the simple task of finding a local mail user, and so that you can see how **mail** itself works. When you test your system over a telephone line, through a modem, if you do not connect properly, or the modem is not dialed at all, there are two files you should review. The first is *c:\UUPlus\lib\hayes.mdm*, particularly the line that specifies the "port speed," and the line that provides an "initialization string" (a set of modem commands). See *\UUPlus\lib\hayes.mdm* for more detail. You should also have your modem manual available for reference purposes. The second file you should review is *systems*.

Recall that the *systems* file contains "definitions" of those systems your local UUCP knows about. Consequently, if you are trying to contact a system named "ewcuucp", then you should also have a line in *systems* similar to the following:

```
ewcuucp Any HAYES57 57600 ATDT5551212 "" <CR> in:-in: nuucp
    ord:-ord: uucpudwm
```

This would be typed on a single line rather than on two as shown here. Without this entry your **uucico** would not know where to call when it received an address like these:

```
mail tmadron@ewcuucp or
mail ewcuucp!tmadron
```

If all this works, and you see your test mail message when next you type mail<Enter> you are about finished, although you will need to test the setup with your smarthost. Do not be dismayed if some additional "tweeking" is required.

WinNET™ MAIL AND NEWS

As we have noted elsewhere, WinNET™ Mail and News is primarily a client-side or leaf implementation of UUCP. As this book was being written announcements were being made concerning other Windows implementations in the works which will provide server functions as well as end-user capabilities. WinNET™ was farther along and provides an excellent leaf implementation which, for the purposes of this book, is more than adequate. According to Michael Tague, President of Computer Witchcraft, Inc., "This UUCP version will just be standard WinNET Mail, with the Alternative Provider selected. In this mode, WinNET as distributed will become shareware. Users will be asked to pay for the software ...." As implied by this statement, if you want WinNET™ for access to the Internet through Computer Witchcraft, then the product is without cost and the installation procedure is completely automatic.

If you will be using the product as part of a private E-Mail system, then some slight additional configuration is required and that is the procedure that is detailed here. First, unzip the distributed system into a *temporary* installation directory by typing:

```
mkdir c:\wnmltmp
cd \wnmltmp
copy a:\wnmail.zip c:\wnmltmp
unzip wnmail
```

The floppy drive "a:\" can also be "b:\" or it could also be in a directory on your hard disk. The hard drive can also be something other than "c:\", as well. The name of your temporary installation directory does not have to be named "wmailtmp," although for purposes of illustration, let's assume that you have used that name. From the *c:\wmailtmp* directory you can start the standard Windows **setup** program from File Manager or Program Manager, by typing

```
c:\wnmltmp\setup ,
```

which, in turn, results in the screen found in Figure 7.8. One of the results of the installation process is a small file called *chat.rc* which you will probably have to modify by hand. A typical *chat.rc* file, along with the document that explains that file distributed with WinNET™ Mail will be found in Appendix E: "Sample WinNET™ *chat.rc* File." Help is available throughout the installation process.

Choosing Your Service Provider

After having clicked on OK to the first screen, the screen illustrated in Figure 7.9 appears giving you two options: 1) choosing Computer Witchcraft as an Internet

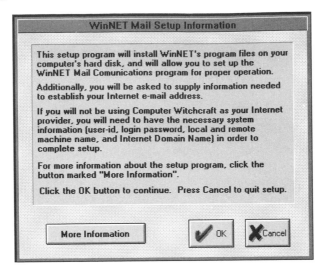

Figure 7.8. WinNET™ setup opening screen

service provider or 2) choosing another service provider. Since we are discussing this product for use in a private UUCP network, we have chosen "alternate provider." With the current implementation of WinNET™, if you wish to use the product for *both* Internet access *and* a private system, then it will be necessary to have two separate installations in separate directories on your hard disk. The reason for this is that Computer Witchcraft has not implemented the equivalent of a *systems/L.sys/sys* or *Permissions/permissn/sys* files (and the ability to read them/it) in their product. To add such a facility would greatly enhance the product, allowing the addition of a "Provider" menu. On the other hand, it would also complicate both the product and the installation.

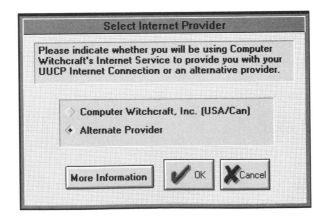

Figure 7.9. Choose your UUCP service provider

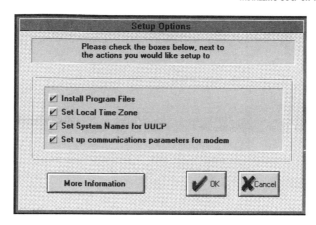

Figure 7.10. Initial setup options

Setup Options

The setup options screen (see Figure 7.10) allows selective installation (or reinstallation) of selected elements of WinNET™. When the installation is complete you will find an icon for **setup** in the WinNET program group in Program Manager. This allows reconfiguration for WinNET without having to do a complete reinstall. The most common use would be to modify either the communications parameters or the UUCP system configuration. For the first-time installation, you should use the defaults, which are to install everything.

Where Do You Want to Install?

You can, of course, install WinNET™ wherever you wish on your hard disk file system. If you have more than one hard disk, or have a large hard disk partitioned into more than one logical drive, you can select the drive, and/or the directory to install from the screen illustrated in Figure 7.11.

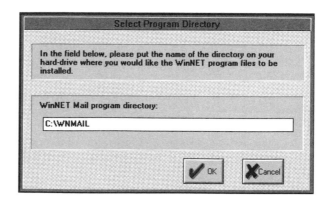

Figure 7.11. Determine disk drive and directory for installation

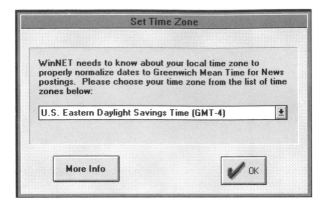

Figure 7.12. Set your current time zone

Time Zone

As with any UUCP system, your UUCP must know the time zone in which you are located. The need for this is a function of the need for UUCP to be able to synchronize itself with Greenwich Mean Time (GMT). Set your current time zone from the screen as illustrated in Figure 7.12 and Figure 7.13. Just click on the down arrow next to the default time zone and select yours from the menu provided.

UUCP **Parameters**

The most difficult part of the setup program is probably getting all the appropriate names properly set up. The various names required by the screen in Figure 7.13 are the same as those required in *UUPlus.cfg* in the UUPlus™ installation de-

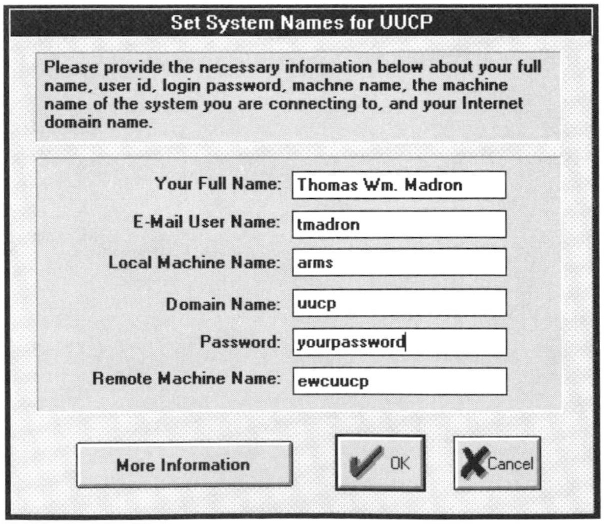

Figure 7.13. User identification parameters

scribed above. Some of the information may be a bit redundant, but assuming that some readers may go directly to the installation of the software they desire, it is reinforced in this section.

A Short Review of Internet Addressing

If you have, or intend to register your UUCP system, then you will need to understand Internet addressing.[1] Even for an unregistered private UUCP network you need to understand the syntax of this addressing scheme. Every system that is connected by the Internet/Usenet networks has a system name and at least one user. Each system also has what is called a domain name, which describes the sub-network of systems to which the system belongs. Your Internet E-Mail address is made up out of the above components, e.g.:

```
user@system.domain
```

The "user" part of your address refers to you personally. It is often the user's first or last name, or a nickname. Some examples of user names are: "jqpublic", "tmadron", "jsmith", "tom", "dick", and "harry". If you have multiple users on your system the user names must be unique in the local system.

The "system" part of your address refers to the computer system on which you are a user. "system" names are sometimes called "machine names". Sometimes the "system" name is the name of a business enterprise, the name of a geographic location or other place, or the name of the computer itself. Some examples of system names are: "lightspeed", "igor", "eniac", "paris_pc". It is common to give systems "cute" names, but be advised that all the "good" system names were taken long ago. Please refer to RFC # 1178 found in Appendix H for detailed suggestions on naming. More prosaic names, such as "ewcuucp" (company initials plus "uucp") are more descriptive and less likely to have already been used.

The "domain" part of the address is usually divided into two or more parts, the formal subnetwork name and a general descriptor of the type of network that it is. For example, Computer Witchcraft's domain is "win.net". "win" is the sub-network name, and "net" is the type of network. Other network types are:

> "com" — (company)
> "edu" — (educational institution/University)
> "gov" — (government entity)
> "mil" — (military network)
> "org" — (general organization)

There are also a variety of networks types specific to countries, such as "uk" for the United Kingdom Internet Network, or, in the United States, names designating states. For an unregistered, private UUCP network, use the name "uucp".

Full Name

Your "real," full name should be specified in this field. The contents of this field will be placed in the header of each mail message you write to indicate the real name of the person sending the mail. Example: "Woodrow Wilson".

User Name

Enter the user name agreed to with your UUCP provider host. As you have already surmised by this time, UUCP networks can be configured in a wide variety of ways. This is the name you are known by on your own system. Depending on how your host is configured, it may or may not be needed on that system. For example, if your mail host is purely passive, it would need to know only your system name, not your user id. If everyone in your mail group used the same login name and password, without system verification, then the host might not even need to know your system, although this would probably be an unwise configuration. On the other hand, if your provider is an Internet mail and news feed, then your user id probably needs to be known to your provider's security services including its *passwd* file.

Machine (System) Name

In this field, enter the system name that you have agreed to with your provider. Some providers do not provide a system name for their users, and expect that the users will log in with the "user" name rather than with a "system" name. If this is the case with your provider, put the first part of your provider's domain name here. For example, if your provider assigns you the address 12345@provider.com, put "provider" in this field. For example, my system name with WinNET is "ewc" (for "Enterprise-Wide Computing, Inc.") and my user id is "tmadron". Remember that their domain name is "win.net". So, my complete E-Mail address on this system is "tmadron@ewc.win.net". When I signed up for this service I entered "ewc" in this field. Regardless of whether you are setting your system up for a private or an Internet connection, you need a unique system name. In Figure 7.13 the machine name is "arms."

Domain Name

This field refers to your UUCP provider or mail server. Here you enter the server's domain name. This should be both the sub-network name and the network-type indicator (a fully qualified domain name), separated by a period (".") character. For example: "win.net". If your provider does not assign system names, put only the network-type identifier in this field, i.e, "com", "net", "gov", "edu", "org" or "mil", etc. For a private, nonregistered domain, use "uucp".

Password

This field allows you to enter the password which your Internet provider or Mail Server has told you will be needed to gain access to your account when you log in to the provider's server. In some cases, there may by a two step log in process that involves more than one password. If this is the case with your provider, give the password which is the unique password for your specific account (rather than a generic password for gaining access to the server initially). Conversely, with a private system, this may be standard for everyone in a mail group.

Remote Machine Name

You must also know, of course, the "machine" or "system" name of the server to which you will be connecting. This should be the uucp "machine" name provided to you by your Internet provider. Refer back to Chapter 2, Figure 2.3; if you were setting up that system, you would enter the system name, "mach1" in this field. The name of my company's system is "ewcuucp."

To summarize this discussion, it may be helpful for look at the files used to set up all of this on both the server and your local system. WinNET™ requires a file called *chat.rc* that provides the login procedure for the host. An example of the file is the following:

```
INITIATE
\,\n
ogin:
nuucp\n
word:
password\n
```

The first two lines simply involve getting the "login:" message from the host. See the file *c:\wnmail\chat.txt* for more information on dealing with *chat.rc*. This file illustrates an implementation for a mail group where all members use the same login and password, "nuucp" and "password", respectively.

On the host side, using Taylor UUCP, there might be an entry in the *sys* file that looks like the following:

```
# System jqpuucp (WINNet Mail for UUCP)
system arms
time Never
port MODEM
speed 2400
commands rmail rnews uucp uux
local-receive /usr/spool/uucppublic
remote-send /usr/spool/uucppublic
remote-receive /usr/spool/uucppublic
```

The first line, of course, is a comment. The system name, "arms" refers to your local system name which should be the same as you entered for your system name in the WinNET setup. The host will never be calling you (third line), the port name is "MODEM" (fourth line, which in this case simply defines a basic Hayes modem), at a speed of 2400 b/s (fifth line). The commands that a remote UUCP system can use are **rmail, rnews, uucp,** and **uux** (sixth line). Incoming and outgoing users can make use only of the directory */usr/spool/uucppublic* (seventh through ninth lines). In this case system verification is required, but the server need not know about you as a user. If I wish to mail you a message, assuming that the server is named "ewcuucp", then the UUCP address would be:

```
ewcuucp!jqpuucp!yourid
```

or possibly,

```
ewcuucp!yourid@jqpuucp.uucp
```

In this instance the first step in getting a message from "me to you" is to dial directly to ewcuucp, which knows directly about you, so that the message can be forwarded to you. Because ewcuucp already knows about you, you do not need these more complicated addresses. Only the following should be required:

```
yourid@arms.uucp
```

The Communications Parameters

Since UUCP is essentially a communications system you will have to set up selected communications parameters as illustrated in Figure 7.14. The default for the system, as you might expect, is the Computer Witchcraft telephone number. The phone number illustrated is my own UUCP system (which is not guaranteed to be up at all times). I have a 2400 b/s Hayes modem running on Com 2. The packet window size and cpu utilization are the defaults and may be left as is. Read the "readme" file that will be in your *c:\wnmail* directory for more on these parameters. Assuming that you have a "Hayes compatible" modem, the basic "AT" commands listed will likely be adequate, although you may be able to improve operation if you are using a high-speed 9600 or 14,400 b/s modem. I have used this setup, however, with both a simple 2400 b/s modem and with higher speed smart modems. If you change modems this screen can be changed later by clicking on the setup icon in Program Manager program group for WinNET. Again, you should probably take a close look at Appendix K if (or when) you experience modem communication problems.

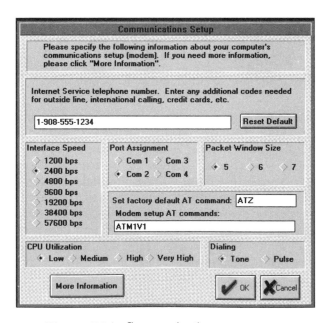

Figure 7.14. Communications parameters

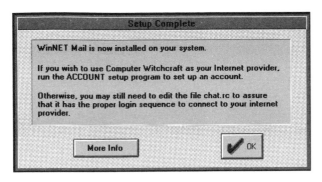

Figure 7.15. Almost finished

Completing the Setup

The two final screens in Figure 7.15 and Figure 7.16, allow you to complete the setup. The first is simply informational. If you want to connect to WinNET, then you will need to run an additional program which will automatically sign you up with their service. If you wish to have **setup** provide you with a Program Manager group for WinNET, then you reply appropriately to the last screen. At this point you are finished and may proceed to use the product. Keep in mind that it may be necessary to "tweak" the *chat.rc* file by hand.

A DOS MAIL SERVER: WAFFLE

All things considered, Waffle is relatively easy to install on DOS machines. It is also available for UNIX systems. This section is an abridged version of the document *\waffle\docs\dos.doc* that comes with the system. The system is reasonably well documented and various documentation files will be found in *\waffle\docs*. As the author of Waffle notes, "It is strongly suggested you read or at least review this [*dos.doc*] entire document before proceeding (and its companion document, MANUAL.DOC; information on some of the more obscure options will be found there)."

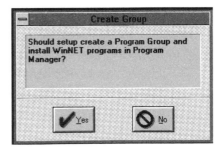

Figure 7.16. Installation complete

System Requirements for the DOS version

The system requirements for Waffle are very moderate. You must have an IBM XT or AT compatible computer with at least 512K of RAM. This means that you could acquire an older AT or inexpensive 386 (AT) to use as a dedicated mail server. In fact, the hard disk, which is required, may be the most expensive part of the system since it will have to be large enough to hold not only the software but also mail and possibly newsgroups. A Hayes compatible modem, one that uses the Hayes AT command set, is also required along with any version of DOS from 3.3 upward.

Software Installation

Waffle will normally be installed on your C:\ drive in the directory *c:\waffle*. Remember that Waffle is more than just UUCP. It is, fundamentally, a bulletin board system and some of the directories needed are dictated by that application. Four directories need to be created "by hand:"

c:\temp	A place to hold temporary files
c:\files	The root directory for the BBS FILES section
c:\user	A user's individual files
c:\spool	The UUCP spool directory

The remaining default directories will be created when the Waffle system is unzipped. The default locations for the directories created when the zipped archive is unzipped are:

```
c:\waffle            c:\waffle\info
c:\waffle\admin      c:\waffle\menus
c:\waffle\bin        c:\waffle\system
c:\waffle\docs       c:\waffle\text
c:\waffle\extern     c:\waffle\uucp
c:\waffle\help       c:\waffle\words
```

To get all these directories, and their contents, you must use **unzip** (on the distribution diskettes). Unzip the *WAF165.ZIP* file using the program **unzip.exe**:

```
unzip waf165
```

Before unzipping the archive, be sure you are in the C:\ (root) directory of your hard disk. You may, of course, unzip into another hard drive than C:\. The entire file system will be unzipped.

Configuration

Waffle's main configuration file is the *static* file which can be found as *c:\waffle\system\static*. Samples of this and other Waffle configuration files may be found in Appendix F, "Sample *Waffle* Configuration Files." Please note the warning in *dos.doc*: "If you placed the directories anywhere other than the default locations (such as setting the main Waffle directory to D:\WAFFLE) you must change the configurations in the static file":

files:	C:\FILES
spool:	C:\SPOOL
temporary:	C:\TEMP
user:	C:\USER
waffle:	C:\WAFFLE

Note that "Waffle's configuration files are distributed in such a way to make installation on drive C: easiest."

You must, of course, tell DOS about Waffle. A **set** command pointing to Waffle must be executed, probably from your *autoexec.bat* file, although it can be accomplished in other ways as well. The **set** command for Waffle itself must be something similar to the following:

```
set waffle=c:\waffle\system\static
```

Your DOS PATH must also be altered to include the C:\WAFFLE\BIN directory. You probably already have a PATH set in your *autoexec.bat* file, but in case you don't, here is an example:

```
path c:\;c:\dos;c:\windows;c:\waffle\bin
```

Also, check to verify that lines similar to those that follow are present in your CONFIG.SYS file:

```
BUFFERS = 48
FILES = 20
SHELL = \COMMAND.COM /E:1000 /P
```

You may have to experiment with the BUFFERS= statement since most sources will suggest that it be set to no more than 10 if you are using a disk caching program (such as **smartdrv**).

Testing Your Installation

First, reboot your machine so that your new PATH statement will be properly set and so that your "set WAFFLE" command will be executed. Then type,

```
login
```

Waffle should display a banner message similar to the following:[2]

```
elf.santa-cruz.ca.us (elf)
Test UUCP & Mail site,
Elf Consulting, Santa Cruz CA.
```

```
Waffle version 1.65, out of the box.
Login or NEW:
```

Waffle is requesting a user name and password from you. The default "factory configuration" password is:

```
Login: system
Password: system
```

This is a "privileged" system account with which you can initially login. A welcome message will be displayed, and you will find yourself at the "main Waffle prompt". Explore the system while you are there.

The *static* File

Like most of the other systems described in this book, Waffle has several configuration files that may need editing. The most important is *waffle**system**static*. Other files let you customize your menus, and in general, "personalize" the public presentation of the system.

Establishing Modem Communications

The next important step will be to get Waffle to answer the phone. You will need to edit the static file, *c:**waffle**system**static*. Set the "device" entry to your COM port (1 or 2), and the "speed" entry to the highest baud rate your modem supports (such as 2400). If you have a high speed internal or external modem it should be set at it maximum speed (56700 or 9600 for example). You may have to experiment a bit with this.

```
device :    1
speed  :    2400
```

From the DOS command prompt, type RUN. The top status bar should appear, your modem should initialize and the following messages should display:

```
Calls: 0
Awaiting Call..
```

If these lines do not come up (for instance, if the first line was printed but not the second), refer to the section in the DOS installation manual entitled, "SETTING UP THE MODEM". That section will tell you how to change the "AT" string sent to initialize the modem, and other important information. Then simply have someone call the modem number. You should see:

```
Calls: 0
Awaiting Call..Ring..
```

```
[connect 2400]
```

If you do not get these lines, or something very similar, go back and check the relevant settings.

Choose a NODE name for your system

Like all systems using a version of UUCP, you must choose a short name for your system. Valid characters are "a" through "z" and "-" (dash). Your system or node name should describe your system in some manner, but it must be unique on the network to which you are connecting. Some examples of node names:

```
Elf Consulting elf.UUCP
The Muffler Palace  muffler.UUCP
```

Edit your static file C:\WAFFLE\SYSTEM\STATIC and set the "node", "alias", and "uucpname" parameters consistent with the node name you choose. The "alias" is any alternative name by which your system might be known. The ability to use an alias is particularly useful if, for some reason, you must change your node name but would like to minimize the impact of that change on the broader network. In that instance you can set your *alias* to the old node name so that is what the broader network continues to use. A normal UUCP-only site would probably set the three something like the following:

```
node :    elf.UUCP
alias   :    elf.UUCP
uucpname :    elf
```

If you have registered your site, for example, within the .US domain, the three parameters might be the following:

```
node :    elf.santa-cruz.ca.us
alias   :    elf.UUCP
uucpname :    elf
```

In the event that your site is registered within a domain:

```
site :    oval.white-house.gov
alias   :    oval.UUCP
uucpname :    oval
```

Bear in mind that if you are not in a registered domain, *DO NOT USE* anything except a name ending with .UUCP as your NODE name. Mail software *WILL NOT DELIVER* any mail to unregistered domains although the unofficial .UUCP domain is recognized by some undefined number of hosts.

Your Organization's Name

The "organ" parameter in *static* should be set to the name of your company, school, BBS, or whatever organization that operates the system. In general, it should not be a person, since it is used to display the originating system for messages sent over a network.

Name Your SMARTHOST

When your system is connected to some UUCP-based network, the appropriate next point of contact should be a smarthost to which you can send mail that isn't addressed to a system to which you are directly attached. Your smarthost can choose to send mail to its own smarthost which in turn can send to another smarthost. If you connect to only one host, you can probably define it as your smarthost. In a private UUCP network, yours may be the smarthost for everyone else, which you having another smarthost. If this is the case you can simply enter your own node name as the smarthost, implying that all mail stops here. An entry such as

```
smarthost :   ewcuucp
```

would normally be a neighbor one hop away, and that neighbor will either be a UNIX site running pathalias, or an Internet site. Remotely connected sites, however, may define the SMARTHOST to be a "bang path" (a bang is a ! sign) in which case addresses will be rewritten to direct mail towards the smarthost:

```
smarthost :   earth!enterprise!universe
```

Set Timezone

The time zone, also in the static file, consists of three fields — your timezone, the number of hours West of Greenwich, and the daylight savings time zone, if there is one. Set these according to your timezone:

```
timezone  :     PST 8 PDT (for US Pacific Time)
timezone  :     EST 5 EDT (for US Eastern Time)
```

If your area has no daylight savings, omit it:

```
timezone  :     GMT 0
```

Other Messages, Menus, and Files

You can customize Waffle extensively and you will probably wish to do so for various text messages and menus, particularly if you also use the system as a standard BBS. There are at least two forum specific parameters in *static*, LOCAL and USENET, that you may also wish to set properly. For these issues please consult the installation guide.

Waffle on a LAN

One of the challenges in designing and installing a UUCP network is what to do with local area network (LAN) users. How do we include all the members of the LAN in the UUCP-based E-Mail network? With Waffle (as well as with many other packages) the solution is relatively simple. In Figure 7.17 you will find a view of the Waffle directory/file system. Under normal conditions you would probably install the *waffle* directory and its subdirectories and files on drive C:\\. On a LAN, however, you might install the Waffle file system on a file server (on something like a Novell network, for example) or on a shared directory in a peer-to-peer LAN (Windows for Workgroups, for instance). In either instance the basic installation would be as illustrated.

Assuming that the base installation of Waffle is in a shared directory on a PC on a peer-to-peer LAN, on drive C:\\, then two important subdirectories would be the following:

```
c:\waffle\bin
c:\waffle\system
```

The first contains all the executable programs for the system and the second contains a number of setup files, including *static*. We have tested the system and

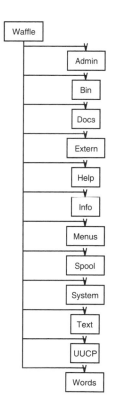

Figure 7.17. Waffle directory/file system

it works from the PC on which it was installed. Now, however, we want to set up several LAN users to be able to use this single shared file system. To do so we need to create the simplified file system illustrated in Figure 7.18.

Basically, on a LAN, the only thing that needs to happen is to have individual users set up a simplified Waffle system that points to the files and directories on the shared disk and directories. The owner of the shared system can simply share his or her entire drive C:\ in the simplest case. In the "directories" section of the *static* file the base system will be defined as in Table 7.1. On each LAN user's workstation, instead of the complete Waffle subdirectory system, the only subdirectories needed are *waffle**bin* and *waffle**system*. The first will contain only the **login.bat** file, the **waffle.exe** program (which is executed from **login**), and a small batch file I have named **setwaf.bat**. The second will have only a copy of *static*, with the appropriate changes in disk names. Thus, in the illustrative case, the first LAN user has defined the shared disk containing the base Waffle installation as "D:\" and the second LAN user has defined that shared disk as "F:\". The locations of the appropriate directories in the LAN users copies of *static* must, therefore, be revised to reflect what those users are calling the base directory system (D:\ and F:\ in the illustration). The content of the **setwaf.bat** files for both LAN users is the following:

```
@ECHO OFF
cd \waffle\bin
set WAFFLE=c:\waffle\system\static
login
```

When **setwaf.bat** is executed it changes directories into its own *c:\waffle\bin* directory, executes a set command that tells the local system where Waffle can find the modified *static* file, and then executes the Waffle **login** command (which lets the LAN user log into Waffle). All the pointers to Waffle files and resources are now pointed to the shared file system, not to the local file system, and at this point both LAN users can access a single Waffle installation. This, in turn, allows the sending and receiving of UUCP/E-Mail as well as making available any BBS capabilities the installation supports. **setwaf.bat** can be called from a Windows "pif" file and is, therefore, accessible through Windows as a DOS application.

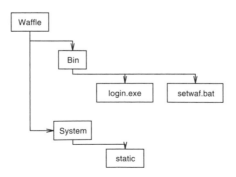

Figure 7.18. LAN user Waffle directory/file system

TABLE 7.1. Waffle Files on Base System and for LAN Users

Type of File	Base System	First LAN User	Second LAN User
Files	c:\files	d:\files	f:\files
Spool	c:\waffle\spool	d:\waffle\spool	f:\waffle\spool
Temporary	c:\temp	d:\temp	f:\temp
User	c:\user	d:\user	f:\user
Waffle	c:\waffle	d:\waffle	f:\waffle

There are, of course, other ways a LAN installation might be handled. A mail user agent such as **pcelm** should be able to be configured to access the appropriate Waffle mail files, for example. The method illustrated is probably the easiest and most straightforward, however. The network operating system itself (NOS) should take care of the problem protecting multiple users from writing to the same file at the same time, or the DOS **share** command will have already been executed to accomplish the same protection.

OS/2 AND MACINTOSH IMPLEMENTATIONS OF uucp

This chapter has been designed to provide you with the information necessary to do a successful installation of UUPlus™, WinNET™, and Waffle on a DOS or Windows system. In the next chapter we will look at the software necessary to create, read, and send mail. In that chapter we will discuss both DOS and Windows software as distributed with this book. Before completing this chapter, however, it will be worthwhile noting some installation issues regarding OS/2 and Macintosh implementations of uucp.

THE OS/2 IMPLEMENTATION

An OS/2 implementation of UUPlus™ is planned, but at this writing was unavailable. The principle OS/2 version is uupc/Extended, and is virtually identical to the DOS version, except that it requires OS/2 executables rather than DOS programs. The sources for acquiring uupc/Extended are noted in Chapter 4 and in Appendix C. If you are using a version of OS/2 that supports Windows, you may also be able to use **cmm** (Cinetics Mail Manager) as your mail user agent (MUA). One advantage of using OS/2, rather than DOS, is that it should be possible to have multiple copies of **uucico** running as alternate processes, each controlling a different communications port. Thus, if you wanted to implement a mail server with multiple modems or other communications attributes, without using a UNIX operating system, then uupc on OS/2 may be the right thing for you.

UUCP **FOR THE MACINTOSH**

When your target machine is a Macintosh, you will either *macgnu.sit* or *uupc3.sea*, and possibly something like *eudora.sea* as a mail reader/composer. Sources for these systems may also be found in Chapter 4 and Appendix C. *eudora.sea* contains an MUA, while *macgnu.sit* and *uupc3.sea* are Mac versions of UUCP. All were described in Chapter 4 and are noted here for the sake of completeness. To use these archives it will be necessary to copy them to a diskette capable of being read by your Mac, then to de-archive them using the appropriate Mac software.

REFERENCES

1. This section is a lightly edited version of the help file distributed with WinNET™ Mail and News.
2. This example is taken directly from the Waffle installation manual.

8

Creating, Reading, and Sending Mail

As you should now know, in order to actually use UUCP to send and receive mail it is necessary to have at least two additional components: a Mail User Agent (MUA), and a Mail Delivery Agent (MDA). Although not a formal part of UUCP, any system that supports UUCP will have one or more MUAs and one or more MDAs. In this chapter we will present three MUAs and illustrate how they are related to the MDAs. The original plan was to distribute all of the products discussed in this chapter, but constraints on disk space precluded that. The three we will discuss are the UNIX-style **mail** commands, **elm** and **pcelm** for UNIX and DOS respectively, and **cmm** (Cinetics Mail Manager), an MUA for Windows, along with the more integrated approach found in WinNET™ Mail and News. Sources for all these systems may be found in Appendix C.

AN INTRODUCTION TO INTERNET STANDARD MAIL

There are at least three mail commands that are commonly used in UNIX environments: **/bin/mail**, **elm**, and **mailx**. **mailx** is a System V MUA. In addition, on BSD systems there is a second "mail" program, **/usr/bin/mail**. The original program from AT&T was **/bin/mail**. It is this program that is closely integrated with UUCP, and on which several implementations of **mail** on non-UNIX platforms are based. The third MUA is **elm**, a screen-oriented, menu-driven mail agent reviewed earlier. In this chapter we will discuss and describe in further detail **/bin/mail**, or simply **mail**, **elm**, **pcelm** (for DOS), and a Windows MUA, **cmm**, the

Cinetics Mail Manager. These programs will be compared to the integrated approach found in WinNET™. In this section, we will confine ourselves to the basic **mail** command. There are a number of variations of the **mail** command. The variations arise as different distributors and value added resellers of UNIX seek to enhance the versions they sell. For this reason, it is important that you read the *manual* pages or other documentation for **mail** on the system you are using, since the details may vary from what is presented here.

Although details of the **mail** command may vary, they all have a number of elements in common. The reason why they all have some elements in common is that there is a standard, embodied in a document labeled RFC # 822, that defines the format for Internet (and by implication, UUCP-based) mail systems. The full text of RFC # 822 may be found in Appendix G. In order to conform to RFC # 822, an MDA and an MUA must be able to understand the format of an incoming message and deal with it, to produce an outgoing message that also conforms to the standard. If you wish to bypass the introduction to E-Mail messages and go directly to how to install and use the MUA, skip to the next section. This section, by the way, is based directly on RFC # 822 and stays close to the wording of that document.

First of all, messages consist of lines of text. No special provisions are made for encoding drawings, facsimile, speech, or structured text. No significant consideration has been given to questions of data compression or to transmission and storage efficiency, and the standard tends to be free with the number of bits consumed. For example, field names are specified as free text, rather than as special terse codes. This has led to variations in mail implementations in order to transfer graphics, sound, and other multimedia information.

A general "memo" framework is used, divided into two parts: a set of rigidly formatted information called a "header," followed by the main part of the message, with a format that is not specified by RFC # 822. The syntax of several fields of the rigidly-formatted ("headers") section is defined in RFC # 822, and some of these fields must be included in all messages. The syntax that distinguishes between header fields is specified separately from the internal syntax for particular fields. This separation is intended to allow simple parsers to operate on the general structure of messages, without concern for the detailed structure of individual header fields. Appendix B [in RFC # 822] is provided to facilitate construction of these parsers. From time to time, as header fields in addition to those specified in 822 come into common use, revisions will be made to standardize their implementation. Users may also wish to extend the set of fields they use privately. Such "user-defined fields" are also permitted.

The framework established for these messages results in a utilitarian rather than a "pretty" document and is designed to be useful for intra-organization communications and well-structured, inter-organization communication. It also can be used for some types of inter-process communication, such as simple file transfer and remote job entry. A more robust framework might allow for multi-font, multi-color, multi-dimension encoding of information. A less robust framework would more severely constrain the ability to add fields and the decision to include specific fields. In contrast with paper-based communication, it is interesting to note that the RECEIVER of a message can exercise an extraordinary amount of control over the message's appearance. The amount of actual control available to message receivers is contingent upon the capabilities of their MUAs.

Much like a paper-based postal service, messages are viewed as having an envelope and contents. The envelope contains whatever information is needed to accomplish transmission and delivery. The contents compose the object to be delivered to the recipient. RFC # 822 applies only to the format and some of the semantics of message contents. It contains no specification of the information in the envelope. Some message systems may use information from the contents to create the envelope. It is intended that RFC # 822 facilitate the acquisition of such information by programs.

Although most UNIX-based E-Mail systems store messages in the format specified by RFC # 822, some message systems may store messages in other formats. RFC # 822 is intended strictly as a definition of what message content format is to be passed *between* hosts. There was no intent to dictate the internal formats used by sites, the specific message system features that they are expected to support, or any of the characteristics of user interface programs that create or read messages. This is why there are variations in the implementations of **mail** and in more elaborate MUAs while conforming to 822. Moreover, a distinction should be made between what the specification *requires* and what it *allows*. Messages can be made complex and rich with formally-structured components of information or can be kept small and simple, with a minimum of such information. Also, the standard simplifies the interpretation of differing visual formats in messages providing only the visual aspect of a message is affected and not the interpretation of information within it. Implementors may choose to retain such visual distinctions. The international standards, X.400 and X.500, also address some of these same issues, and at some point over the next decade, Internet standards will be drawn into conformance with those guidelines.

With the rapidly increasing number of E-Mail products on the market, both for *intra-* and *inter-*organizational use, the problem of how we get a given message from one system to another without the end-user having to use multiple mail services becomes more intense. Largely because of cost there is no one (or good) answer to that issue at present. In general, the problem is solved through the use of one or more mail gateways. There are a number of such gateways available of varying complexity and cost, and there are service suppliers (CompuServe is one that comes to mind) that provide "mail hub" connections. These connections allow the transfer of a single message from among a wide variety of mail services. RFC # 822 also addresses this issue briefly. During transmission through heterogeneous networks, it may be necessary to force data to conform to a network's local conventions. For example, it may be required that a carriage return <CR> be followed either by a line feed <LF>, making a <CRLF>, or by <null>, if the <CR> is to stand alone. Such transformations are reversed when the message exits that network.

When crossing network boundaries, the message should be treated as passing through two modules. It will enter the first module containing whatever network-specific transformations that were necessary to permit migration through the "current" network. It then passes through the modules:

- Transformation Reversal
  The "current" network's idiosyncrasies are removed, and the message is returned to the form specified in 822.
- Transformation
  The "next" network's local idiosyncrasies are imposed on the message. This is depicted in the simple flow diagram in Figure 8.1.

In summary, then, a formal definition of a message in the context of RFC # 822, and one which is applicable to this chapter and this book, is the following: A message consists of header fields and, optionally, a body. The body is simply a sequence of lines containing ASCII characters. It is separated from the headers by a null line (i.e., a line with nothing preceding the <CRLF>).

MAIL DELIVERY AGENTS (MDA)

An MDA is a program that is invoked by one or more other programs to determine from an address on an E-Mail message where to send the message. Depending on the system being used, it may be called **rmail** or the functions may be distributed across two programs, **rmail** and **smail**. On some UNIX systems there are additional programs that enhance either the reception and delivery of E-Mail or of network news. If you have access to a UNIX system that uses the Berkeley **sendmail** software (actually available on all modern UNIX systems), these addi-

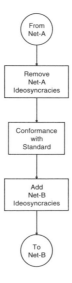

Figure 8.1. Message transmission across heterogeneous systems

tional programs may be available to you. However, they only work on some systems, and are not germane to the discussions in this book. Under UNIX, and UNIX-like systems, MDAs are usually separated from MUAs. The functions (especially those for outgoing mail) can be integrated in a single software package. In most instances, once installed, these programs need never again be directly accessed by an end-user since they are invoked by **mail** (or its equivalent) for outgoing messages, and by **uux** or **uuxqt** for incoming messages. Since you may have to deal with MDAs in the installation process, however, it is of some importance that you learn something about them.

In general, **rmail** is invoked on a remote system to determine whether mail is to be delivered locally on *that* system or forwarded on to another system. It is designed to be called by other programs, such as **mail**, not as a command directly invoked by an end-user. On some UNIX systems **rmail** works in tandem with **smail**, a program that allows users to address mail to remote sites using abbreviated pathnames or Internet addresses. **smail** accomplishes these addressing tasks by accessing the database processed by **pathalias** from UUCP map files. Illustrative of **rmail** in UNIX or UNIX-like (such as Coherent) operating systems, it receives mail from UUCP, reads and interprets the address on the mail, and either delivers it on the local machine (if this is where it is addressed), or passes it on to the next machine named in the message's UUCP path. In contrast, **smail** queues mail locally for delivery to remote systems. UUPlus™ does not, unfortunately, have facilities that will access and manipulate UUCP map data (although some other DOS email utilites do). Only one DOS UUCP system that I know of has a DOS version of **pathalias**: DOSGATE.

Although the UUPlus™ **rmail** is discussed elsewhere, it is instructive to include a brief comment at this point since it illustrates the functions that must take place when mail is sent or received. In UUPlus™ other programs, normally **mail** (when composing and sending E-Mail) and **uuxqt** (when receiving E-Mail from a remote system) pass E-Mail messages to **rmail** which handles the actual writing to local mailboxes and/or queuing for remote systems. **rmail** may, in general, do an 822 parse of the address as well as directing the message to the appropriate user. Proper address parsing is accomplished by UUPlus™, which also has **rmail** functions built into some of its other programs, although a version of **rmail** is provided to facilitate linking with other software, such as **cmm** and **pcelm**.

Another way to think about what happens when you deal with mail is to visualize the problem as a three-stage sequence: the E-Mail must 1) be composed or read by an end-user; it 2) must be routed to the appropriate recipient; and 3) it must be delivered. Under Coherent (and perhaps other UNIX-style systems) these three functions are actually operationalized in specific commands. There, for example, **mail** is the *user agent*, **rmail** and **smail** are *routing agents*, and **lmail** and **uux** are delivery agents for local and remote mail, respectively. Remember that **uux** sets up the instructions for command execution on a remote system, while **uuxqt** executes the commands on a local system requested by a remote system. If we sometimes seem to use the two arbitrarily, it is because they are both required, **uux** at the sending end and **uuxqt** at the receiving end.

Fortunately, unless you are into some form of network programming, you will not have to deal directly with MDAs. If, however, you have cause to put together a software system that must notify someone on the network that some action has taken place, then your software would interact with one or more of these programs—most likely some version of **rmail**.

MAIL USER AGENTS

UNIX-style mail

To give some flavor of the variations that can be found in UNIX-style mail commands, note the following:

Coherent

Send or read mail:
```
mail [-mpqrv] [-f file] [user ...]
```

SunOS (System V)

Read /usr/ucb/mail ...:
```
Mail [ -deHinNUv ] [ -f [ filename | +folder ] ]
     [ -T file ] [ -u user ]
```
Send /usr/ucb/mail ...:
```
Mail [ -dFinUv ] [ -h number ] [ -r address ]
     [ -s subject ] recipient ...
```

UUPlus™ (DOS)

Read mail:
```
mail [-f username]
```
Send mail:
```
mail [-i] [-r filename] [-s subject] recipient
     [recipient ...]
```
Setup Dump: mail -a

Without getting into the meaning of the various options (the letters following the hyphens), suffice it to say that there are a number of variations of **mail**. Moreover, when reading E-Mail, there are some commands that can be issued concerning the disposition of the mail. The dispositions that are common to virtually all the variations of **mail** can be found in Table 8.1.

In all these cases, the actual use of **mail** is somewhat simpler than it may appear. To read a message sent to you, you need only type

```
mail .
```

and to send a message, type:

```
mail addressee.
```

TABLE 8.1. Common Mail Dispositions

Options	Meaning
<Return>	No disposition on this item of mail; it will still be there the next time mail is read; the next piece of mail is then displayed.
d	Delete this item of mail; next piece of mail is then displayed.
s *file*	Save this piece of mail in *file*; next piece of mail is then displayed.
q	Quit reading mail; any unread pieces will be there the next time mail is read; all deletions become permanent.
x	Quit reading mail; any pieces of mail that were deleted will be restored.

Since you may have installed UUPlus™ by now, you should read the instructions for the **mail** command distributed with the system which may be accessed online by typing the command

```
man mail
```

In the preceding examples, *addressee (user, recipient,* etc.) may be in either the UUCP address format, `system!userid`, or in the Internet format, `userid@system.domain`.

ELM AND PCELM

The ELectronic Mailer (ELM) was written by Dave Taylor of HP (Hewlett Packard) Labs several years ago in recognition that many people starting to use UNIX at that time wanted something beyond the line-oriented software that is still characteristic of UNIX systems. **elm** is an MUA designed to replace **/bin/mail** and **mailx**. The software system that comprises *elm* includes programs like **frm** to list a "table of contents" of your mail, **printmail** to quickly paginate mail files, and **autoreply**, a system-wide daemon that can autoanswer mail for people while they're on vacation without having multiple copies spawned on the system. PCElm is a PC-, MS/DOS-based MUA with a user interface closely modeled after **elm**. Apart from an intellectual relationship, PCElm, first produced in 1988 by Wolfgang Siebeck and Martin Freiss, is unrelated to the original **elm**. PCElm is distributed as shareware.

The ELectronic Mailer (elm)

The most significant difference between Elm and earlier mailers is that Elm is screen-oriented. According to Taylor, "users will find that Elm is also quite a bit easier to use, and quite a bit more 'intelligent' about sending mail and so on." Elm was originally written under HP-UX, HP's proprietary version of UNIX System V, with a little BSD thrown in. It has since been ported to most UNIX systems. The system conforms to RFC # 822, which was an early objective of the author. The differences in the user interface between **elm** and **mail**, as described above, can be easily seen in Figure 8.2, which is a typical **elm** screen.

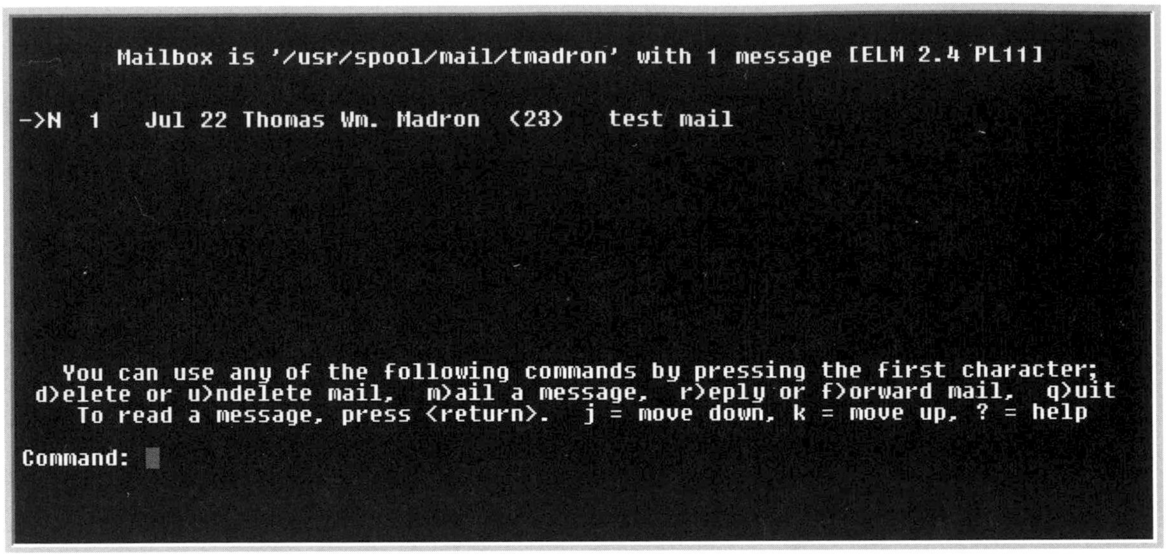

```
        Mailbox is '/usr/spool/mail/tmadron' with 1 message [ELM 2.4 PL11]

->N  1    Jul 22 Thomas Wm. Madron  <23>     test mail




    You can use any of the following commands by pressing the first character;
  d)elete or u)ndelete mail,  m)ail a message,  r)eply or f)orward mail,  q)uit
    To read a message, press <return>.  j = move down, k = move up, ? = help

Command: ▉
```

Figure 8.2. UNIX ELectronic Mail (ELM) screen

The primary design objectives were, according to Taylor, the following:

- To have a mail system that exploited the CRT instead of assuming a teletype.
- To have a mailer that was 100% RFC # 822 compliant.
- To create a system that needed no documentation for the casual user, but was still powerful enough and sophisticated enough for a mail expert.
- To write a "significant" piece of software as a learning experience.
- To find out how reasonable it is to try to modify a program to meet the expectations of the users, rather than vice-versa.
- To basically correct some of the dumb things that the current mailers do, like letting you send mail to addresses that it could trivially figure out are going to result in "dead.letter."
- To make use of **pathalias** and to have the computer parse the addresses rather than the end-user.

Motivations not dissimilar to Taylor's led Siebeck and Freiss to put together PCElm, which was able, by 1988, to make use of UUCP systems being written for DOS machines.

PCElm

An interesting difference between the motivations behind **elm** and **pcelm** is that **pcelm** was originally devised to be used in the context of packet radio among Ham radio operators. It actually had the twofold objective: to be used as a drop-in replacement for **BM** when using the KA9Q NOS package (a TCP/IP system for packet radio), or to be used as a replacement for **mail** when using DOS-based UUCP systems such as UUPlus™. It can also be used for other mail systems, as all relevant things for compatibility with MTA's (Message Transfer Agents) are configurable.

Like its progenitor, PCElm has a full-screen user interface, with relatively easy to learn and easy-to-use commands. UNIX users will already be familiar with the more important commands. It can be made to work with most of the DOS-based UUCP mail systems since it makes no assumptions at all about the underlying network software. Finally, PCElm is multilingual; all messages can be made to appear in your favorite language. Message files for English and German currently exist as might be anticipated since the authors are German. A typical PCElm screen may be seen in Figure 8.3.

PCElm in ham radio mode creates text- and workfiles directly usable by the appropriate software for distribution with the Simple Mail Transfer Protocol (SMTP) of TCP/IP. In UUCP mode, PCElm executes a UUCP mailer (usually **rmail**) to feed mail to your UUCP program. Since there are many UUCP systems for PCs, it is up to you to find the right way to execute the mailer, although the *pcelm.rc* configuration file makes this task relatively straightforward. Functionality, to the extent it is possible on a DOS system, is similar to **elm**. From

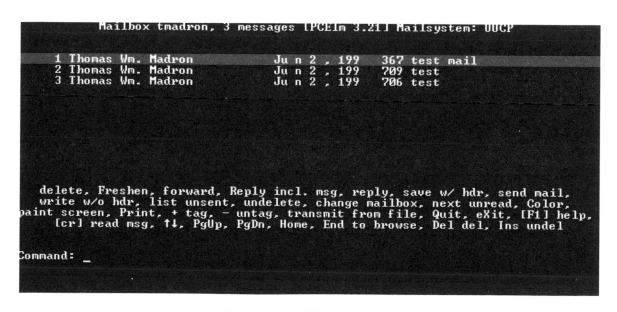

Figure 8.3. PCElm DOS screen

the two figures cited it is possible to see the extent to which **pcelm** has inherited traits from **elm**.

A complete installation manual is provided in the archive in a file named *pcelm.man*. Before you install **pcelm**, you should print and read that document. There are, however, a few highlights that may make this task a bit easier. First, assuming that you are also implementing UUPlus™, you may wish to place the PCElm files in a *pcelm* subdirectory under *UUPlus*, just to keep everything together. The **pcelm.exe** executable can either be copied to the *UUPlus* directory, or a small batch file can be written that resides in the *UUPlus* directory pointing to **pcelm.exe** in its own subdirectory. The primary problem is in properly configuring the *pcelm.rc* file and adding one or more "set" commands to your *autoexec.bat* file.

Several parameters may be set either in the *pcelm.rc* file or as DOS environment variables using the DOS **set** command. The most flexible means of doing this is with the **set** command because that allows more than one mail user to access mail on the same machine. For example, I have, in *UUPlus**bin* the following batch file named *setpcelm.bat*:

```
rem Batch File SETPCELM.BAT
rem Usage: SETPCELM username full_name
set MAILBOX=%1
set MAILDIR=c:/UUPlus/spool/mail
set NAME=%2
set HOME=c:/UUPlus/home/%1
```

There are two parameters that must be given: your mail username and your full name. When you specify your full name in this manner you may not include any spaces, so just use an underline character wherever a space would normally be put. In the *pcelm.rc* file, the entries for "mailbox", "maildir", "name", and "home" are left empty or commented out. If a parameter appears in both places, the entry in *pcelm.rc* takes precedence. The batch file listed above can be called from your *autoexec.bat* file so that it is executed everytime your start or restart your computer.

The most important task is to set the environment variable "HOME" to point to the directory where PCElm's configuration file and alias file reside. This environment variable is mandatory! PCElm will *not* start up without it. If you are installing **pcelm** in conjunction with UUPlus™, then you may put these files in your *UUPlus* directory or in a pcelm directory and set the variable "HOME" as follows:

```
set HOME=c:/UUPlus
set HOME or c:/pcelm
```

The executable, **pcelm.exe**, should probably be placed in *fsuupc**bin* or handled as indicated above. You may wish to experiment a bit with the location of the several files for the most convenient method for you.

Either English or German is selected by copying the appropriate message file (*pcelm.eng* or *pcelm.deu* respectively) and copying it to a file named *pcelm.msg*. This message file must also reside in whatever directory you have defined as "HOME." Once these housekeeping chores are completed, *pcelm.rc* must be properly set up. PCElm needs to know several things about your UUCP environment, and about your computer to function properly. *Before starting PCElm for the first time, you must edit PCElm's configuration file, pcelm.rc. As the authors insist, "DO NOT USE THE EXAMPLE pcelm.rc DISTRIBUTED IN THIS PACKAGE AS-IS. Edit it first with an ASCII-Editor of your choice."*

pcelm.rc is an ASCII file. Lines that start with a pound sign ("#"), or empty lines, are regarded as comments. Other lines are of the form,

```
<keyword> <blank> <information>.
```

The keywords that PCElm knows about are explained in detail *pcelm.man*. Note that ASCII space is used as a delimiter; if you need to include a space in the information field, you can put double quotes ("") around it. If (for whatever reason) you need to insert control characters into a line, write them as escaped decimals (i.e. \001 would be Ctrl-A). Other escape sequences PCElm recognizes are:

```
\n, newline,
\r, carriage return,
\\ backslash, and
\t, tab.
```

Note that PCElm follows the UNIX convention and uses slashes in pathnames, not backslashes. That is, you must write a path like "c:\uupc\spool\mail" as "c:/uupc/spool/mail."

Keywords are case insensitive, so it does not matter whether they are all in lower case, upper case, or a combination (which would be easier to read). The set of keywords (in **boldface** type), along with one of my configurations (in *italics*) that need to be modified are:

> **\<keyword\>** *\<information\>*
> **uucphost** *madron.uucp* [only a single system or machine name is appropriate]
> # If this entry is commented out, the value of the environment variable
> #"mailbox" is used.
> # **user** tmadron
> # If this entry is commented out, the value of the environment variable
> #"name" is used.
> # **fullname** "Tom Madron"
> # **reply** *madron!tmadron*
> **zone** *EST*
> **maxlet** *300*
> **edit** *vde*

```
# If this entry is commented out, the value of the environment variable
#"maildir" is used.
# smtp c:/UUPlus/home/tmadron
queuedir c:/UUPlus/spool
video 0
SOH-UUCP mmdf
SOH-ham "From"
ham-ext ".txt"
uucp-ext "."
START uucp
COLORS 1f,4f,2f,07,6f
# For my version of UUPlus, the following line works:
uucpcall "rmail % $ " [the "%" and "$" are used by pcelm as variables]
sequence sequence.seq
print lpt1
weedout "Reply-To: From: To: Subject: Received: Message-Id: From\32
    Status:"
```

You should refer to *pcelm.man* for the detailed meanings of these parameters, but two or three require some comment. **user** is the equivalent to UUPlus's "logname" and should be the same as the name you gave to the *UUPlus.cfg* file. The **uucphost** must be the same as the "sysname" name in *UUPlus.cfg*. Although *pcelm.man* seems to suggest that **video** should be set to "1", which enables direct video writes, a more stable environment is one that uses more standard calls (set to zero, "0"). A few of the parameters are for use only in a ham radio environment and may be left as in the sample *pcelm.rc* file. To ensure that **pcelm** starts in UUCP mode rather than in ham radio mode, **START** must be set to *uucp*. **uucpcall** names the MDA (**rmail**), using the "-f" (file) option. The "$" and "%" must be left, since they are symbols for parameters ($=filename) that are passed from **pcelm** to **rmail**.

pcelm, once configured properly, is a good alternative to **mail**. It is, without question, more friendly and easier to follow. If, however, you generally work in a Windows environment, then **cmm** is probably the product for you.

The Cinétics Mail Manager (cmm)

In some respects **cmm** is a Windows implementation of **elm**. There are some vague similarities in "look and feel," but as a Windows 3.x application it works very smoothly and can be kept running all the time as a minimized icon. Since it periodically checks the UUPlus™ spool and mail directories, if **rmail** and **uucico** (from UUPlus™) run in minimized DOS windows, with Windows running in 386 Enhanced Mode, you can create a very smooth running E-Mail system. The basic **cmm** window may be seen in Figure 8.4. All the accoutrements of Windows applications are used by **cmm**: drop-down menus, mouse control, on-line help, and so forth. The Cinétics Mail Manager is a shareware product that should be registered if you use it extensively.

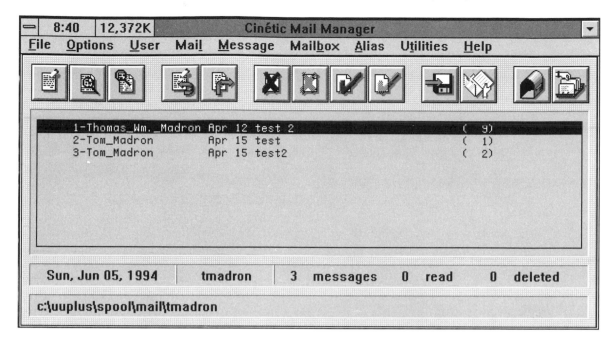

Figure 8.4. Cinétics Mail Manager (CMM) opening Screen

The Cinétics Mail Manager is a mail reader/composer that let you manage Internet and UUCP mail under Windows. The main purpose of CMM is to let the user read, reply, forward and create messages. There are also other functions to simplify the reader's task. CMM is not a mail transport package or a UUCP system, it acts as a front end to such packages. To send a mail message, CMM calls a third party mailer program that does the transport part of the mailing process. Current directly supported systems are:

- •UUPlus™ Utilities by UUPlus Development.
- •UUPC/Extended by Kendra Electronic Wonderworks.
- •PC-NFS from Sun Micro Systems Inc.
- •PC/TCP by FTP Software Inc.
- •Pathway by The Wollongong Group Inc.

Cinétics Mail Manger is configurable to support other systems. Since CMM is configurable, you may use your PC as a multi-user mail system by creating as many users as you wish.

Configuring **cmm** if *very* simple. You simply click on "options" from the menu, then click on "System Setup," at which point you obtain the screen seen in Figure 8.5. First, however, edit the line in the *cmm.ini* file that looks like the following:

FSUUCP by Fubar Systems=Uuplus mailer, fsuucp.pif $R $F $U to
UUPlus by UUPlus Development=UUPlus mailer,uuplus.pif $R $F $U,

to reflect the change in names of the product. Then rename the *fsuucp.pif* file to uuplus.pif. Edit the pif file to reflect changes in directory names from *fsuucp* to *uuplus*. By the time you acquire a copy of the Cinétics Mail Manager these changes may already have been made, but the distribution version current at this writing still reflected the old "fsuucp" nomenclature. You then execute **cmm**, click on "System Setup," click on the down-arrow button next to "Name" and select UUPlus from the drop down menu. At that point your set up is nearly complete. Enter *your* machine name (not mine), and your default domain name (again, not mine). You skip from field to field using the <tab> key, or to go back, the <backtab> "key", the <shift><tab> combination. Depending on where you unzipped CMM, you may have to move the files **cmm.exe,** *cmm.hlp,* and *UUPlus.pif* to your Windows subdirectory or to a directory that is on your DOS path. I keep them in a general purpose directory I have for such things called *c:\utility*. They could also be easily moved to the *\UUPlus* directory. You should also check the *UUPlus.pif* file to ensure that the path specified to the UUPlus **rmail** program is correct (it will probably need to be edited).

At this point you should then open Program Manager and add **cmm** to some existing program group, such as "accessories", or if you want it to start when Windows starts, put it in the "startup" group. You do this by clicking on "file", then on "new" in the "file" menu. If you are just in Program Manager without a group

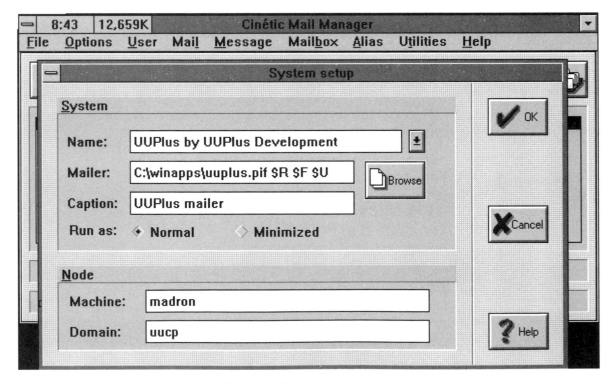

Figure 8.5. cmm setup screen

open you can create a new group, or better, get out of the process and open a group, such as "startup", then click on "file", "new", and "program item." You will then be asked for the file name of **cmm.exe**, which if you have put it in *\UUPlus\bin* should be fully qualified as

```
d:\UUPlus\bin\cmm.exe
```

The default startup directory should also be specified as the directory containing **cmm.exe**. Click "OK" on all this and you are in business.

When you are finished configuring **cmm** a *cmm.ini* file will be created in your Windows subdirectory. At this point you are ready to test **cmm**. There are some other options that you may wish to change, but the basics are finished. Use the "help" facility in **cmm** to obtain further detail and information on the installation and use of the product.

INTEGRATED SYSTEMS (WinNET™ MAIL AND NEWS)

Products written for Microsoft Windows, and probably for the Macintosh, are often more integrated that those for UNIX or MS/DOS. This is at least true from an end-user perspective even when it is not true from the standpoint of software architecture. An example is WinNET™ from Computer Witchcraft. If you decided to use that package one of the obvious things you will find is that the MDA and MUA are tightly integrated. **uucico** is still a separate and distinct program that can either be called from **wnmail.exe** or called as an independent program. We have already presented various screens from WinMail and will not repeat a description of those screens here. Suffice it to say that in this product all the functions discussed in this chapter are present in a single integrated system that is presented in that way to the end-user.

The setup for WinNET™ is pretty much like any other Windows product. First, unzip the archive file to a temporary directory. Then, from either File Manger or Program Manager select "run," find the directory into which you just unzipped the distribution archive, and start the **setup** program. Answer the questions appropriately as they are asked, and when you are finished you will have a completed installation. The only thing you may have to do is edit a file called *chat.rc*. That file contains the expect/send script to get you logged onto your host UUCP system. The login sequence may a general one used by many host users, or your host system may require that the login be specific to you. This is information that comes from your host system's manager.

CONCLUDING NOTES

If you have followed one or another of the paths described in Chapters 7 and 8 you have installed both a complete UUCP system and a reasonably decent MUA so that you can easily read and compose mail. If you are an end-user in a developing network, you are finished. Providing that whoever is managing your mail server is finished with his or her tasks, you can now send mail to that server. If you wish to sign up for a service to link you into the Internet, then you also need to read and digest Chapter 10. If you are the one responsible for finally getting your mail network running, you need to seriously consider the suggestions in Chapter 9. If all those things have been accomplished, you are finished. You should be able to start using your new E-Mail network.

9

Completing and Managing the Network

Now that we have operating software on the individual machines, it is still necessary to integrate those machines (and the people who own them) into a working and functional network. There is not a single "best way" to do this. The national and international network of UUCP systems, called Usenet, as well as the broader Internet, are not centrally and rigidly managed systems. Configurations appropriate for large organizations with many dispersed offices will differ from small groups where the model depicted in Figure 9.1 is accurate and appropriate. There are three general issues we must now address ourselves: 1) completing (integrating) the network; 2) maintaining the network, and 3) planning for the expansion of the network. This chapter will discuss each of these.

COMPLETING THE NETWORK

By the term "completing the network" we mean the integration of the individual components into a single whole, much in the same way individuals or family groups come together to form villages, towns, cities, states, and nations. For an E-Mail network based on UUCP this means configuring the main mail server, as well as individual user sites, so that messages can be sent and received in an orderly and timely fashion.

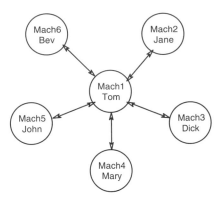

Figure 9.1. Basic star network

COMPLETING THE MAIL SERVER

Depending on your situation, you may not need a mail server that is any more complicated than the workstations of the individual mail users. The only difference is that the mail server will normally be a passive system, simply sitting and waiting for calls. It will not often poll other sites. This means that you will initially bring the server up in "slave" as distinguished from "master" mode. For a small system, like that depicted in Figure 9.1, it may be possible to even limit the number of hours a day the server is waiting for calls, since for only five remote users everyone could call in within a short period of time. This is true even if the mail server has only one port and one modem dedicated to UUCP. This means that it would not be necessary to dedicate a machine to the server function.

However, if you are planning a larger network, however, and/or if you want mail users to be able to call at any time, either a small dedicated mail server would be required, or a multi-user system capable of performing the mail function along with other activities. If you already have a substantial UNIX system available, you may already have a system that can easily be configured to act as a mail server. Alternatively, you might acquire an 80386 or 80486 system and equip it with UNIX or a UNIX-like operating system, such as Coherent. An appropriate DOS system for this purpose is Waffle, distributed with this book. Since we are focused on "low cost" mail systems, Coherent, at $99, would be a good alternative running on an 80386 or 80486 machine with 8 MB of memory, four serial ports, and four modems. This would provide a low-cost, relatively powerful dedicated mail server operating almost identically to a UNIX system. Such a system could easily handle mail services for a reasonably large number of users. The upper limit is a function of how often and with what duration the average mail user called, and these issues are ones of organizational policy as much as technology.

A final issue to be resolved before configuring the server is the level of security required on the system. The last paragraph of the manual page for UUCP dated 12/16/76, which happens to be in the "BUGS" section, noted the following:

"As usual, you have a choice of getting more work done or worrying about protecting what you already did; this choice is perhaps more acute if you use UUCP."

The observation is no less true today than it was nearly 20 years ago. The easy way to set up the server is with little security and allow anonymous logins. The problem with this is that the server is then open to any other people outside the local network that may acquire the appropriate telephone number.

Mail Server Configuration

The server will probably need a *Systems/L.sys* file that defines all members regardless of whether or not it ever dials out to the members of the mail system:

```
#       Sample Mail Server systems/L.sys file
#
mach2 Any ACU 2400 phone_number gin:-gin: nuucp word:-word: mailserv
mach3 Any ACU 2400 phone_number gin:-gin: nuucp word:-word: mailserv
mach4 Any ACU 2400 phone_number gin:-gin: nuucp word:-word: mailserv
mach5 Any ACU 2400 phone_number gin:-gin: nuucp word:-word: mailserv
mach6 Any ACU 2400 phone_number gin:-gin: nuucp word:-word: mailserv

or,

#       Sample Mail Server systems/L.sys file with Greater Security
#
mach2 Any ACU 2400 phone_number gin:-gin: jane word:-word: passwd
mach3 Any ACU 2400 phone_number gin:-gin: dick word:-word: passwd
mach4 Any ACU 2400 phone_number gin:-gin: mary word:-word: passwd
mach5 Any ACU 2400 phone_number gin:-gin: john word:-word: passwd
mach6 Any ACU 2400 phone_number gin:-gin: bev word:-word: passwd
```

The first version assumes that each remote (user) system has been configured with a login name of "nuucp" and a password of "mailserv." The alternative is for each remote system to require a unique login name and a unique password. Since the mail server will only rarely, if ever, be calling the remote sites, this is not too critical unless the remote sites have some special security needs. These examples will work with Coherent or most UNIX systems and on some DOS systems (with the change of "ACU" to "HAYES24", or something appropriate), although the chat script may need modification. If you are using Waffle as your mail server, remember that the Waffle *systems* file has a somewhat different (though similar) format (see Chapter 7, section on Waffle installation, and Appendix F for sample files).

The *Permissions* file for the mail server can be either simple (with relatively low security) or more complex (with increasing security). Examples include those found below. The first is a low security option with the advantage that it is very easy to maintain. This might be an appropriate starting point or you might wish to use the *passwd* file as the primary means of maintaining security. Conversely, you might want a relatively open system. As long as you restrict the directories that can be read and written, and the commands that remote systems can execute on your server, this should actually be sufficient.

```
#    Sample Permissions file for low Security Mail Server
#
LOGNAME=nuucp MACHINE=sbw SENDFILES=yes REQUEST=yes \
   WRITE=/usr/spool/uucppublic READ=/usr/spool/uucppublic \
   COMMANDS=rmail:rnews:uucp
```

A similar entry in a Taylor UUCP *sys* file will be found below.

Security can, of course, be upgraded significantly by requiring the checking of machine names as the following example illustrates. The disadvantage is the time and effort it takes to maintain such a file, since there would have to be an entry for each remote system, although the LOGNAME is the same in each case.

```
#    Sample Permissions file for Mail Server
#
LOGNAME=nuucp VALIDATE=mach2 MACHINE=mach2 \
   SENDFILES=yes REQUEST=yes READ=/usr/spool/uucppublic \
   WRITE=/usr/spool/uucppublic
LOGNAME=nuucp VALIDATE=mach3 MACHINE=mach3 \
   SENDFILES=yes REQUEST=yes READ=/usr/spool/uucppublic \
   WRITE=/usr/spool/uucppublic
LOGNAME=nuucp VALIDATE=mach4 MACHINE=mach4 \
   SENDFILES=yes REQUEST=yes READ=/usr/spool/uucppublic \
   WRITE=/usr/spool/uucppublic
LOGNAME=nuucp VALIDATE=mach5 MACHINE=mach5 \
   SENDFILES=yes REQUEST=yes READ=/usr/spool/uucppublic \
   WRITE=/usr/spool/uucppublic
LOGNAME=nuucp VALIDATE=mach6 MACHINE=mach6 \
   SENDFILES=yes REQUEST=yes READ=/usr/spool/uucppublic \
   WRITE=/usr/spool/uucppublic
```

An even more secure system would be the following one in which there are unique LOGNAMEs as well as machine validation.

```
#    Sample Permissions file for Mail Server for Greater Security
#
LOGNAME=jane VALIDATE=mach2 MACHINE=mach2 \
   SENDFILES=yes REQUEST=yes READ=/usr/spool/uucppublic \
   WRITE=/usr/spool/uucppublic
LOGNAME=dick VALIDATE=mach3 MACHINE=mach3 \
   SENDFILES=yes REQUEST=yes READ=/usr/spool/uucppublic \
   WRITE=/usr/spool/uucppublic
LOGNAME=mary VALIDATE=mach4 MACHINE=mach4 \
   SENDFILES=yes REQUEST=yes READ=/usr/spool/uucppublic \
   WRITE=/usr/spool/uucppublic
```

```
LOGNAME=john VALIDATE=mach5 MACHINE=mach5 \
    SENDFILES=yes REQUEST=yes READ=/usr/spool/uucppublic \
    WRITE=/usr/spool/uucppublic
LOGNAME@comp = =bev VALIDATE=mach6 MACHINE=mach6 \
    SENDFILES=yes REQUEST=yes READ=/usr/spool/uucppublic \
    WRITE=/usr/spool/uucppublic
```

The advantage with either of the first two *Permissions* examples just given is that they require a *passwd* file with only two entries since they reference only a single LOGNAME. This could be made even simpler (and less secure) by not requiring a password for "user" uucp. The disadvantage of the foregoing illustration is, of course, it is not very secure. A much more secure *passwd* file is one that matches the foregoing *Permissions* file, but it has all the disadvantages of being more difficult to maintain and would require one entry for every mail user. As noted above, the Waffle *permits* file has a similar, though slightly different, structure. The default *permits* file is the following:

```
; Neighbors are allowed to execute RNEWS and RMAIL. Also they can
; access
; the anonymous UUCP directories if you uncomment the up and
; down load lines.

default    /system=known
           /account=any
           /commands=rnews,rmail
           /download=anonymous
           /upload=uploads
           /time=any

; For anonymous UUCP login. Provide a "uucp" account calling
; uucico with
; -panonymous -uanonymous to access this permit if you want anon
; uucp.

anonymous  /system=any
           /account=anonymous
           /commands=""
           /download="anonymous"
           /upload="uploads"
           /time=any
```

This default *permits* file allows any system to communicate via UUCP, although each remote system must be defined in the *systems* file in order to be accepted by Waffle for communications. The remote system must also have the appropriate login name and password, of course, but that can be a common one among group members. With Taylor UUCP each remote system must be defined in the *sys* file even though a common login name and password may be used. A typical (and relatively minimal) *sys* file definition is the following:

```
# System ARMS (WINNet Mail for UUCP)
system arms                               system/machine name
time Never                           we will never call "arms"
port MODEM                           connection is via modem
speed 2400                           maximum speed is 2400 b/s
commands rmail rnews uucp uux        commands for a remote system
local-receive /usr/spool/uucppublic  |
remote-send /usr/spool/uucppublic    | usable directories
remote-receive /usr/spool/uucppublic |
```

If Tom is to be able to communicate with the others on the mail network, it would be useful to define an alias file. The alias file is very simple with a record for each member of the network. It allows the user (in this case "Tom") to communicate with a simple, easily-remembered nickname, rather than having to give the full address each time. This is similar to a phone book file found in some other software packages. The first field is the short name, the second fields is the person's full name, enclosed in double quotes, and the third field is the address of the mail user with whom you wish to correspond. The alias systems for WinNET™, UUPlus™, and Waffle all operate in somewhat the same manner. An alias name is equated with a specific address. The most extensive aliasing system is found in Waffle. It allows for both a system-wide alias file and individual user alias files. The basic syntax of both files is:

```
<alias><white space><address>
```

It is also possible to set up distribution groups:

```
<alias><space><address1><space><address2> ... <address?>
```

The Waffle alias system has other options and \waffle\docs\manual.doc should be consulted for details.

The Mail User's Configuration Files

The configuration files for each individual mail user are relatively simple because with this design a mail user must contact only a single system—the Mail Server. To accomplish that task each user must have the following *SYSTEMS/L.sys* file, or if they already have such a file, they must add a line similar to the following:

```
#    Sample user systems/L.sys file to access Mail Server
#
mach1 Any ACU 2400 phone_number gin:—gin: nuucp  word:—word: passwd
```

or for UUPlus™:

```
mach1 Any HAYES24 2400 ATDT5551212 "" <CR> ogin:—ogin: nuucp ord: ord: passwd
```

This is simply an entry that defines how to reach the Mail Server. The machine name of the mail server is "mach1," the local system can dial it at any time of the day or night, it uses a Hayes 2400 bps modem with some phone number, the "g" protocol, and logs in with the login name "uucp" and the password "passwd."

Unless you are using Waffle as your "end-user" access to another mail server, which does require the *permits* file, neither UUPlus™ nor WinNET™ Mail require a *Permissions* file. Other DOS systems, however, may require the equivalent of *Permissions*.

Mail Forwarding

In various examples in this book you may have noticed somewhat strange addresses for each mail user. First, **mail** in most contemporary uucp packages can usually decode either uucp addresses ("bang path") of the form *systemname!userid* or the Internet format, *userid@systemname.domain*.[1] If the path from your system to another system must go through an intermediate machine, then a compound address may be constructed. In the uucp format, the first system name you would list would be the system you are calling. In our examples, that would be the mail server, "mach1." The second system name could be another intermediate system or the final destination if only a single intermediate system is required (as is the case with our mail network). Thus, for Bev to send a message to Jane, she might address it as follows:

```
mach1!mach2!jane
```

The forms may be able to be mixed, although it is not considered good form since it may be subject to misinterpretation on some systems.

```
mach1!jane@mach2.uucp
```

Remember that "mach1" is the mail server, and "mach2" is Jane's machine. This ability to forward mail from system to system is one of the things that makes a mail server feasible and simplifies the configuration of each mail user.

For our sample private mail network, it would not normally be necessary to use an extended bang path for Jane to address Bev. So long as all the machines are defined in the *Permissions* or *sys* (Taylor) file of the mail server (assuming a UNIX or UNIX-like system), or in the *systems* file of Waffle, then a simple address, such as

```
bev@mach6 or
mach6!bev
```

would be necessary. All three of the systems distributed with this book will accept either domain-style addressing or bang paths. Since the mail server "knows about" mach6, it is not necessary for your local system to "know about" mach6. Note that it would be possible to set up a mail server to prevent this automatic forwarding, but for our purposes we would probably not wish to do so.

If the **pathalias** program is available, and can be used by your MUA, a set of "maps" could be constructed so that **mail** (or its substitute) could read the database constructed by **pathalias**, and from those data construct the extended address needed to get a message "from here to there." In a small mail network, such as that illustrated, that probably is not necessary. In a large system, it might become more of a requirement and become an issue in the selection of the software to be used.

Note that on many systems you may not be able to use forwarding with the **uucp** command. Forwarding is always enabled for **mail** messages. The reason for the restriction on forwarding using **uucp** is that the owners of any given system usually have the right to determine what they will pay for, and they may not wish to pay for your file to be sent to someone else. Even with **mail**, however, forwarding software may be configured to allow even mail messages of only limited sizes (typically 64K-100K). For the private E-Mail system we are designing and building, no such limitations have been built in. Remember, however, that you still may be using long distance lines which result in a charge to someone.

Various implementations of UUCP have different methods for controlling forwarding. In BSD 4.x systems a special command, **uusend**, is provided rather than **uucp**. The problem with this is that each computer in the forwarding chain must have implemented **uusend**. In System V-derived UNIX systems there are two files, *ORIGFILE* and *FWDFILE* that control forwarding. Taylor UUCP controls forwarding in the *sys* file with the `forward-to systemlist`, the `forward-from systemlist`, and `forward systemlist` options. If *"systemlist"* is coded as "ANY," then all forwarding is enabled. The `forward systemlist` combines the other two so coding `forward ANY` would enable all forwarding. If you happen to be using Taylor UUCP for your mail server, as you would if you used Coherent 4.2 or later, then you may want to enable forwarding in this manner. The default is to disable forwarding, although mail forwarding continues to function even when general **uucp** transfers may not include forwarding. As we have already noted in Chapter 7, Waffle also provides various options for forwarding and for these you should read the appropriate "doc" files that are distributed with that package.

Integrating LANs

If a node on our mail network was connected to a local area network (LAN), integrating all the LAN users into the mail network would be very simple. First, all the users on the LAN would use the same file system for mail. If the DOS drive name used all LAN users to access a directory on the LAN's file server is "F:" for example; the directory structure for Waffle might be: "F:/waffle/...". Each LAN user would need access to a copy of **waffle.exe** and **login.bat** in their own *waffle* directory. They would also need their own version of *waffle.cfg* and have their own Waffle environmental variables set properly. In addition, it might be appropriate for each user to have his/her own *waffle**extern* subdirectory with tailored versions of some of those configuration files. All users on the LAN would be addressed by the same system (machine) name, but with individual user names. **rmail** would regard all LAN users as local and deliver mail appropriately. **uucp** and other UUCP commands would not be used since each workstation can see the Waffle file structure as if it were located on a local disk drive rather than on the file server.

If there is a UNIX system on the LAN, the problem is only a little more complicated. The key is still to allow all machines on the LAN to use the same file system. This can be accomplished on the DOS machines by running a PC-based NFS (Network File System) program and by having NFS running on the UNIX machine. Through this technique a common mail file system could be defined used by both the UNIX and DOS machines and the PC workstations could simply appear as directories for the UNIX machine to deposit mail. In this case the UNIX machine would act as the mail server rather than a DOS machine operating Waffle or some other DOS package.

MANAGING THE NETWORK

There are several ways we might approach network management. One way would be to take a look at UUCP administration itself. That would entail discussions of the contents of the *spool* directory; methods of tracking UUCP activity; polling issues; and troubleshooting techniques. Unfortunately many of these issues tend to be system-dependent. For that reason, I refer you to the documentation of the particular implementation of the UUCP system you are using. For a discussion of UUCP administration on UNIX systems, see O'Reilly and Todino.[2]

Another way of looking at network administration is to address the very practical issues such as adding and deleting users; scheduling access to the server; and security. This is the approach we will use here since these can be among the more irritating and time-consuming chores. Moreover, they are also important when designing the mail system in the first place because some designs will be more or less efficient than others.

Adding and Deleting Users

An E-Mail system is a multiuser system. Otherwise there is no need for it. It shares with all multiuser systems the need to maintain the database of users. With any version of UUCP this means that whomever administers the mail system will have to work out a process to easily accomplish this chore in a timely fashion. The typical way is to edit the appropriate files, mostly (though not exclusively) on the mail server. When discussing the configuration of the mail server, above, we noted simple and more complex configuration files that had to be created or modified. This must happen every time a new user is added or one is deleted. In addition, an installation and configuration of the system on the user's workstation must also take place. Since the actual procedures to be used are dependent upon specific configurations, it is necessary to produce the instructions for this function after the installation is complete and working.

Scheduling Access to the Server

One technique that can assist you in managing a mail network, either as a mail user or as the manager of the mail server, is through the use of a task scheduler.

This is so that mail will be sent to and received from the server at regular intervals; at the most cost-effective times, and without much, if any, human intervention. The task scheduler that comes with UNIX is called **cron**. **cron** is a daemon that executes commands at preset times. Once each minute, cron searches for commands to execute.

For each entry in each command file, **cron** compares the current time with the scheduled execution time and executes the command if the times match. When it finishes the search, **cron** sleeps until the next minute. Because it never exits, **cron** should be executed only once (customarily by */etc/rc*). **cron** is designed for commands that must be executed regularly. Temporal commands that need to be executed only once should be handled with the command **at**.

There are a number of **cron**-like programs available for both DOS and Windows. As we have mentioned elsewhere, a number of software utility systems, such as *PC Tools*, also come with schedulers. Examples include **cronjr** for DOS and **wcron** for Windows (See Appendix C). **wcron** is a periodic task scheduler inspired by UNIX's cron utility. It is very commonly used on UNIX systems. **cron** (and **wcron** for that matter) is most useful for machines that run 24 hours a day, but it can be of a great help even for casual user. **wcron** lets you specify the time of execution of specific tasks. It can be used for one-shot executions and for periodic executions. People use it to make regular backups, remind them of something, start background tasks like file transfer or automated systems and more. The typical application for a scheduler for electronic mail is to have **wcron** or something else, execute a program that will request mail be sent or received from a remote system.

The particular port used for **uucico** on my system is also used by other communications processes. Normally it supports Procomm Plus for Windows running in host mode so that, for example, I can dial back into my system whenever I am on the road. So, at 11 and 3, Procomm/Host is terminated, then **go2.pif** is executed, followed by an execution of Procomm/Host so that I can again dial into the system. Once a week I also have a similar sequence timed to call out to the Naval Observatory, get the correct time, and reset my system clock. All this is done without my intervention by **wcron**. If cost were a factor, I could have the dialout made in the dead of night at the lowest telephone rates.

Similarly, on my UUCP host system, I could simply have the port and modem in answer mode only during specified hours rather than all the time. Some scheduling is also possible through parameters on records in the *systems* file. Through the use of **cron** or **wcron** relatively complicated scheduling procedures that take place on a regular basis can be set up.

Security

Network security involves the measures taken to protect a network from unauthorized access; accidental or willful interference with normal operations or destruction, including protection of physical facilities, software, and personnel security. The measures can range from instituting good operating procedures with periodic backups, to highly sophisticated access systems. For the sort of low-profile networks described in this book, security is not a top priority, but prudence would dictate that we give some reasonable thought and attention to the degree to which we should protect our mail network. Bear in mind that most security threats stem not from unauthorized access from the outside, but from people on the inside. There are also costs associated with taking security measures in the form of performance, more hassle, and the personnel resources required to maintain security.[3]

The most widely-publicized security incident in recent times, that of Robert Morris and the Internet Worm in November, 1988, resulted when Morris took advantage of flaws in the UNIX operating system and in the Internet protocols TCP/IP and SMTP (Simple Mail Transfer Protocol). While many of the openings that Morris' Worm used have since been closed, the case is quite instructive. Briefly, the Morris Worm took advantage of the standard *finger* program in networked UNIX systems; the *sendmail* program designed to route mail in a heterogeneous internetwork, and an attack on the file(s) used to contain UNIX passwords (which are user readable on a world-wide basis, although the passwords themselves are encrypted). By exploiting services provided by these elements, Morris' Worm was able to propagate itself across some 6,000 BSD (Berkeley) UNIX systems. Please note that the Worm infected *only* BSD UNIX systems, *not* MS/DOS (on PCs), UNIX V, VM, MVS, or VMS operating systems. One unfortunate aspect of this incident, among others, was that in exploiting what previously were thought of as features rather than flaws, some degradation of connective service will eventually be the outcome.

Although Morris was not accessing the Internet through UUCP, from the discussion of the UUCP configuration files earlier in this chapter it should be apparent that we can open our own systems to a similar attack. If we allow remote systems to read and write files at will on our local system and to execute many—if not most—of the programs on our system, someone could deposit something like Morris' worm and consume us. For this reason some modicum of concern must be exercised regarding our configuration. We also need to assess, even if informally, the cost of security versus the cost of a security threat becoming a reality.

There are many ways in which a system can become insecure. Modern computer systems, even single-user desktop computers, are complex devices. If a program is run that can alter one or more programs, the potential for viral infection exists. When a user runs a program written by someone else, compiled by a compiler, or linked to run-time libraries, use is made of code written by a large number of people (mostly unknown). All computing is a cooperative enterprise—even on a stand-alone workstation.

EXPANDING MAIL SERVICES

Once an electronic mail system is up and running, there are a variety of ways in which it can be expanded to provide additional services. On UNIX the mail system has for many years been used for event notification. File transfer is, of course, the purpose of UUCP itself, but transferring files with **mail** can often make the task less arduous.

Event Notification

Almost from the inception of UNIX, E-Mail has been used as a technique for informing appropriate people about the status of the system or of system events, such as failed backups. Similarly, applications developers have built into their software various mail notifications. One accounting package, for example, has an alert feature that can send a mail message to the corporate controller when requests are made that would put a department's expenditures over its budget. Other operating systems have not made such extensive use of mail. On single-user machines, such as IBM (compatible) or Macintoshes, notification by mail is hardly necessary because the user is typically at the machine when something happens. On multiuser systems governed by other operating systems, accessing the mail system has not been as easy or convenient as on UNIX.

However, once PCs are grouped together in a network event notification can become as important as it is on a multiuser UNIX system. The set of programs that come with implementations of uucp under DOS provide the tools for issuing event notifications with E-Mail. Such things as the success or failure of unattended backups of a LAN file server, along with error messages, specific notifications from programs, and similar activities could be sent to appropriate people for followup.

Moving Files

uucp itself, of course, was designed as a file transfer system between UNIX machines. To use uucp in this fashion is very simple:

```
uucp myfile yoursystem!/usr/spool/uucppublic
```

or, in terms of our ongoing illustrations, if I, as "Tom," wanted to send a file to "Bev:"

```
uucp myfile mach6!/usr/spool/uucppublic
```

or, since Bev has a DOS system running UUPlus™,

```
uucp myfile mach6
```

Note that "Bev" is not mentioned in the forgoing **uucp** command. When transferring files from one system to another using **uucp**, we are limited by the *Permissions (permissn)* granted us at the remote site. The file *myfile*, will therefore, simply be transferred to the remote directory */usr/spool/uucppublic* or to *\uuplus\spool*. I will still have to phone or E-Mail Bev to let her know that there should be a file waiting for her.

An alternative is to use E-Mail and send the file attached as an E-Mail message. This way, when the file arrives, Bev will be notified that the mail has arrived. The MUA will display the "subject" line so that through the subject line you can inform her that she has a file waiting rather than "real" mail. The only "glitch" in this procedure is that a mail header (and your signature file) will be attached to the file and that header may need to be removed. Also, some versions of **mail** do not provide a menu of waiting messages, so the header information may simply scroll by. In the case of the version of **mail** distributed with UUPlus™, it will list all waiting messages and it provides a means for saving a message in a file. Some fairly elementary procedures can be set up, however, that take care of most of these problems.

First, large files will be transferred more quickly if they are compressed into smaller files. Second, those files that can be classed as binary files such as programs, compressed files, some kinds of word processing files (WordPerfect files, for example), and graphics files, may need to be processed through programs that will turn them into files composed only of printable characters. Furthermore, if you are communicating with a system, or your files must pass through a system, that uses a 7-bit word length in their asynchronous communications, then your files will also have to processed in this fashion. A useful compression utility is the GNU program, **gzip**. **gzip** has been ported to DOS and is, of course, available on UNIX. It works the same way on both systems. Learn how to use it by typing, at the DOS prompt,

```
gzip -h
```

The "standard" UNIX programs for processing files to run in a 7–bit environment are **uuencode** and **uudecode**. These two encode and decode files, respectively, into a 7-bit space. The methods for doing this are somewhat limited, so the size of the file may end up being larger than the original.

One way to use these programs easily would be to write a short batch file that will call them, then call the mail program. The individual commands would be written as follows for an original file named *test.aaa*:

```
gzip test.aaa
```

The result of running **gzip** is a file named *test.aaz*. **uuencode** is then run:

```
uuencode test.aaz > test.uue
```

resulting in a compressed and uuencoded file, *test.uue*. It is *test.uue* that we will now mail:

```
mail -s "File test.uue" tmadron < test.uue
```

The subject of the mail message is the quoted phrase following the "-s" option. The subject line is followed by the address ("tmadron"), and what is to be sent is the file *test.uue*.

When we type the **mail** command, we will get something like the following sequence, which indicates that we have several files. This one happens to be message 7:

Author, Christopher J. Ambler

c:\uuplus\spool\mail\tmadron: 5 messages, 0 new 2 unread
  R1 Thomas Wm. Madron   15/434 "test from waffle on server"
  R2 Thomas Wm. Madron   19/516 "Test of forwarding fromWinnet to UU-
Plus"
 >U3 Thomas_Wm._Madron   44/939 ""
  U4 Thomas_Wm._Madron   30/1313 "uuencoded config file"
  R5 Thomas_Wm._Madron   14/377 "test"

>>4

From tmadron Thu Mar 03, 1994 14:45:10 EST
Received: by madron.uucp (UUPlus-1.50)
    id D4815oK Thu Mar 03, 1994 14:45:10 EST
From: tmadron@madron.uucp (Thomas_Wm._Madron)
Message-Id: <9403031445.D4815oK@madron.uucp>
X-Mailer: FSMail version 1.42
Date: Thu Mar 03, 1994 14:45:10 EST
Subject: uuencoded config file
To: tmadron@madron.uucp
Status: R

```
begin 666 uuplus.cfg
 M(R!!#;VYF#:6=U<F%%T:6]N(&9I;&4@9F]R($\93555#4"!697]S6;]N(#(#($(-
 M"B@,.-"B@,3&EN97,7,@8F5G;:6YN6YG('=I=&@@,B@,B@(B&R921C;;VUM96YT<PT*
 M(R!";;;&%N:R!L;6YE<R!A<F4@:6=N;W)E9 T*(R!!(5;]M870*870Z('R!!&EO
 M(@D)=F%L=64@-64@-"B@,.-"B@,T&5AI-R!F:6QE(&)E6]E960;#.691960@&\@
 M(65E="*!Y;;;;W5R('-P96-I9FEC(&-;;VYF:6=U<F%T:6]N#OH-"B@,H-"B@,@
 M4WES=&5M($5N9F]R6%T:6]N#OIS5(@-N86UE"'OEM861R;VXB+V5C+875U;(]G
 M;F%M90D);6%D<F]N(&US;WIU<V5R+F%5A;87);GT@-"G-M87]T&:&]S=S= EE
 M=V-U-U=&6-P#OI=8-87()()<6%I;&X&=&R861R;6]E"40-"FES=W-G&VQ%D90.
 M#OIC86QL9!P#9%)A9&!$6@T&@O#HC($$$II=&5C=&1]R2!])F90.<FUA=BE$O;]M
 M9090D)8SI<9G-UR&=6-!"A064"-"G-P#"YL"OEC.E"0F<FW58!888W!!!<W!O;VP-"FQI
 M8F%II<@D))8S!)<9G-UR&=6-!"Q8!@@@@<J<'5B'5B965"OEC.EQQ5888BW5888!<P[VX
 M=7C<C%0'P[)L=6QE"XY9B6S8"L-"@@@&ME$:)$I6L;([6,7$[]7!M%E;0D)99])&E[%-
 --MORE--
```
<spacebar>

```
 M.EQF<W58W5888!<<W!O;VP;7VQL;7W5E '@@@@@@-75C<%QL;;$L==V%=9BA==@E)&E]
 M#OIH&Y5"0B@@1&5!5!@:2?B5R92!)O;9O$<$&5E"Q064692'.O.E%5V:7-U[(%)=86@;)R!G;9I
 M.E'V&1!'G&]]@&S@D(;7@(MY.RD)5999Y>F&%T:6]N(&)E6]E960@'X7]L]R6]]]^;$+E-
 :<V4M5VED&E$92!#;;OV&T;P.&:S<EG8&VW.:6Z6!!6@GE]
```

end

>>s c:\test.txt

>>q

The characters in **boldface** type are my input from the keyboard. In this instance I wanted to read message #4 then write it (using the "s" command) to a file called *test.txt*. The name you save the message to is entirely arbitrary because the original filename that was uuencoded is part of the message itself. I was then returned to the **mail** prompt (">>") so that I could go on reading mail. The use of the "s" command retains the mail header, while if I had used the "w," the file (in this case, just the uuencoded file) would contain only the message without the header. At that point I typed "q" for quit.

The file that was delivered was the following:

```
From tmadron Thu Mar 03, 1994 14:45:10 EST
Received: by madron.uucp (UUPlus-1.50)
id D4815oK Thu Mar 03, 1994 14:45:10 EST
From: tmadron@madron.uucp (Thomas_Wm._Madron)
Message-Id: <9403031445.D4815oK@madron.uucp>
X-Mailer: FSMail version 1.42
Date: Thu Mar 03, 1994 14:45:10 EST
Subject: uuencoded config file
To: tmadron@madron.uucp
Status: R
begin 666 uuplus.cfg
M(R!!#;;;;VYF:6=;U<F%T:6]N(&9I;&4@9F]R($($93555#4"!697)S:6]N(#$$$N-#((-
M"B,-"B,,@3&EN97?,@8F5G;;6YN:6YG(&'=I=&=&'-&&(;,B,B(&%R92!C;;VUM96YT<PT*
M(R!";;&&%N:R;L;&6YE<R!A<F&4@:6=N;W)E9 T*(R!!&;;W)M870@@M870O7Z#HOC&&]P=&$E$
M;;@@D)D)=F5L=64-""&'-""&'@@5&'AI<R!F:6QE(&%S($&&&UU@@8@:D)D:691960@=&\@
M;65E="=!Y;W55R('-96-I9FEC('-Y;2!C;VYF:6=U<F%T:6]N.H-""B,-""B,,@@
M4WES=&5M($$EN9F]R;6%T:6]N.IS>7-&UE"@;86UE''40=&'4=;4'=%.W=5<C T&]G9G]G
M;F%M90D);6%D<F]N('5U8W D86Y0;64-&4F-87&']T*;&'4&85T<;2!;;&YS= EE
M=V5U<6-$P#96G6;87&96#'04 T*;6,&'='6&9&]'&]96.$[,V-96FE[&&R1861E"40-""&'YFE.
M;#OIC86:9L==CV)A&A9&&Z@=H@`A$I&<F%C=!S=5)R2!);X2R!)9&90=;?UA&=;]M
M90D)8SI<9G-=U=6-P#7&&A/780;;064#"-"G-P@-"G&];7"$$2;=0#?;$O&$C$EF<5;&JF
M8F8F1I<@@@D)8SI<9G-=U&-P@7&&]QI8@T*<'$%85893E;9&&'%9E<F0&%'&]YP;@]O.C&&]MO&Z
M=75C<$<%Q%8;;$09L;8:;,T*]D;F9;&;6Y9S=5;&'<:1;;;&O&;&N9=7,@=&?56;;4'4&'&'!
M.E&?F?&=VX@F9O<;@@d)8#:<@9E8:$:.%$$$&:D]F97?@-""&'D86YS;69E<@;86UE"#:<89
M&EE8:.$=#0@T*;6=&=$5*@&&;T;&6;&>=;&^5<:49&&9=,&'40;9=4@&&'6'&04&'&&=#3=#'$#&2;;&'E
M9;&P#&N9#$A(;.#9&&&6=4D?X&&9`]&'&$!@7&/F&)#;;&'4#'79;;/&;YF<2=;?19%3#&#$&
:<V4M5VED92!#;VUP=71I;F<@8V]F:6=U<F%T:6]N('5U5G-&>5VLG"G1
```

```
end
```

The actual file transferred was the material that extends from the word "begin" to the word "end." The information at the beginning is the standard E-Mail header, and the information at the bottom could be signature file information. In order to **uudecode** this file we simply issue the command,

```
uudecode test.uue
```

which results in the file *uuplus.cfg*. You can see this file name on the line above that begins with "begin". The **uudecode** program ignores everything outside the "begin" and "end" keywords so you do not have to manually deal with the mail header and the signature information. One of the reasons for uuencoding files is that some systems may not be able to accept full 8-bit data. This means that any characters above ASCII 127 would become corrupted. In addition, the "control" characters, ASCII 0-31, sometimes carry information that can interfere with a network (some equipment may be turned off with an XOFF character, for example). Thus, only the printable ASCII characters 32-127 are used to uuencode information. By saving the file without the mail header information (using the "w" command) only the message portion of the mail message would be saved. In this illustration the file transferred was not compressed. If it had been compressed, however, we are now ready to uncompress the file, which we do with **gzip** using the "-d" option.

This process may seem a bit arduous, but it ensures that the files that are transferred, regardless of the systems through which they pass, will arrive precisely as they started out. At the very least, even if you do not uuencode the file, unless it is very small, it should probably be processed with **gzip**. This will minimize the transfer time but it makes the file that is transferred more difficult with which to deal and may require that you remove the header and signature information by hand. Moreover, MUAs such as **cmm** in Windows and **pcelm** in DOS, make the process a bit easier, particularly **cmm** since it has built-in uuencode/uudecode facilities. Literally any file can be transferred in the manner illustrated. Other compression programs could, of course, be used as long as they are available for decompression on the other end.

Compression is an increasingly important issue in that some "small" files can grow to enormous proportions. For example, if you embedded a sound bite as an object in a Windows **Write** file, with only a few lines of text, the size of the file could easily be well over 100,000 bytes. If we added a graphic, say a .bmp file that illustrated what the sound bite described, it could grow to a million bytes. Even when transferring such a file with a reasonably high-speed modem it will take a while to transfer. If you can reduce the size of the file by around 50%, you will have effectively doubled the transfer rate. This is exactly what the newer modems do that have compression facilities. The problem is that even today not everyone can take advantage of the "smart" modems, so some additional compression technique is desirable.

The description I have just given for transferring files is fairly standard operating procedure for UUCP. The use of compression techniques and uuencoding can be used with the **uucp** command as well as with **mail**. The advantage of using **mail** for this purpose is that the file ends up in your own home directory, one over which you always have complete control. This issue is not as critical on a single-user DOS system as it might be on a UNIX machine or on a LAN. On the latter two, however, it could be a real productivity problem for your file to always be deposited in the public directory of the system.

The process using Waffle is similar to the illustration given using UUPlus™. If you are using WinNet™ Mail, however, then the process of extracting an embedded uuencoded file is more automatic. In that instance when you click on the "Mail" menu item, another drop-down menu presents itself. There are two relevant options: "Attach Binary File" and "Detach Binary File." If you are composing mail and wish to include a file in uuencoded format, you use the "Attach" option. If you are reading mail and wish to uudecode a file, then you use the "Detach" option. Remember that many files, such as WordPerfect or many other word processing files, programs, and spreadsheet files, among others, must all be treated as binary files. Of course, even text files may be treated that way.

Sending Faxes and Other Enhancements

On a final note for this chapter we might speculate a little about features you may be able to build into your E-Mail system. These are given as ideas you may wish to explore rather than as final solutions to problems you may face or requests you may receive. The first possibility that comes to mind is adding the ability to send E-Mail out a FAX/MODEM board in a PC so that people solely dependent on FAX can also be part of your E-Mail network. A couple of possibilities come to mind as to how this might be implemented in the context of a UUCP-based mail system. First, with Waffle there is an explicit procedure available for adding FAX capabilities. Second, with other systems it may be possible to redirect the mail message to the FAX board, given some additional software. There is available, for example, a small subsystem for Waffle called XFAX, which provides inbound (receiving) FAX capabilities for Waffle. It is available in the Simtel archive on the Internet.[4]

Other enhancements which might be investigated for some circumstances would be text-to-speech software and hardware that would read the text of messages to the user. The ability to use multimedia devices and techniques to enhance mail messages is also of some utility and is developing a growing demand. Such facilities are available today, but it remains to be seen whether they can be made effective to use.

REFERENCES

1. The UUCP "address" is actually more analogous to a path than to a file than to an address as used with the Internet. A "bang path" is one in which there is one or more machines listed with the recipient's username the last in the list. Each of these elements is separated by an exclamation point, which in this context is called a "bang."

2. Tim O'Reilly and Grace Todino, *Managing UUCP and Usenet* (Sebastopol, CA: O'Reilly & Associates, Inc., 1990), Chapter 6.

3. For a complete treatment of network security, see Thomas Wm. Madron, *Network Security in the '90s: Issues and Solutions for Managers* (New York: John Wiley & Sons, 1992).

4. If you do not have access to the Internet, the Simtel MS-DOS archive is also available on CDROM from the following: Walnut Creek CDROM, Suite 260, 1547 Palos Verdes Mall, Walnut Creek, CA 94596; Telephone: 510-675-0783; or via E-Mail: infor@cdrom.com. This CDROM contains Waffle, a number of Waffle add-ons, as well as other DOS-based UUCP software.

10

Beyond Your Private Network

Many of the materials available concerning UUCP, usually address one of two topics: very technical details about the system, or what a great invention Usenet is. To the extent that Usenet and the Internet are related, much the same can be said for books on the Internet (and there are a huge number with new ones weekly). In this book I have taken a considerably different approach by trying to show how to design and implement a private E-Mail network based on UUCP. For a variety of reasons, I would be remiss in not devoting one chapter to the issue of networking beyond the private system. Depending on your specific local situation it may or may not be useful to be connected to the national and world networks. But this overview should give you some information upon which to make a decision to accept or reject it.

USENET AND INTERNET

In this chapter, I will try to give a short introduction to the issues and character of Usenet and the Internet. As mentioned above, a large number of books are available on the topic of the Internet, and virtually all of them devote some space to Usenet. If you need more information than is presented here, I would suggest that you acquire some of the currently available literature.[1]

An internet is a network comprised of a collection of networks interconnected with routers. The Internet (and enthusiasts often say it reverentially and with emphasis) is the largest internet in the world. It is a three-level hierarchy composed of backbone networks (e.g., NSFNET, MILNET), mid-level networks, and sub-networks. The Internet is a multiprotocol internet, although networks in the Internet normally use TCP/IP. They provide electronic mail, remote login, and file transfer services.

Usenet, sometimes confused with the Internet, is a collection of thousands of topically named newsgroups, the computers that run the protocols, and the people who read and submit Usenet news. Not all Internet hosts subscribe to Usenet and not all Usenet hosts are on the Internet. Usenet computers depend to a large (though not exclusive) extent on UUCP to provide the transport for news. The news travels on whatever medium is available, including the public telephone system. It may, however, also travel over the facilities (through gateways) of the Internet, BITNET, and EASYnet, using protocols such as NNTP and Notes as well as UUCP. As will be noted below, if you wish to obtain a registered domain name, one of the items of information you will have to furnish is a mail and news "feed" that is itself attached to the Internet.

If you have not, or do not intend to, register your system name, you will have to arrange for a mail and news feed as a user local and subordinate to a machine that acts as your mail server. Mail, as this book attests, is also carried by UUCP, but while the mail may be transported across the UUCP paths, it is often carried across Internet routes as well. This has led some, incorrectly, to call the network "UUCP." This lack of precision of language has even crept into RFC #1392, the "Internet Users' Glossary," where it is claimed that "Today, the term [UUCP] is more commonly used to describe the large international network which uses the UUCP protocol to pass news and electronic mail."[2] Obviously, some of these issues are confusing, even to those who use the resources extensively. It can be even more confusing to those just starting out.

A number of documents are available on the Internet and Usenet attempting to explain what they are. Unfortunately, if you do not already have access, they are very difficult to obtain. If you decide you want to expand your network horizons, the first thing you should probably do is sign up for some service that offers at least E-Mail access to the Internet, through Gateways, to much of Usenet. There are many such service providers including obvious ones like CompuServe, BIX, and others. Moreover, if you intend to register your UUCP system, you must have access to national/international E-Mail services.

ENTERING USENET

Since this is a book about the use of UUCP, we will concentrate on illustrating how to establish contact with Usenet rather than with the Internet *per se. Because of the close relationship between the two, however, especially in the areas of naming and addressing, there will be some shifting back and forth between discussions of Internet and Usenet issues. As a UUCP* host site you can, and should, apply for an Internet address even though you will access and be accessed through the network of UUCP sites rather than by the Internet directly.

One document, entitled "What is Usenet?" by Chip Salzenberg (chip@count.tct.com, last revised December 2, 1991) is widely distributed across Usenet. Some of this section is a very lightly edited rendition of Salzenberg's article.

What Usenet is Not (Quoted From Salzenberg)[3]

1. Usenet is not an organization.

   No person or group has authority over Usenet as a whole. No one controls who gets a news feed, which articles are propagated where, who can post articles, or anything else. There is no "Usenet Incorporated," nor is there a "Usenet User's Group." You are on your own.

   Various activities are organized by means of Usenet newsgroups. The newsgroup creation process is one such activity—but it would be a mistake to equate Usenet with the organized activities it makes possible. If those activities were to stop tomorrow, Usenet would go on without them.

2. Usenet is not a democracy.

   Since there is no person or group in charge of Usenet as a whole—i.e., there is no Usenet "government"—it follows that Usenet cannot be a democracy, autocracy, or any other kind of "-acy." (But see "The Camel's Nose?" below.)

3. Usenet is not fair.

   After all, who shall decide what's fair? For that matter, if someone is behaving unfairly, who is going to stop him or her?

4. Usenet is not a right.

   Some people misunderstand their local right of "freedom of speech" to mean that they have a legal right to use others' computers to say what they wish in whatever way they wish, and the owners of said computers have no right to stop them.

   Those people are wrong. Freedom of speech also means freedom not to speak. If I choose not to use my computer to aid your speech, that is my right. Freedom of the press belongs to those who own one.

5. Usenet is not a public utility.

   Some Usenet sites are publicly-funded or subsidized. Most of them, however, are not. There is no government monopoly on Usenet, and little or no government control over its activities.

6. Usenet is not an academic network.

   It is no surprise that many Usenet sites are universities, research labs or other academic institutions. Usenet originated with a link between two universities, and the exchange of ideas and information is what such institutions are all about. But the passage of years has changed Usenet's character. Today, most Usenet sites are commercial entities.

7. Usenet is not an advertising medium.

Because of Usenet's roots in academia, and because Usenet depends so heavily upon cooperation (sometimes among competitors), custom dictates that advertising be kept to a minimum. It is tolerated if it is infrequent, informative, and low-hype.

The "comp.newprod" newsgroup is NOT an exception to this rule: product announcements are screened by a moderator in an attempt to keep the hype-to-information ratio in check.

If you must engage in flackery for your company, use the "biz" hierarchy, which is explicitly "advertising-allowed", and which (like all of Usenet) is carried only by those sites that want it.

8. Usenet is not the Internet.

The Internet is a wide-ranging network, parts of which are subsidized by various governments. It carries many kinds of traffic, of which Usenet is only one. And the Internet is only one of the various networks carrying Usenet traffic.

9. Usenet is not a UUCP network.

UUCP is a protocol (actually a "protocol suite," but that's a technical quibble) for sending data over point-to-point connections, typically using dialup modems. Sites use UUCP to carry many kinds of traffic, of which Usenet is only one. UUCP is only one of the various transports carrying Usenet traffic.

10. Usenet is not a United States network.

It is true that Usenet originated in the United States, and the fastest growth in Usenet sites has been there in the U.S. Nowadays, however, Usenet extends worldwide.

The heaviest concentrations of Usenet sites outside the U.S. seem to be in Canada, Europe, Australia, and Japan.

Keep Usenet's worldwide nature in mind when you post articles. Even those who can read your language may have a culture wildly different from yours. When your words are read, they might not mean what you think they mean.

11. Usenet is not a UNIX network.

Don't assume that everyone is using "rn" on a UNIX machine. Among the systems used to read and post to Usenet are: Vaxen running VMS, IBM mainframes, Amigas, and MS-DOS PCs.

12. Usenet is not an ASCII network.

Those IBM mainframes used to participate in Usenet use (shudder) EBCDIC. Other sites use special character sets for non-English postings. Ignore non-ASCII sites if you like, but they exist.

13. Usenet is not software.

There are dozens of software packages used at various sites to transport and read Usenet articles. Thus, no one program or package can be called "the Usenet software."

Software designed to support Usenet traffic can be (and is) used for other kinds of communication, usually without risk of mixing the two.

Such private communication networks are typically kept distinct from Usenet by the invention of newsgroup names different from the universally-recognized ones.

What Usenet Is (Quoted from Salzenberg)

Usenet is the set of people who exchange articles tagged with one or more universally-recognized labels, called "newsgroups" (or "groups" for short). (Note that the term "newsgroup" is correct, while "area," "base," "board," "bboard," "conference," "round table," "SIG," etc. are incorrect. If you want to be understood, be accurate.)

Usenet History

Usenet came into being in late 1979, shortly after the release of V7 UNIX with UUCP. Two Duke University graduate students in North Carolina, Tom Truscott and Jim Ellis, thought of hooking computers together to exchange information with the UNIX community. Steve Bellovin, a graduate student at the University of North Carolina, put together the first version of the news software using shell scripts and installed it on the first two sites: "unc" and "duke."

At the beginning of 1980 the network consisted of those two sites and "phs" (another machine at Duke), and was described at the January Usenix conference. Steve Bellovin later rewrote the scripts into C programs, but they were never released beyond "unc" and "duke." Shortly thereafter, Steve Daniel did another implementation in C for public distribution. Tom Truscott made further modifications, and this became the "A" news release.[4]

In 1981, at U. C. Berkeley, graduate student Mark Horton and high school student Matt Glickman rewrote the news software to add functionality and to cope with the ever increasing volume of news—"A" News was intended for only a few articles per group per day. This rewrite was the "B" News version. The first public release was version 2.1 in 1982; the 1.* versions were all beta test. As the network grew, the news software was expanded and modified.

One of the reasons for the confusion between Usenet and the Internet is that a good deal of Usenet traffic takes place over the Internet. In March 1986 a package was released implementing news transmission, posting, and reading using the Network News Transfer Protocol (NNTP) (as specified in RFC 977). This protocol allows hosts to exchange articles via TCP/IP connections rather than using the traditional UUCP. It also permits users to read and post news (using a modified version of "rn" or other user agents) from machines which cannot or choose not to install the Usenet news software.

Reading and posting are done using TCP/IP messages to a server host which does run the Usenet software. Sites which have many workstations, like the Sun and Apollo products, find this a convenient way to allow workstation users to read news without having to store articles on each system. Many of the Usenet hosts that are also on the Internet exchange news articles using NNTP because the load impact of NNTP is much lower than UUCP (and NNTP ensures much faster propagation).

NNTP grew out of independent work in 1984-1985 by Brian Kantor at U.C. San Diego and Phil Lapsley at U. C. Berkeley. NNTP was developed at U. C. Berkeley by Phil Lapsley with help from Erik Fair, Steven Grady, and Mike Meyer, among others.

WHY DO IT?

After reading some of the "stuff" traveling around the newsgroups, one is tempted to say that there will never be a good reason for making the connection. Much of the information is wrong, misleading, insipid, and sophomoric. Yet, there are reasons for being connected. A primary reason is for access to a very broad-based E-Mail system that reaches around the world. A second is for the reasons the ARPANET, the predecessor of the Internet, was originally established by the U. S. Department of Defense: to support collaborative research by providing access to computer systems not available locally and/or to foster the writing of the results of research. The Internet is still widely used for these central purposes and not everyone can use the facilities in the same way.

The backbone networks in the United States have been largely funded by the U.S. Government. One of those networks is NSFNET, supported by the National Science Foundation, which has an "acceptable use policy" that suggests that transmission of commercial information or traffic is forbidden for transport across the NFS backbone. This is neither easy to regulate nor, on reflection, clearly interpretable. Obvious commercial examples might be purchase orders, invoices, and unsolicited advertising. Yet the policy also suggests that all information in support of academic research by universities and governments is acceptable. Presumably, if a research project were to send purchase orders to a vendor across the Internet, that is okay. Moreover, with commercial services now providing access to the Internet, the service provider's own networks may not have the same restrictions (probably will not) as the NSF.

Some people in academic and other not-for-profit environments suggest that the commercial service providers should not be allowed to profit from offering Internet services. If this opinion were followed it would severely restrict access to a small elite currently attached to an educational or other public institution. This is a point-of-view clearly at odds with the proposals for the Information Highway by Vice President Al Gore and others. These proposals generally assume open access to networking services. If this is to become a long-term reality then public policy will have to be established that encourages the development of low-cost internet services priced in a way that the vast majority of the American public can participate. The telephone system, and the fact that by 1980 virtually every household in the United States had at least minimal access to a telephone, was the result of policies enacted in the 1930s and delegated to the Federal Communications Commission to put into effect.

However, after all our reservations are noted there are two compelling reasons for connecting with the outside world. First, the extended E-Mail system available means that users can contact a very large and growing number of people. The reasons to do this are manifold. It may be a convenient way for the members of an organization, located in many different places to keep in touch. It may be a way of doing collaborative work of various kinds. It may provide users with the ability to deal, in a timely fashion, with associates in other parts of the world. The key to remember here is that even though no one (presumably) reviews E-Mail traffic for appropriateness, it is not a secure system. Anyone who needs high security needs a private system. Whatever you may not be able to reach through a private E-Mail system may be reachable through the national and international network of UUCP sites, and through gateways to the Internet and other E-Mail providers.

If we are sufficiently critical in our evaluation of the information we receive, the Usenet news groups can be a useful source of information. Regardless of the type of information you need, with the approximately 6,000 (more, if you include similar Internet facilities) news groups currently available, you can find several that address issues of concern to you, whether those concerns be professional or personal.

WHAT'S OUT THERE?

The amount of literature on the resources available on-line in the world is a large, and it is growing. I am not going to try to summarize it here. However, I will suggest a few sources that may get you started. Your service provider will be able to furnish you with lists of news groups to which you can "subscribe." These lists are available separately for Usenet and Internet. Both lists are sizeable. They are distributed electronically, and the Usenet file is currently about 150KB in size while the Internet list is about 550KB.

A number of easily-available books can point you in the appropriate direction. There are two classes of books that you may find useful. The first is books giving instruction on the use of Internet and/or Usenet. The second group is comprised of books listing resources on the networks. In the first category I have found the following four books useful:

> Tracey LaQuey and Jeanne C. Ryer, *The Internet Companion: A Beginner's Guide to Global Networking* (Reading, MA: Addison-Wesley Publishing Company, 1993), ISBN 0-201-62224-6.
>
> April Marine, Susan Kirkpatrick, Vivian Neou, and Carol Ward, *INTERNET: Getting Started* (Englewood Cliffs, NJ: PTR Prentice Hall, 1993), ISBN 0-13-327933-2.
>
> Tim O'Reilly and Grace Todino, *Managing uucp and Usenet* (Sebastopol, CA: O'Reilly & Associates, Inc., 1990), ISBN 0-937175-93-5. This is a more technical discussion than the others.
>
> Grace Todino and Dale Dougherty, *Using UUCP and Usenet* (Sebastopol, CA: O'Reilly & Associates, Inc., 1991), ISBN 0-937175-10-2.

Guides to resources are also becoming common. Any large bookstore will have several, and if these prove useful to you, you may have to pick up new editions periodically, since Usenet and Internet resources change and increase on virtually a daily basis. You might investigate the following:

> Edward T. L. Hardie and Vivian Neou (eds.), *INTERNET: Mailing Lists, 1993 Edition* (Englewood Cliffs, NJ: PTR Prentice Hall, 1993), ISBN 0-13-327941-3.
>
> Ed Krol, *The Whole Internet: User's Guide & Catalog* (Sebastopol, CA: O'Reilly & Associates, Inc., 1992), ISBN 1-56592-025-2.
>
> Peter Rutten, Albert F. Bayers III, and Kelly Maloni, *net guide: Your Map to the Services, Information and Entertainment on the Electronic Highway* (New York: Random House Electronic Publishing, 1994), ISBN 0-679-75106-8. This is literally a list of information resources on a wide variety of networks including the Internet and Usenet but extending beyond them.

Additional literature is listed in Appendix A.

HOW-TO-GET

A variety of books and articles are available that give instructions on how to get connected with Usenet and/or the Internet, and I will give only a brief outline here. Much of the information comes from a useful little article from Usenet by Jonathan Kamens titled, "How to become a USENET site."[5] One of the assumptions made by Kamens, and one that must be emphasized, is that you "already have some sort of USENET access ... or at the very least, that you have ftp or mail server access to get to some of the files mentioned in it, and that you are trying to configure your own site to be on the USENET after using some other site for some period of time." He goes on to add, if "this assumption is incorrect, then ask whoever made this article available to you to help you get access to the resources mentioned below." If you have not already done so, therefore, you should immediately join one of the easily accessed commercial services that offer, at a minimum, E-Mail gatewayed to the Internet. These services are widely available, but they include large ones such as CompuServe, BIX, Delphi, and others, and small ones such as WinNET. The latter, by the way, provides full UUCP access to Usenet.

Kamens suggests that "there are five basic steps involved in configuring a machine to be a USENET site." These five steps are reproduced from Kamens' article:

> **1.** Make the decision—do you really want to do this?
>
> If you just want to read USENET yourself, then putting your machine onto the USENET is probably not what you want to do. The process of doing so can be time-consuming, and regular maintenance

is also required. Furthermore, the resources consumed by a full USENET setup on a machine are significant:

- disk space for the programs (a few Mb for the binaries, another couple of MB for any sources you keep online),
- disk space for the articles—currently approaching 400MB a month,
- modem time (possibly long-distance) transferring the articles to your machine (assuming that you are using a modem rather than an Internet NNTP connection),
- fees (if you are paying someone to provide you with a news feed).

You might choose, instead, to get an account on a public-access USENET site on which you can read news by dialing up.

Even if there are no public-access USENET sites which are a local phone call away from you, you might still choose this approach, especially if you only read a few low-traffic groups. Using a public-access site, which is accessible via PC Pursuit or some other packet network might be cheaper and/or easier than setting up the feed, transferring the news and configuring your machine to store news locally.

You should be sure that the benefits you are going to get by storing news locally, are going to outweigh the costs before deciding to proceed. However, this decision is not always a clear one. To explain why, let me include an alternative perspective, from joe@jshark.rn.com, on why getting a feed may be appropriate even for a single-user machine.

When you get to long distance calls, reading the news on-line gets the cost rising fast. A few seconds to skip an article you've no interest in, maybe a minute to take in a good one plus more time to save it and download it later. But when the whole lot is batched together (as news), a) it only takes a few minutes and b) it's all conveniently automated. Sure, configuring the hardware and software may take a (small) time—but it's something you only do once.

And unless you want to get comp.*, the disk space needed is not that great. (20MB disks are about 100 dollars over here; the savings in phone charges would pay for that in a few months.)

I also find that replying takes time, and this is where on-line "reading" would start to really burn dollars! The alternative, { download - logout - compose reply - dial back in - login - post (or mail) reply}, is a) inconvenient and b) still costly.

Perhaps I see "news administration" as a simple task because I only provide news to one other site and get a very limited feed. (No overflowing disks, no "disappearing nodes," neither angry users nor management.) The initial stages were a bit fraught (200kb batches being bounced back because of permission problems), but very little effort now.

2. Find a site to feed news and/or mail to you.

In order to make your machine a USENET site, you need to find other sites on the USENET that are willing to feed news and/or mail to you. You might want to locate more than one such site if you want higher reliability.

Finding feeds for a UUCP site.

If you are going to be using a modem (and, presumably, UUCP) to transfer your news and mail, then there are several resources you can use when trying to locate a feed site:

a. Comp.mail.maps

Find the postings in the comp.mail.maps news group for your state, country, or whatever. Look through it for sites that sound like they are local to you. Contact their administrators, and ask if they would be willing to give you a feed.

Comp.mail.maps is archived at several anonymous ftp and mail server sites, including uunet.uu.net, so you can examine map entries even if the maps have expired at your news-reading site (or if you do not currently have USENET access). See the article entitled "UUCP map for README" in the comp.mail.maps news-group or archives for more information about the maps.

The comp.mail.maps postings are also archived in pit-manager.mit.edu's periodic posting archive, which was mentioned in detail above.

b. News.admin

Post a message to news.admin. If at all possible, post it with a restricted distribution, so that only people who are likely to be able to give you a feed will have to get it (e.g. if you have posting access on a machine in Massachusetts, and the site you are setting up is going to be in Massachusetts, then post with a distribution of "ne").

Note that you can post to news.admin even if you do not have direct USENET access right now, as long as you have E-Mail access—send your message to news-admin@ucbvax.berkeley.edu. However, if you use ucbvax's gateway, you probably cannot use a restricted distribution as described above, since ucbvax probably is not in the distribution you want to post to, and besides, it's not clear that it listens to the "Distribution:" header in postings that are mailed to it.

When posting your message, try to be as specific as possible. Mention where you are, how you intend to transfer news from your feed site to you (e.g. what kind of modem, how fast), approximately how many news groups you are going to want to get and from which hierarchies, and perhaps what kind of machine is being used. A descriptive Subject line such as "news feed wanted—Boston, MA" is also useful.

If there is a regional hierarchy for the distribution in which you want a feed, then you might want to post a message in one of the regional newsgroups as well, or cross-post your message to one of the regional newsgroups. Look first for an "admin" group (e.g.

"ne.admin"), then (if there is no admin group) a "config" group, then for a "wanted" group.

c. Commercial services

If all else fails, you may have to resort to paying someone to provide you with a feed. [A list of such service providers may be found in Appendix B.]

Some regional network service providers, especially in large urban areas, offer both UUCP and TCP/IP service via modem or leased line. If you can find such a company, the cost of a dedicated (leased line) Internet connection will often be cheaper and more desirable than a UUCP connection, if you plan on using it for a full newsfeed or for frequent downloading. Some companies can offer combined voice and data connections using T1 links, for large-scale users seeking both Internet access and low-cost toll telephone service. For more information about the possibility of hooking up to the network, see the "How to Get Information about Networks" posting in news.announce.newusers.

d. European users

In Europe, you can get a feed from one of EUNet's national networks. They charge for feeds but are "non-commercial," which means (I assume) that the fees go to the maintenance of the networks. Most provide help on getting started, as well as can sources for the mail and news software and lists of sites which have indicated that will provide feeds. They also act as Internet forwarders (see below for more information on this). To contact them, try sending mail to postmaster@country.eu.net or newsmaster@country.eu.net. The "country" in this case should be whatever country you are in.

Note that the national networks have a "no redistribution" policy and have the option to cut off sites which break this rule. There are other groups (such as sublink); see (a) and (b) above for suggestions on how to contact them.

Note that it is to your advantage to try to find a feed site that is directly on the Internet, if you are not going to be. Getting a feed from a site on the Internet will allow that site to act as your MX forwarder (see section 5 below), and the fact that you are only one hop off of the Internet will make both mail and news delivery fast (assuming that the feed you get from the Internet site is for both mail and news; of course, if you can only find someone willing to forward mail to you but not to traffic with you the heavier load of a news feed, then your mail delivery will still be fast).

Finding feeds for an Internet site.

If you are on the Internet and would like your news feed to be over the Internet rather than over a modem link, then you might want to look in the UUCP maps in comp.mail.maps, as mentioned above, since many USENET sites that are on the Internet are mentioned there. News.admin and the commercial services listed above are also viable options. Another option which is relevant only to Internet sites is to send mail to the mailing list nntp-managers@ucbvax.berkeley.edu, and ask if anyone on that list is willing to provide you with a news feed. If you do this, be specific, just as if you were posting to news.admin as described above.

3. Get the software.

The "USENET Software" posting referenced above goes into quite a bit of detail about the software that is available. There are three components in the software at a USENET site: (a) the software that transports the news (usually using either UUCP or NNTP), (b) the software that stores the news on the local disks, expires old articles, etc., and (c) the news-readers for looking at the news.

For example, if you are a UNIX site on the Internet and you will be getting your news feed over the Internet, then you are probably going to want to get the NNTP and C news packages mentioned in the "USENET Software" posting, as well as one or more of the UNIX news readers mentioned there.

Since you are probably going to be exchanging mail as well as news, and the mail software that is shipped with the OS you are using might not be powerful enough to handle mail exchanging with the rest of the USENET, you might want to obtain new mail software as well. There are several packages you might choose you use. Discussion of them is beyond the scope of this document; the books referenced below will probably provide some useful information in this area.

Europeans can ask their national backbone site, which will usually also be a software archive, or be closely associated with one. UKC, for example, provide an information pack explaining what is needed and where (and how) to get it.

4. Do what it says.

Most of the software available for news transport or storage comes with installation instructions. Follow them. This part should be self-explanatory (although the instructions might not be :-).

5. Register your site on the network.

[The remaining information in Kamens' article, which deals with how sites are registered and what is necessary for registration, is incorporated into the section below, entitled, "Getting a Domain Name."]

Naming Your Computer

RFC # 1178 set guidelines for naming your own machine and is reprinted in Appendix H. If you elect to obtain a DNN (Internet) name, the domain name(s) will be assigned to you. See Appendix I for further details on obtaining a name in the "us" domain. The suggestions made below are well taken for the naming of your own system for either Usenet or Internet purposes. As noted elsewhere, when you set up your *Permissions* (or *sys* if using Taylor uucp) file you have the opportunity to specify the "MYNAME" option. This lets you be known by one name locally and by another name to a specific remote system if, for some reason, you cannot manage consistent names. It would be simpler, however, to use the same name locally and remotely when logging onto the system that provides news and mail feeds.

As the author of RFC # 1178 notes, "in order to easily distinguish between multiple computers, we give them names. Experience has taught us that it is as easy to choose bad names as it is to choose good ones." RFC # 1178 presents guidelines for deciding what makes a name good or bad. As soon as you deal with more than one computer, you need to distinguish between them. For example, to tell your system administrator that your computer is busted, you might say, "Hey Ken. Goon is down!" Computers also have to be able to distinguish between themselves. Thus, when sending mail to a colleague at another computer, you might use the command "mail libes@goon".

Selecting the "right" name for your computer can, therefore, be quite important. Among the most common mistakes people make is to use "cute" names such as "startrek" or "enterprise" or something similar. First, since there are now several million people networked via Usenet and Internet, all the "good" (translation: "fun") names are taken. Second, your machine name should probably be somewhat more descriptive of yourself or your organization, although the use of your own name should also be avoided just to decrease the confusion factor. These and other issues are discussed in RFC # 1178 and will not be repeated here. Suffice it to say that this particular RFC should be read regardless of whether you will be connecting to the world or limiting your mail network to private uses.

Getting a Domain Name[6]

The past several years have witnessed a dramatic increase in the number of sites choosing to register host names in the Internet Domain Name Service (DNS) hierarchy, in addition to getting a host entry added to the UUCP maps. The former is a formal and "official" service; the latter a voluntary but useful service sponsored by the USNIX organization. Full instructions for registering a name with DNS may be found in RFC # 1480 (June, 1993), reprinted in Appendix I. If you choose not to register your name with DNS, then E-Mail will come to you through the domain name of your UUCP service provider. The DNS hierarchy is becomingly increasingly standardized, and DNS name service is more reliable than the UUCP maps. Therefore, if you register a DNS name for your site, put that DNS name in your UUCP map entry as an alias for your site, and use the DNS address rather than the UUCP host name in your mail and USENET postings. Both UUCP hosts and hosts that do DNS will be able to get mail to you more efficiently and reliably. Please refer to Appendix I for full instructions on obtaining DNS registration. This section will only provide a brief overview of the process.

The Domain Name System (DNS) provides for the translation between hostnames and addresses. Within the Internet, this means translating from a name such as "venera.isi.edu," to an IP address such as "128.9.0.32." The DNS is a set of protocols and databases. The protocols define the syntax and semantics for a query language to ask questions about information located by DNS-style names. The databases are distributed and replicated. There is no dependence upon a single central server, and each part of the database is provided in at least two servers.

Even if you are not going to be connecting directly to Internet at the start, if your site is using any TCP/IP-based equipment, you should request a block of IP addresses, to save future transition headaches. Request one Class C address per subnet, or a Class B if your site has more than a few hundred systems. The assignment of the 32-bit IP addresses is a separate activity. IP addresses are delegated by the central Internet Registry to regional authorities (such as the RIPE NCC for Europe) and the network providers. To have a network number assigned, contact your network service provider or regional registration authority. To determine who this is (or as a last resort), you can contact the central Internet Registry at Hostmaster@INTERNIC.NET. As Kamens has remarked, "If you don't understand any of this and don't intend on getting on the Internet, don't worry about it. If/when you do decide to get onto the Internet, your service provider should be prepared to help you understand what needs to be done."

In addition to translating names to addresses for hosts that are on the Internet, the DNS provides for registering DNS-style names for other hosts reachable (via electronic mail) through gateways or mail relays. The records for such name registrations point to an Internet host (one with an IP address) that acts as a mail forwarder for the registered host. For example, the host "bah.rochester.ny.us" is registered in the DNS with a pointer to the mail relay "relay1.uu.net". This type of pointer is called an MX record. There are actually two types of DNS host records that are relevant here. If you have opted to contract with a company for a direct connection to the Internet, then you are probably going to want to register an address record advertising what your address will be on the Internet. Hosts which understand DNS can then use that record to connect directly to your machine and deliver mail to it. If, on the other hand, you are going to be getting your mail via UUCP from some other site, then the host record you will be registering is a Mail eXchange (MX) record.

The function of the MX record is to announce to the world that mail destined to your host can be directed instead to another host that is directly on the Internet. That host is your "MX forwarder," and it must be one of your feed sites that knows how to deliver mail to you. It is possible to have multiple MX records if you have multiple feeds on the Internet and want it to be possible for mail to be routed through more than of them. If you use a commercial service provider for your mail feed, it will probably also be your MX forwarder.

The procedure for registering a DNS record is relatively simple and usually takes a month or less. Note that many commercial network providers, such as UUNET, will take care of this for you for a small fee. Whether you decide to register an address record or an MX record, you need to decide what your DNS host name is going to be. Since the DNS is arranged in a hierarchy, you need to decide what hierarchy your name will appear in. For example, you might choose to be in the ".us" domain if you are in the United States and want to be in the United States geographical hierarchy. Alternatively, you might choose ".edu" for a University, ".org" for a non-profit organization, ".com" for a commercial company. For the purposes of this book, however, the use of the ".us" domain would be adequate. If you are not in the U.S., theoretically you are supposed to have no choice about the top-level domain—it should always be the two-letter ISO code for your country (".fr", ".de", etc.). If you want to find out how to get a host name in a particular European domain, you can probably start by sending mail to hostmaster@mcsun.eu.net and asking for more information.

You will need to ensure that you are listed with a "name server" that will advertise your host name to anyone who asks for it. Assuming that you have opted to register in the ".us" domain, there are currently seven name servers available:

```
venera.isi.edu
ns.isi.edu
rs.internic.net
ns.csl.sri.com
ns.uu.net
adm.brl.mil
excalibur.usc.edu
```

See RFC # 1480 for details. Once your application has been approved and your name entered into your name servers' databases, update the mail software on your system and on your MX forwarder's system to recognize and use the new domain.

The UUCP Mapping Project

The "traditional" method of advertising your site to the rest of the USENET after setting it up is to get an entry for it added to the UUCP maps. Since many USENET sites still rely exclusively on the UUCP maps for routing mail, you will almost certainly want to register in the maps that are maintained by the *UUCP Mapping Project* is a working group of the USENIX organization. The USENIX instructions for map registration may be found in Appendix J. The *UUCP Mapping Project* is a voluntary group of people who collect information from all sites that communicate via UUCP. The information available to any other site on the network of UUCP systems. Through the use of the maps, in conjunction with the program **pathalias,** you and your E-Mail software can compute the most efficient path between one site and another.

WHERE TO GET SERVICES

There is a growing list of organizations that provide mail and news feeds. If you happen to be part of a university, a government agency, or a large corporation, you may be able to obtain services directly and at low or no cost. These are typically the organizations that have paid the high price of high speed, full-time access to the Internet. Some of these organizations may also sell the service to outsiders. If you are like me, the sole proprietor of a very small company, or if your organization cannot legally or ethically obtain services from a governmental, academic, or large corporate entity, then you will have to go to one or another of the service providers that now exist to take care of the rest of us. I have provided, in Appendix B, a list of commercial service providers. The best known, although not necessarily the best priced, of these is UUNET, Inc., which was originally started as a non-profit corporation (which it still is) by USENIX. Prices and services range all the way from the ridiculously low to the absurdly high. When/if you are in the market for such a service, you should shop around.

When shopping for a mail and news feed there are several issues to take into consideration:

1. Are full UUCP access services available?
   a. Are those services accessible via dial access? What kind of dial access: long distance (the most expensive); 800 numbers; X.25 service networks?
   b. Are those service available only over leased lines?
   c. Is the connection a Host-to-Host service (which is what you want if you are using this book to design an E-Mail network)?
2. How much do they cost and how are charges assessed?
3. Will the service provider help you through the maize of registering your site? How much will it cost?
4. Does the service provide a direct link to the Internet?
5. What kind of technical support is available?
6. How easily available is are these people when problems or questions occur? Can you reach them by telephone or FAX as well as by E-Mail? Do they return calls promptly, or at all? Can you get a "live" person on the phone if necessary?

You should ask these and other questions that may occur to you when you contact a potential service provider.

CONCLUDING NOTE

If you have followed all the suggestions up to this point in this book you have either thrown up your hands in despair, or you have a working UUCP-based E-Mail network available to you. In addition, if you have connected your own network to the outside world you are ready to start making use of what will likely develop into the Electronic Highway over the next few years.

REFERENCES

1. Two books I have already cited several times should be specifically noted in connection with UUCP and Usenet: Tim O'Reilly and Grace Todino, *Managing UUCP and Usenet* (Sebastopol, CA: O'Reilly and Associates, Inc., 1990); and

Grace Todino and Dale Dougherty, *Using UUCP and Usenet* (Sebastopol, CA: O'Reilly and Associates, Inc., 1991). For the Internet see Ed Krol, *The Whole Internet* (Sebastopol, CA: O'Reilly and Associates, Inc., 1992); April Marine, Susan Kirkpatrick, Vivian Neou, Carol Ward, *Internet: Getting Started* (Englewood Cliffs, NJ: Prentice Hall, 1993); Edward T. L. Hardie and Vivian Neou (eds.), *Internet: Mailing Lists* (Englewood Cliffs, NJ: Prentice Hall, 1993). One of the most successful of the Internet books is Tracy LaQuey and Jeanne C. Ryer, *The Internet Companion: A Beginner's Guide to Global Networking* (Reading, MA: Addison-Wesley Publishing Company, 1993).

2. G. Malkin and T. LaQuey Parker (eds.), "Internet Users' Glossary," Request for Comments 1392 (FYI: 18), Network Working Group, January, 1993.

3. In the sections quoted from Salzenberg, material contained in brackets ("[]") are my comments. TWM.

4. This short history of Usenet is abstracted and only lightly edited from a document circulating on Usenet by Gene Spafford: Archive-name: usenet-software/part1, Original from: spaf@purdue (Gene Spafford), Last-change: 18 Oct 1992 by spaf@purdue (Gene Spafford).

5. Jonathan Kamens, Moderator, news.answers, "How to become a USENET site," jik@MIT.Edu, MIT Information Systems/Athena.

6. This section was taken largely from Kamens and from RFC # 1480.

A

Suggested Additional Reading

There are a great many resources available once you gain access to Usenet and/or the Internet generally. Among these are such items as bibliographies concerning various specialties. As you might anticipate, there are bibliographies concerning E-Mail and use of Usenet and Internet. The following, reprinted in its entirety, follows closely my own review of the literature in preparation for this book. You should, however, also consult the endnotes of each chapter for additional reading.

```
+ - - - - - - - - - - - - - - - - - - - - - - - - - - + - - - - - - - - - - - - - - - - - - - - - - - - - - - - - - - +
|  James H. Thompson                |  jimmy_t@verifone.com      (Internet)  |
|  VeriFone Inc.                     |  uunet!verifone!jimmy_t    (UUCP)      |
|  100 Kahelu Avenue                 |  808-623-2911              (Phone)     |
|  Mililani, HI 96789                |  808-625-3201              (FAX)       |
+ - - - - - - - - - - - - - - - - - - - - - - - - - - + - - - - - - - - - - - - - - - - - - - - - - - - - - - - - - - +
```

1. Recommended Reading

        "The Matrix - Computer Networks and Conferencing Systems Worldwide"
        Author: John S. Quarterman
        Copyright: 1990
        Publisher: Digital Press
                TEL: 800-DIGITAL
                Modem: 800-234-1998

        "The User's Directory of Computer Networks"
        Author: Tracy L LaQuey

```
Copyright: 1990
Publisher: Digital Press
         TEL: 800-DIGITAL
         Modem: 800-234-1998

"!%@:: A Directory of Electronic Mail Addressing and Networks"
Author: Donnalyn Frey and Rick Adams
Publisher: O'Reilly & Associates, Inc
         103 Morris Street, Suite A
         Sebastopol, CA 95472
Email: nuts@ora.com
Phone: 800-338-6887
       707-829-0515
FAX:   707-829-0104

"Managing UUCP and the Usenet"
Publisher: O'Reilly & Associates, Inc
         103 Morris Street, Suite A
         Sebastopol, CA 95472
Email: nuts@ora.com
Phone: 800-338-6887
       707-829-0515
FAX:   707-829-0104

BoardWatch Magazine
5970 South Vivian Street
Littleton, CO 80127
Tel: 800-933-6038
     303-973-4222
FAX: 303-973-3731
Email: jrickard@boardwatch.com
Price: $36/year

"How to become a USENET site"
Author: Jonathan I. Kamens <jik@athena.mit.edu>
Latest Version: 22 Mar 92 06:00:52 GMT
Where to get: Posted periodically in newsgroups:
    news.admin,news.announce.newusers,news.answers
Summary: Periodic posting about the basic steps involved
getting connected to USENET.
```

If you are new to Usenet the following articles which are posted periodically in the newsgroup: news.answers (unless noted otherwise) may be useful:

```
"What is Usenet?"
Original-author: chip@tct.com (Chip Salzenberg)
Last-change: 2 Dec 91 by chip@tct.com (Chip Salzenberg)

"A Primer on How to Work With the Usenet Community
Latest Version: 24 Feb 92 06:10:16 GMT
```

Original-author: chuq@apple.COM (Chuq Von Rospach)
Last-change: 20 Feb 92 by spaf@cs.purdue.edu (Gene Spafford)

"USENET Software: History and Sources"
Original-author: spaf@cs.purdue.edu (Gene Spafford)
Last-change: 20 Feb 92 by spaf@cs.purdue.edu (Gene Spafford)

"Hints on writing style for Usenet"
Original-author: ofut@hubcap.clemson.edu (A. Jeff Offutt VI)
Last-change: 30 Nov 91 by spaf@cs.purdue.edu (Gene Spafford)

"Rules for posting to Usenet"
Original-author: mark@stargate.com (Mark Horton)
Last-change: 30 Nov 91 by spaf@cs.purdue.edu (Gene Spafford)

"Answers to Frequently Asked Questions [about USENET]"
Original-author: jerry@eagle.UUCP (Jerry Schwarz)
Last-change: 21 Feb 92 by spaf@cs.purdue.edu (Gene Spafford)

"List of Active Newsgroups"
Last-change: 21 Feb 1992 by spaf@cs.purdue.edu (Gene Spafford)

"How to Get Information about Networks"
Original-author: Randall Atkinson <randall@uvaarpa.virginia.edu>
Last-change: 20 Feb 92 by spaf@cs.purdue.edu (Gene Spafford)

"FAQ: How to find people's E-mail addresses"
Newsgroups: comp.mail.misc,soc.net-people,
            news.newusers.questions,news.answers
Author: jik@athena.mit.edu (Jonathan I. Kamens)
Latest Version: 1 APR 92 06:00:28 GMT

"Updated Internet Services List"
Newsgroups: alt.bbs.internet,alt.bbs.ads,comp.misc,biz.comp.services
Author: yanoff@csd4.csd.uwm.edu (Scott A. Yanoff)
Date: 7 Apr 92 21:56:27 GMT
Summary: A list of services available via the network

"UNIX E-Mail Software - a Survey"
Newsgroups: news.admin,comp.mail.misc,news.answers
Author: Chris Lewis <clewis@ferret.ocunix.on.ca>
Update Frequency: every 2 weeks
Summary: How to set up Email systems

"alt.bbs.internet Frequently asked Questions (with answers)"
Newsgroups: alt.bbs.internet
Last-modified: 15 Mar 92 00:00:01 EST

"How to find sources"
Newsgroups: comp.sources.wanted,alt.sources.wanted,news.answers

From: jik@athena.mit.edu (Jonathan I. Kamens)
Date: 18 Mar 92 06:00:36 GMT
Summary: How to find and retrieve source files

"List of Periodic Informational Postings, Part I"
Newsgroups: news.lists,news.announce.newusers,news.answers
From: jik@athena.mit.edu (Jonathan I. Kamens)
Date: 11 Mar 92 06:01:07 GMT

"Welcome to news.newusers.questions! (weekly posting)"
Newsgroups: news.newusers.questions,news.answers
From: jik@athena.mit.edu (Jonathan I. Kamens)
Date: 18 Mar 92 06:01:07 GMT

B

Commercial UUCP Network Connections

You may wish to gain access to Usenet through your new UUCP system. In order to do so you must have identified a "mail and news feed." Unfortunately, many of the reference materials on UUCP and Usenet suggest informal arrangements with local educational institutions, and it is certainly true that you may be able to find a friendly system administrator willing to provide the service to you. Unfortunately, such an informal arrangement probably ranges from the unethical to the illegal, depending on the state in the United States in which you reside and the institution with which you are dealing. If, of course, the institution has arrangements for "commercial" accounts by people not related to it, then you can certainly avail yourself of the service. On the other hand, many institutions have explicit prohibitions against outside sale of computer resources and the system manager that allows you to have an account may be flaunting the rules of the organization that pays his or her salary.

Fortunately, over the past few years, restrictions on the use of the Internet have relaxed and there has grown up a small, but apparently flourishing group of commercial service providers that can often provide you with relatively low-cost mail and news feeds. If, of course, you are faculty, staff, or student at an educational institution with an Internet connection, there may be internal arrangements for providing UUCP services. If, however, you have graduated, or represent a commercial firm, or simply do not want to spend the money to become a "real" Internet node (real in the sense of a high-speed, permanent connection with full services), then one or more of the services listed below may be useful. If you have looked at WinNET™ Mail and News, you will already recognize that the product is a "front end" for the networking services provided by Computer Witchcraft, Inc. The list of commercial UUCP network connections that follows was more-or-less current when I was writing this book, but these businesses tend to go out of and come into business with some frequency. Moreover, some of the operators of the regional Internet networks also sell similar services, although they tend to be more oriented to high speed connections. This list, though not an endorsement of any of the businesses listed, will start you on your way in a search for a service provider. You should probably also investigate possible service providers in your own community.

Anterior Technology
P.O. Box 1206
Menlo Park, CA 94026-1206
Telephone: 415-328-5615
FAX: 415-322-1753
Email: info@radiomail.net

DMConnection
267 Cox St.
Hudson, Ma. 01749
Telephone: 508-568-1618
FAX: 508-562-1133
email: dmc$info@dmc.com, dmc@dmc.com, info@dmc.com

MSEN, Inc.
628 Brooks Street
Ann Arbor, MI 48103
Phone: 313-741-1120
email: info@msen.com

Netcom
4000 Moorpark Avenue, Suite 209
San Jose, CA 95117
Telephone: 408-554-UNIX
FAX: 408-241-9145
Email: info@netcom.com

Performance Systems International Inc.
11800 Sunrise Valley Drive, #1100
Reston, VA 22091
Telephone: 800-827-7482 or 703-620-6651
FAX: 703-620-4586
Email: info@psi.com
all-info@psi.com (for an automatic reply with
            a summary of services)

UUNET Communications Services
3110 Fairview Park Drive, Suite 570
Falls Church, VA 22042
Telephone: 703-876-5050
Fax: 703-876-5059
Email: info@uunet.uu.net

WinNET™
Computer Witchcraft, Inc.
Post Office Box 4189
Louisville, KY 40204
Telephone: 502-589-6800
Fax: 502-589-7300
Internet Mail: winnet@win.net
CompuServe Mail: 76130,1463.

C

UUCP Product Directory

Although this information is provided in endnotes throughout this book, this list of products discussed is presented here for your convenience. This is not a complete list of all the UUCP products available. It is, however, a good list and specifically covers all the products discussed in this book.

SHAREWARE UUCP PRODUCTS

1. **UUPlus Utilities by UUPlus Development**. UUPlus Utilities (formerly FSUUCP), Christopher Ambler, author, may be obtained from UUPlus Development, P. O. Box 8, Camarillo, CA 93011; Telephone/FAX: 805-485-0057; Internet Mail: info@uuplus.com.

2. **WinNET**™ Mail and News for Windows by Computer Witchcraft, Inc. Computer Witchcraft, Inc., may be reached at Post Office Box 4189, Louisville, KY 40204; Telephone: (502) 589-6800; Fax: (502) 589-7300; Internet Mail: winnet@win.net; CompuServe Mail: 76130,1463. While the current version is distributed with this book, it can also be acquired from the simtel msdos/windows3 directory.

3. Waffle is a product of Darkside International, Thomas E Dell, Post Office Box 4436, Mountain View CA 94040-0436; The preferred method of contact is via electronic mail; you can contact the author at: dell@vox.darkside.com (...vox!dell). If you don't have EMail access, you can contact the author by sending FEEDBACK at: The Dark Side of

the Moon; 300/1200/2400 bps 24 hours 8N1; +1 408/245-7726. There also exists the comp.bbs.waffle and alt.bbs.waffle Usenet news groups. Waffle is normally available in the Simtel msdos/waffle directory.

4. **Gnu UUCP for Mac ported by Jim O'Dell.** Information may be requested from Jim O'Dell, Fort Pond Research, 15 Fort Pond Road, Acton, MA 01720; Email: fpr!jimuu.psi.com, or you might try, from CompuServe, >INTERNET:jimuu@psi.com.

5. **UUPC 3.0 for the Mac coordinated by Dave Platt.** Macintosh UUPC 3.0 is coordinated by Dave Platt who may be reached by EMail at dplatt@snulbug.mtview.ca.us, or, presumably, through CompuServe at >INTERNET:dplatt@snulbug.mtview.ca.us. The product can be downloaded from the Macintosh Communications forum on CompuServe.

6. **Mini-Host for Windows from SuperPhysica Center, St.Petersburg, Russia.** Just as this book was about to go to press, we discovered Mini-Host. This product is "an integrated software package for E-Mail and data processing" for use with Microsoft Windows. The difference between this product and WinMail™ is that Mini-Host can be used as either a leaf or a host system. A demonstration version can be acquired through the Internet from *ftp.cica.indiana.edu:/pub/pc/win3/ demo/mhdemo11.zip* or directly from its authors who may be contacted via EMail at *minihost@sph.spb.su*; SuperPhysica Center, 190031, POB 418, St.Petersburg, Russia; telephone: +7 (812) 310-4631 or +7 (812) 232-1661.

OTHER DOS UUCP SYSTEMS

7. **DOSGATE by Ammon R. Campbell.** The author, Ammon R. Campbell, may be contacted via CompuServe mail at: 71441,2447 or UUCP mail at: or uunet!compuserve!71441.2447 or uunet!sequent-!jli!ionz!ammon or Internet mail at: >INTERNET:71441.2447@compuserve.com.

8. **The UUPC Products.** UUPC/Extended for DOS, OS/2, and Windows is currently supported by Drew Derbyshire, Kendra Electronic Wonderworks, Post Office Box 132, Arlington, MA 02174-0002. The latest versions of the UUPC products are usually available via anonymous **ftp** at *omnigate.clarkson.edu:/pub/msdos/uupc/**.

COMMERCIAL PRODUCTS

9. **The MKS Toolkit from Mortice Kern Systems.** Mortice Kern Systems, Inc., 35 King St., N, Waterloo, ON, CD N2J 2W9; 800-265-2797; 519-884-2251; FAX: 519-884-8861; Tech support: 519-884-2270.

This product is listed in the materials from UUNET, an international networking organization providing domestic and international communications and information services to its customers including services as an UUCP mail and news feeder.

10. **Late Night Software**, 671 28th Street, San Francisco, CA 94131, Telephone: 415-695-7727. During the writing of this book I placed several calls to Late Night Software requesting information on their product. None were returned nor was any information forthcoming by U. S. Mail.

11. **UULINK from Vortex Technology**. Vortex Technology may be reached at P. O. Box 1323, Topanga, CA 90290; Telephone: 310-455-9300.

12. **"UMail" UUCP for the Macintosh by ICE Engineering.** ICE Engineering may be reached at 8840 Main St., Whitmore Lake, MI 4818; Voice: (313) 449 8288; EMail: time@oxtrap.aa.ox.com or uunet!oxtrap!time.

13. **UUCP/Connect (for the Macintosh) by Intercon.** Intercon may be contacted through Clint Heiden at 703-709-5503 or via CompuServe Mail's Internet connection at address >INTERNET:clint@intercon.com.

14. **Coherent 4.2 with Taylor** UUCP from the Mark Williams Company. Coherent is a UNIX look-alike selling at the very reasonable price of $99.00. It is available from the Mark Williams Company, 60 Revere Drive, Northbrook, IL 60062; Telephone: 708-291-6700; FAX: 708-291-6750.

MAIL USER AGENTS (MUA)

15. **Cinetics Mail Manager (CMM) for Windows by Cinetic Systems.** Cinetic Systems may be reached at 4933 Verreau, Montreal, Quebec, Canada, H1M 2C7; or by Email at Internet: Cinetic@Speedy.CAM.ORG or Compuserve: 71640,666.

16. PCElm (for DOS) by Wolfgang Siebeck and Martin Freiss. PCELM is a shareware product. Support may be acquired from the authors at the following addresses:

Wolfgang Siebeck	-or-	Martin Freiss
Rosstr. 38-40		Muehlenfloessstr. 60
D-W 5100 Aachen		D-W 4792 Bad Lippspringe
Germany		Germany
EMail:		EMail:
siebeck@infoac.rmi.de		freiss.pad@sni.de

17. **Fernmail and Eudora for the MAC.** Both of these are available from the Macintosh/Communications Forum on CompuServe.

SCHEDULING SOFTWARE (CRON)

18. **WCRON for Windows from Cinetic Systems.** See the endnote for Cinetics Mail Manager for an appropriate address.
19. **CRON for DOS.** *CronJr ver 2.36*, Software Shorts, Suite 101, 14101 Yorba Street, Tustin, CA 92680, U.S.A., author unknown.

RELATED PRODUCTS

20. **PC-NFS from Sunselect (Sun Micro Systems Inc, a commercial product).** For more information call SunSelect, 2 Elizabeth Dr., Chelmsford, MA 01824, (508) 442-2300.
21. **PC/TCP by FTP Software Inc.** For more information, contact The Wollongong Group, 1129 San Antonio Rd., Palo Alto, Calif. 94303; (415) 962-7100.
22. **Pathway by The Wollongong Group Inc.** For more information, contact The Wollongong Group, 1129 San Antonio Rd., Palo Alto, Calif. 94303; (415) 962-7100.

D

Sample UUPlus™ Configuration Files

These files, *systems*, *uuplus.cfg*, and *mailrc*, are samples of the UUPlus configuration files. They are given here for your reference only. Without modification, they will (except for *mailrc*) not work on your system "as is."

SAMPLE SYSTEMS FILE

```
# systems file - Version 1.50
#
# This file controls how uucico.exe logs into the remote machine. Here are a
# few example systems scripts. Probably the hardest part of setting up a mail
# and news feed is getting this to work correctly. Have patience and be
# observant.
#
# Lines beginning with "#" are comments. Blank lines are ignored.
#
# ESCAPE CODES SUPPORTED:
#
# \b  - send break
# \r  - send return
# \n  - send newline
# \t  - send tab
# \d  - flush line, delay 1 second
# \s  - send space
```

```
# \c  - do NOT send a return at the end of this line (default is to do so)
# \\  - send a backslash
#
# EXPECT/SEND/EXPECT
#
# expect strings may have conditional retry in the format
#
#    expect1-send-expect2
#
# whereas if [expect1] isn't seen in the time specified by the "timeout"
# variable in the .CFG file, the text [send] will be sent, and [expect2]
# will be scanned for.
#
# a string of the format
#
#    expect1—expect2
#
# will cause a single return to be sent should [expect1] not be seen
#
# login through some sort of network. Send returns until you see something,
# at the "NET >" prompt, turn on a binary connection, then connect to the
# system and procede as normal.
#
tomservo Any Hayes 2400 ATDT5551000 "" <CR> NET\s> set\sbinary\son NET\s>
c\sunix ogin:—ogin: fsuucp ssword:—ssword mst3000
# Window request level for g protocol. Default is 7. Valid values are from
# 1 to 7
#
configure  g_window    7
#
# Packet request level for g protocol. Default is 64. Valid values are from
# 64 bytes, to 4096 in powers of 2. NOTE that some UNIX systems will behave
# unpredictably if you send a packet request other than 64. Experimentation
# is the best way to go.
#
configure  g_packet    64
#
configure  ulimit          disable
#
# gradechar may be either 'p' or 'v' depending on host requirements
#
configure  gradechar   p
#
# 3 retries at 60, 120, and 180 second delays
#
configure  retries          3
configure  retrytimes  60,120,180
#
# Most simple login. Note that it has the packet size set to 256
#
```

```
crow Any Hayes 2400 ATDT5413958 "" <CR> ogin: fsuucp ssword: mst3000
configure   g_window   7
configure   g_packet   256
#
# Direct connection. Note the ABSENCE of the dialing command, since direct
# connections are already connected.
#
cambot Any Direct 9600 "" <CR> ogin: fsuucp ssword: mst3000
configure   g_window   7
configure   g_packet   256
```

SAMPLE *UUPLUS.CFG* FILE

```
# Configuration file for UUPlus Utilities 1.50
#
# Lines beginning with "#" are comments
# Blank lines are ignored
# Format:
# option          value
#
# This file must be modified to meet your specific system configuration

# System Information
sysname         arms.uucp
logname         arms
username        twm
fullname        Thomas Wm. Madron
smarthost  ewcuucp
gradechar  p
mailgrade  D
newsgrade  N
callgrade  Z

# Directory Information
home       c:\uuplus\home
spool      c:\uuplus\spool
libdir         c:\uuplus\lib
pubdir         c:\uuplus\spool\uucp\public
news       c:\uuplus\news
logfile        c:\uuplus\spool\uucp\logfile
#ramdisk        (none)

# Feature Information
editor          visual
visual          c:\utility\vde.com
autosig         on
organization    Enterprise-Wide Computing, Inc.
```

SAMPLE *MAILRC* FILE

```
# Default mailrc file for UUPlus Utilities 1.50
set askcc on
set dot on
set ignoreeof off
set nosave off
set record off
set metoo off
set escape ~
set crt 24
set prompt &
```

E

Sample WinNET™ *chat.rc* File

When configuring WinNET™ Mail and News for a UUCP environment other than WinNET itself, the *chat.rc* file will almost always require some manual editing. This is not arduous since the *chat.rc* file need be only a few lines. It is well to keep in mind that this file is the WinNET version of the *chat* scripts found most frequently in *Systems/L.sys*.

```
INITIATE
\,\r

ogin:
nuucp\r

word:
uucpudwm\r
```

The following is the complete *chat.txt* file that documents *chat.rc*. It is found in the distribution archive and is reprinted here for your convenience.

```
Editing   the   chat   script

If you are reading this while setting up WinNET with
the setup program, you will probably also want to refer
```

to this file later when you edit your chat.rc file.
The file you are reading is called CHAT.TXT and is
installed along with WinNET to your \wnmail directory.

What is the chat.rc file?

The chat.rc file controls the log-in process between the
time that your modem connects to the remote site to the
time when the uucico (unix-to-unix-copy-in-copy-out)
protocol starts up. (uucico is the basic mail/news
transfer program that handles data transfer under uucp).

A default chat.rc file is put in the directory where you
installed WinNET by the setup program. The chat.rc that
is created by default may not be adequate to actually
log in to your remote uucp site, so you'll have to
modify it so that it is complete.

When your modem connects and established a link/protocol
with the remote site, the remote site will start sending
various log-in prompts that your WinNET uucico module
needs to respond to to successfully log in. In the
simplest type of log-in sequence, the remote site will
spawn some type of banner with information about itself
(such as the brand name of its operating system and some
sort of welcome message), and then emit the prompt

login:

After receiving input for log-in, the remote will typically
then emit

password:

After receiving input for password, it will verify the
inputs and, if they are correct, start up its own uucico
and then mail / news transfer takes place.

So, the chat.rc script is to control the scripting just of
this simple log-in phase. However, in the 'real world',
the log-in process can become more complicated. Many
uucp provider sites have several layers of logging in. In
most cases, you have to log in in 2 steps; first, you have
to log in to a generic terminal server front end; after you
get past the terminal server, you can then log in pretty
much as described above. The precise sequence is
something that your uucp provider should be able to provide.

Before Configuring your chat.rc File...

It is almost always a good idea to fire up a terminal
emulation program like Window's 'Terminal' or 'Procomm'
to directly dial the telephone number of your uucp provider
and try logging on to the remote system manually before
trying to configure chat.rc.

This exercise gives you a very clear idea of the behavior of
the remote system, and also allows you to verify that the
log-in name(s) and password(s) that your provider has given
you are actually correct.

Doing this may well save you hours of exasperation trying
to configure your chat.rc file, particularly if you don't
have the correct login/password information to begin with!

For uucp, you can tell that you've successfully logged in
when you see the output:

    Shere=remote_name

from the remote site, where 'remote_name' is the machine
name of the remote system. When you get this far, it
means that you've logged in completely, and the remote site
has permitted you access to uucico. (You'll have to hang
up your modem at this point though, unless you know how to
manually enter the correct sequence to continue with
uucico!)

Now, let's look at how the chat.rc script works.

The chat.rc script is designed to be able to do what you
could do manually if you called your uucp provider with a
terminal emulation program (like procomm or terminal for
Windows) and visually looked for the various prompts and
then typed in the proper inputs. In each case, you 'expect'
to see a prompt and then 'send' (type) the correct
response. The chat.rc file allows you the script these
expect/send pairs for up to 15 levels.

For each prompt that is expected, you create an entry in
the chat.rc file. Each entry consists of 2 lines, and each
entry is separated by a blank line. Here is the syntax
format of an entry in chat.rc, followed by a realistic
example:

expect text
send text

; example entry
login:

hullaballoo\n

Let's break down each of the 2 lines in detail:

1. expect text

This line shows the literal text of the prompt that is
expected from the remote uucp site. In most cases, this
will be case sensitive. Spaces are acceptable, but it is
also fine just to use the last few characters of the
prompt if you know that these characters will not be
repeated in any of the other output from the remote. Our
example expect text could usually be abbreviated as
'ogin:', for example.

2. send text

This line lists the literal text of what our system should
send to the remote as input for the prompt listed in the
expect text line. This will also generally be case
sensitive.

It is also *crucial* to remember that the send text line will
almost always have to end with the correct line termination
character for the system you are connecting to (the
equivelent of hitting the ENTER or RETURN key of your
keyboard). For this purpose, there are several special
characters that you can enter preceded by a backspace. These
characters are not literal representations of the characters
that will be emited to the remote site, but rather,
placeholders or symbols that will be replaced when the
program actually runs by the correct control characters.
Presently, the following special characters are
implemented:

    \n   unix-style 'new line' character (ASCII 10)
    \r   carriage return (ASCII 13)
    \\   backslash
    \b   space character (you can enter a space directly,
            \b is just included to improve readability).
    \,   pause one second

AS A RULE OF THUMB, IF YOU ARE CONNECTING TO A UNIX SYSTEM,
MAKE SURE TO TERMINATE EACH LINE OF THE SEND TEXT LINE
WITH A \n   IF THE SYSTEM YOU ARE CONNECTED TO IS *NOT* A
UNIX SYSTEM, INSTEAD TERMINATE EACH LINE OF THE SEND TEXT
LINE WITH A \r

Intiating Output

In some cases, when your modem connects to the remote site,
the remote site will not emit its prompts until it has
received some cuing or prompting from your system. In most
cases where this is true, the remote will wait for one or
more end of line characters from your system before emiting
its first log-in prompt. (If you called with a terminal
emulater, you'd have to hit the RETURN/ENTER key a few times
before seeing any output from the remote site). This can
be tricky, because the number of carriage returns and the
interval of time between them can be unpredictable; it
doesn't always work exactly the same way twice!
(Sometimes you have to hit ENTER twice, sometimes three or
four times).

To initiate unprompted output the chat.rc file provides a
special statement called the "INITIATE" statement. The
syntax is:

INITIATE
send text

The send text line of the INITIATE statement can be
whatever you like, but in most situations where you would
want to use an INITIATE statement, it will be
something like \,\n\,\n\,\n\,\n which indicates
pause-newline-pause-newline-pause-newline,
pause-newline, a sequence that will sufficiently 'cue'
most terminal servers.

Comments

You can put comments at the TOP of your chat.rc file. Once
the script proper begins, NO comments are allowed.
If you wish to put a comment(s) at the top of the
script, put a semi-colon charater in column one of
each line that you intend as a comment. It is also OK
to use blank lines in the chat.rc (with or without
comment semi-colons), up to the point where the script
actually begins — BUT, once the script begins, blank
lines are syntactically significant, indicating the end
of an entry, so make sure that your entries are
separated by just 1 blank line once the script
begins.

A Complete Sample chat.rc

; sample chat.rc
; the \,\r\, in the INITIATE statement indicates that
; the communications program should initiate the login
; process by pausing one second, issuing a carriage return

; character (ascii 13) and pausing again for one second.

```
INITIATE
\,\r\,

name:
baxter\n

word:
7UpGirl\n

ogin:
cyborg\n

word:
Ten.PM\n
```

F

Sample *Waffle* Configuration Files

THE *SYSTEMS* FILE

```
#       Tokens are as follows:
# 1             system name
# 2             Time to call (Any, Never, Evening, Night are few valid entries)
# 3             Protocol to use (must be g)
# 4             Name of dialer with a corresponding entry in
#                   'dialers' file (which includes baud rate).
# 5             Name of connection script.  The corresponding
#                   script in the 'scripts' file is performed after
#                   the dialers script has finished.
# 6             Telephone number to call (for \T).  When a \T is
#                   encountered in the 'dialers' script, this
#                   number is inserted.
# 7             log-in name to use (for \L).
# 8             Password to use (for \P).
#
Pittz     Never g   Hayes2400 toUnix    1201xxxxxxx  uucp     uucp
lisajous  Any   g   TB19200   toWaffle  245xxxx      UUozone  noogie
```

SAMPLE *SCRIPTS* FILE

This is the Waffle equivalent of the chat scripts usually found in *Systems/L.sys* on UNIX UUCP systems.

```
toUnix     in:-in: \L word: \P
toWaffle   NEW:-NEW: \d\L word: \P
toNull
toNasty    "" \r\p\r in:-in:-in: \L word: \P
toCisco    "" \r\p\p\p\r\c > login\s\L word: \P > open\s\S\s540 in:   \L rd: \P
```

SAMPLE *DIALERS* FILE

Note that the ">" sign in the "DALLAS" configuration is only a typographical symbol indicating that the tokens that follow are to be typed on the same line, not on an additional line.

```
Hayes2400   Default   2400    "" ATV1&D2 OK ATDT\T CONNECT \m\c
TB9600      Default   9600    "" ATX3V1S51=4S52=1S58=2S66=1S111=30 OK ATDT\T CONNECT \m\c
TB19200     Default   19200   "" ATX3V1S51=5S52=1S58=2S66=1S111=30 OK ATDT\T CONNECT \m\c
Null.2400   Default   2400
Null.9600   Default   9600
DALLAS      Default   9600    "" ATZ OK ATQ0V1M1&C1&D3S95=2S0=
  0S36=7S95=255&Q0$C0$E0X4 OK ATDT\T >
  CONNECT \m\c
HAYES57     Default   57600   "" ATZ OK ATQ0V1M1&C1&D2S36=7S0=
  0&Q0$C0$E0 OK ATDT\T CONNECT \m\c
```

SAMPLE *PERMITS* FILE

```
;  Neighbors are allowed to execute RNEWS and RMAIL. Also they can access
;  the anonymous UUCP directories if you uncomment the up and download lines.

default    /system=known
           /account=any
           /commands=rnews,rmail
           /download=anonymous
           /upload=uploads
           /time=any
```

```
;   For anonymous UUCP login. Provide a "uucp" account calling uucico with
;   -panonymous -uanonymous to access this permit if you want anon uucp.

anonymous    /system=any
             /account=anonymous
             /commands=""
             /download="anonymous"
             /upload="uploads"
             /time=any
```

G

RFC # 822

You will find in the documentation to **mail** and other MUA references to RFC # 822. The purpose of RFC # 822 is to provide a standard for what MUAs and other components of a mail system must conform to for the transfer of Internet messages. This applies also to MUAs that "front-end" UUCP. Those of you that need or want to delve more deeply into how the mail system works may wish to read this document. Since it is normally available in machine-readable form, it is often not accessible to those who are just starting the process of using UNIX-style mail systems as they are currently used. Consequently, this RFC, though relatively long, is presented here in its entirety.

RFC # 822

Obsoletes: RFC #733 (NIC #41952)

STANDARD FOR THE FORMAT OF

ARPA INTERNET TEXT MESSAGES

August 13, 1982

Revised by

David H. Crocker

Dept. of Electrical Engineering
University of Delaware, Newark, DE 19711
Network: DCrocker @ UDel-Relay

Standard for ARPA Internet Text Messages

TABLE OF CONTENTS

Standard for ARPA Internet Text Messages

PREFACE

By 1977, the Arpanet employed several informal standards for
the text messages (mail) sent among its host computers. It was
felt necessary to codify these practices and provide for those
features that seemed imminent. The result of that effort was
Request for Comments (RFC) #733, "Standard for the Format of ARPA
Network Text Message", by Crocker, Vittal, Pogran, and Henderson.
The specification attempted to avoid major changes in existing
software, while permitting several new features.

This document revises the specifications in RFC #733, in
order to serve the needs of the larger and more complex ARPA
Internet. Some of RFC #733's features failed to gain adequate
acceptance. In order to simplify the standard and the software
that follows it, these features have been removed. A different
addressing scheme is used, to handle the case of inter-network
mail; and the concept of re-transmission has been introduced.

This specification is intended for use in the ARPA Internet.
However, an attempt has been made to free it of any dependence on
that environment, so that it can be applied to other network text
message systems.

The specification of RFC #733 took place over the course of
one year, using the ARPANET mail environment, itself, to provide
an on-going forum for discussing the capabilities to be included.
More than twenty individuals, from across the country, partici-
pated in the original discussion. The development of this
revised specification has, similarly, utilized network mail-based
group discussion. Both specification efforts greatly benefited
from the comments and ideas of the participants.

The syntax of the standard, in RFC #733, was originally
specified in the Backus-Naur Form (BNF) meta-language. Ken L.
Harrenstien, of SRI International, was responsible for re-coding
the BNF into an augmented BNF that makes the representation
smaller and easier to understand.

Standard for ARPA Internet Text Messages

1. INTRODUCTION

1.1. SCOPE

This standard specifies a syntax for text messages that are sent among computer users, within the framework of "electronic mail". The standard supersedes the one specified in ARPANET Request for Comments #733, "Standard for the Format of ARPA Network Text Messages".

In this context, messages are viewed as having an envelope and contents. The envelope contains whatever information is needed to accomplish transmission and delivery. The contents compose the object to be delivered to the recipient. This standard applies only to the format and some of the semantics of message contents. It contains no specification of the information in the envelope.

However, some message systems may use information from the contents to create the envelope. It is intended that this standard facilitate the acquisition of such information by programs.

Some message systems may store messages in formats that differ from the one specified in this standard. This specification is intended strictly as a definition of what message content format is to be passed BETWEEN hosts.

Note: This standard is NOT intended to dictate the internal formats used by sites, the specific message system features that they are expected to support, or any of the characteristics of user interface programs that create or read messages.

A distinction should be made between what the specification REQUIRES and what it ALLOWS. Messages can be made complex and rich with formally-structured components of information or can be kept small and simple, with a minimum of such information. Also, the standard simplifies the interpretation of differing visual formats in messages; only the visual aspect of a message is affected and not the interpretation of information within it. Implementors may choose to retain such visual distinctions.

The formal definition is divided into four levels. The bottom level describes the meta-notation used in this document. The second level describes basic lexical analyzers that feed tokens to higher-level parsers. Next is an overall specification for messages; it permits distinguishing individual fields. Finally, there is definition of the contents of several structured fields.

Standard for ARPA Internet Text Messages

1.2. COMMUNICATION FRAMEWORK

Messages consist of lines of text. No special provisions
are made for encoding drawings, facsimile, speech, or structured
text. No significant consideration has been given to questions
of data compression or to transmission and storage efficiency,
and the standard tends to be free with the number of bits consumed. For example, field names are specified as free text,
rather than special terse codes.

A general "memo" framework is used. That is, a message consists of some information in a rigid format, followed by the main
part of the message, with a format that is not specified in this
document. The syntax of several fields of the rigidly-formated
("headers") section is defined in this specification; some of
these fields must be included in all messages.

The syntax that distinguishes between header fields is
specified separately from the internal syntax for particular
fields. This separation is intended to allow simple parsers to
operate on the general structure of messages, without concern for
the detailed structure of individual header fields. Appendix B
is provided to facilitate construction of these parsers.

In addition to the fields specified in this document, it is
expected that other fields will gain common use. As necessary,
the specifications for these "extension-fields" will be published
through the same mechanism used to publish this document. Users
may also wish to extend the set of fields that they use
privately. Such "user-defined fields" are permitted.

The framework severely constrains document tone and appearance and is primarily useful for most intra-organization communications and well-structured inter-organization communication.
It also can be used for some types of inter-process communication, such as simple file transfer and remote job entry. A more
robust framework might allow for multi-font, multi-color, multi-
dimension encoding of information. A less robust one, as is
present in most single-machine message systems, would more
severely constrain the ability to add fields and the decision to
include specific fields. In contrast with paper-based communication, it is interesting to note that the RECEIVER of a message
can exercise an extraordinary amount of control over the
message's appearance. The amount of actual control available to
message receivers is contingent upon the capabilities of their
individual message systems.

Standard for ARPA Internet Text Messages

2. NOTATIONAL CONVENTIONS

This specification uses an augmented Backus-Naur Form (BNF) notation. The differences from standard BNF involve naming rules and indicating repetition and "local" alternatives.

2.1. RULE NAMING

Angle brackets ("<", ">") are not used, in general. The name of a rule is simply the name itself, rather than "<name>". Quotation-marks enclose literal text (which may be upper and/or lower case). Certain basic rules are in uppercase, such as SPACE, TAB, CRLF, DIGIT, ALPHA, etc. Angle brackets are used in rule definitions, and in the rest of this document, whenever their presence will facilitate discerning the use of rule names.

2.2. RULE1 / RULE2: ALTERNATIVES

Elements separated by slash ("/") are alternatives. There-fore "foo / bar" will accept foo or bar.

2.3. (RULE1 RULE2): LOCAL ALTERNATIVES

Elements enclosed in parentheses are treated as a single element. Thus, "(elem (foo / bar) elem)" allows the token sequences "elem foo elem" and "elem bar elem".

2.4. *RULE: REPETITION

The character "*" preceding an element indicates repetition. The full form is:

<l>*<m>element

indicating at least <l> and at most <m> occurrences of element. Default values are 0 and infinity so that "*(element)" allows any number, including zero; "1*element" requires at least one; and "1*2element" allows one or two.

2.5. [RULE]: OPTIONAL

Square brackets enclose optional elements; "[foo bar]" is equivalent to "*1(foo bar)".

2.6. NRULE: SPECIFIC REPETITION

"<n>(element)" is equivalent to "<n>*<n>(element)"; that is, exactly <n> occurrences of (element). Thus 2DIGIT is a 2-digit number, and 3ALPHA is a string of three alphabetic characters.

Standard for ARPA Internet Text Messages

2.7. #RULE: LISTS

A construct "#" is defined, similar to "*", as follows:

<l>#<m>element

indicating at least <l> and at most <m> elements, each separated by one or more commas (","). This makes the usual form of lists very easy; a rule such as '(element *("," element))' can be shown as "1#element". Wherever this construct is used, null elements are allowed, but do not contribute to the count of elements present. That is, "(element),,(element)" is permitted, but counts as only two elements. Therefore, where at least one element is required, at least one non-null element must be present. Default values are 0 and infinity so that "#(element)" allows any number, including zero; "1#element" requires at least one; and "1#2element" allows one or two.

2.8. ; COMMENTS

A semi-colon, set off some distance to the right of rule text, starts a comment that continues to the end of line. This is a simple way of including useful notes in parallel with the specifications.

Standard for ARPA Internet Text Messages

3. LEXICAL ANALYSIS OF MESSAGES

3.1. GENERAL DESCRIPTION

A message consists of header fields and, optionally, a body. The body is simply a sequence of lines containing ASCII characters. It is separated from the headers by a null line (i.e., a line with nothing preceding the CRLF).

3.1.1. LONG HEADER FIELDS

Each header field can be viewed as a single, logical line of ASCII characters, comprising a field-name and a field-body. For convenience, the field-body portion of this conceptual entity can be split into a multiple-line representation; this is called "folding". The general rule is that wherever there may be linear-white-space (NOT simply LWSP-chars), a CRLF immediately followed by AT LEAST one LWSP-char may instead be inserted. Thus, the single line

        To: "Joe & J. Harvey" <ddd @Org>, JJV @ BBN

can be represented as:

        To: "Joe & J. Harvey" <ddd @ Org>,
                JJV@BBN

and

        To: "Joe & J. Harvey"
                        <ddd@ Org>, JJV
          @BBN

and

        To: "Joe &
        J. Harvey" <ddd @ Org>, JJV @ BBN

The process of moving from this folded multiple-line representation of a header field to its single line representation is called "unfolding". Unfolding is accomplished by regarding CRLF immediately followed by a LWSP-char as equivalent to the LWSP-char.

Note: While the standard permits folding wherever linear-white-space is permitted, it is recommended that structured fields, such as those containing addresses, limit folding to higher-level syntactic breaks. For address fields, it is recommended that such folding occur

Standard for ARPA Internet Text Messages

between addresses, after the separating comma.

3.1.2. STRUCTURE OF HEADER FIELDS

Once a field has been unfolded, it may be viewed as being composed of a field-name followed by a colon (":"), followed by a
field-body, and terminated by a carriage-return/line-feed.
The field-name must be composed of printable ASCII characters
(i.e., characters that have values between 33. and 126.,
decimal, except colon). The field-body may be composed of any
ASCII characters, except CR or LF. (While CR and/or LF may be
present in the actual text, they are removed by the action of
unfolding the field.)

Certain field-bodies of headers may be interpreted according
to an internal syntax that some systems may wish to parse.
These fields are called "structured fields". Examples
include fields containing dates and addresses. Other fields,
such as "Subject" and "Comments", are regarded simply as
strings of text.

Note: Any field which has a field-body that is defined as
      other than simply <text> is to be treated as a struc-
      tured field.

      Field-names, unstructured field bodies and structured
      field bodies each are scanned by their own, independent
      "lexical" analyzers.

3.1.3. UNSTRUCTURED FIELD BODIES

For some fields, such as "Subject" and "Comments", no structuring is assumed, and they are treated simply as <text>s, as
in the message body. Rules of folding apply to these fields,
so that such field bodies which occupy several lines must
therefore have the second and successive lines indented by at
least one LWSP-char.

3.1.4. STRUCTURED FIELD BODIES

To aid in the creation and reading of structured fields, the
free insertion of linear-white-space (which permits folding
by inclusion of CRLFs) is allowed between lexical tokens.
Rather than obscuring the syntax specifications for these
structured fields with explicit syntax for this linear-white-
space, the existence of another "lexical" analyzer is assumed.
This analyzer does not apply for unstructured field bodies
that are simply strings of text, as described above. The
analyzer provides an interpretation of the unfolded text

Standard for ARPA Internet Text Messages

composing the body of the field as a sequence of lexical symbols.

These symbols are:

- individual special characters
- quoted-strings
- domain-literals
- comments
- atoms

The first four of these symbols are self-delimiting. Atoms
are not; they are delimited by the self-delimiting symbols and
by linear-white-space. For the purposes of regenerating
sequences of atoms and quoted-strings, exactly one SPACE is
assumed to exist, and should be used, between them. (Also, in
the "Clarifications" section on "White Space", below, note the
rules about treatment of multiple contiguous LWSP-chars.)

So, for example, the folded body of an address field

    ":sysmail"@ Some-Group. Some-Org,
    Muhammed.(I am the greatest) Ali @(the)Vegas.WBA

Standard for ARPA Internet Text Messages

is analyzed into the following lexical symbols and types:

:sysmail	quoted string
@	special
Some-Group	atom
.	special
Some-Org	atom
,	special
Muhammed	atom
.	special
(I am the greatest)	comment
Ali	atom
@	atom
(the)	comment
Vegas	atom
.	special
WBA	atom

The canonical representations for the data in these addresses are the following strings:

":sysmail"@Some-Group.Some-Org

and

Muhammed.Ali@Vegas.WBA

Note: For purposes of display, and when passing such structured information to other systems, such as mail protocol services, there must be NO linear-white-space
between <word>s that are separated by period (".") or
at-sign ("@") and exactly one SPACE between all other
<word>s. Also, headers should be in a folded form.

Standard for ARPA Internet Text Messages

3.2. HEADER FIELD DEFINITIONS

These rules show a field meta-syntax, without regard for the particular type or internal syntax. Their purpose is to permit detection of fields; also, they present to higher-level parsers an image of each field as fitting on one line.

```
field       =  field-name ":" [ field-body ] CRLF

field-name  =  1*<any CHAR, excluding CTLs, SPACE, and ":">

field-body  =  field-body-contents
               [CRLF LWSP-char field-body]

field-body-contents =
               <the ASCII characters making up the field-body, as
                defined in the following sections, and consisting
                of combinations of atom, quoted-string, and
                specials tokens, or else consisting of texts>
```

Standard for ARPA Internet Text Messages

3.3. LEXICAL TOKENS

The following rules are used to define an underlying lexical analyzer, which feeds tokens to higher level parsers. See the ANSI references, in the Bibliography.

```
                                          ; (  Octal, Decimal.)
CHAR        = <any ASCII character>       ; (  0-177,  0.-127.)
ALPHA       = <any ASCII alphabetic character>
                                          ; (101-132, 65.- 90.)
                                          ; (141-172, 97.-122.)
DIGIT       = <any ASCII decimal digit>   ; ( 60- 71, 48.- 57.)
CTL         = <any ASCII control          ; (  0- 37,  0.- 31.)
              character and DEL>          ; (    177,     127.)
CR          = <ASCII CR, carriage return> ; (     15,      13.)
LF          = <ASCII LF, linefeed>        ; (     12,      10.)
SPACE       = <ASCII SP, space>           ; (     40,      32.)
HTAB        = <ASCII HT, horizontal-tab>  ; (     11,       9.)
<">         = <ASCII quote mark>          ; (     42,      34.)
CRLF        = CR LF

LWSP-char   = SPACE / HTAB                ; semantics = SPACE

linear-white-space = 1*([CRLF] LWSP-char) ; semantics = SPACE
                                          ; CRLF => folding

specials    = "(" / ")" / "<" / ">" / "@" ; Must be in quoted-
            / "," / ";" / ":" / "\" / <"> ;  string, to use
            / "." / "[" / "]"             ;  within a word.

delimiters  = specials / linear-white-space / comment

text        = <any CHAR, including bare   ; => atoms, specials,
              CR & bare LF, but NOT       ;  comments and
              including CRLF>             ;  quoted-strings are
                                          ;  NOT recognized.

atom        = 1*<any CHAR except specials, SPACE and CTLs>

quoted-string = <"> *(qtext/quoted-pair) <">; Regular qtext or
                                          ;  quoted chars.

qtext       = <any CHAR excepting <">,    ; => may be folded
              "\" & CR, and including
              linear-white-space>

domain-literal = "[" *(dtext / quoted-pair) "]"
```

Standard for ARPA Internet Text Messages

```
dtext        =   <any CHAR excluding "[",    ; => may be folded
                 "]", "\" & CR, & including
                 linear-white-space>

comment      =   "(" *(ctext / quoted-pair / comment) ")"

ctext        =   <any CHAR excluding "(",    ; => may be folded
                 ")", "\" & CR, & including
                 linear-white-space>

quoted-pair  =   "\" CHAR                    ; may quote any char

phrase       =   1*word                      ; Sequence of words

word         =   atom / quoted-string
```

3.4. CLARIFICATIONS

3.4.1. QUOTING

Some characters are reserved for special interpretation, such
as delimiting lexical tokens. To permit use of these characters as uninterpreted data, a quoting mechanism is provided.
To quote a character, precede it with a backslash ("\").

This mechanism is not fully general. Characters may be quoted
only within a subset of the lexical constructs. In particular, quoting is limited to use within:

> - quoted-string
> - domain-literal
> - comment

Within these constructs, quoting is REQUIRED for CR and "\"
and for the character(s) that delimit the token (e.g., "(" and
")" for a comment). However, quoting is PERMITTED for any
character.

> Note: In particular, quoting is NOT permitted within atoms.
>   For example when the local-part of an addr-spec must
>   contain a special character, a quoted string must be
>   used. Therefore, a specification such as:

> Full\ Name@Domain

> is not legal and must be specified as:

> "Full Name"@Domain

Standard for ARPA Internet Text Messages

3.4.2. WHITE SPACE

> Note: In structured field bodies, multiple linear space ASCII
>   characters (namely HTABs and SPACEs) are treated as
>   single spaces and may freely surround any symbol. In
>   all header fields, the only place in which at least one
>   LWSP-char is REQUIRED is at the beginning of continua-
>   tion lines in a folded field.

When passing text to processes that do not interpret text
according to this standard (e.g., mail protocol servers), then
NO linear-white-space characters should occur between a period
(".") or at-sign ("@") and a <word>. Exactly ONE SPACE should
be used in place of arbitrary linear-white-space and comment
sequences.

> Note: Within systems conforming to this standard, wherever a
>   member of the list of delimiters is allowed, LWSP-chars
>   may also occur before and/or after it.

Writers of mail-sending (i.e., header-generating) programs
should realize that there is no network-wide definition of the
effect of ASCII HT (horizontal-tab) characters on the appearance of text at another network host; therefore, the use of
tabs in message headers, though permitted, is discouraged.

3.4.3. COMMENTS

A comment is a set of ASCII characters, which is enclosed in
matching parentheses and which is not within a quoted-string
The comment construct permits message originators to add text
which will be useful for human readers, but which will be
ignored by the formal semantics. Comments should be retained
while the message is subject to interpretation according to
this standard. However, comments must NOT be included in
other cases, such as during protocol exchanges with mail
servers.

Comments nest, so that if an unquoted left parenthesis occurs
in a comment string, there must also be a matching right
parenthesis. When a comment acts as the delimiter between a
sequence of two lexical symbols, such as two atoms, it is lex-
ically equivalent with a single SPACE, for the purposes of
regenerating the sequence, such as when passing the sequence
onto a mail protocol server. Comments are detected as such
only within field-bodies of structured fields.

If a comment is to be "folded" onto multiple lines, then the
syntax for folding must be adhered to. (See the "Lexical

Standard for ARPA Internet Text Messages

Analysis of Messages" section on "Folding Long Header Fields" above, and the section on "Case Independence" below.) Note that the official semantics therefore do not "see" any unquoted CRLFs that are in comments, although particular parsing programs may wish to note their presence. For these programs, it would be reasonable to interpret a "CRLF LWSP-char" as being a CRLF that is part of the comment; i.e., the CRLF is kept and the LWSP-char is discarded. Quoted CRLFs (i.e., a backslash followed by a CR followed by a LF) still must be followed by at least one LWSP-char.

3.4.4. DELIMITING AND QUOTING CHARACTERS

The quote character (backslash) and characters that delimit syntactic units are not, generally, to be taken as data that are part of the delimited or quoted unit(s). In particular, the quotation-marks that define a quoted-string, the parentheses that define a comment and the backslash that quotes a following character are NOT part of the quoted-string, comment or quoted character. A quotation-mark that is to be part of a quoted-string, a parenthesis that is to be part of a comment and a backslash that is to be part of either must each be preceded by the quote-character backslash ("\"). Note that the syntax allows any character to be quoted within a quoted-string or comment; however only certain characters MUST be quoted to be included as data. These characters are the ones that are not part of the alternate text group (i.e., ctext or qtext).

The one exception to this rule is that a single SPACE is assumed to exist between contiguous words in a phrase, and this interpretation is independent of the actual number of LWSP-chars that the creator places between the words. To include more than one SPACE, the creator must make the LWSP-chars be part of a quoted-string.

Quotation marks that delimit a quoted string and backslashes that quote the following character should NOT accompany the quoted-string when the string is passed to processes that do not interpret data according to this specification (e.g., mail protocol servers).

3.4.5. QUOTED-STRINGS

Where permitted (i.e., in words in structured fields) quoted-strings are treated as a single symbol. That is, a quoted-string is equivalent to an atom, syntactically. If a quoted-string is to be "folded" onto multiple lines, then the syntax for folding must be adhered to. (See the "Lexical Analysis of

Standard for ARPA Internet Text Messages

Messages" section on "Folding Long Header Fields" above, and
the section on "Case Independence" below.) Therefore, the
official semantics do not "see" any bare CRLFs that are in
quoted-strings; however particular parsing programs may wish
to note their presence. For such programs, it would be reasonable to interpret a "CRLF LWSP-char" as being a CRLF which
is part of the quoted-string; i.e., the CRLF is kept and the
LWSP-char is discarded. Quoted CRLFs (i.e., a backslash followed by a CR followed by a LF) are also subject to rules of
folding, but the presence of the quoting character (backslash)
explicitly indicates that the CRLF is data to the quoted
string. Stripping off the first following LWSP-char is also
appropriate when parsing quoted CRLFs.

3.4.6. BRACKETING CHARACTERS

There is one type of bracket which must occur in matched pairs
and may have pairs nested within each other:

o   Parentheses ("(" and ")") are used to indicate com-
    ments.

There are three types of brackets which must occur in matched
pairs, and which may NOT be nested:

o   Colon/semi-colon (":" and ";") are used in address
    specifications to indicate that the included list of
    addresses are to be treated as a group.

o   Angle brackets ("<" and ">") are generally used to
    indicate the presence of a one machine-usable refer-
    ence (e.g., delimiting mailboxes), possibly including
    source-routing to the machine.

o   Square brackets ("[" and "]") are used to indicate the
    presence of a domain-literal, which the appropriate
    name-domain is to use directly, bypassing normal
    name-resolution mechanisms.

3.4.7. CASE INDEPENDENCE

Except as noted, alphabetic strings may be represented in any
combination of upper and lower case. The only syntactic units

Standard for ARPA Internet Text Messages

which requires preservation of case information are:

- text
- qtext
- dtext
- ctext
- quoted-pair
- local-part, except "Postmaster"

When matching any other syntactic unit, case is to be ignored. For example, the field-names "From", "FROM", "from", and even "FroM" are semantically equal and should all be treated identically.

When generating these units, any mix of upper and lower case alphabetic characters may be used. The case shown in this specification is suggested for message-creating processes.

Note: The reserved local-part address unit, "Postmaster", is an exception. When the value "Postmaster" is being interpreted, it must be accepted in any mixture of case, including "POSTMASTER", and "postmaster".

3.4.8. FOLDING LONG HEADER FIELDS

Each header field may be represented on exactly one line consisting of the name of the field and its body, and terminated by a CRLF; this is what the parser sees. For readability, the field-body portion of long header fields may be "folded" onto multiple lines of the actual field. "Long" is commonly interpreted to mean greater than 65 or 72 characters. The former length serves as a limit, when the message is to be viewed on most simple terminals which use simple display software; however, the limit is not imposed by this standard.

Note: Some display software often can selectively fold lines, to suit the display terminal. In such cases, sender-provided folding can interfere with the display software.

3.4.9. BACKSPACE CHARACTERS

ASCII BS characters (Backspace, decimal 8) may be included in texts and quoted-strings to effect overstriking. However, any use of backspaces which effects an overstrike to the left of the beginning of the text or quoted-string is prohibited.

Standard for ARPA Internet Text Messages

3.4.10. NETWORK-SPECIFIC TRANSFORMATIONS

During transmission through heterogeneous networks, it may be
necessary to force data to conform to a network's local conventions. For example, it may be required that a CR be followed either by LF, making a CRLF, or by <null>, if the CR is
to stand alone). Such transformations are reversed, when the
message exits that network.

When crossing network boundaries, the message should be
treated as passing through two modules. It will enter the
first module containing whatever network-specific transformations that were necessary to permit migration through the
"current" network. It then passes through the modules:

o   Transformation Reversal

The "current" network's idiosyncracies are removed and
the message is returned to the canonical form specified in this standard.

o   Transformation

The "next" network's local idiosyncracies are imposed
on the message.

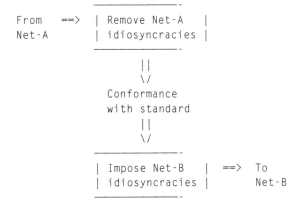

Standard for ARPA Internet Text Messages

4. MESSAGE SPECIFICATION

4.1. SYNTAX

Note: Due to an artifact of the notational conventions, the syn-
        tax indicates that, when present, some fields, must be in
        a particular order. Header fields   are   NOT   required to
        occur in any particular order, except that the message
        body must occur AFTER the   headers. It is recommended
        that, if present, headers be sent in the order "Return-
        Path", "Received", "Date", "From", "Subject", "Sender",
        "To", "cc", etc.

        This specification permits multiple occurrences of most
        fields. Except   as   noted, their interpretation is not
        specified here, and their use is discouraged.

        The following syntax for the bodies of various fields should
be thought of as describing each field body as a single long
string (or line). The "Lexical Analysis of Message" section on
"Long Header Fields", above, indicates how such long strings can
be represented on more than one line in the   actual   transmitted
message.

```
message     =  fields *( CRLF *text )      ; Everything after
                                           ;  first null line
                                           ;  is message body

fields      =    dates                     ; Creation time,
                 source                     ;  author id & one
              1*destination                 ;  address required
               *optional-field              ;  others optional

source      = [  trace ]                    ; net traversals
                 originator                 ; original mail
              [  resent ]                   ; forwarded

trace       =    return                     ; path to sender
              1*received                    ; receipt tags

return      =  "Return-path" ":" route-addr ; return address

received    =  "Received"    ":"            ; one per relay
                 ["from" domain]            ; sending host
                 ["by"   domain]            ; receiving host
                 ["via"  atom]              ; physical path
               *("with" atom)               ; link/mail protocol
                 ["id"   msg-id]            ; receiver msg id
                 ["for"  addr-spec]         ; initial form
```

Standard for ARPA Internet Text Messages

```
                    ":"    date-time           ; time received

originator  =   authentic                      ; authenticated addr
                [ "Reply-To"    ":" 1#address] )

authentic   =   "From"          ":"   mailbox  ; Single author
            / ( "Sender"        ":"   mailbox  ; Actual submittor
                "From"          ":" 1#mailbox) ; Multiple authors
                                               ;  or not sender

resent      =   resent-authentic
                [ "Resent-Reply-To"  ":" 1#address] )

resent-authentic =
            =   "Resent-From"       ":"   mailbox
            / ( "Resent-Sender"     ":"   mailbox
                "Resent-From"       ":" 1#mailbox  )

dates       =   orig-date                      ; Original
                [ resent-date ]                ; Forwarded

orig-date   =   "Date"          ":"   date-time

resent-date =   "Resent-Date" ":"   date-time

destination =   "To"            ":" 1#address  ; Primary
            /   "Resent-To"     ":" 1#address
            /   "cc"            ":" 1#address  ; Secondary
            /   "Resent-cc"     ":" 1#address
            /   "bcc"           ":"  #address  ; Blind carbon
            /   "Resent-bcc"    ":"  #address

optional-field =
            /   "Message-ID"          ":"   msg-id
            /   "Resent-Message-ID"   ":"   msg-id
            /   "In-Reply-To"         ":"  *(phrase / msg-id)
            /   "References"          ":"  *(phrase / msg-id)
            /   "Keywords"            ":"   #phrase
            /   "Subject"             ":"  *text
            /   "Comments"            ":"  *text
            /   "Encrypted"           ":" 1#2word
            /   extension-field             ; To be defined
            /   user-defined-field          ; May be pre-empted

msg-id      =   "<" addr-spec ">"              ; Unique message id
```

Standard for ARPA Internet Text Messages

extension-field =

                <Any field which is defined in a document
                published as a formal extension to this
                specification; none will have names beginning
                with the string "X-">

user-defined-field =

                <Any field which has not been defined
                in this specification or published as an
                extension to this specification; names for
                such fields must be unique and may be
                pre-empted by published extensions>

4.2. FORWARDING

Some systems permit mail recipients to forward a message, retaining the original headers, by adding some new fields. This standard supports such a service, through the "Resent-" prefix to field names.

Whenever the string "Resent-" begins a field name, the field has the same semantics as a field whose name does not have the prefix. However, the message is assumed to have been forwarded by an original recipient who attached the "Resent-" field. This new field is treated as being more recent than the equivalent, original field. For example, the "Resent-From", indicates the person that forwarded the message, whereas the "From" field indicates the original author.

Use of such precedence information depends upon participants' communication needs. For example, this standard does not dictate when a "Resent-From:" address should receive replies, in lieu of sending them to the "From:" address.

Note: In general, the "Resent-" fields should be treated as containing a set of information that is independent of the set of original fields. Information for one set should not automatically be taken from the other. The interpretation of multiple "Resent-" fields, of the same type, is undefined.

In the remainder of this specification, occurrence of legal "Resent-" fields are treated identically with the occurrence of

Standard for ARPA Internet Text Messages

fields whose names do not contain this prefix.

4.3. TRACE FIELDS

Trace information is used to provide an audit trail of message handling. In addition, it indicates a route back to the
sender of the message.

The list of known "via" and "with" values are registered
with the Network Information Center, SRI International, Menlo
Park, California.

4.3.1. RETURN-PATH

This field is added by the final transport system that
delivers the message to its recipient. The field is intended
to contain definitive information about the address and route
back to the message's originator.

Note: The "Reply-To" field is added by the originator and
       serves to direct replies, whereas the "Return-Path"
       field is used to identify a path back to the origina-
       tor.

While the syntax indicates that a route specification is
optional, every attempt should be made to provide that information in this field.

4.3.2. RECEIVED

A copy of this field is added by each transport service that
relays the message. The information in the field can be quite
useful for tracing transport problems.

The names of the sending and receiving hosts and time-of-
receipt may be specified. The "via" parameter may be used, to
indicate what physical mechanism the message was sent over,
such as Arpanet or Phonenet, and the "with" parameter may be
used to indicate the mail-, or connection-, level protocol
that was used, such as the SMTP mail protocol, or X.25 transport protocol.

Note: Several "with" parameters may be included, to fully
       specify the set of protocols that were used.

Some transport services queue mail; the internal message identifier that is assigned to the message may be noted, using the
"id" parameter. When the sending host uses a destination
address specification that the receiving host reinterprets, by

Standard for ARPA Internet Text Messages

expansion or transformation, the receiving host may wish to record the original specification, using the "for" parameter. For example, when a copy of mail is sent to the member of a distribution list, this parameter may be used to record the original address that was used to specify the list.

4.4. ORIGINATOR FIELDS

The standard allows only a subset of the combinations possible with the From, Sender, Reply-To, Resent-From, Resent-Sender, and Resent-Reply-To fields. The limitation is intentional.

4.4.1. FROM / RESENT-FROM

This field contains the identity of the person(s) who wished this message to be sent. The message-creation process should default this field to be a single, authenticated machine address, indicating the AGENT (person, system or process) entering the message. If this is not done, the "Sender" field MUST be present. If the "From" field IS defaulted this way, the "Sender" field is optional and is redundant with the "From" field. In all cases, addresses in the "From" field must be machine-usable (addr-specs) and may not contain named lists (groups).

4.4.2. SENDER / RESENT-SENDER

This field contains the authenticated identity of the AGENT (person, system or process) that sends the message. It is intended for use when the sender is not the author of the message, or to indicate who among a group of authors actually sent the message. If the contents of the "Sender" field would be completely redundant with the "From" field, then the "Sender" field need not be present and its use is discouraged (though still legal). In particular, the "Sender" field MUST be present if it is NOT the same as the "From" Field.

The Sender mailbox specification includes a word sequence which must correspond to a specific agent (i.e., a human user or a computer program) rather than a standard address. This indicates the expectation that the field will identify the single AGENT (person, system, or process) responsible for sending the mail and not simply include the name of a mailbox from which the mail was sent. For example in the case of a shared login name, the name, by itself, would not be adequate. The local-part address unit, which refers to this agent, is expected to be a computer system term, and not (for example) a generalized person reference which can be used outside the network text message context.

Standard for ARPA Internet Text Messages

Since the critical function served by the "Sender" field is
identification of the agent responsible for sending mail and
since computer programs cannot be held accountable for their
behavior, it is strongly recommended that when a computer program generates a message, the HUMAN who is responsible for
that program be referenced as part of the "Sender" field mailbox specification.

4.4.3. REPLY-TO / RESENT-REPLY-TO

This field provides a general mechanism for indicating any
mailbox(es) to which responses are to be sent. Three typical
uses for this feature can be distinguished. In the first
case, the author(s) may not have regular machine-based mailboxes and therefore wish(es) to indicate an alternate machine
address. In the second case, an author may wish additional
persons to be made aware of, or responsible for, replies. A
somewhat different use may be of some help to "text message
teleconferencing" groups equipped with automatic distribution
services: include the address of that service in the "Reply-
To" field of all messages submitted to the teleconference;
then participants can "reply" to conference submissions to
guarantee the correct distribution of any submission of their
own.

Note: The "Return-Path" field is added by the mail transport
       service, at the time of final deliver. It is intended
       to identify a path back to the orginator of the mes-
       sage. The "Reply-To" field is added by the message
       originator and is intended to direct replies.

4.4.4. AUTOMATIC USE OF FROM / SENDER / REPLY-TO

For systems which automatically generate address lists for
replies to messages, the following recommendations are made:

o   The "Sender" field mailbox should be sent notices of
    any problems in transport or delivery of the original
    messages. If there is no "Sender" field, then the
    "From" field mailbox should be used.

o   The "Sender" field mailbox should NEVER be used
    automatically, in a recipient's reply message.

o   If the "Reply-To" field exists, then the reply should
    go to the addresses indicated in that field and not to
    the address(es) indicated in the "From" field.

Standard for ARPA Internet Text Messages

> o If there is a "From" field, but no "Reply-To" field, the reply should be sent to the address(es) indicated in the "From" field.

Sometimes, a recipient may actually wish to communicate with the person that initiated the message transfer. In such cases, it is reasonable to use the "Sender" address.

This recommendation is intended only for automated use of originator-fields and is not intended to suggest that replies may not also be sent to other recipients of messages. It is up to the respective mail-handling programs to decide what additional facilities will be provided.

Examples are provided in Appendix A.

4.5. RECEIVER FIELDS

4.5.1. TO / RESENT-TO

This field contains the identity of the primary recipients of the message.

4.5.2. CC / RESENT-CC

This field contains the identity of the secondary (informational) recipients of the message.

4.5.3. BCC / RESENT-BCC

This field contains the identity of additional recipients of the message. The contents of this field are not included in copies of the message sent to the primary and secondary recipients. Some systems may choose to include the text of the "Bcc" field only in the author(s)'s copy, while others may also include it in the text sent to all those indicated in the "Bcc" list.

4.6. REFERENCE FIELDS

4.6.1. MESSAGE-ID / RESENT-MESSAGE-ID

This field contains a unique identifier (the local-part address unit) which refers to THIS version of THIS message. The uniqueness of the message identifier is guaranteed by the host which generates it. This identifier is intended to be machine readable and not necessarily meaningful to humans. A message identifier pertains to exactly one instantiation of a particular message; subsequent revisions to the message should

Standard for ARPA Internet Text Messages

each receive new message identifiers.

4.6.2. IN-REPLY-TO

The contents of this field identify previous correspondence which this message answers. Note that if message identifiers are used in this field, they must use the msg-id
specification format.

4.6.3. REFERENCES

The contents of this field identify other correspondence
which this message references. Note that if message identifiers are used, they must use the msg-id specification format.

4.6.4. KEYWORDS

This field contains keywords or phrases, separated by
commas.

4.7. OTHER FIELDS

4.7.1. SUBJECT

This is intended to provide a summary, or indicate the
nature, of the message.

4.7.2. COMMENTS

Permits adding text comments onto the message without
disturbing the contents of the message's body.

4.7.3. ENCRYPTED

Sometimes, data encryption is used to increase the
privacy of message contents. If the body of a message has
been encrypted, to keep its contents private, the "Encrypted"
field can be used to note the fact and to indicate the nature
of the encryption. The first <word> parameter indicates the
software used to encrypt the body, and the second, optional
<word> is intended to aid the recipient in selecting the
proper decryption key. This code word may be viewed as an
index to a table of keys held by the recipient.

Note: Unfortunately, headers must contain envelope, as well
      as contents, information. Consequently, it is neces-
      sary that they remain unencrypted, so that mail tran-
      sport services may access them. Since names,
      addresses, and "Subject" field contents may contain

Standard for ARPA Internet Text Messages

        sensitive information, this requirement limits total message privacy.

        Names of encryption software are registered with the Network Information Center, SRI International, Menlo Park, California.

4.7.4. EXTENSION-FIELD

        A limited number of common fields have been defined in this document. As network mail requirements dictate, additional fields may be standardized. To provide user-defined fields with a measure of safety, in name selection, such extension-fields will never have names that begin with the string "X-".

        Names of Extension-fields are registered with the Network Information Center, SRI International, Menlo Park, California.

4.7.5. USER-DEFINED-FIELD

        Individual users of network mail are free to define and use additional header fields. Such fields must have names which are not already used in the current specification or in any definitions of extension-fields, and the overall syntax of these user-defined-fields must conform to this specification's rules for delimiting and folding fields. Due to the extension-field publishing process, the name of a user-defined-field may be pre-empted

Note: The prefatory string "X-" will never be used in the names of Extension-fields. This provides user defined fields with a protected set of names.

Standard for ARPA Internet Text Messages

5. DATE AND TIME SPECIFICATION

5.1. SYNTAX

```
date-time   =   [ day "," ] date time        ; dd mm yy
                                              ;  hh:mm:ss zzz

day         =   "Mon"  / "Tue"  / "Wed"  / "Thu"
            /   "Fri"  / "Sat"  / "Sun"

date        =   1*2DIGIT month 2DIGIT         ; day month year
                                              ;  e.g. 20 Jun 82

month       =   "Jan"  /  "Feb"  /  "Mar"  /  "Apr"
            /   "May"  /  "Jun"  /  "Jul"  /  "Aug"
            /   "Sep"  /  "Oct"  /  "Nov"  /  "Dec"

time        =   hour zone                     ; ANSI and Military

hour        =   2DIGIT ":" 2DIGIT [":" 2DIGIT]
                                              ; 00:00:00 - 23:59:59

zone        =   "UT"  /  "GMT"                ; Universal Time
                                              ; North American : UT
            /   "EST" / "EDT"                 ;  Eastern:  - 5/ - 4
            /   "CST" / "CDT"                 ;  Central:  - 6/ - 5
            /   "MST" / "MDT"                 ;  Mountain: - 7/ - 6
            /   "PST" / "PDT"                 ;  Pacific:  - 8/ - 7
            /   1ALPHA                        ; Military: Z = UT;
                                              ;  A:-1; (J not used)
                                              ;  M:-12; N:+1; Y:+12

            / ( ("+" / "-") 4DIGIT )          ; Local differential
                                              ;  hours+min. (HHMM)
```

5.2. SEMANTICS

   If included, day-of-week must be the day implied by the date
specification.

   Time zone may be indicated in several ways. "UT" is Universal Time (formerly called "Greenwich Mean Time"); "GMT" is permitted as a reference to Universal Time. The military standard
uses a single character for each zone. "Z" is Universal Time.
"A" indicates one hour earlier, and "M" indicates 12 hours earlier; "N" is one hour later, and "Y" is 12 hours later. The
letter "J" is not used. The other remaining two forms are taken
from ANSI standard X3.51-1975. One allows explicit indication of
the amount of offset from UT; the other uses common 3-character
strings for indicating time zones in North America.

August 13, 1982   - 26 -   RFC #822

Standard for ARPA Internet Text Messages

6. ADDRESS SPECIFICATION

6.1. SYNTAX

```
address     =  mailbox                      ; one addressee
            /  group                        ; named list

group       =  phrase ":" [#mailbox] ";"

mailbox     =  addr-spec                     ; simple address
            /  phrase route-addr             ; name & addr-spec

route-addr  =  "<" [route] addr-spec ">"

route       =  1#("@" domain) ":"            ; path-relative

addr-spec   =  local-part "@" domain         ; global address

local-part  =  word *("." word)              ; uninterpreted
                                             ; case-preserved

domain      =  sub-domain *("." sub-domain)

sub-domain  =  domain-ref / domain-literal

domain-ref  =  atom                          ; symbolic reference
```

6.2. SEMANTICS

   A mailbox receives mail. It is a conceptual entity which
does not necessarily pertain to file storage. For example, some
sites may choose to print mail on their line printer and deliver
the output to the addressee's desk.

   A mailbox specification comprises a person, system or process name reference, a domain-dependent string, and a name-domain
reference. The name reference is optional and is usually used to
indicate the human name of a recipient. The name-domain reference specifies a sequence of sub-domains. The domain-dependent
string is uninterpreted, except by the final sub-domain; the rest
of the mail service merely transmits it as a literal string.

6.2.1. DOMAINS

   A name-domain is a set of registered (mail) names. A name-
domain specification resolves to a subordinate name-domain
specification or to a terminal domain-dependent string.
Hence, domain specification is extensible, permitting any
number of registration levels.

Standard for ARPA Internet Text Messages

Name-domains model a global, logical, hierarchical addressing
scheme. The model is logical, in that an address specification is related to name registration and is not necessarily
tied to transmission path. The model's hierarchy is a
directed graph, called an in-tree, such that there is a single
path from the root of the tree to any node in the hierarchy.
If more than one path actually exists, they are considered to
be different addresses.

The root node is common to all addresses; consequently, it is
not referenced. Its children constitute "top-level" name-
domains. Usually, a service has access to its own full domain
specification and to the names of all top-level name-domains.

The "top" of the domain addressing hierarchy — a child of the
root — is indicated by the right-most field, in a domain
specification. Its child is specified to the left, its child
to the left, and so on.

Some groups provide formal registration services; these constitute name-domains that are independent logically of
specific machines. In addition, networks and machines implicitly compose name-domains, since their membership usually is
registered in name tables.

In the case of formal registration, an organization implements
a (distributed) data base which provides an address-to-route
mapping service for addresses of the form:

person@registry.organization

Note that "organization" is a logical entity, separate from
any particular communication network.

A mechanism for accessing "organization" is universally available. That mechanism, in turn, seeks an instantiation of the
registry; its location is not indicated in the address specification. It is assumed that the system which operates under
the name "organization" knows how to find a subordinate registry. The registry will then use the "person" string to determine where to send the mail specification.

The latter, network-oriented case permits simple, direct,
attachment-related address specification, such as:

user@host.network

Once the network is accessed, it is expected that a message
will go directly to the host and that the host will resolve

Standard for ARPA Internet Text Messages

the user name, placing the message in the user's mailbox.

6.2.2. ABBREVIATED DOMAIN SPECIFICATION

Since any number of levels is possible within the domain
hierarchy, specification of a fully qualified address can
become inconvenient. This standard permits abbreviated domain
specification, in a special case:

> For the address of the sender, call the left-most
> sub-domain Level N. In a header address, if all of
> the sub-domains above (i.e., to the right of) Level N
> are the same as those of the sender, then they do not
> have to appear in the specification. Otherwise, the
> address must be fully qualified.

> This feature is subject to approval by local sub-
> domains. Individual sub-domains may require their
> member systems, which originate mail, to provide full
> domain specification only. When permitted, abbrevia-
> tions may be present only while the message stays
> within the sub-domain of the sender.

> Use of this mechanism requires the sender's sub-domain
> to reserve the names of all top-level domains, so that
> full specifications can be distinguished from abbrevi-
> ated specifications.

For example, if a sender's address is:

> sender@registry-A.registry-1.organization-X

and one recipient's address is:

> recipient@registry B.registry-1.organization-X

and another's is:

> recipient@registry-C.registry-2.organization-X

then ".registry-1.organization-X" need not be specified in the
the message, but "registry-C.registry-2" DOES have to be
specified. That is, the first two addresses may be abbreviated, but the third address must be fully specified.

When a message crosses a domain boundary, all addresses must
be specified in the full format, ending with the top-level
name-domain in the right-most field. It is the responsibility
of mail forwarding services to ensure that addresses conform

Standard for ARPA Internet Text Messages

with this requirement. In the case of abbreviated addresses, the relaying service must make the necessary expansions. It should be noted that it often is difficult for such a service to locate all occurrences of address abbreviations. For example, it will not be possible to find such abbreviations within the body of the message. The "Return-Path" field can aid recipients in recovering from these errors.

Note: When passing any portion of an addr-spec onto a process which does not interpret data according to this standard (e.g., mail protocol servers). There must be NO LWSP-chars preceding or following the at-sign or any delimiting period (".") , such as shown in the above examples, and only ONE SPACE between contiguous <word>s.

6.2.3. DOMAIN TERMS

A domain-ref must be THE official name of a registry, network, or host. It is a symbolic reference, within a name sub-domain. At times, it is necessary to bypass standard mechanisms for resolving such references, using more primitive information, such as a network host address rather than its associated host name.

To permit such references, this standard provides the domain-literal construct. Its contents must conform with the needs of the sub-domain in which it is interpreted.

Domain-literals which refer to domains within the ARPA Internet specify 32-bit Internet addresses, in four 8-bit fields noted in decimal, as described in Request for Comments #820, "Assigned Numbers." For example:

[10.0.3.19]

Note: THE USE OF DOMAIN-LITERALS IS STRONGLY DISCOURAGED. It is permitted only as a means of bypassing temporary system limitations, such as name tables which are not complete.

The names of "top-level" domains, and the names of domains under in the ARPA Internet, are registered with the Network Information Center, SRI International, Menlo Park, California.

6.2.4. DOMAIN-DEPENDENT LOCAL STRING

The local-part of an addr-spec in a mailbox specification (i.e., the host's name for the mailbox) is understood to be

Standard for ARPA Internet Text Messages

whatever the receiving mail protocol server allows. For example, some systems do not understand mailbox references of the
form "P. D. Q. Bach", but others do.

This specification treats periods (".") as lexical separators.
Hence, their presence in local-parts which are not quoted-
strings, is detected. However, such occurrences carry NO
semantics. That is, if a local-part has periods within it, an
address parser will divide the local-part into several tokens,
but the sequence of tokens will be treated as one uninterpreted unit. The sequence will be re-assembled, when the
address is passed outside of the system such as to a mail protocol service.

For example, the address:

First.Last@Registry.Org

is legal and does not require the local-part to be surrounded
with quotation-marks. (However, "First Last" DOES require
quoting.) The local-part of the address, when passed outside
of the mail system, within the Registry.Org domain, is
"First.Last", again without quotation marks.

6.2.5. BALANCING LOCAL-PART AND DOMAIN

In some cases, the boundary between local-part and domain can
be flexible. The local-part may be a simple string, which is
used for the final determination of the recipient's mailbox.
All other levels of reference are, therefore, part of the
domain.

For some systems, in the case of abbreviated reference to the
local and subordinate sub-domains, it may be possible to
specify only one reference within the domain part and place
the other, subordinate name-domain references within the
local-part. This would appear as:

mailbox.sub1.sub2@this-domain

Such a specification would be acceptable to address parsers
which conform to RFC #733, but do not support this newer
Internet standard. While contrary to the intent of this standard, the form is legal.

Also, some sub-domains have a specification syntax which does
not conform to this standard. For example:

sub-net.mailbox@sub-domain.domain

Standard for ARPA Internet Text Messages

uses a different parsing sequence for local-part than for
domain.

Note: As a rule, the domain specification should contain
        fields which are encoded according to the syntax of
        this standard and which contain generally-standardized
        information. The local-part specification should con-
        tain only that portion of the address which deviates
        from the form or intention of the domain field.

6.2.6. MULTIPLE MAILBOXES

An individual may have several mailboxes and wish to receive
mail at whatever mailbox is convenient for the sender to
access. This standard does not provide a means of specifying
"any member of" a list of mailboxes.

A set of individuals may wish to receive mail as a single unit
(i.e., a distribution list). The <group> construct permits
specification of such a list. Recipient mailboxes are specified within the bracketed part (":" - ";"). A copy of the
transmitted message is to be sent to each mailbox listed.
This standard does not permit recursive specification of
groups within groups.

While a list must be named, it is not required that the contents of the list be included. In this case, the <address>
serves only as an indication of group distribution and would
appear in the form:

                        name:;

Some mail services may provide a group-list distribution
facility, accepting a single mailbox reference, expanding it
to the full distribution list, and relaying the mail to the
list's members. This standard provides no additional syntax
for indicating such a service. Using the <group> address
alternative, while listing one mailbox in it, can mean either
that the mailbox reference will be expanded to a list or that
there is a group with one member.

6.2.7. EXPLICIT PATH SPECIFICATION

At times, a message originator may wish to indicate the
transmission path that a message should follow. This is
called source routing. The normal addressing scheme, used in
an addr-spec, is carefully separated from such information;
the <route> portion of a route-addr is provided for such occasions. It specifies the sequence of hosts and/or transmission

Standard for ARPA Internet Text Messages

services that are to be traversed. Both domain-refs and
domain-literals may be used.

Note: The use of source routing is discouraged. Unless the
        sender has special need of path restriction, the choice
        of transmission route should be left to the mail tran-
        sport service.

6.3. RESERVED ADDRESS

It often is necessary to send mail to a site, without know-
ing any of its valid addresses. For example, there may be mail
system dysfunctions, or a user may wish to find out a person's
correct address, at that site.

This standard specifies a single, reserved mailbox address
(local-part) which is to be valid at each site. Mail sent to
that address is to be routed to a person responsible for the
site's mail system or to a person with responsibility for general
site operation. The name of the reserved local-part address is:

                        Postmaster

so that "Postmaster@domain" is required to be valid.

Note: This reserved local-part must be matched without sensi-
        tivity to alphabetic case, so that "POSTMASTER", "postmas-
        ter", and even "poStmASteR" is to be accepted.

Standard for ARPA Internet Text Messages

7. BIBLIOGRAPHY

ANSI. "USA Standard Code for Information Interchange," X3.4. American National Standards Institute: New York (1968). Also in: Feinler, E. and J. Postel, eds., "ARPANET Protocol Handbook", NIC 7104.

ANSI. "Representations of Universal Time, Local Time Differentials, and United States Time Zone References for Information Interchange," X3.51-1975. American National Standards Institute: New York (1975).

Bemer, R.W., "Time and the Computer." In: Interface Age (Feb. 1979).

Bennett, C.J. "JNT Mail Protocol". Joint Network Team, Rutherford and Appleton Laboratory: Didcot, England.

Bhushan, A.K., Pogran, K.T., Tomlinson, R.S., and White, J.E. "Standardizing Network Mail Headers," ARPANET Request for Comments No. 561, Network Information Center No. 18516; SRI International: Menlo Park (September 1973).

Birrell, A.D., Levin, R., Needham, R.M., and Schroeder, M.D. "Grapevine: An Exercise in Distributed Computing," Communications of the ACM 25, 4 (April 1982), 260-274.

Crocker, D.H., Vittal, J.J., Pogran, K.T., Henderson, D.A. "Standard for the Format of ARPA Network Text Message," ARPANET Request for Comments No. 733, Network Information Center No. 41952. SRI International: Menlo Park (November 1977).

Feinler, E.J. and Postel, J.B. ARPANET Protocol Handbook, Network Information Center No. 7104 (NTIS AD A003890). SRI International: Menlo Park (April 1976).

Harary, F. "Graph Theory". Addison-Wesley: Reading, Mass. (1969).

Levin, R. and Schroeder, M. "Transport of Electronic Messages through a Network," TeleInformatics 79, pp. 29-33. North Holland (1979). Also as Xerox Palo Alto Research Center Technical Report CSL-79-4.

Myer, T.H. and Henderson, D.A. "Message Transmission Protocol," ARPANET Request for Comments, No. 680, Network Information Center No. 32116. SRI International: Menlo Park (1975).

Standard for ARPA Internet Text Messages

NBS. "Specification of Message Format for Computer Based Message Systems, Recommended Federal Information Processing Standard." National Bureau of Standards: Gaithersburg, Maryland (October 1981).

NIC. Internet Protocol Transition Workbook. Network Information Center, SRI-International, Menlo Park, California (March 1982).

Oppen, D.C. and Dalal, Y.K. "The Clearinghouse: A Decentralized Agent for Locating Named Objects in a Distributed Environment," OPD-T8103. Xerox Office Products Division: Palo Alto, CA. (October 1981).

Postel, J.B. "Assigned Numbers," ARPANET Request for Comments, No. 820. SRI International: Menlo Park (August 1982).

Postel, J.B. "Simple Mail Transfer Protocol," ARPANET Request for Comments, No. 821. SRI International: Menlo Park (August 1982).

Shoch, J.F. "Internetwork naming, addressing and routing," in Proc. 17th IEEE Computer Society International Conference, pp. 72-79, Sept. 1978, IEEE Cat. No. 78 CH 1388-8C.

Su, Z. and Postel, J. "The Domain Naming Convention for Internet User Applications," ARPANET Request for Comments, No. 819. SRI International: Menlo Park (August 1982).

Standard for ARPA Internet Text Messages

APPENDIX

A. EXAMPLES

A.1. ADDRESSES

A.1.1. Alfred Neuman <Neuman@BBN-TENEXA>

A.1.2. Neuman@BBN-TENEXA

These two "Alfred Neuman" examples have identical semantics, as far as the operation of the local host's mail sending
(distribution) program (also sometimes called its "mailer")
and the remote host's mail protocol server are concerned. In
the first example, the "Alfred Neuman" is ignored by the
mailer, as "Neuman@BBN-TENEXA" completely specifies the recipient. The second example contains no superfluous information, and, again, "Neuman@BBN-TENEXA" is the intended recipient.

Note: When the message crosses name-domain boundaries, then
these specifications must be changed, so as to indicate
the remainder of the hierarchy, starting with the top
level.

A.1.3. "George, Ted" <Shared@Group.Arpanet>

This form might be used to indicate that a single mailbox
is shared by several users. The quoted string is ignored by
the originating host's mailer, because "Shared@Group.Arpanet"
completely specifies the destination mailbox.

A.1.4. Wilt . (the Stilt) Chamberlain@NBA.US

The "(the Stilt)" is a comment, which is NOT included in
the destination mailbox address handed to the originating
system's mailer. The local-part of the address is the string
"Wilt.Chamberlain", with NO space between the first and second
words.

A.1.5. Address Lists

Gourmets: Pompous Person <WhoZiWhatZit@Cordon-Bleu>,
           Childs@WGBH.Boston, Galloping Gourmet@
           ANT.Down-Under (Australian National Television),
           Cheapie@Discount-Liquors;,
   Cruisers: Port@Portugal, Jones@SEA;,
     Another@Somewhere.SomeOrg

Standard for ARPA Internet Text Messages

This group list example points out the use of comments and the mixing of addresses and groups.

A.2. ORIGINATOR ITEMS

A.2.1. Author-sent

George Jones logs into his host as "Jones". He sends mail himself.

    From: Jones@Group.Org

or

    From: George Jones <Jones@Group.Org>

A.2.2. Secretary-sent

George Jones logs in as Jones on his host. His secretary, who logs in as Secy sends mail for him. Replies to the mail should go to George.

    From: George Jones <Jones@Group>
    Sender: Secy@Other-Group

A.2.3. Secretary-sent, for user of shared directory

George Jones' secretary sends mail for George. Replies should go to George.

    From: George Jones<Shared@Group.Org>
    Sender: Secy@Other-Group

Note that there need not be a space between "Jones" and the "<", but adding a space enhances readability (as is the case in other examples.

A.2.4. Committee activity, with one author

George is a member of a committee. He wishes to have any replies to his message go to all committee members.

    From: George Jones <Jones@Host.Net>
    Sender: Jones@Host
    Reply-To: The Committee: Jones@Host.Net,
                             Smith@Other.Org,
                             Doe@Somewhere-Else;

Note that if George had not included himself in the

Standard for ARPA Internet Text Messages

enumeration of The Committee, he would not have gotten an implicit reply; the presence of the "Reply-to" field SUPER-SEDES the sending of a reply to the person named in the "From" field.

A.2.5. Secretary acting as full agent of author

George Jones asks his secretary (Secy@Host) to send a message for him in his capacity as Group. He wants his secretary to handle all replies.

```
From:     George Jones <Group@Host>
Sender:   Secy@Host
Reply-To: Secy@Host
```

A.2.6. Agent for user without online mailbox

A friend of George's, Sarah, is visiting. George's secretary sends some mail to a friend of Sarah in computerland. Replies should go to George, whose mailbox is Jones at Registry.

```
From:     Sarah Friendly <Secy@Registry>
Sender:   Secy-Name <Secy@Registry>
Reply-To: Jones@Registry.
```

A.2.7. Agent for member of a committee

George's secretary sends out a message which was authored jointly by all the members of a committee. Note that the name of the committee cannot be specified, since <group> names are not permitted in the From field.

```
From:    Jones@Host,
         Smith@Other-Host,
         Doe@Somewhere-Else
Sender:  Secy@SHost
```

Standard for ARPA Internet Text Messages

A.3. COMPLETE HEADERS

A.3.1. Minimum required

```
Date:      26 Aug 76 1429 EDT       Date:    26 Aug 76 1429 EDT
From:      Jones@Registry.Org   or  From:    Jones@Registry.Org
Bcc:                                To:      Smith@Registry.Org
```

Note that the "Bcc" field may be empty, while the "To" field is required to have at least one address.

A.3.2. Using some of the additional fields

```
Date:      26 Aug 76 1430 EDT
From:      George Jones<Group@Host>
Sender:    Secy@SHOST
To:        "Al Neuman"@Mad-Host,
           Sam.Irving@Other-Host
Message-ID:  <some.string@SHOST>
```

A.3.3. About as complex as you're going to get

```
Date     :  27 Aug 76 0932 PDT
From     :  Ken Davis <KDavis@This-Host.This-net>
Subject  :  Re: The Syntax in the RFC
Sender   :  KSecy@Other-Host
Reply-To :  Sam.Irving@Reg.Organization
To       :  George Jones <Group@Some-Reg.An-Org>,
            Al.Neuman@MAD.Publisher
cc       :  Important folk:
               Tom Softwood <Balsa@Tree.Root>,
               "Sam Irving"@Other-Host:,
            Standard Distribution:
               /main/davis/people/standard@Other-Host,
               "<Jones>standard.dist.3"@Tops-20-Host>;
Comment  :  Sam is away on business. He asked me to handle
            his mail for him. He'll be able to provide  a
            more  accurate  explanation  when  he  returns
            next week.
In-Reply-To: <some.string@DBM.Group>, George's message
X-Special-action:  This is a sample of user-defined field-
            names. There could also be a field-name
            "Special-action", but its name might later be
            preempted
Message-ID: <4231.629.XYzi-What@Other-Host>
```

Standard for ARPA Internet Text Messages

B. SIMPLE FIELD PARSING

Some mail-reading software systems may wish to perform only minimal processing, ignoring the internal syntax of structured field-bodies and treating them the same as unstructured-field-bodies. Such software will need only to distinguish:

o   Header fields from the message body,

o   Beginnings of fields from lines which continue fields,

o   Field-names from field-contents.

The abbreviated set of syntactic rules which follows will suffice for this purpose. It describes a limited view of messages and is a subset of the syntactic rules provided in the main part of this specification. One small exception is that the contents of field-bodies consist only of text:

B.1. SYNTAX

```
message       =    *field *(CRLF *text)

field         =     field-name ":" [field-body] CRLF

field-name    =  1*<any CHAR, excluding CTLs, SPACE, and ":">

field-body    =    *text [CRLF LWSP-char field-body]
```

B.2. SEMANTICS

Headers occur before the message body and are terminated by a null line (i.e., two contiguous CRLFs).

A line which continues a header field begins with a SPACE or HTAB character, while a line beginning a field starts with a printable character which is not a colon.

A field-name consists of one or more printable characters (excluding colon, space, and control-characters). A field-name MUST be contained on one line. Upper and lower case are not distinguished when comparing field-names.

Standard for ARPA Internet Text Messages

C. DIFFERENCES FROM RFC #733

The following summarizes the differences between this standard and the one specified in Arpanet Request for Comments #733,
"Standard for the Format of ARPA Network Text Messages". The
differences are listed in the order of their occurrence in the
current specification.

C.1. FIELD DEFINITIONS

C.1.1. FIELD NAMES

These now must be a sequence of printable characters. They
may not contain any LWSP-chars.

C.2. LEXICAL TOKENS

C.2.1. SPECIALS

The characters period ("."), left-square bracket ("["), and
right-square bracket ("]") have been added. For presentation
purposes, and when passing a specification to a system that
does not conform to this standard, periods are to be contiguous with their surrounding lexical tokens. No linear-white-
space is permitted between them. The presence of one LWSP-
char between other tokens is still directed.

C.2.2. ATOM

Atoms may not contain SPACE.

C.2.3. SPECIAL TEXT

ctext and qtext have had backslash ("\") added to the list of
prohibited characters.

C.2.4. DOMAINS

The lexical tokens <domain-literal> and <dtext> have been
added.

C.3. MESSAGE SPECIFICATION

C.3.1. TRACE

The "Return-path:" and "Received:" fields have been specified.

Standard for ARPA Internet Text Messages

C.3.2. FROM

The "From" field must contain machine-usable addresses (addr-spec). Multiple addresses may be specified, but named-lists (groups) may not.

C.3.3. RESENT

The meta-construct of prefacing field names with the string "Resent-" has been added, to indicate that a message has been forwarded by an intermediate recipient.

C.3.4. DESTINATION

A message must contain at least one destination address field. "To" and "CC" are required to contain at least one address.

C.3.5. IN-REPLY-TO

The field-body is no longer a comma-separated list, although a sequence is still permitted.

C.3.6. REFERENCE

The field-body is no longer a comma-separated list, although a sequence is still permitted.

C.3.7. ENCRYPTED

A field has been specified that permits senders to indicate that the body of a message has been encrypted.

C.3.8. EXTENSION-FIELD

Extension fields are prohibited from beginning with the characters "X-".

C.4. DATE AND TIME SPECIFICATION

C.4.1. SIMPLIFICATION

Fewer optional forms are permitted and the list of three-letter time zones has been shortened.

C.5. ADDRESS SPECIFICATION

Standard for ARPA Internet Text Messages

C.5.1. ADDRESS

The use of quoted-string, and the ":"-atom-":" construct, have been removed. An address now is either a single mailbox reference or is a named list of addresses. The latter indicates a group distribution.

C.5.2. GROUPS

Group lists are now required to to have a name. Group lists may not be nested.

C.5.3. MAILBOX

A mailbox specification may indicate a person's name, as before. Such a named list no longer may specify multiple mailboxes and may not be nested.

C.5.4. ROUTE ADDRESSING

Addresses now are taken to be absolute, global specifications, independent of transmission paths. The <route> construct has been provided, to permit explicit specification of transmission path. RFC #733's use of multiple at-signs ("@") was intended as a general syntax for indicating routing and/or hierarchical addressing. The current standard separates these specifications and only one at-sign is permitted.

C.5.5. AT-SIGN

The string " at " no longer is used as an address delimiter. Only at-sign ("@") serves the function.

C.5.6. DOMAINS

Hierarchical, logical name-domains have been added.

C.6. RESERVED ADDRESS

The local-part "Postmaster" has been reserved, so that users can be guaranteed at least one valid address at a site.

Standard for ARPA Internet Text Messages

D. ALPHABETICAL LISTING OF SYNTAX RULES

```
address      =  mailbox                          ; one addressee
             /  group                            ; named list
addr-spec    =  local-part "@" domain            ; global address
ALPHA        =  <any ASCII alphabetic character>
                                                 ; (101-132, 65.- 90.)
                                                 ; (141-172, 97.-122.)
atom         =  1*<any CHAR except specials, SPACE and CTLs>
authentic    =  "From"          ":"    mailbox   ; Single author
             / ( "Sender"       ":"    mailbox   ; Actual submittor
                 "From"         ":" 1#mailbox)   ; Multiple authors
                                                 ;  or not sender
CHAR         =  <any ASCII character>            ; (  0-177,  0.-127.)
comment      =  "(" *(ctext / quoted-pair / comment) ")"
CR           =  <ASCII CR, carriage return>      ; (      15,      13.)
CRLF         =  CR LF
ctext        =  <any CHAR excluding "(",         ; => may be folded
                ")", "\" & CR, & including
                linear-white-space>
CTL          =  <any ASCII control               ; (  0- 37,  0.- 31.)
                character and DEL>               ; (     177,     127.)
date         =  1*2DIGIT month 2DIGIT            ; day month year
                                                 ;  e.g. 20 Jun 82
dates        =    orig-date                      ; Original
                [ resent-date ]                  ; Forwarded
date-time    =  [ day "," ] date time            ; dd mm yy
                                                 ;  hh:mm:ss zzz
day          =  "Mon"  / "Tue" / "Wed"  / "Thu"
             /  "Fri"  / "Sat" / "Sun"
delimiters   =  specials / linear-white-space / comment
destination  =  "To"             ":" 1#address   ; Primary
             /  "Resent-To"      ":" 1#address
             /  "cc"             ":" 1#address    ; Secondary
             /  "Resent-cc"      ":" 1#address
             /  "bcc"            ":"  #address    ; Blind carbon
             /  "Resent-bcc" ":"  #address
DIGIT        =  <any ASCII decimal digit>        ; ( 60- 71, 48.- 57.)
domain       =  sub-domain *("." sub-domain)
domain-literal = "[" *(dtext / quoted-pair) "]"
domain-ref   =  atom                             ; symbolic reference
dtext        =  <any CHAR excluding "[",         ; => may be folded
                "]", "\" & CR, & including
                linear-white-space>
extension-field =
                <Any field which is defined in a document
                published as a formal extension to this
                specification; none will have names beginning
                with the string "X-">
```

Standard for ARPA Internet Text Messages

```
field      =  field-name ":" [ field-body ] CRLF
fields     =    dates                      ; Creation time,
                source                     ;   author id & one
              1*destination                ;   address required
                *optional-field            ;   others optional
field-body =  field-body-contents
              [CRLF LWSP-char field-body]
field-body-contents =
              <the ASCII characters making up the field-body, as
              defined in the following sections, and consisting
              of combinations of atom, quoted-string, and
              specials tokens, or else consisting of texts>
field-name =  1*<any CHAR, excluding CTLs, SPACE, and ":">
group      =  phrase ":" [#mailbox] ";"
hour       =  2DIGIT ":" 2DIGIT [":" 2DIGIT]
                                           ; 00:00:00 - 23:59:59
HTAB       =  <ASCII HT, horizontal-tab>   ; (    11,       9.)
LF         =  <ASCII LF, linefeed>         ; (    12,      10.)
linear-white-space =  1*([CRLF] LWSP-char) ; semantics = SPACE
                                           ; CRLF => folding
local-part =  word *("." word)             ; uninterpreted
                                           ; case-preserved
LWSP-char  =  SPACE / HTAB                  ; semantics = SPACE
mailbox    =  addr-spec                     ; simple address
           /  phrase route-addr             ; name & addr-spec
message    =  fields *( CRLF *text )         ; Everything after
                                           ;   first null line
                                           ;   is message body
month      =  "Jan" / "Feb" / "Mar" / "Apr"
           /  "May" / "Jun" / "Jul" / "Aug"
           /  "Sep" / "Oct" / "Nov" / "Dec"
msg-id     =  "<" addr-spec ">"            ; Unique message id
optional-field =
           /  "Message-ID"          ":"  msg-id
           /  "Resent-Message-ID" ":"  msg-id
           /  "In-Reply-To"        ":"  *(phrase / msg-id)
           /  "References"         ":"  *(phrase / msg-id)
           /  "Keywords"           ":"  #phrase
           /  "Subject"            ":"  *text
           /  "Comments"           ":"  *text
           /  "Encrypted"          ":"  1#2word
           /  extension-field            ; To be defined
           /  user-defined-field         ; May be pre-empted
orig-date  =  "Date"           ":"  date-time
originator =    authentic                    ; authenticated addr
              [ "Reply-To"     ":"  1#address] )
phrase     =  1*word                        ; Sequence of words
```

Standard for ARPA Internet Text Messages

```
qtext        =  <any CHAR excepting <">,     ; => may be folded
                 "\" & CR, and including
                 linear-white-space>
quoted-pair  = "\" CHAR                       ; may quote any char
quoted-string = <"> *(qtext/quoted-pair) <">; Regular qtext or
                                              ;   quoted chars.
received     = "Received"      ":"            ; one per relay
                  ["from" domain]            ; sending host
                  ["by"   domain]            ; receiving host
                  ["via"  atom]              ; physical path
                 *("with" atom)              ; link/mail protocol
                  ["id"   msg-id]            ; receiver msg id
                  ["for"  addr-spec]         ; initial form
                   ";"    date-time          ; time received

resent       =   resent-authentic
               [ "Resent-Reply-To"  ":" 1#address] )
resent-authentic =
             =   "Resent-From"       ":"   mailbox
             / ( "Resent-Sender"     ":"   mailbox
                 "Resent-From"       ":" 1#mailbox   )
resent-date  = "Resent-Date" ":"   date-time
return       = "Return-path" ":" route-addr ; return address
route        = 1#("@" domain) ":"           ; path-relative
route-addr   = "<" [route] addr-spec ">"
source       = [ trace ]                     ; net traversals
                 originator                  ; original mail
               [ resent ]                    ; forwarded
SPACE        = <ASCII SP, space>             ; (    40,      32.)
specials     = "(" / ")" / "<" / ">" / "@"  ; Must be in quoted-
               / "," / ";" / ":" / "\" / <"> ;   string, to use
               / "." / "[" / "]"             ;   within a word.
sub-domain   = domain-ref / domain-literal
text         = <any CHAR, including bare     ; => atoms, specials,
                CR & bare LF, but NOT        ;   comments and
                including CRLF>              ;   quoted-strings are
                                             ;   NOT recognized.
time         = hour zone                     ; ANSI and Military
trace        =   return                      ; path to sender
                1*received                   ; receipt tags
user-defined-field =
             <Any field which has not been defined
              in this specification or published as an
              extension to this specification; names for
              such fields must be unique and may be
              pre-empted by published extensions>
word         = atom / quoted-string
```

Standard for ARPA Internet Text Messages

```
zone        =   "UT"  / "GMT"              ; Universal Time
                                           ; North American : UT
            /   "EST" / "EDT"              ;  Eastern:   - 5/ - 4
            /   "CST" / "CDT"              ;  Central:   - 6/ - 5
            /   "MST" / "MDT"              ;  Mountain:  - 7/ - 6
            /   "PST" / "PDT"              ;  Pacific:   - 8/ - 7
            /   1ALPHA                     ; Military: Z = UT;
<">         =   <ASCII quote mark>         ; (     42,      34.)
```

$\overline{\text{H}}$

RFC # 1178

RFC # 1178 sets guidelines for naming your own machine. If you elect to obtain a DNN (Internet) name, the domain name(s) will be assigned to you. See Appendix I for further details on obtaining a name in the "us" domain. The suggestions made below are well taken for the naming of your own system for either Usenet or Internet purposes. As noted elsewhere, when you set up your Permissions (permissn) (or sys if using Taylor UUCP) file you have the opportunity to specify the "MYNAME" option. This lets you be known by one name locally and by another name to a specifc remote system if, for some reason, you cannot manage consistent names. It would be simpler, however, to use the same name locally and remotely when logging onto the system that provides news and mail feeds.

Network Working Group   D. Libes
Request for Comments: 1178   Integrated Systems Group/NIST
FYI: 5   August 1990

                    Choosing a Name for Your Computer

Status of this Memo

    This FYI RFC is a republication of a Communications of the ACM
    article on guidelines on what to do and what not to do when naming
    your computer [1]. This memo provides information for the Internet
    community. It does not specify any standard.

    Distribution of this memo is unlimited.

Abstract

    In order to easily distinguish between multiple computers, we give
    them names. Experience has taught us that it is as easy to choose
    bad names as it is to choose good ones. This essay presents
    guidelines for deciding what makes a name good or bad.

    Keywords: domain name system, naming conventions, computer
    administration, computer network management

Introduction

    As soon as you deal with more than one computer, you need to
    distinguish between them. For example, to tell your system
    administrator that your computer is busted, you might say, "Hey Ken.
    Goon is down!"

    Computers also have to be able to distinguish between themselves.
    Thus, when sending mail to a colleague at another computer, you might
    use the command "mail libes@goon".

    In both cases, "goon" refers to a particular computer. How the name
    is actually dereferenced by a human or computer need not concern us
    here. This essay is only concerned with choosing a "good" name. (It
    is assumed that the reader has a basic understanding of the domain
    name system as described by [2].)

    By picking a "good" name for your computer, you can avoid a number of
    problems that people stumble over again and again.

    Here are some guidelines on what NOT to do.

Libes

Don't overload other terms already in common use.

Using a word that has strong semantic implications in the current context will cause confusion. This is especially true in conversation where punctuation is not obvious and grammar is often incorrect.

For example, a distributed database had been built on top of several computers. Each one had a different name. One machine was named "up", as it was the only one that accepted updates. Conversations would sound like this: "Is up down?" and "Boot the machine up." followed by "Which machine?"

While it didn't take long to catch on and get used to this zaniness, it was annoying when occasionally your mind would stumble, and you would have to stop and think about each word in a sentence. It is as if, all of a sudden, English has become a foreign language.

Don't choose a name after a project unique to that machine.

A manufacturing project had named a machine "shop" since it was going to be used to control a number of machines on a shop floor. A while later, a new machine was acquired to help with some of the processing. Needless to say, it couldn't be called "shop" as well. Indeed, both machines ended up performing more specific tasks, allowing more precision in naming. A year later, five new machines were installed and the original one was moved to an unrelated project. It is simply impossible to choose generic names that remain appropriate for very long.

Of course, they could have called the second one "shop2" and so on. But then one is really only distinguishing machines by their number. You might as well just call them "1", "2", and "3". The only time this kind of naming scheme is appropriate is when you have a lot of machines and there are no reasons for any human to distinguish between them. For example, a master computer might be controlling an array of one hundred computers. In this case, it makes sense to refer to them with the array indices.

While computers aren't quite analogous to people, their names are. Nobody expects to learn much about a person by their name. Just because a person is named "Don" doesn't mean he is the ruler of the world (despite what the "Choosing a Name for your Baby" books say). In reality, names are just arbitrary tags. You cannot tell what a person does for a living, what their hobbies are, and so on.

Don't use your own name.

> Even if a computer is sitting on your desktop, it is a mistake
> to name it after yourself. This is another case of
> overloading, in which statements become ambiguous. Does "give
> the disk drive to don" refer to a person or computer?

> Even using your initials (or some other moniker) is
> unsatisfactory. What happens if I get a different machine
> after a year? Someone else gets stuck with "don" and I end up
> living with "jim". The machines can be renamed, but that is
> excess work and besides, a program that used a special
> peripheral or database on "don" would start failing when it
> wasn't found on the "new don".

> It is especially tempting to name your first computer after
> yourself, but think about it. Do you name any of your other
> possessions after yourself? No. Your dog has its own name, as
> do your children. If you are one of those who feel so inclined
> to name your car and other objects, you certainly don't reuse
> your own name. Otherwise you would have a great deal of
> trouble distinguishing between them in speech.

> For the same reason, it follows that naming your computer the
> same thing as your car or another possession is a mistake.

Don't use long names.

> This is hard to quantify, but experience has shown that names
> longer than eight characters simply annoy people.

> Most systems will allow prespecified abbreviations, but why not
> choose a name that you don't have to abbreviate to begin with?
> This removes any chance of confusion.

Avoid alternate spellings.

> Once we called a machine "czek". In discussion, people
> continually thought we were talking about a machine called
> "check". Indeed, "czek" isn't even a word (although "Czech"
> is).

> Purposely incorrect (but cute) spellings also tend to annoy a
> large subset of people. Also, people who have learned English
> as a second language often question their own knowledge upon
> seeing a word that they know but spelled differently. ("I
> guess I've always been spelling "funxion" incorrectly. How
> embarrassing!")

By now you may be saying to yourself, "This is all very
silly...people who have to know how to spell a name will learn
it and that's that." While it is true that some people will
learn the spelling, it will eventually cause problems
somewhere.

For example, one day a machine named "pythagoris" (sic) went
awry and began sending a tremendous number of messages to the
site administrator's computer. The administrator, who wasn't a
very good speller to begin with, had never seen this machine
before (someone else had set it up and named it), but he had to
deal with it since it was clogging up the network as well as
bogging down his own machine which was logging all the errors.
Needless to say, he had to look it up every time he needed to
spell "pythagoris". (He suspected there was an abbreviation,
but he would have had to log into yet another computer (the
local nameserver) to find out and the network was too jammed to
waste time doing that.)

Avoid domain names.

For technical reasons, domain names should be avoided. In
particular, name resolution of non-absolute hostnames is
problematic. Resolvers will check names against domains before
checking them against hostnames. But we have seen instances of
mailers that refuse to treat single token names as domains.
For example, assume that you mail to "libes@rutgers" from
yale.edu. Depending upon the implementation, the mail may go
to rutgers.edu or rutgers.yale.edu (assuming both exist).

Avoid domain-like names.

Domain names are either organizational (e.g., cia.gov) or
geographical (e.g., dallas.tx.us). Using anything like these
tends to imply some connection. For example, the name "tahiti"
sounds like it means you are located there. This is confusing
if it is really somewhere else (e.g., "tahiti.cia.gov is
located in Langley, Virginia? I thought it was the CIA's
Tahiti office!"). If it really is located there, the name
implies that it is the only computer there. If this isn't
wrong now, it inevitably will be.

There are some organizational and geographical names that work
fine. These are exactly the ones that do not function well as
domain names. For example, amorphous names such as rivers,
mythological places and other impossibilities are very
suitable. ("earth" is not yet a domain name.)

Libes

Don't use antagonistic or otherwise embarrassing names.

Words like "moron" or "twit" are good names if no one else is going to see them. But if you ever give someone a demo on your machine, you may find that they are distracted by seeing a nasty word on your screen. (Maybe their spouse called them that this morning.) Why bother taking the chance that they will be turned off by something completely irrelevant to your demo.

Don't use digits at the beginning of the name.

Many programs accept a numerical internet address as well as a name. Unfortunately, some programs do not correctly distinguish between the two and may be fooled, for example, by a string beginning with a decimal digit.

Names consisting entirely of hexadecimal digits, such as "beef", are also problematic, since they can be interpreted entirely as hexadecimal numbers as well as alphabetic strings.

Don't use non-alphanumeric characters in a name.

Your own computer may handle punctuation or control characters in a name, but most others do not. If you ever expect to connect your computer to a heterogeneous network, you can count on a variety of interpretations of non-alphanumeric characters in names. Network conventions on this are surprisingly nonstandard.

Don't expect case to be preserved.

Upper and lowercase characters look the same to a great deal of internet software, often under the assumption that it is doing you a favor. It may seem appropriate to capitalize a name the same way you might do it in English, but convention dictates that computer names appear all lowercase. (And it saves holding down the shift key.)

Now that we've heard what not to do, here are some suggestions on names that work well.

Use words/names that are rarely used.

While a word like "typical" or "up" (see above) isn't computer jargon, it is just too likely to arise in discussion and throw off one's concentration while determining the correct referent. Instead, use words like "lurch" or "squire" which are unlikely to cause any confusion.

You might feel it is safe to use the name "jose" just because no one is named that in your group, but you will have a problem if you should happen to hire Jose. A name like "sphinx" will be less likely to conflict with new hires.

Use theme names.

Naming groups of machines in a common way is very popular, and enhances communality while displaying depth of knowledge as well as imagination. A simple example is to use colors, such as "red" and "blue". Personality can be injected by choices such as "aqua" and "crimson".

Certain sets are finite, such as the seven dwarfs. When you order your first seven computers, keep in mind that you will probably get more next year. Colors will never run out.

Some more suggestions are: mythical places (e.g., Midgard, Styx, Paradise), mythical people (e.g., Procne, Tereus, Zeus), killers (e.g., Cain, Burr, Boleyn), babies (e.g., colt, puppy, tadpole, elver), collectives (e.g., passel, plague, bevy, covey), elements (e.g., helium, argon, zinc), flowers (e.g., tulip, peony, lilac, arbutus). Get the idea?

Use real words.

Random strings are inappropriate for the same reason that they are so useful for passwords. They are hard to remember. Use real words.

Don't worry about reusing someone else's hostname.

Extremely well-known hostnames such as "sri-nic" and "uunet" should be avoided since they are understood in conversation as absolute addresses even without a domain. In all other cases, the local domain is assumed to qualify single-part hostnames. This is similar to the way phone numbers are qualified by an area code when dialed from another area.

In other words, if you have choosen a reasonable name, you do not have to worry that it has already been used in another domain. The number of hosts in a bottom-level domain is small, so it shouldn't be hard to pick a name unique only to that domain.

Libes

There is always room for an exception.

> I don't think any explanation is needed here. However, let me add that if you later decide to change a name (to something sensible like you should have chosen in the first place), you are going to be amazed at the amount of pain awaiting you. No matter how easy the manuals suggest it is to change a name, you will find that lots of obscure software has rapidly accumulated which refers to that computer using that now-ugly name. It all has to be found and changed. People mailing to you from other sites have to be told. And you will have to remember that names on old backup media labels correspond to different names.

> I could go on but it would be easier just to forget this guideline exists.

Conclusion

Most people don't have the opportunity to name more than one or two computers, while site administrators name large numbers of them. By choosing a name wisely, both user and administrator will have an easier time of remembering, discussing and typing the names of their computers.

I have tried to formalize useful guidelines for naming computers, along with plenty of examples to make my points obvious. Having been both a user and site administrator, many of these anecdotes come from real experiences which I have no desire to relive. Hopefully, you will avoid all of the pitfalls I have discussed by choosing your computer's name wisely.

Credits

Thanks to the following people for suggesting some of these guidelines and participating in numerous discussions on computer naming: Ed Barkmeyer, Peter Brown, Chuck Hedrick, Ken Manheimer, and Scott Paisley.

This essay first appeared in the Communications of the ACM, November, 1989, along with a Gary Larson cartoon reprinted with permission of United Press Syndicate. The text is not subject to copyright, since it is work of the National Institute of Standards and Technology. However, the author, CACM, and NIST request that this credit appear with the article whenever it is reprinted.

Libes

RFC 1178   Name Your Computer   August 1990

References

[1] Libes, D., "Choosing a Name for Your Computer", Communications
of the ACM, Vol. 32, No. 11, Pg. 1289, November 1989.

[2] Mockapetris, P., "Domain Names - Concepts and Facilities",
RFC 1034, USC/Information Sciences Institute, November 1987.

Security Considerations

Security issues are not discussed in this memo.

Author's Address

Don Libes
Integrated Systems Group
National Institute of Standards and Technology
Gaithersburg, MD 20899

Phone: (301) 975-3535

E-Mail: libes@cme.nist.gov

I

RFC # 1480

RFC # 1386 explains in detail the procedure for obtaining a "us" domain name.
The information contained in this document applies to Usenet and Internet alike.
Read it with care.

Network Working Group   A. Cooper
Request for Comments: 1480   J. Postel
Obsoletes: 1386   June 1993

                          The US Domain

Status of this Memo

   This memo provides information for the Internet community. It does
   not specify an Internet standard. Distribution of this memo is
   unlimited.

Table of Contents

RFC 1480   The US Domain   June 1993

1. INTRODUCTION

1.1 The Internet Domain Name System

The Domain Name System (DNS) provides for the translation between
hostnames and addresses. Within the Internet, this means translating
from a name such as "venera.isi.edu", to an IP address such as
"128.9.0.32". The DNS is a set of protocols and databases. The
protocols define the syntax and semantics for a query language to ask
questions about information located by DNS-style names. The
databases are distributed and replicated. There is no dependence on
a single central server, and each part of the database is provided in
at least two servers.

The assignment of the 32-bit IP addresses is a separate activity. IP
addresses are delegated by the central Internet Registry to regional
authorities (such as the RIPE NCC for Europe) and the network
providers.

To have a network number assigned please contact your network service
provider or regional registration authority. To determine who this
is (or as a last resort), you can contact the central Internet
Registry at Hostmaster@INTERNIC.NET.

In addition to translating names to addresses for hosts that are on
the Internet, the DNS provides for registering DNS-style names for
other hosts reachable (via electronic mail) through gateways or mail
relays. The records for such name registrations point to an Internet
host (one with an IP address) that acts as a mail forwarder for the
registered host. For example, the host "bah.rochester.ny.us" is
registered in the DNS with a pointer to the mail relay
"relay1.uu.net". This type of pointer is called an MX record.

This gives electronic mail users a uniform mail addressing syntax and
avoids making users aware of the underlying network boundaries.

The reason for the development of the domain system was growth in the
Internet. The hostname to address mappings were maintained by the
InterNIC in a single file, called HOSTS.TXT, which was FTP'd by all
the hosts on the Internet. The network population was changing in
character. The time-share hosts that made up the original ARPANET
were being replaced with local networks of workstations. Local
organizations were administering their own names and addresses, but

had to wait for the NIC to make changes in HOSTS.TXT to make the
changes visible to the Internet at large. Organizations also wanted
some local structure on the name space. The applications on the
Internet were getting more sophisticated and creating a need for
general purpose name service. The idea of a hierarchical name space,
with the hierarchy roughly corresponding to organizational structure,
and names using "." as the character to mark the boundary between
hierarchy levels was developed. A design using a distributed
database and generalized resources was implemented.

The DNS provides standard formats for resource data, standard methods
for querying the database, and standard methods for name servers to
refresh local data from other name servers.

1.2 Top-Level Domains

The top-level domains in the DNS are EDU, COM, GOV, MIL, ORG, INT,
and NET, and all the 2-letter country codes from the list of
countries in ISO-3166. The establishment of new top-level domains is
managed by the Internet Assigned Numbers Authority (IANA). The IANA
may be contacted at IANA@ISI.EDU.

Even though the original intention was that any educational
institution anywhere in the world could be registered under the EDU
domain, in practice, it has turned out with few exceptions, only
those in the United States have registered under EDU, similarly with
COM (for commercial). In other countries, everything is registered
under the 2-letter country code, often with some subdivision. For
example, in Korea (KR) the second level names are AC for academic
community, CO for commercial, GO for government, and RE for research.
However, each country may go its own way about organizing its domain,
and many have.

There are no current plans of putting all of the organizational
domains EDU, GOV, COM, etc., under US. These name tokens are not
used in the US Domain to avoid confusion.

Currently, only four year colleges and universities are being
registered in the EDU domain. All other schools are being registered
in the US Domain.

There are also concerns about the size of the other top-level domains
(especially COM) and ideas are being considered for restructuring.

Other names sometimes appear as top-level domain names. Some people
have made up names in the DNS-style without coordinating or
registering with the DNS management. Some names that typically
appear are BITNET, UUCP, and two-letter codes for continents, such as

"NA" for North America (this conflicts with the official Internet code for Namibia).

For example, the DNS-style name "KA7EEJ.CO.USA.NA" is used in the amateur radio network. These addresses are never supposed to show up on the Internet but they do occasionally. The amateur radio network people created their own naming scheme, and it interferes sometimes with Internet addresses.

1.3 The US Domain

The US Domain is an official top-level domain in the DNS of the Internet community. The domain administrators are Jon Postel and Ann Westine Cooper at the Information Sciences Institute of the University of Southern California (USC-ISI).

US is the ISO-3166 2-letter country code for the United States and thus the US Domain is established as a top-level domain and registered with the InterNIC the same way other country domains are.

Because organizations in the United States have registered primarily in the EDU and COM domains, little use was initially made of the US domain. In the past, the computers registered in the US Domain were primarily owned by small companies or individuals with computers at home. However, the US Domain has grown and currently registers hosts in federal government agencies, state government agencies, K12 schools, community colleges, technical/vocational schools, private schools, libraries, city and county government agencies, to name a few.

Initially, the administration of the US Domain was managed solely by the Domain Registrar. However, due to the increase in registrations, administration of subdomains is being delegated to others.

Any computer in the United States may be registered in the US Domain.

2. NAMING STRUCTURE

The US Domain hierarchy is based on political geography. The basic name space under US is the state name space, then the "locality" name space, (like a city, or county) then organization or computer name and so on.

For example:

        BERKELEY.CA.US
        PORTLAND.WA.US

There is of course no problem with running out of names.

The things that are named are individual computers.

If you register now in one city and then move, the database can be updated with a new name in your new city, and a pointer can be set up from your old name to your new name. This type of pointer is called a CNAME record.

The use of unregistered names is not effective and causes problems for other users. Inventing your own name and using it without registering is not a good idea.

In addition to strictly geographically names, some special names are used, such as FED, STATE, AGENCY, DISTRICT, K12, LIB, CC, CITY, and COUNTY. Several new name spaces have been created, DNI, GEN, and TEC, and a minor change under the "locality" name space was made to the existing CITY and COUNTY subdomains by abbreviating them to CI and CO. A detailed description follows.

Below US, Parallel to States:
_____ -

"FED" - This branch may be used for agencies of the federal government. For example: <org-name>.<city>.FED.US

"DNI" - DISTRIBUTED NATIONAL INSTITUTES - The "DNI" branch was created directly under the top-level US. This branch is to be used for distributed national institutes; organizations that span state, regional, and other organizational boundaries; that are national in scope, and have distributed facilities. For example: <org-name>.DNI.US.

Name Space Within States:
_____

"locality" - cities, counties, parishes, and townships. Subdomains under the "locality" would be like CI.<city>.<state>.US, CO.<county>.<state>.US, or businesses. For example: Petville.Marvista.CA.US.

"CI" - This branch is used for city government agencies and is a subdomain under the "locality" name (like Los Angeles). For example: Fire-Dept.CI.Los-Angeles.CA.US.

"CO" - This branch is used for county government agencies and is a subdomain under the "locality" name (like Los Angeles). For example: Fire-Dept.CO.San-Diego.CA.US.

"K12" - This branch may be used for public school districts. A special name "PVT" can be used in the place of a school district name for private schools. For example: <school-name>.K12.<state>.US and <school-name>.PVT.K12.<state>.US.

"CC" - COMMUNITY COLLEGES - This branch was established for all state wide community colleges. For example: <school-name>.CC.<state>.US.

"TEC" - TECHNICAL AND VOCATIONAL SCHOOLS - The branch "TEC" was established for technical and vocational schools and colleges. For example: <school-name>.TEC.<state>.US.

"LIB" - LIBRARIES (STATE, REGIONAL, CITY, COUNTY) - This branch may be used for libraries only. For example: <lib-name>.LIB.<state>.US.

"STATE" - This branch may be used for state government agencies. For example: <org-name>.STATE.<state>.US.

"GEN" - GENERAL INDEPENDENT ENTITY - This branch is for the things that don't fit easily into any other structure listed — things that might fit in to something like ORG at the top-level. It is best not to use the same keywords (ORG, EDU, COM, etc.) that are used at the top-level to avoid confusion. GEN would be used for such things as, state-wide organizations, clubs, or domain parks. For example: <org-name>.GEN.<state-code>.US.

++

VIEW OF SECOND LEVEL DOMAINS UNDER US

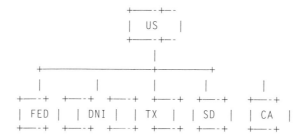

++

RFC 1480   The US Domain   June 1993

```
+++++++++++++++++++++++++++++++++++++++++++++++++++++++++++++++++++++++
SCHOOL AND LIBRARY VIEW
                              +--+++
                              | CA |
                              +--+++
                                |
              +--------------------------------+
              |          |          |           |           |
           +--+      +---+ +--+    +------+   +--+-+-+    +--+
           | K12 |   | CC |  | TEC |   | LOS ANGELES |   | LIB |
           +--+      +---+ +--+    +------+   +--+-+-+    +--+
            / \       /|\     /|\          /|\            /|\
      +---+ +--+  +--+ +-----+  +------+   +----+-+    +---+
      |sch dist| |PVT| |SJC| |WM TRADE|   |pvt school|   |MALIBU|
      +---+ +--+  +--+ +-----+  +-----+   +----+-+    +---+
       /|\       /|\
     +----+ +----+--+
     |sch name| |sch name|
     +----+ +----+--+
+++++++++++++++++++++++++++++++++++++++++++++++++++++++++++++++++++++++++


VIEW OF STATE, REGIONAL, and GENERAL AGENCIES

                              +--+++
                              | CA |
                              +--+++
                                |
                  +----------------+------+
                  |          |           |
              +---+      +--------+ +--+ +--+
              | STATE |    |DISTRICT|   | GEN |
              +---+      +--------+ +--+ +--+
               /|\        /|\        /|\
              +----+      +----+ +-----+-++--+
              |CALTRANS|   |SCAQMD|  |domain pk|
              ----+      +----+ +----+-++--+
                 |
              +----+--+
              |TCEW100E|
              +----+--+
+++++++++++++++++++++++++++++++++++++++++++++++++++++++++++++++++++++++
```

```
++++++++++++++++++++++++++++++++++++++++++++++++++++++++++++++++++++++++++
VIEW OF LOCALITY
```

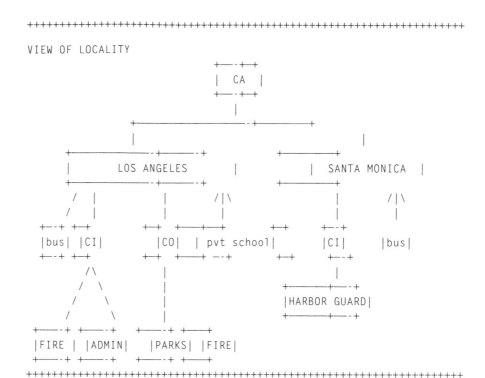

2.1 State Codes

The state codes are the two letter US Postal abbreviations. For
example: "CA" California.

2.2 Locality Names

Within the state name space there are "locality" names, some may be
cities, some may be counties, some may be local names, but not
incorporated entities.

Registered names under "locality" could be like:

```
<hostname>.CI.<locality>.<state>.US    ==>   city gov't agency
<hostname>.CO.<locality>.<state>.US,   ==>   county gov't agency
<hostname>.<locality>.<state>.US       ==>   businesses
```

In the cases where the locality name is a county, there is a branch
under the locality name, called "county" or "CO", that is used by the
county government. Businesses are registered directly under the
locality name.

Under the city locality name space there is a "city" or "CI" branch
for city government agencies. As usual, businesses and private
schools may register directly under the city name.

In the case where there is both a county and a city with the same
locality name there is no problem, since the names will be unique
with the "CO" or "CI" keyword. In our area the county has a fire
department and the city has its own fire department. They could have
names like:

```
Fire-Dept.CI.Los-Angeles.CA.US
Fire-Dept.CO.Los-Angeles.CA.US
```

Cities may be named (designated) by their full name (spelled out with
hyphens replacing spaces (e.g., Los-Angeles or Fort-Collins), or by a
city code. The first choice is the full city name. In some cases it
may be appropriate to use the well-known city abbreviation known
throughout a locality. However, it is very desirable that all users
in the same city use the same designator for the city. That is, any
particular locality should have just one DNS name.

Some users would like names associated with a greater metropolitan
area or region like the "Bay Area" or "Tri-Cities". One problem with
this is that these names are not necessarily unique within a state.
The best thing to do in this case is to use the larger metropolitan
city in your hostname. Cities and counties are used.

Should all the names be obvious? Trying to do this is desirable and
also impossible. There will come a point when the obviously right
name for an organization is already taken. As the system grows this
will happen with increasing frequency. While ease of use to the end
user is desirable, a higher priority must be placed on having a
system that operates. This means that the manageability of the
system must have high consideration.

The reason the DNS was created was to subdivide the problem of
maintaining a list of hosts in the Internet into manageable portions.

The happy result is that this subdivision makes name uniqueness
easier and promotes logical grouping. What is a "logical grouping"
though, always depends on the viewer.

Many levels of delegation are needed to keep the zone files
manageable. Many sections of the name space are needed to allow
unique names to be easily added.

Cooper & Postel

RFC 1480   The US Domain   June 1993

Way back in the olden days, when the Internet was invented, some thought that an 8-bit network number would be more than enough to number all the networks that would ever exist. Today, there are over 10,000 networks operating in the Internet, and arguments are made about the doubling time being 2 years versus 4 years.

One concern is that things will continue to grow dramatically, and this will require more subdivision of the domain name management. Maybe the plan for the US Domain is overkill on growth planning, but there has never been overplanning for growth yet.

When things are bigger, names have to be longer. There is an argument that with only 8-character names, and in each position allow a-z, 0-9, and -, you get $37**8 = 3,512,479,453,921$ or 3.5 trillion possible names. It is a great argument, but how many of us want names like "xs4gp-7q". It is like license plate numbers, sure some people get the name they want on a vanity plate, but a lot more people who want something specific on a vanity plate can't get it because someone else got it first. Structure and longer names also let more people get their "obviously right" name.

2.3 Schools

K12 schools are connecting to the Internet and registering in the Internet DNS. A decision has been made by the IANA (after consultation with the new InterNIC Internet Registry and the Federal Networking Council (FNC)) to direct these school registrations to the US domain using the naming structure described here.

There is a need for competent, experienced, volunteers to come forward to act as third and perhaps fourth level registries and to operate delegated portions of the DNS.

There are two reasons for registering schools in the US Domain. (1) uniqueness of names, and (2) management of the database.

  1. Name Uniqueness:

     There are many "Washington" high schools, only one can be "Washington.EDU" (actually none can be, since that name is used by a University. There will be many name conflicts if all schools attempt to register directly under EDU.

     In addition, in some districts, the same school name is used at different levels, for example, Washington Elementary School and Washington High School. We suggest that when necessary, the keywords "Elementary", "Middle", and "High" be used to distinguish these schools. These keywords would only be used

when they are needed, if the school's name is unique without
such keywords, don't use them.

2. Database Management:

One goal of the DNS is to divide up the management of the name
database in to small pieces. Each piece (or "zone" in DNS
terminology) could be managed by a distinct administrator.
Adding all the high schools to the EDU domain will make the
already large zone file for EDU even larger, possibly to the
point of being unmanageable.

For both these reasons it is necessary to introduce structure into
names. Structure provides a basis for making common names unique in
context, and for dividing the management responsibility.

The US Domain has a framework established and has registered many
schools already in this structured scheme. The general form is:

    <school>.<district>.K12.<state>.US.

        For example: Hamilton.LA-Unified.K12.CA.US

Public schools are usually organized by districts which can be larger
or smaller than a city or county. For example, the Portland school
district in Oregon, is in three or four counties. Each of those
counties also has non-Portland districts.

It makes sense to name schools within districts. However districts
often have the same name as a city or county so there has to be a way
to distinguish a public school district name from some other type of
locality name. The keyword "K12" is used for this.

For example, typical K12 school names currently used are:

        IVY.PRS.K12.NJ.US
        DMHS.JCPS.K12.KY.US
        OHS.EUNION.K12.CA.US
        BOHS.BREA.K12.CA.US

These names are generally longer than the old alternative of shorter
names in the EDU domain, but that would not have lasted long without
a significant number of schools finding that their "obviously
correct" name has already been used by some other school.

Cooper & Postel

RFC 1480   The US Domain   June 1993

When there are many things to name some of the names will be long.
In some cases there may be appropriate abbreviations that can be
used. For example Hamilton High School in Los Angeles could be:

     Hami.Hi.LA.K12.CA.US

If a school has a number of PCs, then each PC should have a name.
Suppose they are named "alpha", "beta", ... then if they belong to a
school named "Lincoln.High.Lakewood.K12.CA.US" their names would be:

       alpha.Lincoln.High.Lakewood.K12.CA.US.
       beta.Lincoln.High.Lakewood.K12.CA.US

       ...

The K12 subdomain provides two points at which to delegate a branch
of the database to distinct administrators — the K12 Administrator
for each state, and the district administrator for each district
within a state.

The US Domain Administrator will delegate a branch of the US domain
to an appropriate party. In some cases, this may be a particular
school, a school district, or ever all of K12 for a state.

The responsibility for managing a K12 branch or sub-branch may be
delegated to an appropriate volunteer. We envision that such
delegations of the schools' DNS service may eventually migrate to
someone else "more appropriate" from an administrative organizational
point of view. The "obvious" state agency to manage the schools' DNS
branch may take some time to get up to speed on Internetting. In the
meantime, we can have the more advanced schools up and running.

Special Schools and Service Units

In many states, there are special schools that are not in districts
that are run directly by the state or by consortiums. There are also
service units that provide "educational services" ranging from books
and computers to janitorial supplies and building maintenance. Often
these service units do not have a one-to-one relationship with
districts.

There is some concern about naming these schools and service units
within the naming structure for schools established in this memo.
There are several possibilities. For a state with many service units
creating a "pseudo district" ESU (or whatever, the common terminology
is in that state) is a possibility. For example, the Johnson service
unit could be JOHNSON.ESU.K12.CA.US. For a state with a few such
service units (and avoiding conflicts with district names) the
service units could be directly under K12. For example,

    TIES.K12.MN.US.

    The special public funded schools can be handled in a similar
    fashion. If there are many special schools in a state, a "pseudo
    district" should be established and all the special schools listed
    under it. For example, suppose there is a "pseudo district" in
    Massachusetts called SPCL, and there is a special school called the
    Progressive Computer Institute, then that school could have the name
    PCI.SPCL.K12.MA.US. If there are only a few special schools, they
    can be listed directly under K12 (avoiding name conflicts with
    district names). For example, the California Academy of Math and
    Science is CAMS.K12.CA.US. CAMS is sponsored by seven schools, the
    California Department of Education, and a University.

    "PVT" Private Schools

    Private schools may be thought of as businesses. Public schools are
    in districts, and districts provide a natural organizational
    structure for naming and delegation. For private schools there are
    no districts and they really do operate like businesses. But, many
    people are upset to think about their children in a private school
    being in a business category and not in K12 with the rest of the
    children. To accommodate both public and private schools, in each
    state's K12 branch, we've added an artificial district called private
    or "PVT". This gives a private school the option of registering like
    a business under "locality" or in the PVT.K12.<state-code>.US branch.

    For example:

       Crossroads.PVT.K12.CA.US
       Crossroads-Santa-Monica.CA.US

    A public school "Oak High" in the "Woodward" school district in
    California would have a name like "Oak-High.Woodward.K12.CA.US".

    A private school "Old Trail" in Pasadena, California could have the
    <locality> based name "Old-Trail.Pasadena.CA.US" or the private
    school base name "Old-Trail.PVT.K12.CA.US".

    Some suggest that for private schools instead of a special pseudo
    district PVT to use a locality name. One reason to use district
    names is that, in time, it seems likely that school district
    administrators will take over the operation of the DNS for their
    district. One needs to be able to delegate at that branch point.
    One implication of delegation is that the delegatee is now in charge
    of a chunk of the name space and will be registering new names. To
    keep names unique one can't have two different people registering new
    things below identically named branches.

Cooper & Postel

For example, if there is a school district named Pasadena and a city
named Pasadena, the branch of the name space PASADENA.K12.CA.US might
be delegated to the administrator of that public school district. If
a private school in Pasadena wanted to be registered in the DNS, it
would have to get the public school district administrator to do it
(perhaps unlikely) or not be in the K12 branch at all (unless there
is the PVT pseudo district).

So, if private schools are registered by
<school>.<locality>.K12.<state-code>.US and public schools are
registered by <school>.<district>.K12.<state-code>.US, there can't be
any locality names that are the same as district names or the
delegation of these will get very tricky later.

If it is all done by locality names rather than district names, and
public and private schools are mixed together, then finding an
appropriate party to delegate the locality to may be difficult.

Another suggestion was that private schools be registered directly
under K12, while public schools must be under a district under K12.
This would require the operator of the K12 branch to register all
districts and private schools himself (checking for name uniqueness),
he couldn't easily delegate the registration of the private schools
to anyone else.

Community Colleges and Technical Schools

To distinguish Community Colleges and Technical/Vocational schools,
the keywords "CC" and "TEC" have been created.

Some School Examples

```
Hamilton.High.LA-Unified.K12.CA.US          <== a public school
Sherman-Oaks.Elem.LA-Unified.K12.CA.US      <== a public school
John-Muir.Middle.Santa-Monica.K12.CA.US     <== a public school
Crossroads-School.Santa-Monica.CA.US        <== a private school
SMCC.CC.CA.US                               <== a community college
TECMCC.CC.CA.US                             <== a community college
Brick-and-Basket-Institute.TEC.CA.US        <== a technical college
Northridge.CSU.STATE.CA.US                  <== a state university
```

RFC 1480   The US Domain   June 1993

2.4 State Agencies

Several states are setting up networks to interconnect the offices of
state government agencies. The hosts in such networks should be
registered under the STATE.<state-code>.US branch.

A US Domain name space has been established for the state government
agencies. For example, in the State of Minnesota, the subdomain is
STATE.MN.US.

    State Agencies:
    _____-

    Senate.STATE.MN.US   <== State Senate
    MDH.STATE.MN.US   <== Dept. of Health
    CALTRANS.STATE.CA.US   <== Dept. of Transportation
    DMV.STATE.CA.US   <== Dept. of Motor Vehicles

2.5 Federal Agencies

A federal name space has been established for the federal government
agencies. For example, the subdomain for the Federal Reserve Bank of
Minneapolis is MNPL.FRB.FED.US. Other examples are listed below.

    Federal Government Agencies:
    _____-

    Senate.FED.US   <==== US Senate
    DOD.FED.US   <==== US Defense Dept.
    USPS.FED.US   <==== US Postal Service
    VA.FED.US   <==== US Veterans Administration
    IRS.FED.US   <==== US Internal Revenue Service
    Yosemite.NPS.Interior.FED.US   <==== A Federal agency

2.6 Distributed National Institutes

The "DNI" branch was created directly under the top-level US. This
is to be used for organizations that span state, regional, and other
organizational boundaries; are national in scope, and have
distributed facilities. An example would be:

    Distributed National Institutes:
    _____

    MetaCenter.DNI.US   <==== The MetaCenter Supercomputer Centers

Cooper & Postel

RFC 1480   The US Domain   June 1993

The MetaCenter domain encompasses the four NSF sponsored
supercomputer centers. These are:

    San Diego Supercomputer Center (SDSC)
    National Center for Supercomputing Applications (NCSA)
    Pittsburgh Supercomputing Center (PSC)
    Cornell Theory Center (CTC)

The MetaCenter Network will enable applications and services like
file systems and archival storage to be operated in a distributed
fashion; thus, allowing the resources at the four centers to appear
integrated and "seamless" to users of the centers.

2.7   General Independent Entities

This name space was created for organizations that don't really fit
anywhere else, such as state-wide associations, clubs, and "domain
parks". Think of this as the miscellaneous category.

The examples are state-wide clubs. For example, the Garden Club of
Arizona, might want to be "GARDEN.GEN.AZ.US". Such a club has
membership from all over the state and is not associated with any one
city (or locality). Another example is "domain parks" that have been
established up-to-now as entities in ORG. For example, there is
"LONESTAR.ORG", which is a kind of computer club in Texas that has
lots of dial-in computers registered. In the US Domain such an
entity might have a name like "LONESTAR.GEN.TX.US".

The organizations registered in GEN may typically be non-profit
entities. These organizations don't fit in a <locality> and are not
a school, library, or state agency. Ordinary businesses are not
registered in GEN.

Some suggest that these kinds of organizations are just like all the
other things and ought to be registered under some <locality>. This
may be true, but sometimes one just can't find any way to convince
the applicant that it is the right thing to do. One can argue that
any organization has to have a headquarters, or an office, or
something about it that is in a fixed place, and thus the
organization could be registered in that place.

Some suggest that no token is needed, these entities could be
directly under the <state-code>. The problem with not having a
token, is that you can't delegate the responsibility for registering
these entities to someone separate from whoever is responsible for
the <state-code>. You want to be able to delegate for both name-
uniqueness reasons, and operational management reasons. Having a
token there makes both easy.

Cooper & Postel

General Independent Entities:
_____-

CAL-Comp-Club.GEN.CA.US   <==== The Computer Club of California

2.8 Examples of Names

For small entities like individuals or small businesses, there is
usually no problem with selecting locality based names.

        For example: Zuckys.Santa-Monica.CA.US

For large entities like large corporations with multiple
facilities in several cities or states this often seems like an
unreasonable constraint (especially when compared with the
alternative of registering directly in the COM domain). However,
a company does have a headquarters office in a particular locality
and so could register with that name. Example: IBM.Armonk.NY.US

PRIVATE (business or individual)
================================

```
Camp-Curry.Yosemite.CA.US         <==== a business
IBM.Armonk.NY.US                  <==== a business
Dogwood.atl.GA.US                 <==== a business
Geo-Petrellis.Culver-City.CA.US   <==== a restaurant
Zuckys.Santa-Monica.CA.US         <==== a restaurant
Joe-Josts.Long-Beach.CA.US        <==== a bar
Holodek.Santa-Cruz.CA.US          <==== a personal computer
```

FEDERAL
=======

```
Senate.FED.US              <==== US Senate
DOD.FED.US                 <==== US Defense Dept.
DOT.FED.US                 <==== US Transportation Dept.
USPS.FED.US                <==== US Postal Service
VA.FED.US                  <==== US Veterans Administration
IRS.FED.US                 <==== US Internal Revenue Service
Yosemite.NPS.Interior.FED.US   <==== a federal agency
MNPL.FRB.FED.US.       <==== US Fed. Reserve Bank of Minneapolis
```

```
STATE
=====

Senate.STATE.MN.US          <====  state Senate
House.STATE.MN.US           <====  state House of Reps
MDH.STATE.MN.US             <====  state Health Dept.
HUD.STATE.CA.US             <====  state House and Urban Dev. Dept.
DOT.STATE.MN.US             <====  state Transportation Dept.
CALTRANS.STATE.CA.US        <====  state Transportation Dept.
DMV.STATE.CA.US             <====  state Motor Vehicles Dept.
Culver-City.DMV.STATE.CA.US <====  a local office of DMV


DNI   (distributed national Institutes)
=======================================

METACENTER.DNI.US           <==== a distributed nat'l Inst.


GEN (General Independent Entities)
==================================

GARDEN.GEN.AZ.US            <==== a garden club of Arizona


CITY | CI | COUNTY | CO (locality)
==================================

Parks.CI.Culver-City.CA.US          <====  a city department
Fire-Dept.CI.Los-Angeles.CA.US      <====  a city department
Fire-Dept.CO.Los-Angeles.CA.US      <====  a county department
Planning.CO.Fulton.GA.US.           <====  a county department
Main.Library.CI.Los-Angeles.CA.US   <====  a city department
MDR.Library.CO.Los-Angeles.CA.US    <====  a county department


TOWNSHIP | PARISH (locality)
============================

Police.TOWNSHIP.Green.OH.US            <====  a township department
Administration.PARISH.Lafayette.LA.US <====  a parish department
```

```
DISTRICT | LIBRARY (agency)
============================

SCAQMD.DISTRICT.CA.US                    <==== a regional district
Bunker-Hill-Improvement.DISTRICT.LA.CA.US <==== a local district

Huntington.LIB.CA.US                     <==== a private library
Venice.LA-City.LIB.CA.US                 <==== a city library
MDR.LA-County.LIB.CA.US                  <==== a county library

K12 | PRIVATE SCHOOLS (PVT) | CC | TEC
======================================

Hamilton.High.LA-Unified.K12.CA.US       <==== a public school
Sherman-Oaks.Elem.LA-Unified.K12.CA.US   <==== a public K12 school
John-Muir.Middle.Santa-Monica.K12.CA.US  <==== a public K12 school
Culver-High.CCSD.K12.CA.US               <==== a public K12 school

St-Monica.High.Santa-Monica.CA.US        <==== a private school
Crossroads-School.Santa-Monica.CA.US     <==== a private school
Mary-Ellens.Montessori-School.LA.CA.US   <==== a private school
Progress-Learning-Center.PVT.K12.CA.US   <==== a private school

SMCC.Santa-Monica.CC.CA.US       <==== a public community college
Trade-Tech.Los-Angeles.CC.CA.US  <==== a public community college
Valley.Los-Angeles.CC.CA.US      <==== a public community college

Brick-and-Basket-Institute.TEC.CA.US     <== a technical college


When appropriate, subdomains are delegated and partioned in
various categories, such as:

   <locality>.<state>.US  =   city/locality based names
          K12.<state>.US  =   kindergarten thru 12th grade
      PVT.K12.<state.US    =   private kindergarten thru 12th grade
           CC.<state>.US  =   community colleges
          TEC.<state>.US  =   technical or vocational schools
          LIB.<state>.US  =   libraries
        STATE.<state>.US  =   state government agencies
       <org-name>.FED.US  =   federal government agencies
       <org-name>.DNI.US  =   distributed national institutes
 <org-name>.GEN.<state>.US. = statewide assoc,clubs,domain parks

The Appendix-I contains the current US Domain Names BNF.
```

RFC 1480   The US Domain   June 1993

3. REGISTRATION

There are two types of registrations (1) Delegation, where a branch
of the US Domain is delegated to an organization running name servers
to support that branch; or (2) Direct Registration, in which the
information is put directly into the main database.

In Direct Registration there are two cases: (a) an IP-host (with an
IP address), and (b) non-IP host (for example, a UUCP host). Any
particular registration will involve any one of these three
situations.

3.1 Requirements

Anyone requesting to register a host in the US Domain is sent a copy
of the "Instructions for the US Domain Template", and must fill out a
US Domain template.

The US Domain template, is similar to the InterNIC Domain template,
but it is not the same. To request a copy of the US Domain template,
send a message to the US Domain registrar (us-domain@isi.edu).

If you are registering a name in a delegated zone, please register
with the contact for that zone. You can FTP the file "in-notes/us-
domain-delegated.txt" from venera.isi.edu, via anonymous FTP. This
information is also available via email from RFC-INFO@ISI.EDU
(include as the only text in the message
"Help: us_domain_delegated_domains").

The key people must have electronic mailboxes (that work). Please
provide all the information indicated in the "Administrator" and
"Technical Contact" slots.

The administrator will be the point of contact for any administrative
and policy questions about the domain. The administrator is usually
the person who manages the organization being registered.

The technical contact can also be administrator, or the systems
person, or someone who is familiar with the technical details of the
Internet. The technical contact should have a valid working email
address. This is necessary in case something goes wrong.

It is important that your "Return-Path" and "From" field indicate an
Internet-style address. UUCP-style addresses such as "host1!user"
will not work. This is fine within the UUCP world, but not the
Internet. If you want people on the Internet to be able to send mail
to you, your return path needs to be an Internet-style address such
as: host1!user@Internet.gateway.host or user@Internet.gateway.host.

It is also possible to register through one of the Internet service providers that have established working relationships with the US Domain Administrator.

If everything checks out, the turn around time for registering a host is usually a few days. The name servers are updated anywhere from 12 to 24 hours later.

There are two ways to be registered in the US Domain, directly, or by delegation.

3.2 Direct Entries

Direct entry in the database of the US Domain appeals most to individuals and small companies. You may fill out the application and send it directly to the US Domain Administrator. If you are in an area where the zone is delegated to someone else your request will be forwarded to the zone administrator for your registration. Or, you may send the form directly to the manager of a delegated zone (see Section 3.1).

3.2.1 IP-Hosts

These are hosts with IP addresses which correspond to "A" records in the DNS database.

3.2.2 Non-IP Hosts

Many applicants have hosts in the UUCP world. Some are one hop away, some two and three hops away from their "Internet Forwarder", this is acceptable. What is important is getting an Internet host to be your forwarder. If you do not already have an Internet forwarder, there are several businesses that provide this service for a fee, such as UUNET.UU.NET (postmaster@uunet.uu.net), PSI (postmaster@UU2.PSI.COM) and CERFNET (help@cerf.net). Sometimes local colleges in your area are already on the Internet and may be willing to act as an Internet Forwarder. You would need to work this out with the systems administrator as we cannot make these arrangements for you.

Although we work with UUCP service providers, the Internet US Domain registration is not affiliated with the registration of UUCP Map entries. The UUCP map entry does not provide us with sufficient information. If you do not have a copy of the US Domain questionnaire template, please send a message to: us-domain@isi.edu and request one. See Appendix-II.

Cooper & Postel

RFC 1480   The US Domain   June 1993

The example below is not an appropriate registration for the US Domain.

```
#N starl
#S Amiga 2500; AmigaDOS 2.04; Dillon's AmigaUUCP 1.15D
#O Starlight BBS
#C Stephen Baker
#E starl!sbaker
#T +1 305 378 1161
#P 1107 SW 200th St #303B Miami, Fl. 33157
#L 25 47 N / 88 10 W [city]
#R
#U mthvax
#W starl!sbaker (Stephen Baker); Mon Feb 24 19:58:24 EST 1992
  starl         mthvax(DAILY)
```

If you are registering your host as a central site for a USENET group where other UUCP sites will feed from you, that's fine. These UUCP sites do not need to register. If however, the other sites become a subdomain of your hostname, then we will need to register them individually or add a wildcard record. (See Section 4.4. Wildcards).

```
        For example:          bah.rochester.ny.us
                        host1.bah.rochester.ny.us
                        host2.bah.rochester.ny.us
```

To use US Domain names for non-IP hosts, there must be a forwarder host that is an IP host. There must be an administrative agreement and a technical procedure for relaying mail between the non-IP host and the forwarder host.

Case 1:
——-

Your host is not an IP host but does talk directly with a host that is an IP host.

```
                                        +——-+——-+
                                        |           |
+——-+——-+        +——-+--+           |           |
|your-host |—-UUCP—-|forwarder|—IP/TCP— |    INTERNET      |
+——-+——-+        +——-+--+           |           |
                                        +——-+——-+
```

"Forwarder" must be an IP host on the Internet.

You must ask "forwarder" if they are willing to be the Internet forwarder for "your-host".

In the US Domain of the DNS data base there must be an entry like this:
        "your-host" MX   10 "forwarder"

Cooper & Postel

This must be entered by the US Domain Administrator.

In the "forwarder" routing tables there must be information about
"your-host" with a rule like: If I see mail for "your-host" I will
send it via uucp by calling phone number "123-4567".

Case 2:
─── -

In this case your hosts talks to another host that ... that talks to
an IP host. In other words, there are multiple hops between your host
and the Internet.

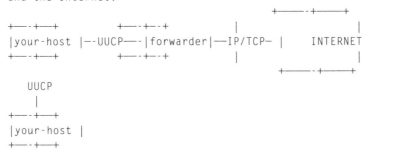

"Forwarder" must be an IP host on the Internet.

You must ask "forwarder" if they are willing to be the Internet
Forwarder for "Your-Host". You must ask "path-host" to relay your
mail.

In the US Domain of the DNS Database there must be an entry like this:

        "your-host"   MX   10   "forwarder"

This must be entered by the US Domain Administrator.

In the "forwarder" routing tables there must be information about
"your-host" with a rule like: If I see mail for "your-host" I will
send it via UUCP to "path-host" by calling phone number "123-4567".
and "path-host" must also know how to relay the mail to "your-host".

Note: It is assumed that "path-host" is already MXed to "forwarder".
It is not appropriate to ask to MX "your-host" to "path-host" (this
is sometimes called double MXing). The host on the right hand side
of an MX entry must be a host on the Internet with an IP address
(e.g., 128.9.2.32).

3.3 Delegated Subdomains

Many branches of the US Domain are delegated. There must be a knowledgeable and competent technical contact, familiar with the Internet DNS. This requirement is easily satisified if the technical contact already runs some other name servers.

Examples of delegations are K12.TX.US for the Kindergarten through 12th Grade public schools in Texas, the locality "berkeley.ca.us", or the LIB.MN.US branch for the libraries in Minnesota.

The administrator of the US Domain is responsible for the assignment of all the DNS names that end with ".US". Of course, one person or even one group can't handle all this in the long run so portions of the name space are delegated to others.

The major concern in selecting a designated manager for a domain is that it be able to carry out the necessary responsibilities, and have the ability to do an equitable, just, honest, and competent job.

The key requirement is that for each domain there be a designated manager for supervising that domain's name space.

These designated authorities are trustees for the delegated domain, and have a duty to serve the community.

The designated manager is the trustee of the domain for the domain itself and the global Internet community.

Concerns about "rights" and "ownership" of domains are inappropriate. It is appropriate to be concerned about "responsibilities" and "service" to the community.

The designated manager must be equitable to all groups in the domain that request domain names.

This means that the same rules are applied to all requests. All requests must be processed in a nondiscriminatory fashion, and academic and commercial (and other) users are treated on an equal basis. No bias shall be shown regarding requests that may come from customers of some other business related to the manager — e.g., no preferential service for customers of a particular data network provider. There can be no requirement that a particular mail system (or other application), protocol, or product be used.

There are no requirements on subdomains beyond the requirements on higher-level domains themselves. That is, the requirements are applied recursively. In particular, all subdomains shall be allowed

RFC 1480   The US Domain   June 1993

to operate their own domain name servers, providing in them whatever information the subdomain manager sees fit (as long as it is true and correct).

Significantly interested parties in the domain should agree that the designated manager is the appropriate party.

The US Domain Administrator tries to have any contending parties reach agreement among themselves, and generally takes no action to change things unless all the contending parties agree; only in cases where the designated manager has substantially neglected their responsibilities would the US Domain Administrator step in.

The designated manager must do a satisfactory job of operating the DNS service for the domain.

That is, the actual management of the assigning of domain names, delegating subdomains and operating name servers must be done with technical competence. This includes keeping the US Domain Administrator or other higher-level domain managers advised of the status of the domain, responding to requests in a timely manner, and operating the database with accuracy, robustness, and resilience.

There must be a primary and a secondary name server that have IP connectivity to the Internet and can be easily checked for operational status and database accuracy by the US Domain Administrator.

One of the aspects of having two name servers for each domain (or zone), is for robustness. One concern under this heading is that the name service not go out entirely if there is a local power failure (earthquake, tornado, or other disaster).

Name Servers should be in distinctly separate physical locations. It is appropriate to have more than two name servers, but there must be at least two.

For any transfer of the designated manager trusteeship from one organization to another, the higher-level domain manager must receive communications from both the old organization and the new organization that assures the US Domain Administrator that the transfer in mutually agreed, and that the new organization understands its responsibilities.

It is also very helpful for the US Domain Administrator to receive communications from other parties that may be concerned or affected by the transfer.

Cooper & Postel

Delegation of cities, companies within cities, schools (K12), community colleges (CC), libraries (LIB), state government (STATE), and federal government agencies (FED), etc., is acceptable and practical.

For a delegated portion of the name space, for example a city, no alterations can be made to that name, no abbreviations added, etc. unless applied for.

Sometimes there may be two people running name servers in the same city because different portions of the name space has been delegated to them. For example, someone may be delegated the <city>.<state>.US name space, and someone else from a state government agency may have the .STATE.<state>.US, portion. For example, Fred may run the name servers for Sacramento.CA.US and Joe may run the name servers for STATE.CA.US in Sacramento.

If a company would like to have wildcard records added, or run their own name servers in a city that we have delegated name space to, this is acceptable.

Delegation of the whole State name space is not yet implemented. The delegated part of the name space is in the form of:

```
        .<locality>.<state>.US.
     .CI.<locality>.<state>.US.
     .CO.<locality>.<state>.US.
              .STATE.<state>.US.
                .K12.<state>.US.
            PVT.K12.<state>.US.
                 .CC.<state>.US.
                .TEC.<state>.US.
                .LIB.<state>.US.
                .GEN.<state>.US.
                         .DNI.US.
                         .FED.US.
```

3.3.1. Delegation Requirements

When a subdomain is delegated, the following requirements must be met:

   1) There must be a knowledgeable and competent technical contact, familiar with the Internet DNS. This requirement is easily satisfied if the technical contact already runs some other name servers.

2) Organizations requesting delegations must provide at least two
    independent (robust and reliable) DNS name servers in
    physically separate locations on the Internet.

3) The subdomain must accept all applicants on an equal basis.

4) The subdomain must provide timely processing of requests. To
    do this, it is helpful to have several individuals
    knowledgeable about the procedures so that the operations are
    not delayed due to one persons unavailability (for example, by
    being on vacation).

5) The subdomain manager must tell the US Domain Administrator
    when there are changes in the name servers that should be
    reflected in the US Domain zone files, or changes in the
    contact information.

K12 Administrators

In the long term, registering schools will be a big job. So you
need to have in mind delegating parts of the work to various
school districts. If you can delegate every school district in
the state then you are finished, except for checking that they are
all operating correctly. However, initially you will have quite a
bit to do with educating people, helping them choose names and
getting name servers arranged. You are responsible for seeing
that the naming of schools follow the guidelines suggested in this
memo.

All K12 Administrators will initially be responsible for managing
the "pseudo district" PVT for private schools. Private schools
have the option of registering as <school-name>.PVT.K12.<state>.US
or as a business under the city based names.

Locality Administrators

If you have been delegated a locality subdomain, you will be
responsible for registering not only businesses directly under the
locality, but city and county agencies under the "CI" and "CO"
branches. When appropriate these branches should be delegated.

If you want, you may spell out "CITY" instead of "CI" or "COUNTY"
instead of "CO", but you must be consistent and use only one or
the other in a given locality. The whole city government should
be under one branch.

Cooper & Postel

RFC 1480   The US Domain   June 1993

WHOIS Database

Only the second and third level delegated name spaces will be
entered in the WHOIS database. For example, K12.CA.US would have
an entry in WHOIS. Anything under K12.CA.US will not be listed.
The US Domain Administrator will send the information that you
supplied on your US Domain template to the InterNIC. It is the
hope that in the future, each delegated subdomain will provide
their own WHOIS directory database for their branch.

3.3.2 Delegation Procedures

The procedure that is followed when a subdomain is delegated includes
the following steps:

1) Evaluate the technical contact's experience with DNS. Make
    sure there is a need for the proposed delegation. Make sure
    the technical contact has the information about the US Domain
    and the suggested naming structure. Two contacts with email
    addresses are necessary in case something goes wrong.

2) Add the new technical contact to the "us-dom-adm" mailing list
    for distributing updates concerning the US Domain policies and
    procedures.

3) Delete any hosts from our zone file that belongs in the newly
    delegated subdomain and make sure they now have the hosts in
    their zone file.

4) Send them a copy of the zone file so their initial zone file
    is identical to ours. For example:

```
mil.wi.us.        69582   SOA    spool.mu.edu.
                                 manager.spool.mu.edu. (
                         930119  ;serial
                         28800   ;refresh
                         14400   ;retry
                         3600000 ;expire
                         86400 ) ;minim

mil.wi.us.        69582   NS     spool.mu.edu.
spool.mu.edu.     85483   A      134.48.1.31
mil.wi.us.        69582   NS     sophie.mscs.mu.edu.
sophie.mscs.mu.edu.  85483 A        134.48.4.6
solaria.mil.wi.us.   69582 HINFO    Sun 3/60 SunOs
solaria.mil.wi.us.   69582 MX       10 spool.mu.edu.
nthomas.mil.wi.us.   69582 HINFO    386 Clone DOS
nthomas.mil.wi.us.   69582 MX       10 spool.mu.edu.
```

```
          rwmke.mil.wi.us.      69582    HINFO    UNIX PC UNIX
          rwmke.mil.wi.us.      69582    MX       10 spool.mu.edu.
          milestn.mil.wi.us.    69582    MX       10 spool.mu.edu.
          nrunner.mil.wi.us.    69582    HINFO    MacIntosh System 7
          nrunner.mil.wi.us.    69582    MX       10 spool.mu.edu.
          dawley.mil.wi.us.     69582    HINFO    386 Clone DOS
          dawley.mil.wi.us.     69582    MX       10 spool.mu.edu.
          ...
```

5) The US Domain zone file must have the following records,
    showing the name, address, email, and phone number of the
    technical contact for the delegated subdomain and the name of
    the delegated name space and the names of the name servers.

```
    ;;;;;;;;;;;;;;;;;;;;;;;;;;;;;;;;;;;;;;;;;;;;;;;;;;;;;;;;;;;;;;
    ;
    ;Contact:   Joseph Klein (tjk@spool.mu.edu)
    ;           Marquette University
    ;           (414) 288-6734
    ;
    ;Delegate mil.wi.us zone

    mil.wi.us.      604800    NS     SPOOL.MU.EDU.
                    604800    NS     SOPHIE.MSCS.MU.EDU.

    ; A glue record is not needed this time. Glue records are
    ; needed when the name of the server is a subdomain of the
    ; delegated domain.
    ;;;;;;;;;;;;;;;;;;;;;;;;;;;;;;;;;;;;;;;;;;;;;;;;;;;;;;;;;;;;;;
```

6) Check to see that delegated subdomain name servers are up and
    running, and make sure the delegated hosts are installed in
    their zone file. Now delete any hosts from the US Domain zone
    file that belongs in the newly delegated subdomain.

7) Inform the technical contact of the newly delegated subdomain
    that wildcard records are allowed in the zone file under the
    organizational subdomain but no wildcard records are allowed
    under the "city" or "state" domain.

8) Make sure each administrator has a copy of this RFC and
    follows the guidelines set forth.

3.3.3   Subdomain Contacts

The number of hosts registered under each subdomain is unknown. See
Section 3.1 for information on the delegated domains and the
contacts.

4. DATABASE INFORMATION

4.1. Name Servers

Name servers are the repositories of information that make up the domain database. The database is divided up into sections called zones, which are distributed among the name servers. While name servers can have several optional functions and sources of data, the essential task of a name server is to answer queries using data in its zones. The response to a query can always be generated using only local data, and either contains the answer to the question or a referral to other name servers "closer" to the desired information.

A given zone will be available from several name servers to insure its availability in spite of host or communication link failure. Every zone is required to be available on at least two servers, and many zones have more redundancy than that.

The US Domain is currently supported by seven name servers:

> venera.isi.edu
> ns.isi.edu
> rs.internic.net
> ns.csl.sri.com
> ns.uu.net
> adm.brl.mil
> excalibur.usc.edu

4.2 Zone Files

A "zone" is a registry of domains kept by a particular organization. A zone registry is "authoritative", that is, the master copy of the registry is kept by the zone organization, and this copy is, by definition, always up-to-date. Copies of this registry may be distributed to other places and kept in caches, but these caches are not authoritative, and may be out-of-date.

Every zone has at least one node, and hence domain name, for which it is authoritative, and all of the nodes in a particular zone are connected. Given the tree structure, every zone has a highest node which is closer to the root than any other node in the zone. The name of this node is often used to identify the zone. The data that describes a zone has four major parts:

> 1) Authoritative data for all nodes within the zone.

> 2) Data that defines the top node of the zone
>   (can be thought of as part of the authoritative data).

3) Data that describes delegated subzones, i.e., cuts
   around the bottom of the zone,

4) Data that allows access to name servers for subzones
   (sometimes called "glue" data).

The zone administrator has to maintain the zones at all the name
servers which are authoritative for the zone. When the changes are
made, they must be distributed to all of the name servers.

Copies of the zone files are not available unless you are on the
Internet. To look at the zone files use the "dig" program of the DNS
domain name system.

        dig   @nshost host-your-checking axfr

4.3 Resource Records

Records in the zone data files are called resource records (RRs).
The standard Resource records (RR) are specified in STD 13, RFC 1034
and STD 13, RFC 1035 (3,4). An RR has a standard format as shown.

            <name> [<ttl>] [<class>] <type> <data>

The first field is always the name of the domain record. The second
field is an optional time to live field. This specifies how long
this data will be stored in the data base. The third field is the
address class; the class field specifies the protocol group most
often this is the Internet class "IN". The fourth field states the
type of the resource record. The fields after that are dependent on
the Type of RR. The fifth field is the data field which is defined
differently for each type and class of data. Here is a list of the
current commonly used types:

        SOA   Start of Authority
        NS   Name Server
        A   Internet Address
        CNAME   Canonical Name (nickname pointer)
        HINFO   Host Information
        WKS   Well Known Services
        MX   Mail Exchanger
        PTR   Pointer

What do the fields mean?

```
foo.LA.CA.US.      604800      MX   10     Venera.ISI.EDU.
(1)                (2)         (3)  (4)    (5)
```

1) domain name
2) time to live information
3) mail exchanger record
4) preference value to determine (if more than one
   forwarder) which mailer to use first, lower number
   higher preference
5) the Internet forwarding host.

4.3.1 "A" Records

Internet (IP) Address. The data for an "A" record is an Internet
address in a dotted decimal form. A sample "A" record might look
like:

```
venera.isi.edu.            A      128.9.0.32
   (name)                 (A)    (address)
```

The name field is the machine name, and the address is the network
address. There should be only one "A" record for each address of a
host.

4.3.2 CNAME Records

Canonical Name resource record, CNAME, specifies an alias for a
canonical name. This is essentially a pointer to the official name
for the requested name. All other RRs appear under this official
name. A machine named FERNWOOD.MPK.CA.US may want to have the
nickname ANTERIOR.MPK.CA.US. In that case, the following RR would be
used:

```
anterior.mpk.ca.us.      CNAME       fernwood.mpk.ca.us.
   (alias nickname)                     (canonical name)
```

Nicknames (the name associated with the RR is the nickname) may be
added for awhile when a host changes its name, usually because it
moves to another state. It helps to have this CNAME pointer so if
any mail comes to the old address it will get forwarded to the new
one. There cannot be any other RRs associated with a nickname of the
same class.

4.3.3 MX Records

Mail Exchanger records, MX, are used to specify a machine that knows
how to deliver mail to a machine that is not directly connected to
the Internet. For example, venera.isi.edu is the mail gateway that
knows how to deliver mail to foo.la.ca.us, but other machines on the
network cannot deliver mail directly to foo.la.ca.us. These two
machines may have a private connection or use a different transport
medium (such as uucp). The preference value (10) is the order that a
mailer should follow when there is more than one way to deliver mail
to a single machine. The lower the number the higher the preference.

        foo.LA.CA.US. 604800 MX 10 Venera.ISI.EDU.
        foo.LA.CA.US. 604800 MX 20 relay1.uu.net.

4.3.4   HINFO Records

Host information resource records, HINFO is for host specific data.
This lists the hardware and operating system that are running at the
listed host. It should be noted that a space separates the hardware
information and the operating system information. If you want to
include a space in the machine name you must quote the name. Host
information is not specific to any class, so ANY may be used for the
address class. There should be one HINFO record for each host.

acb.la.ca.us.   HINFO   VAX-11/780   UNIX
                                  (Hardware)   (Operating System)

The official HINFO types can be found in the latest Assigned Numbers
RFC, the most recent edition being STD 2, RFC 1340 [9]. The hardware
type is called the Machine Name, and the software type is called the
System Name.

The information users supply about this is often inconsistent or
incomplete. Please follow the terms in the current "Assigned
Numbers".

4.3.5 PTR Records

A Domain Name Pointer record, PTR, allows special names to point to
some other location in the domain data base. These are typically
used in setting up reverse pointers for the special IN-ADDR.ARPA
domain. PTR names should be unique to the zone.

        0.0.9.128.in-addr.arpa   PTR   isi-net.isi.edu.
          (special name)   (real name)

A PTR record is to be added to the IN-ADDR.ARPA domain for every "A" record registered in the US Domain. These PTR records need to be added by the administrator of the network where the host is connected. The US Domain Administration does not administer the network and cannot make these entries in the DNS database.

4.4 Wildcards

The wildcard records are of the form "*.<anydomain>", where <anydomain> is any domain name. The wildcards potentially apply to descendents of <anydomain>, but not to <anydomain> itself.

For example, suppose a large company located in California with a large, non-IP/TCP, network wanted to create a mail gateway. If the company was called DWP.LA.CA.US, and the IP/TCP capable gateway machine (Internet forwarder) was called ELROY.JPL.NASA.GOV, the following RRs might be entered into the .US zone.

```
     dwp.la.ca.us     MX     10     ELROY.JPL.NASA.GOV
   *.dwp.la.ca.us     MX     10     ELROY.JPL.NASA.GOV
```

The wildcard record *.DWP.LA.CA.US would cause an MX query for any domain name ending in DWP.LA.CA.US to return an MX RR pointing at ELROY.JPL.NASA.GOV. The entry without the "*" is needed so the host dwp can be found.

In the US Domain, wildcard records are allowed in our zone files under the organizational subdomain (and where noted otherwise) but no wildcard records are allowed under the "City" or "State" domain.

> The authors strongly believe that it is in everyone's
> interest and good for the Internet to have each host
> explicitly registered (that is, we believe that wildcards
> should not be used), we also realize that not everyone
> agrees with this belief. Thus, we will allow wildcard
> records in the US Domain under groups or organizations.
> For example, *.DWP.LA.CA.US.

> The reason we feel single entries are the best is by the mere
> fact that if anyone wanted to find one of the hosts in the
> domain name system it would be there, and problems can be
> detected more easily. When using wildcards records all the
> hosts under a subdomain are hidden.

Cooper & Postel

RFC 1480   The US Domain   June 1993

5. REFERENCES

   [1] Stahl, M., "Domain Administrators Guide", RFC 1032, SRI
        International, November 1987.

   [2] Lottor, M., "Domain Administrators Operations Guide" RFC 1033,
        SRI International, November 1987.

   [3] Mockapetris, P., "Domain Names - Concepts and Facilities",
        STD 13, RFC 1034, ISI, November 1987.

   [4] Mockapetris, P., "Domain Names - Implementation and
        Specification", STD 13, RFC 1035, ISI, November 1987.

   [5] Dunlap, K., "Name Server Operations Guide for Bind,
        Release 4.3", UC Berkeley, SMM:11-3.

   [6] Partridge, C., "Mail Routing and the Domain Name System",
        STD 14, RFC 974, BBN, January 1986.

   [7] Albitz, P., C. Liu, "DNS and Bind" Help for UNIX System
        Administrators, O'Reilly and Associates, Inc., October 1992.

   [8] ACM SIGUCCS Networking Taskforce, "Connecting to the Internet -
        What Connecting Institutions Should Anticipate", FYI 16,
        RFC 1359, August 1992.

   [9] Reynolds, J., and J. Postel, "Assigned Numbers", STD 2,
        RFC 1340, ISI, July 1992.

6. Security Considerations

   Security issues are not discussed in this memo.

RFC 1480   The US Domain   June 1993

7. Authors' Addresses

    Ann Cooper
    USC/Information Sciences Institute
    4676 Admiralty Way
    Marina del Rey, CA 90292
    Phone: 1-310-822-1511
    Email: cooper@isi.edu

    Jon Postel
    USC/Information Sciences Institute
    4676 Admiralty Way
    Marina del Rey, CA 90292
    Phone: 1-310-822-1511
    Email: postel@isi.edu

APPENDIX-I: US DOMAIN NAMES BNF
================================

```
<us-domain-name>      ::= <us-name><dot><us>

<us-name>             ::= <state-name><dot><state-code> |
                          <fed-name><dot><fed>
                          <dni-name><dot><dni>

<state-code>          ::= <the two-letter code of a state from the
                          zip code directory>

<state-name>          ::= <local-name><dot><locality> |
                          <state-agency-name><dot><state> |
                          <regional-agency-name><dot><agency>

<fed-name>            ::= <the dotted hierarchical name of a US
                          federal government agency>

<dni-name>            ::= <the dotted hierarchical name of a
                          distributed national institution>

<locality>            ::= <the full name of a city from the
                            zip code directory> |
                          <a short code name for a city> |
                          <the full name of a county, township,
                           or parish> |
                          <other well known and commonly used
                           locality name>

<local-name>          ::= <entity-name> |
                          <city-name><dot><city> |
                          <county-name><dot><county> |
                          <local-agency-name><dot><local-agency>

<state-agency-name> ::= <the dotted hierarchical name of a state
                          government agency>

<regional-agency-name> ::= <the dotted hierarchical name of a
                            special agency or district not an
                            element of the state government and
                            typically larger than a single city or
                            county, for example, the Southern
                            California Air Quality Management District>
```

RFC 1480   The US Domain   June 1993

```
<entity-name>          ::= <the dotted hierarchical name of an
                           entity within a city, for example: a
                           company, business, private school, club,
                           organization, or individual>

<city-name>            ::= <the dotted hierarchical name of a city
                           government agency>

<county-name>          ::= <the dotted hierarchical name of a county,
                           township, or parish government agency>

<local-agency-name> ::= <the dotted hierarchical name of a special
                           agency or district not an element of a
                           city or county government and typically
                           equal or smaller than a single city or
                           county, for example, the Bunker Hill
                           Improvement District>

<city> ::= "CI" | "CITY"

<county> ::= "CO" | "COUNTY" | "TOWNSHIP" | "PARISH"

<dot> ::= "."

<fed> ::= "FED"

<dni> ::= "DNI"

<state> ::= "STATE" | "COMMONWEALTH"

<agency> ::= "AGENCY" | "DISTRICT" | "K12" | "CC" | "LIB" |
             "GEN"    | "TEC"

<local-agency> ::= "AGENCY" | "DISTRICT"

<us> ::= "US"
```

Notes:

Within States:

"K12" may be used for public school districts. A special name
"PVT" can be used in the place of a school district name for
private schools.

"CC" may be used only for public community colleges.

Cooper & Postel

"LIB" may be only used by libraries.

"TEC" is used only for technical and vocational schools and colleges.

"GEN" is for general independent entities, that is, organizations
that don't really fit anywhere else (such as statewide associations,
clubs, and "domain parks").

"STATE" may be used only for state government entities.

Below US, parallel to States:

"FED" is for agencies of the federal government.

"DNI" is for distributed national institutes; organizations that
span state, regional, and other organizational boundaries; that
are national in scope, and have distributed facilities.

Examples:
=========

Geo-Petrellis.Culver-City.CA.US   <== resturant

Joe-Josts.Long-Beach.CA.US   <== bar

IBM.Armonk.NY.US   <== business

Camp-Curry.Yosemite.CA.US   <== business

Yosemite.NPS.Interior.FED.US   <== federal agency

Senate.FED.US   <== US Senate

DOD.FED.US   <== US Defense Dept.

DOT.FED.US   <== US Transportation Dept.

MNPL.FRB.FED.US   <== the Minneapolis branch of
                                             the Federal Reserve Bank

MetaCenter.DNI.US   <== distributed Nat'l Inst

Senate.STATE.MN.US   <== state Senate

House.STATE.MN.US   <== state House of Reps

Assembly.STATE.CA.US   <== state Assembly

```
MDH.STATE.MN.US                           <== state Health Dept.

DOT.STATE.MN.US                           <== state Transportation Dept

CALTRANS.STATE.CA.US                      <== state Transportation Dept

DMV.STATE.CA.US                           <== state Motor Vehicles Dept

Culver-City.DMV.STATE.CA.US               <== local office of DMV

Police.CI.Culver-City.CA.US               <== city department

Fire-Dept.CI.Los-Angeles.CA.US            <== city department

Fire-Dept.CO.Los-Angeles.CA.US            <== county department

Main.Library.CI.Los-Angeles.CA.US         <== city department

MDR.Library.CO.Los-Angeles.CA.US          <== county department

Huntington.LIB.CA.US                      <== private library

SMCC.Santa-Monica.CC.CA.US                <== public community college

Trade-Tech.Los-Angeles.CC.CA.US           <== public community college

Valley.Los-Angeles.CC.CA.US               <== public community college

Hamilton.High.LA-Unified.K12.CA.US        <== public school

Sherman-Oaks.Elem.LA-Unified.K12.CA.US    <== public school

John-Muir.Middle.Santa-Monica.K12.CA.US   <== public school

St-Monicas.High.Santa-Monica.CA.US        <== private school

Crossroads-School.Santa-Monica.CA.US      <== private school

Mary-Ellens-Montessori-School.LA.CA.US    <== private school

Progress-Learning-Center.PVT.K12.CA.US    <== private school

Brick-and-Basket-Institute.TEC.CA.US      <== technical college

Bunker-Hill.DISTRICT.Los-Angeles.CA.US    <== local district

SCAQMD.DISTRICT.CA.US                      <== regional district
```

```
Berkeley.UC.STATE.CA.US                  <== "CAL"

Los-Angeles.UC.STATE.CA.US               <== UCLA

Irvine.UC.STATE.CA.US                    <== UC Irvine

Northridge.CSU.STATE.CA.US               <== CSUN

Los-Angeles.CSU.STATE.CA.US              <== Cal State LA

Leland-Stanford-Jr-University.Stanford.CA.US   <== private school


~~~~~~~~~~~~~~~~~~~~~~~~~~~~~~~~~~~~~~~~~~~~~~~~~~~~~~~~~~~~~~~~~~~~
```

RFC 1480   The US Domain   June 1993

APPENDIX-II: US DOMAIN QUESTIONNAIRE FOR HOST ENTRY

To register a host in the US domain, the US Domain Template must be
sent to the US Domain Registrar (US-Domain@ISI.EDU). The first few
pages explain each question on the attached template. FILL OUT THE
TWO PAGE TEMPLATE AT THE END. Questions may be sent by electronic
mail to the above address, or by phone to Ann Cooper, USC/Information
Sciences Institute, (310) 822-1511.

(1)   Please specify whether this is a new application, modification to
      an existing registration, or deletion.

(2)   The name of the domain. This is the name that will be used in
      tables and lists associating the domain with the domain server
      addresses. See RFC 1480 - The US Domain for more details.

```
 <host>.<city/locality>.<state>.US. =  city/locality based names
<school>.<district>.K12.<state>.US. =  kindergarten thru 12th grade
       <school>.PVT.K12.<state>.US. =  private K thru 12th grade
   <school>.<locality>.<state>.US. =  PVT sch opt: locality names
             <school>.CC.<state>.US. =  community colleges
            <school>.TEC.<state>.US. =  technical or vocational schools
          <lib-name>.LIB.<state>.US. =  libraries
        <org-name>.STATE.<state>.US. =  state government agencies
                 <org-name>.FED.US. =  federal government agencies
                 <org-name>.DNI.US. =  distributed national institutes
             <org>.GEN.<state>.US. =  statewide assoc,clubs,domain parks
```

      For example: networthy.santa-clara.ca.us.

(3)   The name of the entity represented, that is, the organization
      being named. For example: The Networthy Corporation. Not the
      name of the organization submitting the request.

(4)   Please describe the domain briefly.

      For example: The Networthy Corporation is a consulting
      organization of people working with UNIX and the C language
      in an electronic networking environment. It sponsors two
      technical conferences annually and distributes a bimonthly
      newsletter.

(5)   The date you expect the domain to be fully operational.

Cooper & Postel

For every registration, we need both the Administrative and the
Technical contacts of a domain (questions 6 & 7) and we MUST have a
network mailbox for each. If you have a NIC handle (a unique NIC
database identifier) please enter it. (If you don't know what a NIC
handle is leave it blank). Also the title, mailing address, phone
number, organization, and network mailbox.

(6)   The name of the administrative head of the "organization". The
      administrator is the contact point for administrative and policy
      questions about the domain. The Domain administrator should work
      closely with the personnel he has designated as the "technical
      contact" for his domain. In this example the Domain Administrator
      would be the Administrator of the Networthy Corporation, not the
      Administrator of the organization running the name server
      (unless it is the same person).

(7)   The name of the technical and zone contact. The technical and
      zone contact handles the technical aspects of maintaining the
      domain's name server and resolver software, and database files.
      He keeps the name server running. More than likely, this person
      would be the technical contact running the primary name server.

****

PLEASE READ: There are several types of registrations.

   (a)   Delegation (i.e., a portion of the US Domain name space is
         given to an organization running name servers to support that
         branch; For example, K12.TX.US, for all K12 schools in Texas).
         For (a) answer questions 8 and 9.

   (b)   Direct Registration of an IP Host.
         For (b) answer question 10.

   (c)   Direct Registration of a non-IP Host.
         For (c) answer question 11 and 12.

****

QUESTIONS FOR DELEGATIONS

(8)   PRIMARY SERVER Information. It is required to supply both the
      Contact information as well as hardware/software information of
      the primary name server.

(9)* SECONDARY SERVER Information. It is required to supply the
      hardware and software information of all secondary name servers.

Cooper & Postel

RFC 1480   The US Domain   June 1993

Domains must provide at least two independent servers that provide the domain service for translating names to addresses for hosts in this domain. If you are applying for a domain and a network number assignment simultaneously and a host on your proposed network will be used as a server for the domain, you must wait until you receive your network number assignment and have given the server(s) a net- address before sending in the domain application. Establishing the servers in physically separate locations and on different PSNs and/or networks is strongly recommended.

NOTE: For those applicants not able to run name servers, or for non-IP hosts the Name Server information is not applicable. (See #10 and #11).

==

QUESTION FOR DIRECT IP HOSTS (If you answered 8 & 9 do not answer 10, 11, or 12).

(10) What Domain Name System (DNS) Resource Records (RR) and values are to be entered for your IP host (must have an "A" record).

    +++
    Example: RRs for an INTERNET hosts.

    (a) DOMAIN NAME (required)...: Networthy.Santa-Clara.CA.US.
    (b) IP ADDRESS (required)....: A 128.9.3.123 (required)
    (c) HARDWARE (opt)...........: SUN-3/110
    (d) OPERATING SYS (opt)......: UNIX
    (e) WKS (opt)........: 128.9.3.123. UDP (echo tftp) TCP (ftp)
    (f) MX (opt).................: 10 RELAY.ISI.EDU.

It is your responsibility to see that an IN-ADDR pointer record is entered in the DNS database. (For Internet hosts only). Contact the administrator of the IP network your host is on to have this done. The US Domain administration does not administer the network and cannot make these entries in the DNS database.

==

QUESTIONS FOR NON-IP HOSTS (such as UUCP).

   Many applicants have hosts in the UUCP world. Some are one hop away, some two and three hops away from their "Internet Forwarder", this is ok. What is important is getting an Internet host to be your forwarder. If you do not already have an Internet forwarder, there are several businesses that provide this service for a fee, (see RFC 1359 - Connecting to the Internet What Connecting Institutions Should Anticipate, ACM SIGUCCS, August 1992). Sometimes local colleges in your area are already on the Internet and may be willing to act as an Internet Forwarder. You would need to work this out with the systems administrator. We cannot make these arrangements for you.

Cooper & Postel

RFC 1480   The US Domain   June 1993

(11) Internet Forwarding Host Information

    (11a) What is the name of your Internet forwarding host?
          For example: The host Yacht-Club.MDR.CA.US uses
          UUCP to connect to RELAY.ISI.EDU which is an Internet
          host. (i.e., RELAY.ISI.EDU is the forwarding host).

    (11b) What is the name of your contact person at forwarding host?
          The Administrator of RELAY.ISI.EDU must agree to be the
          forwarding host for Yacht-Club.MDR.CA.US, and the
          forwarding host must know a delivery method and route to
          Networthy. No double MXing.

    (11c) What is the mailbox of your contact?
          What is the mailbox of the administrator of the forwarding
          host.

        Example: Contact Name......: John Smith
                  Contact Email.....: js@RELAY.ISI.EDU

(12) What Domain Name System (DNS) Resource Records (RR) and values
    are to be entered for your NON-IP host.

    ++
    Example: RRs for a NON-IP host (uucp).

    (a) DOMAIN NAME (required).....:   Yacht-Club.MDR.CA.US.
    (b) HARDWARE (opt)............:   SUN-3/110
    (c) OPERATING SYS (opt)........:   UNIX
    (d) MX (required).............:   10 RELAY.ISI.EDU.
    ++

PLEASE ALLOW AT LEAST 8 WORKING DAYS FOR PROCESSING THIS APPLICATION

RFC 1480   The US Domain   June 1993

US DOMAIN TEMPLATE   [6/93]

PLEASE SUBMIT THE FOLLOWING TWO PAGE TEMPLATE TO (Us-Domain@isi.edu).
Sections or fields of this form marked with an asterisk (*) may be
copied as many times as necessary. (For example: If you had two phone
numbers for the Administrative Contact, you would use the same number
"6h" twice. PLEASE DO NOT ALTER THIS APPLICATION IN ANY WAY.
===

```
    1.   REGISTRATION TYPE
         (N)ew (M)odify (D)elete..:

    2.*  FULLY-QUALIFIED DOMAIN NAME:

    3.   ORGANIZATION INFORMATION
    3a.  Organization Name.....:
    3b.  Address Line 1........:
    3b.  Address Line 2........:
    3c.  City..................:
    3d.  State.................:
    3e.  Zip/Code..............:

    4.   DESCRIPTION OF ORG/DOMAIN:

    5.   Date Operational......:

    6.   ADMINISTRATIVE CONTACT OF ORG/DOMAIN
    6a.  NIChandle (if known)..:
    6b.  Whole Name............:
    6c.  Organization Name.....:
    6d.  Address Line 1........:
    6d.  Address Line 2........:
    6e.  City..................:
    6f.  State.................:
    6g.  Zip/Code..............:
    6h.* Voice Phone...........:
    6i.* Electronic Mailbox....:

    7.   TECHNICAL AND ZONE CONTACT
    7a.  NIChandle (if known)..:
    7b.  Whole Name............:
    7c.  Organization Name.....:
    7d.  Address Line 1........:
    7d.  Address Line 2........:
    7e.  City..................:
    7f.  State.................:
    7g.  Zip/Code..............:
    7h.* Voice Phone...........:
    7i.* Electronic Mailbox....:
```

RFC 1480   The US Domain   June 1993

FILL OUT QUESTIONS 8 AND 9 FOR DELEGATIONS ONLY (i.e., those
organizations running name servers for a branch of the US Domain
name space, for example: k12.<state>.us).

```
8.    PRIMARY SERVER: CONTACT INFO, HOSTNAME, NETADDRESS
8a.   NIChandle (if known)..:
8b.   Whole Name...........:
8c.   Organization Name.....:
8d.   Address Line 1........:
8d.   Address Line 2........:
8e.   City.................:
8f.   State................:
8g.   Zip/Code.............:
8h.*  Voice Phone..........:
8i.*  Electronic Mailbox....:
8j.   Hostname.............:
8k.*  IP Address...........:
8l.*  HARDWARE.............:
8m.*  OPERATING SYS........:

9. *  SECONDARY SERVER: HOSTNAME, NETADDRESS
9a.*  Hostname.............:
9b.*  IP Address...........:
9c.*  HARDWARE.............:
9d.*  OPERATING SYS........:
```

FILL OUT QUESTION 10 FOR DIRECT REGISTRATIONS IP HOSTS

```
10.   RESOURCE RECORDS (RRs) FOR IP INTERNET HOSTS
10a.  DOMAIN NAME..........:
10b.* IP ADDRESS (required).:
10c.  HARDWARE.............:
10d.  OPERATING SYS........:
10e.  WKS .................:
10f.* MX...................:
```

FILL OUT QUESTIONS 11 AND 12 FOR NON-IP HOSTS (such as UUCP)

```
11.   FORWARDING HOST INFORMATION
11a.  Forwarding Host......:
11b.  Contact Name.........:
11c.  Contact Email........:

12.   RESOURCE RECORDS (RRs) FOR NON-IP HOSTS (UUCP)
12a.  DOMAIN NAME..........:
12b.  HARDWARE.............:
12c.  OPERATING SYS........:
12d.* MX (required)........:
```

Cooper & Postel

J

Registering with the Mapping Project

The attached document was recently sent to me by E-Mail from the USENIX Mapping Project, located at Rutgers University in New Jersey. It provides detailed instructions for registering your UUCP host so that you will appear in the set of UUCP maps that are updated on a monthly basis. This is a voluntary action on your part, but it is useful for anyone trying to contact you via UUCP E-Mail.

```
FROM: Mel Pleasant, INTERNET:pleasant@ptolemaeus.rutgers.edu
TO:   Tom Madron, 71260,704
DAT:  12/6/93 11:16 AM
Re:   Re: uucp mapping
Sender: pleasant@ptolemaeus.rutgers.edu
Received: from ptolemaeus.rutgers.edu by arl-img-1.compuserve.com
(8.6.4/5.930129sam)
      id LAA02876; Mon, 6 Dec 1993 11:14:45 -0500
Received: by ptolemaeus.rutgers.edu (5.59/SMI4.0/RU1.5/3.08)
      id AA24985; Mon, 6 Dec 93 11:14:32 EST
Date: Mon, 6 Dec 93 11:14:31 EST
From: Mel Pleasant <pleasant@ptolemaeus.rutgers.edu>
To: Tom Madron <71260.704@compuserve.com>
Cc: uucp-map <uucpmap@rutgers.edu>
Subject: Re: uucp mapping
In-Reply-To: Your message of 05 Dec 93 21:56:38 EST
Message-Id: <CMM-RU.1.3.755194471.pleasant@ptolemaeus.rutgers.edu>
Hello,
```

My name is Mel Pleasant and I'm with the UUCP Mapping Project group of the USENIX organization. In case you've never heard of us until now, we are a voluntary group of people who collect information from all sites that communicate via UUCP. We make this information available to any other site on the UUCP network. The primary use by most sites of this information is to compute the quickest path between one site and another. There exists a program that will do this for you and we make this program available as well.

As head co-ordinator of the UUCP maps, I'm attempting to cajole those sites which have not published a map entry with us into doing so. Your site has been identified as one of these. This determination was made by examining all of the map entries we do have and identifying links to sites for which we don't have entries. All this means is that some other site has given us a map entry, that their map entry points to your site, and that we don't have a map for the site (your site) that is pointed to.

Below, you'll find a guide for completing a map entry. We'd greatly appreciate it if you would register a map entry with us. If you have any questions or concerns you can address them to me. I'd be happy to help you in most any way. If you do not wish to publish any information on your site, please drop us a message saying so. Believe it or not, this is a computer generated message and if we don't hear from you in one way or another, you'll continue to receive this message once a month or so.

```
-Mel Pleasant
-UUCP Mapping Project Group
This describes the format of the UUCP map data.
It was last updated July 9, 1985 by Erik E. Fair <ucbvax!fair>.
```

The entire map is intended to be processed by pathalias, a program that generates UUCP routes from this data. All lines beginning in '#' are comment lines to pathalias, however the UUCP Project has defined a set of these comment lines to have specific format so that a complete database could be built.

The generic form of these lines is

#<field id letter><tab><field data>

Each host has an entry in the following format. The entry should begin with the #N line, end with a blank line after the pathalias data, and not contain any other blank lines, since there are ed, sed, and awk scripts that use expressions like /^#N $1/,/^$/ for the purpose of separating the map out into files, each containing one site entry.

```
#N    UUCP name of site
#S    manufacturer machine model; operating system & version
#O    organization name
#C    contact person's name
#E    contact person's electronic mail address
#T    contact person's telephone number
#P    organization's address
#L    latitude / longitude
#R    remarks
#U    netnews neighbors
#W    who last edited the entry ; date edited
#
sitename    remote1(FREQUENCY), remote2(FREQUENCY),
       remote3(FREQUENCY)
```

Example of a completed entry:

```
#N    ucbvax
#S    DEC VAX-11/750; 4.3 BSD UNIX
#O    University of California at Berkeley
#C    Robert W. Henry
#E    ucbvax!postmaster
#T    +1 415 642 1024
#P    573 Evans Hall, Berkeley, CA 94720
#L    122 13 44 W / 37 52 29 N
#R    This is also UCB-VAX.BERKELEY.EDU [10.2.0.78] on the internet
#U    decvax ibmpa ucsfcgl ucbtopaz ucbcad
#W    ucbvax!fair (Erik F. Fair); Sat Jun 22 03:35:16 PDT 1985
#
ucbvax    decvax(DAILY/4), ihnp4(DAILY/2),
       sun(POLLED)
```

Specific Field Descriptions

#N   system name

Your system's UUCP name should go here. Either the uname(1) command from System III or System V UNIX; or the uuname(1) command from Version 7 UNIX will tell you what UUCP is using for the local UUCP name.

One of the goals of the UUCP Project is to keep duplicate UUCP host names from appearing because there exist mailers in the world which assume that the UUCP name space contains no duplicates (and attempts UUCP path optimization on that basis), and it's just plain confusing to have two different sites with the same name.

At present, the most severe restriction on UUCP names is that the name must be unique somewhere in the first six characters, because of a poor software design decision made by AT&T for the System V release of UNIX.

This does not mean that your site name has to be six characters or less in length. Just unique within that length.

With regard to choosing system names, HARRIS'S LAMENT:

------------------- ''All the good ones are taken.''

#S ----------------- machine type; operating system

This is a quick description of your equipment. Machine type should be manufacturer and model, and after a semi-colon(;), the operating system name and version number (if you have it). Some examples:

```
DEC PDP-11/70; 2.9 BSD UNIX
DEC PDP-11/45; ULTRIX-11
DEC VAX-11/780; VMS 4.0
SUN 2/150; 4.2 BSD UNIX
Pyramid 90x; OSx 2.1
CoData 3300; Version 7 UniPlus+
Callan Unistar 200; System V UniPlus+
IBM PC/XT; Coherent
Intel 386; XENIX 3.0
CRDS Universe 68; UNOS
```

#O   organization name

This should be the full name of your organization, squeezed to fit inside 80 columns as necessary. Don't be afraid to abbreviate where the abbreviation would be clear to the entire world (say a famous institution like MIT or CERN), but beware of duplication (In USC the C could be either California or Carolina).

#C   contact person

This should be the full name (or names, separated by commas) of the person responsible for handling queries from the outside world about your machine.

#E   contact person's electronic address

This should be just a machine name, and a user name, like 'ucbvax!fair'. It should not be a full path, since we will be able to generate a path to the given address from the data you're giving us. There is no problem with the machine name not being the same as the #N field (i.e. the contact 'lives' on another machine at your site).

Also, it's a good idea to give a generic address or alias (if your mail system is capable of providing aliases) like 'usenet' or 'postmaster', so that if the contact person leaves the institution or is re-assigned to other duties, he doesn't keep getting mail about the system. In a perfect world, people would send notice to the UUCP Project, but in practice, they don't, so the data does get out of date. If you give a generic address you can easily change it to point at the appropriate person.

Multiple electronic addresses should be separated by commas, and all of them should be specified in the manner described above.

#T   contact person's telephone number

Format: +<country code><space><area code><space><prefix><space><number>

Example:

#T   +1 415 642 1024

This is the international format for the representation of phone numbers. The country code for the United States of America is 1. Other country codes should be listed in your telephone book.

If you must list an extension (i.e. what to ask the receptionist for, if not the name of the contact person), list it after the main phone number with an 'x' in front of it to distinguish it from the rest of the phone number.

Example:

#T   +1 415 549 3854 x37

Multiple phone numbers should be separated by commas, and all of them should be completely specified as described above to prevent confusion.

#P   organization's address

This field should be one line filled with whatever else anyone would need after the contact person's name, and your organization's name (given in other fields above), to mail you something in the physical mails. Generally, if there's room, it's best to spell out things like Road, Street, Avenue, and Boulevard, since this is an international network, and the abbreviations will not necessarily be obvious to someone from Finland, for example.

#L   latitude and longitude

This should be in the following format:

#L   NNN MM [SS] E|W / NN MM [SS] N|S [city]

Two fields, with optional third.

First number is Longitude in degrees (NNN), minutes (MM), and seconds (SS), and a E or W to indicate East or West of the Prime Meridian in Greenwich, England.

A Slash Separator.

Second number is Latitude in degrees (NN), minutes (MM), and seconds (SS), and a N or S to indicate North or South of the Equator.

Seconds are optional, but it is worth noting that the more accurate you are, the more accurate maps we can make of the network (including blow-ups of various high density areas, like New Jersey, or the San Francisco Bay Area).

If you give the coordinates for your city (i.e. without fudging for where you are relative to that), add the word 'city' at the end of the end of the specification, to indicate that. If you know where you are relative to a given coordinate for which you have longitude and latitude data, then the following fudge factors can be useful:

```
1 degree     =      69.2 miles    =     111 kilometers
1 minute     =      1.15 miles    =     1.9 kilometers
1 second     =      101.5 feet    =     31 meters
```

The Prime Meridian is through Greenwich, England, and longitudes go no higher than 180 degrees West or East of Greenwich. Latitudes go no higher than 90 degrees North or South of the Equator.

Beware that the distance between two degrees of longitude decreases as you get further away from the Equator. (Imagine all those longitudinal lines converging on the north and south poles...) These numbers are good for the Equator. If you're in Alaska or Norway, for example, they are certainly too large for you to fudge longitude accurately.

#R   remarks

This is for one line of comment. As noted before, all lines beginning with a '#' character are comment lines, so if you need more than one line to tell us something about your site, do so between the end of the map data (the #?\t fields) and the pathalias data.

#U   netnews neighbors

The USENET is the network that moves netnews around, specifically, net.announce. If you send net.announce to any of your UUCP neighbors, list their names here, delimited by spaces. Example:

#U   ihnp4 decvax mcvax seismo

Since some places have lots of USENET neighbors, continuation lines should be just another #U and more site names.

#W   who last edited the entry and when

This field should contain an email address, a name in parentheses, followed by a semi-colon, and the output of the date program. Example:

#W   ucbvax!fair (Erik E. Fair); Sat Jun 22 03:35:16 PDT 1985

The same rules for email address that apply in the contact's email address apply here also. (i.e. only one system name, and user name). It is intended that this field be used for automatic ageing of the map entries so that we can do more automated checking and updating of the entire map. See getdate(3) from the netnews source for other acceptable date formats.

PATHALIAS DATA (or, documenting your UUCP connections & frequency of use)

The DEMAND, DAILY, etc., entries represent imaginary connect costs (see below) used by pathalias to calculate lowest cost paths. The cost breakdown is:

```
LOCAL       25      local area network
DEDICATED   95      high speed dedicated
DIRECT      200     local call
DEMAND      300     normal call (long distance, anytime)
HOURLY      500     hourly poll
EVENING     1800    time restricted call
DAILY       5000    daily poll
```

```
            WEEKLY              30000 irregular poll
            DEAD                    a very high number - not usable path
```

Additionally, HIGH and LOW (used like DAILY+HIGH) are -5 and +5
respectively, for baud-rate or quality bonuses/penalties. Arithmetic
expressions can be used, however, you should be aware that the results
are often counter-intuitive (e.g. (DAILY*4) means every 4 days, not 4
times a day).

The numbers are intended to represent frequency of connection, which
seems to be far more important than baud rates for this type of
traffic. There is an assumed high overhead for each hop; thus,
HOURLY is far more than DAILY/24.

There are a few other cost names that sometimes appear in the map;
these are discouraged. Some are synonyms for the prefered
names above (e.g. POLLED means DAILY), some are obsolete (e.g.
the letters A through F, which are letter grades for connections.)
It is not acceptable to make up new names or spellings (pathalias
gets very upset when people do that...).

LOCAL AREA NETWORKS

For local area networks, (since they are usually completely connected),
there is a list notation for specifying them. Usually there is one
gateway machine to the outside world; it is best that the definition of
the network appear in that system's pathalias entry, and the other
systems just note that they connect to the LAN. An abbreviated map
entry for the sake of example:

```
#N     frobozz
#O     Frobozz Skonk Works
#C     Joe Palooka
#E     frobozz!postmaster
#R     gateway machine to Frobozz Company LAN
#
frobozz     ucbvax(DEMAND), ihnp4(EVENING), seismo(DAILY),
       mcvax(WEEKLY), akgua(EVENING)
#
#     LAN addressed user@host
#
FROBOZZ-ETHER = @{frobozz, frob1, frob2, frob3}(LOCAL)
#
#     LAN addressed BerkNet style host:user
#
FROBOZZ-BERKNET = {frobozz, frob4, frob5, frob6}:(LOCAL)
```

For the other sites on the LAN, their map entries should reflect
who is in charge of the machine, and their pathalias data
would appear like this (again, this example is abbreviated):

```
#N     frob1
#O     Frobozz Skonk Works, Software Development System
#C     Joe Palooka
#E     frobozz!postmaster
#
frob1 FROBOZZ-ETHER
```

HOW TO USE THIS INFORMATION

To most effectively use the data provided by these maps, you will probably want to install a couple of public-domain programs. The "uuhosts" program is a set of tools to automatically unpack the maps, without exposing your filesystem to the outside world. Uuhosts can also be used to easily view the information about one or more hosts. The Honeyman's "pathalias" program reads the map data and builds optimal routes from your site to all hosts and domains in the network. Pathalias is a powerful program, and can be hard for the beginner to use.

Finally, you may want to install one of the automatic mail-routing programs. This programs use the pathalias output to automatically generate full UUCP routes, so users need only know Internet-style addresses like "user@site.domain" Two of the most common routers are "smail" and "uumail."

All of these programs are available from the mod.sources archives; if you are not sure who your closest archive site is, send mail to the moderator at {cbosgd,seismo,cca,pyramid}!mirror!sources-request. You might also try asking your upstream news feed if they can send things to you.

WHAT TO DO WITH THIS STUFF

Once you have finished constructing your pathalias entry, mail it off to {ucbvax,ihnp4,akgua,seismo}!cbosgd!uucpmap, which is a mailing list of the regional map coordinators. They maintain assigned geographic sections of the map, and the entire map is posted on a rolling basis in the USENET newsgroups mod.map over the course of a month (at the end of the month they start over).

Questions or comments about this specification should also be directed at cbosgd!uucpmap.

$\overline{\underline{\mathsf{K}}}$

Common Modem Problems and Other Foibles Experienced with UUCP

Almost everyone experiences some modem problems on the first attempt to establish communications over a UUCP-based network. This appendix covers some of the more common modem/UUCP problems. The assumption here is that you are using a "Hayes compatible" modem. That means that your modem uses the "AT" command "language" originally devised by Hayes. Since the original formulation of the AT command set there have been extensions added, many of which were a by-product of the needs of newer high-speed modems. Every communications package, including UUCP systems, somewhere allows you to set an initialization string of AT commands for your modem. In addition, there will be some means for setting the modem speed (often called "baud rate," but more accurately referred to as "bit-per-second", or b/s or bps). Regardless of how fast your modem can operate, or how smart it is, when you are first attempting to establish communications it is best to start out modestly. Unfamiliar communications terms and acronyms may be found in the Glossary.

INITIAL SETTINGS

At the beginning in the appropriate places or files specified for WinNET™, UU-Plus™, and/or Waffle, use the following:

1. Set speed to not more than 2400 b/s. Go to higher speeds only when you have a basic system working.

2. Unless told differently by your mail server administrator, set your modem to "no parity", a word length of 8 bits, and 1 stop bit.

3. Be sure your software is set to the correct port (COM1 through COM4). You may also need to check to be sure that the correct "IRQ" and port addresses are set both in your software, and if you are using Windows, in the Ports section of Control Panel. The IBM/PC/AT standard settings are:

Port	IRQ	Address
COM1	4	3F8
COM2	3	2F8
COM3	4	3E8
COM4	3	2E8

Note that COM1 and COM3 both use IRQ 4 and COM2 and COM4 both use IRQ 3. Because these IRQs are shared, you may not be able to use both ports simultaneously. This is particularly true if a mouse is attached to one of these ports. Moreover, with your machine, COM3 and COM4 may not be enabled even though you may have the serial port hardware. This can be remedied in a variety of ways. One way is to obtain a program that will enable COM3 and COM4.

4. Set flow control to "Hardware", "CTS/RTS", or "None". You may have to experiment with the settings. The usual default is "XON/XOFF". With newer high-speed modems this can also usually be accomplished in the initialization command string, but may not be standard from modem to modem. For example, my SI-1414i FaxModem board (SIIG, Inc.) uses the AT$F4 to enable hardware CTS/RTS flow control and AT$F5 to disable flow control. My Dallas 96/96 FaxModem board uses AT&K3 and AT&K0, respectively, for the same functions. Check your modem manual for the proper settings for this and other AT commands. In general, CTS should not be set to constantly on or constantly off.

5. Turn off data compression and error correction capabilities. Once you get the connection going, you can try turning these back on. Again, you need to check your modem manual for the AT commands the manufacturer has used for these functions. My SI-1414i uses AT$C0 to disable data compression and AT$E0 for "normal mode" (i.e., no error correction). My Dallas 96/96 uses AT\N0 for "normal mode". There may also other related options that your modem may need to have set.

6. Most UUCP systems require that English result codes be generated by the modem (ATV1), although most modems default to this. Your system, however, may require that the result codes be disabled.

7. DCD should normally track the carrier from the remote modem (AT&C1) and the modem should go on hook and disable auto answer when it detects an ON-to-OFF transition on DTR (AT&D2). Note, however, that not all modems conform to these commands. My Dallas

96/96 uses AT&D3 rather than AT&D2 to accomplish the on hook status.

8. For modern high-speed error correcting modems it is usually the case that the modem-to-PC speed may be different from the modem-to-modem line speed. Moreover, with some software it is possible to "lock" the modem-to-PC speed at a constant b/s rate even though the actual modem-to-modem speed may vary depending on the remote system's capability. If your software system gives you the opportunity to lock the modem-to-PC speed, do so at the highest possible b/s rate. My SI-1414i, for example, can be locked at 57600 b/s and my Dallas 96/96 can be locked at 38400 b/s. Note, however, what has already been suggested about starting out at 2400 b/s.

9. Set timeout parameters generously. Many of the systems discussed come with defaults of 30 seconds. In most cases these should be reset to much longer periods of time, such as 60, 90, or even 120 seconds. The amount of time it takes to acquire carrier and to logon is a function of your own operating conditions plus the operating conditions of your server (host). Issues such as whether your host is communicating via a PBX or other telephone "front end" will affect the time it takes to acquire carrier, regardless of how quickly the host appears to answer the phone. With UUPlus™, for example, you will find in your \uu-plus\lib\modem\hayes.mdm file the following lines:

```
# Timeout to detect carrier.
tcd  90
#
# Timeout for login phase.
tlogin    60
```

The defaults are much shorter than those shown. Those illustrated (90 and 60) are probably more appropriate in many circumstances. Short timeout values may prevent a successful login. Long timeout values will only slow you down a bit if, in fact, there is a problem with logging in.

10. After all of this you may still get a message like "Login Failed." The most likely cause of this error is an incorrect chat script (found in *Systems* or its equivalent for UUPlus™, Waffle, Taylor UUCP, and other UUCPs, or *chat.rc* in WinNET™). The other common cause is line noise—static somewhere on the link between your machine and the machine being called.

CHAT SCRIPT ISSUES

Ordinarily your chat script should first look for part of the the word "login:". You should use only the last part of the word because some systems will use "Login:" and others "login:", and in the UNIX world case is significant. To be certain of the

sequence for your host system, use a terminal emulator program (such as Windows Terminal, Procomm Plus, or something similar), and dial your host. Login using the login name and password *for UUCP*. Watch the screen carefully for any anomalies, including odd characters at the end of the "login:" and "Password:" lines. A noisy line, for example, can generate extraneous characters. By inserting a few extra line feeds (UNIX) or carriage returns (DOS systems), *before you get to your "ogin: logname" expect / send pair* in your chat script, you can usually receive a clean "login:" prompt:

For UUPlus™ (in *systems*):

```
"" <CR>  ogin: logname word: abcxyz              normal
"" \n\d\n\d\n\d\n ogin: logname word: abcxyz      UNIX host
"" \r\d\r\d\r\d\r ogin: logname word: abcxyz      DOS host
```

For WinNET™ (in *chat.rc*):

```
INITIATE                                          1st line
\,\n\,\n\,\n\,\n                                  UNIX host
\,\r\,\r\,\r\,\r                                  DOS host
```

Other UUCP systems:

```
"" \n\d\n\d\n\d\n ogin: logname word: abcxyz      UNIX host
"" \r\d\r\d\r\d\r ogin: logname word: abcxyz      DOS host
```

Note, however, than even with a UNIX host, it may be easier to get its attention using carriage returns (\r) rather than line feeds (\n). *You may have to experiment.* Most UUCP systems also recognize a form such as "ogin:—ogin:" or "word:—word:". These forms have the effect of *expect string / kick-the-host-system / expect string*. It is also possible on most (but not all) systems to place escape characters, such as \r or \n between the two hyphens: ogin:-\n-ogin:. This has the effect of more explicitly "kicking the host" to get the correct login prompt before timing out with the "Login Failed" message. In other words, you may have to experiment before you get the right login combination. It may be useful, in order to see what the login sequence actually looks like, to dial into your mail server with a normal terminal emulator program, then try logging as if you were a UUCP session. Such a session might be the following sample (you type the bolded information given to you by your host administrator):

```
login: logname
Password: password
```

Then, if all goes well, the computer will respond:

```
shere=machine_name
```

If you see anything else, you may have to compensate by adding to your chat script. For example, if the "login:" prompt does not appear until you press <Enter> several times, then your chat script will also have to produce a few carriage returns (\r) or linefeeds (\n) at the beginning. On some systems there can also be a

secondary login sequence for remote users and this sequence will have to be built-in to your chat script.

To login successfully, you must get a clean "login:" prompt. A common problem is static on the line that may introduce spurious characters that the remote system takes to be part of the logname. Chat script processors are relatively simple, so you may have to generate extra linefeeds or carriage returns on noisy lines. The UUPlus™ "<CR>" chat script token automatically generates 10 carriage returns, but even this automatic sequencing of CRs is not foolproof and may not work on all systems.

If there is noise on the line, this noise can be sent to your host in the form of spurious characters which will, of course, affect your ability to login if they show up while your system is trying to send the logname or the password. The presence of noise on the line can have many sources: 1) your own service; 2) the service used by your mail server; 3) long distance circuits; 4) your communications ports/board; 5) the communications port/board of your server; 6) local circuits either at your end or at your server's location; 7) loose cable connections from your computer to your modem; 8) loose cable connections at your server; 9) cables with hairline cracks in the copper wire or poorly soldered or other poor mechanical connections between your DB25 or DB9 connector and your cable; or 10) a host of other possibilities. There are several things that can be done if this problem is persistent.

First, simply try for a connection at another time of day. This may cure the problem. Second, check all your connecting cables and be sure they are firmly seated. Third, if you use a separate communications board or internal modem, pull it out of your machine, reseat it firmly, and screw it down tightly. Fourth, have your telephone company check your local telephone line for noise. Fifth, request that your mail service have their local lines checked for noise. For either the fourth or fifth options you may have to be very firm with your phone company or your mail server manager about getting his or her line checked. Sixth, replace your communications board with a new card containing new serial ports (the cost of such boards today is typically between $10 and $20). Seventh, try explicitly reinitializing your modem by using a terminal emulator program to issue the appropriate "AT" commands to your modem (usually ATZ or AT&F). You may have to read your modem manual carefully.

As implied by this short discussion, it is sometimes difficult to "nail down" the causes of line noise and to determine a permanent cure. Just because you can successfully communicate with one service with a specific item of software does not guarantee that you will be able to communicate successfully with another service at another location with different software. While it is unlikely that the software itself will be a source of noise, some software can provide filtering of some extraneous chatacters, while other software cannot. Debugging this kind of problem can be one of the most vexing aspects of any system that relies on serial, dial-access communications. With some patience, however, it can be accomplished. A visit to your book store to acquire one of the many books on modem communications available that may provide more detail on such problems that we can with this short discussion.

MODEM INITIALIZATION

The failure to communicate properly is, more often than not, due to improperly set modems. The AT command set allows you to change the operating characteristics of your modem and different modems may come with different defaults for one or another of these commands. "Hayes compatible" usually means that the modem uses the AT command set, not necessarily that it is designed to work just like a Hayes modem. You can find out what the initial settings on your modem are by getting into your favorite communications program. First, in order to verify that you are communicating with your modem, type

`AT<Enter>`

The modem should respond with

`OK`

Then type:

`ATZ` and/or `AT&F`.

In either case the modem will respond with OK. The "ATZ" command resets the modem, causing the modem to break a connection if it exists. One of the two stored configuration profiles (see the &W command in your modem manual), numbered "0" or "1", is written over the active parameter profile of the modem. "ATZ" is the same as "ATZ0", or if you wish to see profile 1, then type "ATZ1". The reason for resetting the modem is that we want to see the parameters as they are provided for **uucico**, not as your communications program has reset them. The modem can also be resent to the factory profile by issuing the "&F" command. The results are not necessarily the same as that obtained with the "ATZn" command. On power-up the profile stored in Z0 is the default, although this can be changed by issuing the "&Yn" command, where n=0 or 1.

Almost all communications programs alter the current profile. Consequently, if you have been using your modem for several different applications, and have not turned it off, then the current profile will be the one that was last used unless the final command issued by the last communications program was "ATZn". That is why the initialization strings are important in all communications activities and why they must be reset for each communications program, of which **uucico** is one. Having issued the "ATZ" command and received "OK", you can now issue the "AT&V" command to see the basic profiles of your modem. Not all "Hayes compatible" modems handle the AT&V command the same way. If it is truly Hayes compatible, then typing **AT&V** should give you the stored profiles of both Profile 1 and Profile 2, which should look something like the following:

```
Stored Profile #0
B1   E1   M1   Q0   V1   X4   Y0   &C1   &D0   &E0   &G0   &L0   &P0   &S0   $A1   $B0
```

```
$C1   $E3   $F4   $K1   $L2   $Q2   $R0   $S0   $T5   $X2
S00=002 S01=000 S02=043 S03=013 S04=010 S05=008 S06=002 S07=045 S08=002
S09=006
S10=007 S12=050 S18=000 S25=005 S26=001 S36=000 S37=000

Stored Profile #1
 B1   E1   M1   Q0   V1   X4   Y0   &C1   &D2   &E0   &G0   &L0   &P0   &S0   $A1
$B0
$C1   $E3   $F4   $K1   $L2   $Q2   $R0   $S0   $T5   $X2
S00=000 S01=000 S02=043 S03=013 S04=010 S05=008 S06=002 S07=045 S08=002
S09=006
S10=007 S12=050 S18=000 S25=005 S26=001 S36=007 S37=000

OK
```

Your modem may not have the parameters preceded by the dollar sign ("$") or it may have other parameters, perhaps preceded by a slash ("/") or some other special character. With some modems it may be necessary to issue an "AT&Vn" command, where n=some number specified in your modem manual. To obtain the information listed above for one of my modems, for example, it is necessary to type **AT&V3**.

Some modems will also give additional information, or information in more readable form. For example, the same mode that requires the "AT&V3" command, will also give the following information (I typed the information in bold characters, the modem responded with the other information):

```
at&v1
 B1   PROTOCOL              E1   COMMAND ECHO
 M1   SPEAKER CONTROL       Q0   QUIET MODE
 V1   VERBAL MODE           X4   RESULT CODE
 Y0   DISCONNECT TYPE       &C1  CARRIER CONTROL
&D0   DTR CONTROL           &E0  RETRAIN
&G0   GUARD TONE            &L0  LINE SPEED
&P0   PULSE SPACING         &S0  DSR CONTROL
$A1   ECHO CANCEL LENGTH    $B0  BUFFER SIZE
$C1   COMPRESSION           $E3  ERROR CONTROL
$F4   FLOW CONTROL          $K1  DIAL INTERRUPT
$L2   CHAR LENGTH           $Q2  COMP EQUALIZER
$R0   DISTINCTIVE RING      $S0  SPEED CONVERSION
$T5   Tx LEVEL              $X2  EXTEND RESULT CODE

&Y0   POWER-UP PROFILE

OK
at&v2
S00=002 RING THRESHOLD          S01=000 RING COUNT
S02=043 ESC CHARACTER           S03=013 CR CHARACTER
S04=010 LF CHARACTER            S05=008 BS CHARACTER
S06=002 BLIND DIAL WAIT TIMER   S07=045 CARRIER WAIT TIMER
S08=002 PAUSE TIMER             S09=006 CD DELAY TIMER
```

```
S10=007 CARRIER LOSS TIMER     S12=050 ESC PROMPT DELAY
S18=000 TEST TIMER             S25=005 DTR SYNC DELAY TIMER
S26=001 RTS TO CTS DELAY TIME  S36=000 INACTIVITY TIMER
S37=000 DCE LINE SPEED

OK
```

TIMING ISSUES

When a modem fails, it is necessary to check the register settings of the modem *calling* (usually) modem. A common problem is a modem picking up the line and immediately disconnecting. On a Hayes compatible modem, check the delay values of registers S7, S9, S10, and S25 on the *calling* modem. These registers are defined as follows:[1]

S7   Wait for Carrier after Dial (Carrier Waiting Timer).
      S7 is used for two purposes:
      (1)   During call establishment, this register provides the time that
            the local modem waits for carrier from the remote modem before
            hanging up.
      (2)   Sets the length of time that the modem waits when the "Wait
            For Dial Tone" call progress feature (W in the dial string) is in
            effect.
      Of primary importance here is the first purpose. On three different
      modems I have the default on one is 30 seconds, on another, 45
      seconds, and on the third, 50 seconds. If your call to a mail server
      must go through a switch of some kind, all of these times may be too
      short and you will experience a disconnect. **When your modem is
      initialized, S7 should probably be set to at least 60 and 90 is
      not too much.**

S9   Carrier Detect Response Time
      The range is from 0-255 with each unit measured in 0.1 seconds.
      The typical default is 6 (0.6 seconds), although again, this varies
      across modem manufacturers. One of mine defaults to 7 (0.7 sec-
      onds). This register determines how long a carrier signal must be
      present before the modem recognizes it as a carrier and turns on
      DCD. **As this time is increased, there is less opportunity to
      detect a false carrier due to noise from the telephone (telco)
      line.** You may have to experiment with the settings for this register.

S10   Lost Carrier to Hang Up Delay
      S10 sets the length of time the modem waits before hanging up after
      a loss of carrier. **The S10 value must be greater than S9 or else
      the modem disconnects before it recognizes the carrier.**
      Setting S10 to 255 often disables the hang-up function. The range
      of values is 1-255 with one value defined as 0.1 seconds. Some

modems default S10 to only one second larger than S9, others will default it to higher values such as 14 or more (more than twice the default value of S9). **A value of approximately twice that of S9 is probably most appropriate.**

S25 Delay to DTR

When on-line, S25 specifies the time DTR must be false before the modem accepts a DTR transition as valid. A change in DTR (on to off) that persists for a period shorter than the value held in S25 is ignored by the modem while it is in data made. The valid range is 0-255 in hundredths of a second with a default of 5 (0.05 seconds). When in command mode, DTR is ignored. A change in DTR from on to off normally indicates that the carrier has been or should be dropped. Short transition states can occur, however, when it is not intended that carrier be dropped.

Of all four of these S-registers, the most important one to change is S7. If changing S7 to 60 or 90 seconds does not cure premature hangups, then increase S10. If that does not solve the problem, then increase S25 a little. Some or all these parameters may be changed "automatically" by setting appropriate values in configuration or modem definition files, but when all else fails, they can be set explicitly by using the appropriate modem initialization commands in the modem initialization string.

OTHER ISSUES TO NOTE

Once your modem is dialing out properly, and connecting to another system, if mail or other files are not exchanged, then you review your setup further:

1. Check your chat scripts. Contact the other system's system administrator to be sure that you are expecting the correct prompts in the chat script for the system you are calling.
2. If available, use the debugging mode of uucico to watch communications. Debugging mode is normally accessed using the uucico command suffixed by a ‹-x#› where ‹#› is a number from 1 to 9 which determines the debugging level.
3. If you see messages in your log files that a site would not accept a file from your site, the other site may not have its permissions set to allow you to send files to it, or to write files you are sending to a particular directory you specified.
4. When sending files across systems, watch the length of the sitename you are using. Currently, Coherent, for example, can only work with a 7 character sitename. If you are using an 8 character sitename, Coherent will not properly distribute files transferred from your site.
5. When attaching an external modem to your computer, it is important to use a modem cable that supports all relevant RS-232 signals. It is

probably the better part of valor to buy a commercially made cable rather than trying to construct your own.

Not all modem communication problems can be addressed here. There are several excellent books available that can provide further instruction on dealing with modems and they are probably available in the Computer section of your local book shop.

REFERENCES

1. *Hayes ACCURA User's Guide* (Atlanta, GA: Hayes Microcomputer Products, Inc., 1992), pp. 4-3, 4-4; *Dallas FAX 96/96 PRO & 14.4 PRO PLUS* [User's Guide] (Dallas, TX: Dallas FAX, Inc., 1992), pp. 14, 16–17; and *High-Speed FaxModem Board SI-1414i User's Manual* (SIIG, Inc., 1992), pp. 3-20–3-21, 3-25.

L

Last-Minute Software Notes

One of the problems with writing a book of this sort is that software development seems to take place faster than the book can be written. When I started the current version of Taylor UUCP was 1.04. While the book was in production Version 1.05 was released. WinNET™ Mail and News was at Version 2.10, although it is now at 2.12. We were able to obtain the latest release for the book, however. Similarly, UUPlus™ Utilities was changing until almost the last minute as the author sought to produce its release version. Obscure bugs are sometimes found at inopportune times as well. Just as I was finishing reading the page proofs I received the notice below concerning WinNET™ Mail and News. The notice reflects a small bug in one element of the system that you should probably know about, but is unlikely to be a problem for the uses described in this book. It is appropriate, however, that you be aware of the bug. The notice is, therefore, reproduced in its entirety.

```
From all Fri Jul 22 02:50:23 1994 remote from witch
Subject: Caution: Problem with Queue Editor
Reply-To: help@win.net
Message-Id: <x20250.AA15490@witch.uucp>
Date: 22 Jul 94 02:50:23 EDT (Fri)
From: all@witch.uucp (WinNET Admin)
To: postmaster@ewc.win.net

REPLY-TO: help@win.net
»»»»»»»»»»»»»»»»»»»»»»»»»»
```

Dear WinNET Customer:

We have recently discovered that there is a bug in the Queue Editor Utility program that comes with WinNET Mail & News. This bug is in versions of WinNET from 2.06 through 2.12.

The problem is in the Recycle function - the button labeled

> BACK
> <<<<<<
> Recycle

When you press this button, the Queue Editor is supposed to send the highlighted mail item back to your Incoming mailbox. It does this, but in the process, it may corrupt some of the data files that WinNET uses to keep track of everything. Some of the effects that this appears to produce are:

1. Your E-Mail address placed in the From and Reply-To fields of mail messages is garbled. You can see your E-Mail address if you look in the Help menu About box.

    This error can be recovered easily by rerunning the setup program.

2. Some systems may begin receiving a "No OK from Modem" error message when attempting to contact the server.

3. It appears that in a few cases, the counters that point to mail folders may become corrupted. If this happens, creation of new mail folder can cause old mail folders to be lost. The mail itselt is not actually lost, but the reference to it is.

If you experience either problems 2 or 3, please contact us at Technical Support.

It is ok to use the Queue Editor, but we suggest that you do not use the Recycle button.

A new version of WinNET will be released within the next 10 days which will fix this problem and will include more self-correcting functions to reduce or recover from this kind of problem.

Thank you for using WinNET.

Best Regards,

Michael Tague
WinNET Admin

Glossary

:-): This odd symbol is one of the ways a person can portray "mood" in the very flat medium of computers—by using "smiley faces." This is "metacommunication," and there are literally hundreds of such symbols, from the obvious to the obscure. This particular example expresses "happiness." Don't see it? Tilt your head to the left 90 degrees. Smiles are also used to denote sarcasm.

abstract syntax: A description of a data structure that is independent of machine-oriented structures and encodings. [Source: RFC1208]

Abstract Syntax Notation One (ASN.1): The language used by the OSI protocols for describing abstract syntax. This language is also used to encode SNMP packets. ASN.1 is defined in ISO documents 8824.2 and 8825.2. See also Basic Encoding Rules.

acceptable risk: In *risk analysis*, an assessment that an activity or system meets minimum requirements of security directives.

Acceptable Use Policy (AUP): Many transit networks have policies which restrict the use to which the network may be put. A well known example is NSFNET's AUP which does not allow commercial use. Enforcement of AUPs varies with the network. See also National Science Foundation.

access: 1) In data processing, interaction between a subject and an object which allows information to flow from one to the other; 2) in physical security, the ability to enter a secured building area.

access authorization: Granting permission to an object (i.e., person, terminal, program) to execute a set of operations in the system. Generally, a profile matrix grants access privileges to users, terminals, programs, data elements, type of access (e.g., read, write), and time period.

access control: In a network or its components: the tasks performed by hardware, software, and administrative controls to monitor a system operation, ensure data integrity, perform user identification, record system access and changes, and grant access to users.

Access Control List (ACL): Most network security systems operate by allowing selective use of services. An Access Control List is the usual means by which access to, and denial of, services is controlled. It is simply a list of the services available, each with a list of the hosts permitted to use the service.

access method: A software routine accessible by the network control program that performs the transmitting/receiving of data and may include error detection and correction mechanisms. See also *medium access control.*

active threats: Unauthorized use of a device attached to a communications facility to alter transmitting data or control signals; or to generate spurious data or control signals.

acknowledgment (ACK): A type of message sent to indicate that a block of data arrived at its destination without error. See also Negative Acknowledgement. [Source: NNSC]

ACL: *See* Access Control List.

ACK: *See* Acknowledgment.

AD: *See* Administrative Domain.

address: There are three types of addresses in common use within the Internet. They are E-Mail address; IP, internet or Internet address; and hardware or MAC address. *See also* E-Mail address, IP address, internet address, MAC address.

address mask: A bit mask used to identify which bits in an IP address correspond to the network and subnet portions of the address. This mask is often referred to as the subnet mask because the network portion of the address can be determined by the encoding which is inherent in an IP address.

address resolution: Conversion of an internet address into the corresponding physical address.

Address Resolution Protocol (ARP): Used to dynamically discover the low level physical network hardware address that corresponds to the high level IP address for a given host. ARP is limited to physical network systems that support broadcast packets which can be heard by all hosts on the network. It is defined in RFC 826. *See also* proxy ARP.

Administrative Domain (AD): A collection of hosts and routers, and the interconnecting network(s), managed by a single administrative authority.

Advanced Research Projects Agency Network (ARPANET): A pioneering longhaul network funded by ARPA (now DARPA). It served as the basis for early networking research, as well as a central backbone during the development of the Internet. The ARPANET consisted of individual packet switching computers interconnected by leased lines. See also: Defense Advanced Research Projects Agency. [Source: FYI4]

agent: In the client-server model, the part of the system that performs information preparation and exchange on behalf of a client or server application. [Source: RFC1208]

alias: A name, usually short and easy to remember, that is translated into another name, usually long and difficult to remember.

American National Standards Institute (ANSI): This organization is responsible for approving U.S. standards in many areas, including computers and communications. Standards approved by this organization are often called ANSI standards (e.g., ANSI C is the version of the C language approved by ANSI). ANSI is a member of ISO. See also International Organization for Standardization. [Source: NNSC]

American Standard Code for Information Interchange (ASCII): A standard character-to-number encoding widely used in the computer industry. See also: EBCDIC.

amplifier: In a broadband system, a device for strengthening the radio frequency signal to a level needed by other devices on the system.

answer modem: *See* modem.

Anonymous FTP (File Transfer Protocol): The procedure of connecting to a remote computer, as an anonymous or guest user, in order to transfer public files back to your local computer. (See also: FTP and Protocols). Anonymous FTP allows a user to retrieve documents, files, programs, and other archived data from anywhere in the Internet without having to establish a userid and password. By using the special userid of "anonymous" the network user will bypass local security checks and will have access to publicly accessible files on the remote system. See also archive site, File Transfer Protocol.

ANSI: *See* American National Standards Institute.

API: *See* Application Program Interface.

Appletalk: A networking protocol developed by Apple Computer for communication between Apple Computer products and other computers. This protocol is independent of the network layer on which it is run. Current implementations exist for Localtalk, a 235Kb/s local area network; and Ethertalk, a 10Mb/s local area network. [Source: NNSC]

application: A program that performs a function directly for a user. FTP, mail and Telnet clients are examples of network applications.

application layer: The top layer of the network protocol stack. The application layer is concerned with the semantics of work (e.g., formatting electronic mail messages). How to represent that data and how to reach the foreign node are issues for lower layers of the network. [Source: MALAMUD]

Application Program Interface (API): A set of calling conventions which define how a service is invoked through a software package. [Source: RFC1208]

archie: A system to automatically gather, index and serve information on the Internet. The initial implementation of archie provided an indexed directory of filenames from all anonymous FTP archives on the Internet. Later versions provide other collections of information. See also: archive site, Gopher, Prospero, Wide Area Information Servers.

archive site: A machine that provides access to a collection of files across the Internet. An "anonymous FTP archive site", for example, provides access to this material via the FTP protocol. See also: anonymous FTP, archie, Gopher, Prospero, Wide Area Information Servers.

ARP: *See* Address Resolution Protocol.

ARPA: *See* Defense Advanced Research Projects Agency.

ARPANET: *See* Advanced Research Projects Agency Network.

AS: *See* Autonomous System.

ASCII: *See* American Standard Code for Information Interchange.

ASN.1: *See* Abstract Syntax Notation One.

assigned numbers: The RFC [STD2] that documents the currently assigned values from several series of numbers used in network protocol implementations. This RFC is updated periodically and, in any case, current information can be obtained from the Internet Assigned Numbers Authority (IANA). If you are developing a protocol or application that will require the use of a link, socket, port, protocol, etc., please contact the IANA to receive a number assignment. See also Internet Assigned Numbers Authority, STD. [Source: STD2]

Asynchronous Transfer Mode (ATM): A method for the dynamic allocation of bandwidth using a fixed- size packet (called a cell). ATM is also known as "fast packet".

ASCII: American (National) Standard Code for Information Interchange, X3.4 1968. A seven-bit-plus parity code established by the American National Standards Institute to achieve compatibility among data services and consisting of 96 displayed upper and lower case characters and 32 non-displayed control codes.

asymmetric encryption: *See* public key cryptosystem.

asynchronous transmission: A mode of data communications transmission in which time intervals between transmitted characters may be of unequal length. The transmission is controlled by start and stop elements at the beginning and end of each character; hence it is also called start-stop transmission.

attachment unit interface (AUI): The cable, connectors, and transmission circuitry used to interconnect the physical signaling (PLS) sublayer and MAU.

audit of computer security: As defined by NBS (now NIST) Special Publication 500-57, an independent evaluation of the controls employed to ensure:

1. The appropriate protection of the organization's information assets (including hardware, software, firmware, and data) from all significant anticipated threats or hazards
2. The accuracy and reliability of the data maintained on or generated by an automated data-processing system
3. The operational reliability and performance assurance for accuracy and timeliness of all components of the automated data-processing system

An examination of data security procedures and measures for the purpose of evaluating their adequacy and compliance with established policy.

ATM: *See* Asynchronous Transfer Mode.

AUP: *See* Acceptable Use Policy.

authentication: 1) Ensuring that a message is genuine, has arrived exactly as it was sent and came from the stated source; 2) verifying the identity of an individual, such as a person at a remote terminal or the sender of a message. In OSI nomenclature, authentication refers to the certainty that the data received comes from the supposed origin; it is not extended to include the integrity of the data that are being transmitted. See also, *data origin authentication* and *peer-entry authentication*. Protection against fraudulent tran actions by establishing the validity of messages, stations, individuals or originators.

Autonomous System (AS): A collection of routers under a single administrative authority using a common Interior Gateway Protocol for routing packets.

availability: That aspect of security that deals with the timely delivery of information and services to the user. An attack on availability would seek to sever network connections, tie up accounts or systems.

backbone: The top level in a hierarchical network. Stub and transit networks which connect to the same backbone are guaranteed to be interconnected. See also stub network, transit network.

back door: A feature built into a program by its designer, which allows the designer special privileges which are denied to the normal users of the program. A back door in a logon program, for instance, could enable the designer to log on to a system, even though he or she did not have an authorized account on that system.

bacterium (informal): A program which, when executed, spreads to other users and systems by sending copies of itself; since it *infects* other programs, it may be thought of as a *system virus* as opposed to a *program virus*. It differs from a *rabbit* in that it is not necessarily designed to exhaust system resources.

bandwidth: The range of frequencies assigned to a channel or system. The difference expressed in Hertz between the highest and lowest frequencies of a band. However, as typically used, the amount of data that can be sent through a given communications circuit.

bang: An exclamation point (!) used to separate machine names in an extended UUCP path. *See also* bang path.

bang path: A series of machine names used to direct electronic mail from one user to another, typically by specifying an explicit UUCP path through which the mail is to be routed. *See also* e-mail address, mail path, UNIX-to-UNIX CoPy.

baseband (signaling): Transmission of a signal at its original frequencies, i.e., unmodulated. A transmission medium through which digital signals are sent without complicated frequency shifting. In general, only one communication channel is available at any given time. Ethernet is an example of a baseband network. See also broadband, Ethernet. [Source: NNSC]

Basic Encoding Rules (BER): Standard rules for encoding data units described in ASN.1. Sometimes incorrectly lumped under the term ASN.1, which properly refers only to the abstract syntax description language, not the encoding technique. *See also* Abstract Syntax Notation One. [Source: NNSC]

batch: A group of records or programs that is considered a single unit for processing on a computer.

batch processing: A technique in which a number of data transactions are collected over a period of time and aggregated for sequential processing.

baud: A unit of transmission speed equal to the number of discrete conditions or signal events per second. Baud is the same as "bits per second" only if each signal event represents exactly one bit, although the two terms are often incorrectly used interchangeably.

BBS: *See* Bulletin Board System

BCNU: Be Seein' You

BER: *See* Basic Encoding Rules

Berkeley Internet Name Domain (BIND): Implementation of a DNS server developed and distributed by the University of California at Berkeley. Many Internet hosts run BIND, and it is the ancestor of many commercial BIND implementations.

Berkeley Software Distribution (BSD): Implementation of the UNIX operating system and its utilities developed and distributed by the University of California at Berkeley. "BSD" is usually preceded by the version number of the distribution, e.g., "4.3 BSD" is version 4.3 of the Berkeley UNIX distribution. Many Internet hosts run BSD software, and it is the ancestor of many commercial UNIX implementations. [Source: NNSC]

BGP: *See* Border Gateway Protocol

big-endian: A format for storage or transmission of binary data in which the most significant bit (or byte) comes first. The term comes from "Gulliver's Travels" by Jonathan Swift. The Lilliputians, being very small, had correspondingly small political problems. The Big-Endian and Little-Endian parties debated over whether soft- boiled eggs should be opened at the big end or the little end. *See also* little-endian. [Source: RFC1208]

binary: 1) A base 2 number system with numbers usually symbolized as strings of ones (1) and zeroes (0); 2) executable programs in machine language.

BIND: *See* Berkeley Internet Name Domain

Birds Of a Feather (BOF): A Birds Of a Feather (flocking together) is an informal discussion group. It is formed, often ad hoc, to consider a specific issue and, therefore, has a narrow focus.

BITNET: A cooperative computer network interconnecting over 2,300 academic and research institutions in 32 countries. Originally based on IBM's RSCS networking protocol, BITNET supports mail, mailing lists, and file transfer. Now merged with CSNET and running the RSCS protocol over TCP/IP protocol (BITNET II), the network will be called Computer Research and Education Network (CREN). An academic computer network that provides interactive electronic mail and file transfer services, using a store-and-forward protocol, based on IBM Network Job Entry protocols. Bitnet-II encapsulates the Bitnet protocol within IP packets and depends on the Internet to route them.

bisynchronous transmission: Binary synchronous (bisync) transmission. Data transmission in which synchronization of characters is controlled by timing signals generated at the sending and receiving stations in contrast to asynchronous transmission.

bit-mapped graphics: A method of representing data in a computer for display in which each dot on the screen is mapped to a unit of data in memory.

bit rate: The data throughput on the trunk coaxial medium expressed in hertz.

block: A group of digits, characters, or words that are held in one section of an input/output medium and handled as a unit, such as the data recorded between to interblock gaps on a magnetic tape or a data unit being transmitted over a data communications system; a block may or may not contain control information. A group of N-ary digits, transmitted as unit. An encoding procedure is generally applied to the group of bits or N-ary digits for error=control purposes.

b/s (bits per second): *See* baud.

BNC-connector: A bayonet-type coaxial cable connector of the kind commonly found on RF equipment.

BOF: *See* Birds Of a Feather

BOOTP: The Bootstrap Protocol, described in RFCs 951 and 1084, is used for booting diskless nodes. *See also* Reverse Address Resolution Protocol.

Border Gateway Protocol (BGP): The Border Gateway Protocol is an exterior gateway protocol defined in RFCs 1267 and 1268. It's design is based on experience gained with EGP, as defined in STD 18, RFC 904, and EGP usage in the NSFNET Backbone, as described in RFCs 1092 and 1093. *See also* Exterior Gateway Protocol.

bounce: The return of a piece of mail because of an error in its delivery. [Source: ZEN]

branch cable: The AUI cable interconnecting the data terminal equipment (DTE) and MAU system components.

bridge: The hardware and software necessary for two networks using the same or similar technology to communicate; more specifically the hardware and software necessary to link segments of the same or similar networks at the Data Link Layer of the OSI Reference Model, i.e., a MAC Level Bridge; a router that connects two or more networks and forwards packets among them. Usually, bridges operate at the physical network level. Bridges differ from repeaters because bridges store and forward complete packets while repeaters forward electrical signals. A device which forwards traffic between network segments based on datalink layer information. These segments would have a common network layer address. *See also* gateway, router.

broadband: A communications channel having a bandwidth characterized by high data transmission speeds (10,000 to 500,000 bits per second). Often used when describing communications systems based on cable television technology. In the 802 standards, a system whereby information is encoded, modulated onto a carrier, and band-pass filtered or otherwise constrained to occupy only a limited frequency spectrum on the coaxial transmission medium. Many information signals can be present on the medium at the same time without disruption provided that they all occupy nonoverlapping frequency regions within the cable system's range of frequency transport. A transmission medium capable of supporting a wide range of frequencies. It can carry multiple signals by dividing the total capacity of the medium into multiple, independent bandwidth channels, where each channel operates only on a specific range of frequencies. *See also* baseband.

broadcast: A special type of multicast packet which all nodes on the network are always willing to receive. *See also* multicast.

broadcast storm: An incorrect packet broadcast onto a network that causes multiple hosts to respond all at once, typically with equally incorrect packets which causes the storm to grow exponentially in severity.

brouter: A device which bridges some packets (i.e., forwards based on datalink layer information) and routes other packets (i.e., forwards based on network layer information). The bridge/route decision is based on configuration information. *See also* bridge, router.

BSD: *See* Berkeley Software Distribution

BTW: By The Way

bug: An error in the design or implementation of a program that causes it to do something that neither the user nor the program author had intended to be done.

Bulletin Board System (BBS): A computer, and associated software, which typically provides electronic messaging services, archives of files, and any other services or activities of interest to the bulletin board system's operator. Although BBS's have traditionally been the domain of hobbyists, an increasing number of BBS's are connected directly to the Internet, and many BBS's are currently operated by government, educational, and research institutions. *See also* Electronic Mail, Internet, Usenet. [Source: NWNET]

bus: The organization of electrical paths within a circuit. A specific bus, such as the S-100, provides a standard definition for specific paths.

carrier sense: The signal provided by the physical layer to the access sublayer to indicate that one or more stations are currently transmitting on the trunk cable.

CATV: Community Antenna Television. See broadband.

CCITT: Consultative Committee International Telegraph and Telephone. An organization established by the United Nations to develop worldwide standards for communications technology, as for example *protocols* to be used by devices exchanging data.

central processing unit: *See* CPU.

centralized network: A computer network with a central processing node through which all data and communications flow.

Centronics: A manufacturer of computer printers. Centronics pioneered the use of a parallel interface between printers and computers and that interface, using Centronic standards, is sometimes referred to as a Centronics parallel interface.

character user interface (CUI): Classical character-based system for computer/human communications.

checksum: A fixed-length block produced as a function of every bit in an encrypted message; a summation of a set of data items for error detection; a sum of digits or bits used to verify the integrity of data.

cipher: An algorithm for disguising information according to a logical principle by working within the elements of whatever alphabet is in use, such as by shift substitution of the letters of the alphabet by other letters a certain number of places toward the beginning or end of the alphabet. Not to be confused with a *code*.

ciphertext: Encrypted text that cannot be read without decryption; data in an encrypted form that is cryptologically protected; the opposite of *plaintext* or *cleartext*.

client-server: The model of interaction in a distributed system in which a program at one site sends a request to a program at another site and awaits a response. The requesting program is called a client; the program satisfying the request is called the server. It is usually easier to build client software than server software.

Client-Server Interface: A program that provides an interface to remote programs (called clients), most commonly across a network, in order to provide these clients with access to some service such as databases, printing, etc. In general, the clients act on behalf of a human end-user (perhaps indirectly).

code: A technique by which the basic elements of language, such as syllables, words, phrases, sentences, and paragraphs, are disguised through being replaced by other, usually shorter, arbitrarily selected language elements, requiring a codebook (table) for translation. A term not generally used in relation to encryption. Not to be confused with cipher.

cold-site: DP hardware-ready room, or series of rooms, which is ready to receive hardware for disaster recovery. *See also hot-site* and *warm-site*.

collision: Multiple concurrent transmission on the cable resulting in garbled data.

command languages: Software in which commands are typed in, rather than selected from, a set displayed on the screen.

communications: *See* data communications. Transmission of intelligence between points of origin and reception without alteration of sequence or structure of the information content.

communications network: The total network of devices and transmission media (radio, cables, etc.) necessary to transmit and receive intelligence.

communications security (COMSEC): The protection resulting from the application of cryptosecurity, transmission security, and emission security measures to telecommunications and from the application of physical security measure to communications security information. These measures are taken to deny unauthorized persons information of value which might be derived from the possession and study of such telecommunications. COMSEC include: 1. cryptosecurity; 2. transmission security; 3. emission security; and 4. physical security of communications security materials and information. (a) Cryptosecurity: the component of communications security which results from the provision of technically sound cryptosystems and their proper use. (b) Transmission security: the component of communications security which results from all measures designed to protect transmissions from interception and exploitation by means other than crypt-analysis. (c) Emission security: the component of communications security that results from all measures taken to deny unauthorized persons information of value which might be derived from intercept and analysis of compromising emanations from cryptoequipment and telecommunications systems. (d) Physical security: the component of communications security which results from all physical measures necessary to safe guard classified equipment, material, and documents from access thereto or observation thereof by unauthorized persons.

communications security equipment: Equipment designed to provide security to telecommunications by converting information to a form unintelligible to an unauthorized interceptor and by reconverting such information to its original form for authorized recipients, as well as equipment designed specifically to aid in, or as an essential element of, the conversion process. COMSEC equipment is cryptoequipment, cryptoancillary equipment, cryptoproduction equipment, and authentication equipment.

computer conferencing: A process for holding group discussions through the use of a computer network.

computer network: One or more computers linked with users or each other via a communications network.

computer security: The technological safeguards and managerial procedures that can be applied to computer hardware, programs, data, and facilities to ensure the availability, integrity, and confidentiality of computer-based resources. It can also ensure that intended functions are performed as planned.

confidentiality: The property that information is not made available or disclosed to unauthorized individuals, entities or processes; an attack on confidentiality would seek to view databases, print files, discover a password, etc., to which the attacker was not entitled.

connectionless applications: Those applications that require routing services but do not require connection-oriented services.

connectionless service: A class of service that does not establish a virtual or logical connection and does not guarantee that data-units will be delivered or be delivered in the proper order. Connectionless services are flexible, robust, and provide connectionless application support.

connection-oriented services: Services that establish a virtual connection which appears to the user as an actual end-to-end circuit. Sometimes called a virtual circuit or virtual connection. *See also virtual circuit.*

connectivity: In a local area network, the ability of any device attached to the distribution system to establish a session with any other device.

CP/M: Control Program for Microcomputers. Manufactured and marketed by Digital Research, Inc.

CPU: Central Processing Unit. The "brain" of the general purpose computer that controls the interpretation and execution of instructions. The CPU does not include interfaces, main memory, or peripherals.

CREN: Computer Research and Education Network is the new name for the merged computer networks, BITNET and Computer Science Network (CSNET). It supports electronic mail and file transfer.

cryptochannel: A complete system of cryptocommunications between two or more holders. The basic unit for naval cryptographic communication. It includes: (a) the cryptographic aids prescribed; (b) the holders thereof; (c) the indicators or other means of identification; (d) the area or areas in which it is effective; (e) the special purpose, if any, for which provided; and (f) pertinent notes as to distribution, usage, etc. A cryptochannel is analogous to a radio circuit.

cryptogram: The ciphertext.

cryptography: The branch of cryptology devoted to creating appropriate algorithms.

crypto-information: Information which would make a significant contribution to the cryptanalytic solution of encrypted text or a cryptosystem.

cryptology: The science which treats of hidden, disguised, or encrypted communications. It embraces communications security and communications intelligence. The art of creating and breaking ciphers.

cryptomaterial: All material, including documents, devices, or equipment that contains crypto-information and is essential to the encryption, decryption, or authentication of telecommunications.

CSMA/CD: Carrier Sense Multiple Access with Collision Detection. A network access method for managing collisions of data packets.

CTS/RTS: (clear to send)/(request to send); RS-232 signals sent from the receiving station to the transmitting station that incidates it is ready to accept (CTS) or send (RTS) data. Typically, a means of hardware flow control. See also, *flow control*. Contrast with *XON/XOFF*.

CUI: *See* Character User Interface.

cursor: A position indicator frequently employed in video (CRT or VDT) output devices or terminals to indicate a character to be corrected or a position in which data is to be entered.

cyclic redundancy check (CRC): An algorithm designed to generate a check field used to guard against errors against which may occur in data transmission; the check field is often generated by taking the remainder after dividing all the serialized bits in a block of data by a predetermined binary number.

daemon: A UNIX program that is invisible to users but provides important system services. Daemons manage everything from paging to networking to notification of incoming mail. BSD UNIX has many different daemons: without counting precisely, there are something like two dozen. Daemons normally spend most of their time "sleeping" or waiting for something to do, so that they do not account for a lot of CPU load.

data base: A nonredundant collection of inter-related data items processable by one or more applications.

data communications: The transmission and reception of data, often including operations such as coding, decoding, and validation.

data encryption standard (DES): An algorithm to be implemented in electronic hardware devices and used for the cryptographic protection of digital, binary-coded information. For the relevant publications see "Data Encryption Standard," *Federal Information Processing Standard (FIPS) Publication 46*, 1977 January 15, also published as *American National Standard Data Encryption Algorithm*, American National Standards Institute, Inc., December 30, 1980, and supplemented with "DES Modes of Operation," *Federal Information Processing Standard (FIPS) Publication 81*, 1980 December 2; "Telecommunications: Interoperability and security requirements for use of the data encryption standard in the physical layer of data communications," *Federal Standard of the General Services Administration*, August 3, 1983, FED-STD-1026; "Telecommunications: General security requirements for equipment using the data encryption standard," *Federal Standard of the General Services Administration*, April 14, 1982, FED-STD-1027; and "Telecommunications: Interoperability and security requirements for use of the data encryption standard with CCITT Group 3 Facsimile equipment," *Federal Standard of the General Services Administration*, April 4, 1985, FED-STD-1028.

Data origin authentication: The corroboration that the source of data received is as claimed. For an OSI network, this refers to authentication in the context of a connectionless service.

data file: A collection of related data records organized in a specific manner. In large systems data files are gradually being replaced by data bases in order to limit redundancy and improve reliability and timeliness.

datagram: A finite-length packet with sufficient information to be independently routed from source to destination without reliance on previous transmissions; typically does not involve end-to-end session establishment and may or may not entail delivery confirmation acknowledgement.

datagram service: One that establishes a datagram-based connection between peer entities. In OSI parlance this type of service is called a *connectionless service*. *See also* connectionless service.

data link: An assembly of two or more terminal installations and the interconnecting communications channel operating according to a particular method that permits information to be exchanged.

data link layer: The conceptual layer of control or processing logic existing in the hierarchical structure of a station which is responsible for maintaining control of the data link.

data management system: A system that provides the necessary procedures and programs to collect, organize, and maintain data files or data bases.

data security: Procedures and actions designed to prevent the unauthorized disclosure, transfer, modification, or destruction, whether accidental or intentional, of data.

data set ready: An RS-232 signal that is sent from the modem to the computer or terminal indicating that it is able to accept data. Contrast with *data terminal ready*.

data terminal ready: An RS-232 signal that is sent form the computer or terminal to the modem indicating that it is able to accept data. Contast with *Data Set Ready*.

DB-25: A 25 pin connector commonly used in the United States as the connector of choice for the RS-232-C serial interface standard.

dialog box: A rectangle that appears onscreen, prompting the user to enter data or mutually exclusive selection.

digital signature: A number depending on all the bits of a message and also on a secret key. Its correctness can be verified by using a public key (unlike and authenticator which needs a secret key for its verification).

disaster: A condition in which an organization is deemed unable to function as a result of some natural or human-created occurrence.

disaster recovery operation: The act of recovering from the effects of disruption to a computer facility and restoring, in a preplanned manner, the capabilities of the facility.

disaster recovery plan: The preplanned steps to be taken that make possible the recovery of an organization's computer facility and/or the applications processed there. Also called a contingency plan or business resumption plan.

disk storage (disc storage): Information recording on continuously rotating magnetic platters. Storage may be either sequential or random access.

distributed data processing (DDP): An organization of information processing such that both processing and data may be distributed over a number of different machines in one or more locations.

distributed network: A network configuration in which all node pairs are connected either directly, or through redundant paths through intermediate nodes.

Domain Name System (DNS): The Internet naming scheme which consists of a hierarchical sequence of names, from the most specific to the most general (left to right), separated by dots, for example nic.ddn.mil. (*See also* IP address)

DOS (Disk Operating System): A general term for the operating system used on computers using disk drives. See also operating system.

download: The ability of a communications device (usually a microcomputer acting as an intelligent terminal) to load data from another device or computer to itself, saving the data on a local disk or tape.

DSR: *See* Data Set Ready.

DTR: *See* Data Terminal Ready.

EDI: *See* Electronic data interchange

Electronic Bulletin Board: A shared file where users can enter information for other users to read or download. Many bulletin boards are set up according to general topics and are accessable throughout a network.

electronic data interchange (EDI): The intercompany, computer-to-computer exchange of business documents in standard formats.

electronic mail (E-Mail): A system to send messages between or among users of a computer network and the programs necessary to support such message transfers.

E-Mail message (RFC # 822): A message consists of header fields and, optionally, a body. The body is simply a sequence of lines containing ASCII characters. It is separated from the headers by a null line (i.e., a line with nothing preceding the CRLF).

emulator, terminal: *See* Terminal Emulator.

encryption: The translation of one character string into another by means of a cipher, translation table, or algorithm in order to render the information contained therein meaningless to anyone who does not possess the decoding mechanism. It is the reverse of *de*cryption.

encryption algorithm: A group of mathematically expressed rules that render information unintelligible by producing a series of changes through the use of variable elements controlled by the application of a key to the normal representation of the information.

end-to-end encryption: The encryption of data in a communications network at the point of origin with decryption occurring at the final destination point.

envelope: A group of binary digits formed by a byte augmented by a number of additional bits which are required for the operation of the data network; the boundary of a family of curves obtained by varying a parameter of a wave.

ETHERNET: A local area network and its associated protocol developed by (but not limited to) Xerox. Ethernet is a baseband system.

FAX (facsimile): Devices that consist of three basic components: an image scanner, a FAX modem, and a printer. This setup is often integrated in a single unit with each FAX file treated as a cohesive image (rather than character data).

F-connector: A 75 Ohm F-series coaxial cable connector of the kind commonly found on consumer television and video equipment.

FEP (Front End Processor): A communications device used for entry into a computer system. The FEP typically provides either or both asynchronous or synchronous ports for the system.

fiber optics: A technology for transmitting information via light waves through a fine filament. Signals are encoded by varying some characteristic of the light waves generated by a low-powered laser. Output is sent through a light-conducting fiber to a receiving device that decodes the signal.

file transfer protocol: A communications protocol that can transmit files without loss of data. It implies that it can handle binary data as well as ASCII data.

floppy disks: Magnetic, low cost, flexible data disks (or diskettes) usually either 5.25 inches or 8 inches in diameter.

flow control: A speed matching technique used in data communications to prevent receiving devices from overflow, thus losing data.

frame: In data transmission, the sequence of contiguous bits bracketed by and including beginning and ending flag sequences. A typical frame might consist of a specified number of bits between flags and contain an address field, a control field, and a frame check sequence. A frame may or may not include an information field. A transmission unit that carries a protocol data unit (PDU).

FTP: File Transfer Protocol allows a user to transfer files electronically from remote computers back to the user's computer. Part of the TCP/IP/TELNET software suite.

gateway: The hardware and software necessary to make two technologically different networks communicate with one another; a gateway provides protocol conversion from one network architecture to another and may, therefore, use all seven layers of the OSI Reference Model; a special purpose, dedicated computer that attaches to two or more networks and routes packets from one to the other. The term is loosely applied to any machine that transfers information from one network to another, as in *mail gateway*.

graphical user interface (GUI): A means for computer/human communications characterized by case of use, interaction, and intuitive feel providing visual, direct, immediate feedback in a WYSIWYG environment.

GUI: *See* Graphical User Interface.

handheld password generators (HPGs): Sometimes called tokens, are pocket-sized devices that generate a unique onetime password for each access attempt to a properly equipped host or network.

HDLC: Hierarchical Data Link Control. A highly structured set of standards governing the means by which unlike devices can communicate with each other on large data- communications networks.

headend: In a broadband local area network or CATV system, the point at which a signal processor upconverts a signal from a low inbound channel to a high outbound channel.

Hertz: A unit of frequency equal to one cycle per second. Cycles are referred to as Hertz in honor of the experimenter Heinrich Hertz. Abbreviated as Hz.

highsplit: In a broadband system the organization of the spectrum that places the guard band at about 190 MHz. The midsplit system offers the greatest amount of spectrum for return path channels (14 channels).

Host Computer: In the context of networks, a computer that directly provides service to a user. In contrast to a network server, which provides services to a user through an intermediary host computer.

hot-site: A backup facility that is fully operational and compatible with the site's hardware and software. It provides security, fire protection, and telecommunications capabilities. See also *cold-site* and *warm-site*.

IBM: International Business Machines. One of the primary manufacturers of computer equipment (usually though not exclusively large-scale equipment).

icon: A small graphic image on a computer screen that represents a function or program.

IEEE: Institute of Electrical and Electronic Engineers.

impedance: In a circuit, the opposition that circuit elements present to the flow of alternating current. The impedance includes both resistance and reactance.

information security: The protection of information assets from accidental or intentional but unauthorized disclosure, modification, or destruction or the inability to process that information.

integrity (of data): The property that data have not been altered or destroyed in an unauthorized manner; an attack on integrity would seek to erase a file that should not be erased, alter an element of a database improperly, corrupt the audit trail for a series of events, propagate a virus, etc.

interactive processing: Processing in which transactions are processed one at a time, often eliciting a response from a user before proceeding. An interactive system may be conversational, implying continuous dialogue between the user and the system. Contrast with batch processing.

interface: A shared boundary between system elements defined by common physical interconnections, signals, and meanings of interchanged signals.

Internet: The series of interconnected networks that includes local area, regional, and national backbone networks. Networks in the Internet use the same telecommunications protocol (TCP/IP) and provide electronic mail, remote login, and file transfer services. The Internet is the largest internet in the world. Is a three level hierarchy composed of backbone networks (e.g., NSFNET, MILNET), mid-level networks, and stub networks. The Internet is a multiprotocol internet. *See also* backbone, mid-level network, stub network, transit network, Internet Protocol, Corporation for Research and Educational Networks, National Science Foundation.

IP (Internet protocol): The Internet standard protocol that provides a common layer over dissimilar networks, used to move packets among host computers and through gateways if necessary.

IP Address: The numeric address of a computer connected to the Internet; also called Internet address.

ISO/OSI: International Standards Organization Open Systems Interface. A seven tiered network model.

kernel: The fundamental part of a program, such as an operating system, which resides in memory at all times.

key: A piece of digital information that interacts with cryption algorithms to control cryption of information and, thus, must be protected from disclosure.

key distribution center (KDC): The element in a system that generates and distributes cryptographic key variables.

key generator: An object for encrypting-key generation.

key hashing: The method in which a long key is converted to a native key for use in the encryption/decryption process. Each number or letter of the long key helps to create each digital bit of the native key.

key management: Control of key selection and key distribution in a cryptographic system.

key notarization: A method for encrypting information at a terminal site before transmission to a host computer, over communications media which might not be secure. It is necessary for the host and the terminal to maintain the same encryption key and algorithm. This is frequently accomplished by *downloading* (sending information) from the host to the terminal on key changes. The downloaded information must also be encrypted.

kilohertz: One thousand Hertz. *See also* Hertz.

leaf: In database management, the last node of a tree; in network design and administration, the last (or lowest) node of a hierarchical network.

link encryption: Application of online crypto-operations to a communications system link so that all information passing over the link is encrypted completely. The term also refers to end-to-end encryption within each link in a communications network.

line extender: In a broadband system, an amplifier used to boost signal strength usually within a building.

Listserv Lists (or listservers): Electronic discussion of technical and nontechnical issues conducted by electronic mail over BITNET using LISTSERV protocols. Similar lists, often using the UNIX readnews or rn facilty, are available exclusively on the Internet. Internet users may subscribe to BITNET listservers. Participants subscribe via a central service, and lists often have a moderator who manages the information flow and content.

LLC: *See* Logical Link Control.

local area network (LAN): A computer and communications network which covers a limited geographical area; allows every node to communicate with every other node; and which does not require a central node or processor.

logical link control (LLC): That part of a data station that supports the logical link control functions of one or more logical links.

logical record: A collection of items independent of their physical environment. Portions of the same logical record may be located in different physical records.

logic bomb: A program routine that destroys data; for example, it may reformat the hard disk or randomly insert garbage into data files. A logic bomb may be brought into a personal computer by downloading a public-domain program that has been tampered with. Once executed, it does its damage right away, whereas a virus keeps on destroying (see *virus* and *worm*).

MAC: *See* medium access control or message authentication code.

Mail Transport Agent: The software responsible for transporting mail from source to destination, possibly transforming protocols, addresses, and routing the mail.

Mail User Agent: The user interface to the mail system; the software that the user uses to read mail, store mail, and send mail.

mainframe computer: A large-scale computing system.

malicious software: Any software, such as a virus, worm, logic bomb, bacterium, rabbit, rogue, time bomb, Trojan Horse or something else, that has the *unauthorized* capacity to modify or erase data or software and/or to reproduce itself in an *unauthorized* manner.

Manchester encoding: A means by which separate data and clock signals can be combined into a single, self- synchronizable data stream, suitable for transmission on a serial channel.

manager's workstation: A microcomputer containing an integrated package of software designed to improve the productivity of managers. A workstation will usually, though not exclusively, include a word processor, a spread sheet program, a communications program, and a data manager.

manipulation detection code: *See* MDC.

Masquerading: The attempt to gain access to a system by posing as an authorized client or host.

master-slave computer system: A computer system consisting of a master computer connected to one or more slave computers; the master computer provides the scheduling function and jobs to the slave computers(s).

MDC: Manipulation (Modification) Detection Code. A redundancy check field included in the plaintext of a chain before encipherment, so that changes to the ciphertext (an active attack) will be detected.

medium attachment unit (MAU): The portion of the physical layer between the MDI and AUI that interconnects the trunk cable to the branch cable and contains the electronics which send, receive, and manage the encoded signals impressed on, and recovered from the trunk cable.

medium dependent interface (MDI): The mechanical and electrical interface between the trunk cable medium and the MAU.

medium access control (MAC): The portion of the IEEE 802 data station that controls and mediates the access to the medium.

menu: A multiple choice list of procedures or programs to be executed; a list of command options currently available to the computer user and displayed onscreen.

menu trees: Successions of menu displays that become more detailed.

message: *See* type of message, such as *E-mail message.*

message authentication code (MAC): A method by which cryptographic check digits are appended to the message. They pertain to the transaction type, transaction account number, destination, and point of origin in computer security. Specifically, by using MAC, messages without the additional check digits are rejected by the computer system, and valid transactions cannot be modified without detection.

MHS: 1. (Message Handling Service) An electronic mail system developed by Action Technologies, Inc., and licensed by Novell for its NetWare operating systems. It allows for the transfer and routing of messages between users and provides store and forward capabilities. MHS also provides gateways into IBM's PROFS, Digital's All-in-1 office automation system and X.400 message systems. 2. (Message Handling System) An electronic mail system. MHS often refers to mail systems which conform to the OSI (open systems interconnect) model, which are passed on CCITT's X.400 international message protocol.

microcomputer: A computer system of limited physical size and in former times limited in speed and address capacity. Usually, though not exclusively, a single-user computer.

microprocessor: The central processing unit of a microcomputer which contains the logical elements for manipulating data and performing arithmetic or logical operations on it.

midsplit: In a broadband system the organization of the spectrum which places the guard band at about 140 MHz. The midsplit system offers a substantial amount of spectrum for return path channels (14 channels).

minicomputer: A computer system, usually a timesharing system, sometimes faster than microcomputers but not as fast as large main-frame computers.

modem: MODulator/DEModulator. A device which modulates and demodulates signals transmitted over communication facilities. A modem is sometimes called a data set.

modification detection code: *See* MDC.

MTA: *See* Mail Transport Agent.

MUA: *See* Mail User Agent.

multimedia: Software that permits a mix of text, speech, and static and dynamic visual images.

multitasking: The ability of a computer to perform two or more functions (tasks) concurrently.

multi-user system: A system where two or more people, using different access systems (terminals), can access one computer concurrently or simultaneously. Such system must have multitasking capabilities.

National Institute of Standards and Technology: *See* NIST.

native key: The internal key (string of bits) that is required by the cryption algorithm.

network: *See also* communications network and/or computer network. (1) A system of interconnected computer systems and terminals; (2) a series of points connected by communications channels; (3) the structure of relationships among a project's activities, tasks and events.

network operating system (NOS): A control program that usually resides in a file server within a local area network. It handles the requests for data from all the users (workstations) on the network; on a peer-to-peer LAN the NOS may be distributed across all the attached worksations.

network security: The measures taken to protect a network from unauthorized access, accidental or willful interference with normal operations, or destruction, including protection of physical facilities, software, and personnel security.

NIC (Network Information Center): NIC provides administrative support, user support, and information services for a network.

NIST (National Institute of Standards and Technology): Formerly (prior to 1988) the National Bureau of Standards (NBS) of the U.S. government.

node: Any station, terminal, computer or other device in a computer network.

notarization: The verification (authentication) of a message by a trusted third party similar in logic to classic notarization procedures; normally an automated procedure.

NREN (National Research and Education Network): A proposed national computer network to be built upon the foundation of the NSF backbone network, NSFnet. NREN would provide high speed interconnection between other national and regional networks. SB 1067 is the legislative bill proposing NREN.

object: An entity (e.g., record, page, program, printer) that contains or receives information.

object protection: 1) In computer system security, the mechanisms and rule used to restrict access to objects; 2) in physical security, a means to protect objects such as safes, files, or anything of value that could be removed from a protected area.

object reuse: Reassigning some subject of a magnetic medium that contained one or more objects. To be securely reassigned, such media must contain no residual data from the previously contained object.

octet: A bit-oriented element that consists of eight contiguous binary bits.

off-the-shelf: Production items which are available from current stock and need not be either newly purchased or immediately manufactured. Also relates to computer software or equipment that can be used by customers with little or no adaptation, thereby saving the time and expense of developing their own.

office automation: Refers to efforts to provide automation for common office tasks including word processing, filing, record keeping, and other office chores.

on-line processing: A general data processing term concerning access to computers, in which the input data enters the computer directly from the point of origin or in which output data is transmitted directly to where it is used.

OPAC: Online Public Access Catalog, a term used to describe any type of computerized library catalog.

operating system (OS): A program that manages the hardware and software environment of a computing system.

originate-only-modem: A modem that can originate data communications, but which cannot answer a call from another device.

OSI (Open Systems Interconnection): This is the evolving international standard under development at ISO (International Standards Organization) for the interconnection of cooperative computer systems. An open system is one that conforms to OSI standards in its communications with other systems.

outlet: Access point, with an appropriate connector, to a communications medium.

packet: A block of data for data transmission. Each packet contains control information, such as routing, address and error control. Each also includes data; a group of data and control characters in a specified format, transferred as a whole; a group of binary digits, including data and call control signals, which is switched as a composite whole; the data, all control signals, and possibly error control information are arranged in a specific format.

packet switching: A discipline for controlling and moving messages in a large data-communications network. Each message is handled as a complete unit containing the addresses of the recipient and the originator.

passive threats: Monitoring and/or recording data while data are being transferred over a communications facility; with *release of message contents* an attacker can read user data in messages; with *traffic analysis* the attacker can read user packet headers to identify source and destination information as well as the length and frequency of messages. *See also* threats, active threats.

passphrase: A phrase used instead of a password to control user access.

password: A unique word or string of characters used to authenticate an identity. A program, computer operator, or user may be required to submit a password to meet security requirements before gaining access to data. The password is confidential, as opposed to the user identification.

PBX/PABX: Private branch exchange or private automated branch exchange. A switching network for voice or data.

Peer-entity authentication: The corroboration that a peer entity in an association is the one claimed. This exists in an OSI context only when an association has been established between peer entities.

peer protocol: The sequence of message exchanges between two entities in the same layer that utilize the services of the underlying layers to effect the successful transfer of data and/or control information from one location to another location.

peer systems: Computer/communication systems capable of performing equal or comparable tasks within defined limits or parameters.

peer-to-peer LANs: A local area network regulated by a network operating system that does not require a central server; a LAN where each node on the LAN is capable of performing equal or comparable tasks.

peripheral: Computer equipment external to the CPU performing a wide variety of input and output functions.

personal computer: An alternative name for microcomputer suggesting that the computer is to be used for personal and individual work production or entertainment.

personal identification number (PIN): A sequence of decimal digits (usually four, five, or six) used to verify the identity of the hold of a bank card; a kind of password.

physical access control: The procedures used to authorize and validate requests for physical access to computer, communication, or network physical facilities to help ensure the physical integrity of those systems and facilities.

physical security: Measures necessary to protect the computer and related equipment and their contents from damage by intruders, fire, accident, and environmental hazards.

physical record: A basic unit of data which is read or written by a single input/output command to the computer.

plaintext: Text that has not been encrypted (or has been decrypted) and can be easily read or acted upon.

private key cryptosystem (encryption): A type of encrypting system which uses a single key to both encrypt and decrypt information. Also called *symmetric*, or single-key, encryption.

program: A set of instructions in a programming language used to define an operation or set of operations to a computer.

protocol: A formal set of conventions governing the format and relative timing of message exchange in a communications network.

protocol data unit (PDU): The sequence of contiguous octets delivered as a unit from or to the MAC sublayer. A valid LLC PDU is at least 3 octets in length, and contains two address fields and a control field. A PDU may or may not include an information field in addition.

public key: A cryptographic key used for encipherment but not usable for decipherment. It is therefore possible to make this key public.

public key cryptosystem: An encryption methodology that depends on two keys: a public key—made available to anyone who wants to encrypt information—is used for the encryption process, and a private key—known only to the owner—is used for the decryption process. The two keys are mathematically related. Also termed *asymmetric encryption*.

pull-down menu: A menu that appears onscreen when accessed by a cursor placed on a box or bar at the top of the display.

questionnaire: A method of identity verification which makes use of information known to the authorized user but unlikely to be known to others.

rabbit (informal): A program designed to exhaust some resource of a system (CPU time, disk space, spool space, etc.) by replacing itself without limit; it differs from a *bacterium* in that a rabbit is specifically designed to exhaust resources; it differs from a *virus* in that it is a complete program in itself; it does not infect other programs.

RAM (Random Access Memory): Semiconductor memory devices used in the construction of computers. The time required to obtain data is independent of the location.

reference monitor concept: An information systems access control concept which refers to an abstract machine that mediates all access to objects by subjects.

reliability: In data communications or computer equipment, the extent to which hardware or software operates in a repeatable manner, often characterized (for hardware) as a low mean-time-between-failures.

Remote Access: The ability to access a computer from outside a building in which it is housed, or outside the library. Remote access requires communications hardware, software, and actual physical links, although this can be as simple as common carrier (telephone) lines or as complex as Telnet login to another computer across the Internet; pertaining to communication with a computer by a terminal distant from the computer.

remote batch terminal (RBT): A terminal used for entering jobs and data into a computer from a remote site for later batch processing.

remote job entry (RJE): Input of a batch job from a remote site and receipt of output via a line printer or other device at a remote site.

repeater: A device used to extend the length, topology, or interconnectivity of the physical medium beyond that imposed by a single segment, up to the maximum allowable end-to-end trunk transmission line length by copying electrical signals from one network segment to another. Because repeaters transfer electrical impulses rather than data packets they may also transfer noise.

repudiation: The denial by a message sender that the message was sent, or by a message recipient that the message was received.

resource: Anything used or consumed while performing a function. Categories of resources include time, information, objects (information containers), or processors (the ability to use information).

risk analysis: A process of studying system assets and vulnerabilities to determine an expected loss from harmful events, based upon probabilities of occurrence of those harmful events. The object of risk analysis is to determine the degree of acceptability of each risk to system operation.

ROM: Read-Only-Memory. A memory device used in computers that cannot be altered during normal computer use. Normally a semiconductor device.

router: The hardware and software necessary to link two subnetworks of the same network together; the hardware and software necessary to link two subnetworks at the Network Layer of the OSI Reference Model; any machine responsible for making decisions about which of several paths network traffic will follow. At the lowest level, a physical network bridge is a router because it chooses whether to pass packets from one physical wire to another. Within a long haul network, each individual packet switch is a router because it chooses routes for individual packets. In the Internet, each IP gateway is a router because it uses IP destination addresses to choose routes.

security: *See also* data security, communications security. The state of certainty that computerized data and program files cannot be accessed, obtained, or modified by unauthorized personnel or the computer or its programs. Security is implemented by restricting the physical area around the computer system to authorized personnel, using special software and the security built into the operating procedure of the computer.

security: When applied to computer systems and networks denotes the authorized, correct, timely performance of computing tasks. It encompasses the areas of confidentiality, integrity, and availability.

security audit: *See* audit of computer security.

security mechanisms: Operating procedures, hardware and software features, management procedures, and any combinations of these that are designed to detect and prevent either passive or active threats on any component of an information system.

security service: Activity or provision of an activity that enhances the security of information systems and an organization's information transfer. In the OSI model the defined services consist of five groups: confidentiality, authentication, integrity, non-repudiation, and access control.

security threat: Any action that compromises the security of information owned by an organization. *See also* active threat, and passive threat.

server: A computer in a network that is shared by multiple users such as a file server, print server, or communications server; a computer in a network designated to provide a specific service as distinct from a general purpose, centralized, multi-user computer system.

session: Active connection of one device to another over a communications system, during which interactions do or can occur.

Shareware: Microcomputer software, distributed through public domain channels, for which the author expects to receive compensation.

shell: An outer layer of a program that provides the user interface, or way of commanding the computer. Shells are typically add-on programs created for command-driven operating systems, such as UNIX and DOS. The shell may provide a menu-driven or graphical icon-oriented interface to the system in order to make it easier to use.

software: A term used to contrast computer programs with the "iron" or hardware of a computer system.

socket: The abstraction provided by Berkeley 4.3 BSD UNIX which allows a process to access the Internet. A process opens a socket, specifies the service desired (e.g., reliable stream delivery), binds the socket to a specific destination, and then sends or receives data. While the functional characteristics remain as defined, the concept has been generalized to include processes that access networks other than Internet.

spectrum: A range of wave lengths usually applied to radio frequencies.

spread sheet programs: Computer programs which allow data to be entered as elements of a table or matrix with rows and columns and to manipulate the data. Programs widely available on microcomputers are Lotus 1-2-3 and SUPERCALC.

start-stop transmission: *See* asynchronous transmission.

station: A physical device that may be attached to a shared medium local area network for the purpose of transmitting and receiving information on that shared medium.

subject: An active entity (such as a process, person, or device) that causes information to flow among objects or changes the system's state.

subject security level: The security level of a subject that is the same as the security level of the objects to which it has both read and write access. The clearance of the user the subject is associated with always dominates the security level of the subject.

subsplit: In a broadband system the organization of the spectrum which places the guard band at about 40 MHz. The subsplit system offers the least amount of spectrum for return path channels (4 channels).

symmetric encryption: *See* private key cryptosystem.

vtap: A device which allows an exit from a main line of a communications system.

TCP/IP: Transmission Control Protocol/Internet Protocol is a combined set of protocols which performs the transfer of data between two computers. TCP monitors and ensures correct transfer of data. IP receives the data from TCP, breaks it up into packets, and ships it off to a network within the Internet. TCP/IP is also used as a name for a protocol suite which incorporates these functions and others.

telecommunications: The transfer of data from one place to another over communications lines or channels; the communication of all forms of information including voice and video.

TELNET: A portion of the TCP/IP suite of software protocols which handles terminals. Among other functions, it allows a user to log in to a remote computer from the user's local computer.

teletex: One-way transmission of data via a television system.

terminal: A device that allows input and output of data to a computer. The term is most frequently used in conjunction with a device that has a keyboard for data entry and either a printer or a video tube for displaying data.

Terminal Emulation: Most communications software packages will permit your personal computer or workstation to communicate with another computer or network as if it were a specific type of terminal directly connected to that computer or network.

terminal emulator: A software or software/hardware system for microcomputers that allows the micro to behave like some specified terminal such as a DEC VT100 or an IBM 3278/79.

Terminal Server: A machine that connects terminals to a network by providing host TELNET service.

text editor: A program that provides flexible editing facilities on a computer for the purpose of allowing data entry from a keyboard terminal without regard for the eventual format or medium for publication. With a text editor data (text, copy, or what have you) can be edited easily and quickly.

text formatter: A program for reading a data file created with a text editor and transforming the raw file into a neatly formatted listing.

threats: Threats to an information system or its networks may be either *active* or *passive*. *See also* active threats *and* passive threats.

time bomb: A *logic bomb* activated at a certain time or date. See also, *logic bomb*.

TN3270: A version of TELNET providing IBM full-screen support.

token: (1) (LAN protocols) the symbol of authority that is passed between stations using a token access method to indicate which station is currently in control of the medium; (2) a hand-held password generator designed to provide a unique password for each access attempt to a LAN (or other network) or multi-user computer system (see *HPG*).

token passing: A collision avoidance technique in which each station is polled and must bass the poll along.

transaction processing: A style of data processing in which files are updated and results are generated immediately as a result of data entry.

traffic: The information moved over a communications channel.

traffic analysis: When communication traffic is in cipher form and cannot be understood it may still be possible to get useful information by detecting who is sending messages to whom and in what quantity. This process of detecting information about the sender is traffic analysis.

traffic flow confidentiality: Concealment of the quantity of users' messages in a communication system and their sources or destinations, to prevent traffic analysis.

traffic flow security: The protection resulting from features, inherent in some crypto-equipment, which conceal the presence of valid messages on a communications circuit, normally achieved by causing the circuit to appear busy at all times.

traffic padding: A function that generates a continuous stream of random data or ciphertext, thus making it (1) very difficult for an attacker to distinguish between true data flow and noise; and (2) very difficult to deduce the amount of traffic.

trojan horse: Any program designed to do things that the user of the program did not intend to do. An example of this would be a program that simulates the logon sequence for a computer and, rather than logging the user on, simply records the user's userid and password in a file for later collection. Rather than logging the user on, it steals the user's password so that the Trojan Horse's designer can long on as the user.

trunk cable: The trunk (usually coaxial) cable system.

trusted computer system: A system that can process simultaneously a spectrum of sensitive or classified information, because it employs sufficient hardware and software security measures.

trusted computing base (TCB): Refers to the hardware, firmware, and software protection mechanisms within a computer system that are responsible for enforcing a security policy.

trusted path: The way in which a person at a terminal can communicate directly with the trusted computing base. Only the person or the trusted computing base can activate this mechanism; it cannot be imitated by untrusted software.

trusted software: A trusted computing base's software segment.

turn-key system: A system in which the manufacturer or distributor takes full responsibility for complete system design and installation, and supplies all necessary hardware, software, and documentation.

twisted pair: The two wires of a signaling circuit, twisted around each other to minimize the effects of inductance

UNIX: A multi-tasking, multi-user operating system developed by Ken Thompson, Dennis Ritchie and coworkers at Bell Laboratories (AT&T); a powerful operating system implemented on wide variety of computers from mainframes to microcomputers.

upload: Refers to the ability to send data from an originating terminal (usually a microcomputer) to another computer or terminal.

videotex: A two-way method of communications integrating video and a related communications system.

UNIX-to-UNIX CoPy (UUCP): This was initially a program that ran under the UNIX operating system that allowed one UNIX system to send files to another UNIX system via dial-up phone lines. Today, the term is often, if somewhat inaccurately, used to describe the large international network which uses the UUCP protocols to pass news and electronic mail. See also Electronic Mail, Usenet, uucp.

Usenet: A collection of thousands of topically named newsgroups, the computers which run the protocols, and the people who read and submit Usenet news. Not all

Internet hosts subscribe to Usenet and not all Usenet hosts are on the Internet. See also: Network News Transfer Protocol, UNIX-to-UNIX CoPy. [Source: NWNET]

user: A human being or computer process that possesses the right to login to a particular computer system.

uucp (Unix-to-Unix CoPy): A system of closely integrated programs providing file transfer capabilities; originated in the UNIX world, but has expanded to many other operating environments. "uucp" can also apply to the uucp command which is party of the the uucp system, thus resulting in some confusion. See also: UNIX-to-UNIX CoPy.

virtual circuit: A communication arrangement in which data from a source user may be passed to a destination user over various real circuit configurations during a single period of communication (during a single session). Also called a logical circuit. *See also* connection-oriented service.

virus: A program that is used to infect a computer. After virus code is written, it is buried within an existing program. Once that program is executed, the virus code is also activated and it attaches copies of itself to other programs in the system. Whenever an infected program is run, the virus copies itself to other programs. A virus cannot be attached to data. It must be attached to an executable program that is installed on a computer. The virus-attached program must be executed in order to activate the virus. *See* logic bomb, *and* worm.

warm-site: Similar to a cold site but with telecommunications facilities. See also, *cold-site* and *warm-site*.

wide area network: In communications, a network that interconnects other networks and computers across geographical boundaries such as cities, states, or nations.

Winchester disks: Hard magnetic disk storage media in sealed containers. Not all sealed disks are Winchester drives.

window: A rectangular onscreen image where the user accesses particular features of a system. With operating environment software windowing is often combined with multi-tasking capabilities.

windows (Microsoft): The graphical user interface (Gui) developed by Microsoft for use on microcomputers using Intel 80286 and higher cpu chips.

windows uucp leaf system: A Microsoft Windows-based uucp system that is the last node in an hierarchically arranged network using uucp as the method for communications. *See also* leaf, uucp.

word processing: The transformation of ideas and information into a human readable form of communication through the management of procedures, equipment and personnel. Generally refers to text editing and formatting on a computer.

worm: (1) A destructive program that replicates itself throughout disk and memory, using up the computer's resources and eventually putting the system down (See *virus* and *logic bomb*); (2) a program that moves throughout a network and deposits information at each node for diagnostic purposes, or causes idle computers to share some of the processing workload; (3) WORM (Write Once Read Many) a storage device that uses an optical medium which can be recorded only once. Updating requires destroying the existing data (zeroes [0] made ones [1]), and writing the revised data to an unused part of the disk.

WYSIWYG: What You See Is What You Get.

XON/XOFF: In communications, a simple asynchronous protocol that keeps the receiving device in synchronization with the sending device. When the buffer in the receiving device if full, it sends and *xoff* signal (transmit off) to the sending device, telling it to stop transmitting. When the receiving device is ready to accept more, it sends the sending device an *xon* signal (transmit on) to start again. A means of software flow control. *See also* flow control. Contrast with *CTS/RTS*.

Z39.50 Protocol: The name of the national standard developed by the National Information Standards Organization (NISO) that defines an applications level protocol by which one computer can query another computer and transfer result records, using a canonical format. This protocol provides the framework for OPAC users to search remote catalogs on the Internet using the commands of their own local systems. Projects are now in development to provide Z39.50 support for catalogs on the Internet. SR (Search and Retrieval), ISO Draft International Standard 10162/10163 is the international version of Z39.50.

INDEX